PROGRAMMER'

murach's
CICS
desk
reference

Raul Menendez

Doug Lowe

MIKE MURACH & ASSOCIATES, INC.

2560 West Shaw Lane, Suite 101 • Fresno, CA 93711-2765

Author:	Raul Menendez
Editor:	Judy Taylor
Cover design:	Zylka Design
Production:	Tom Murach
Special thanks:	To CICS expert Bob Yelavich of Yelavich Consulting for his technical review of portions of this book.

Books in the Murach series

Murach's CICS for the COBOL Programmer

Murach's OS/390 and z/OS JCL

Murach's Structured COBOL

Murach's Beginning Java 2

Murach's Beginning Visual Basic .NET

Murach's Visual Basic 6

Other books for IBM programmers

DB2 for the COBOL Programmer, Part 1 & Part 2

IMS for the COBOL Programmer, Part 1 & Part 2

MVS TSO, Part 1 & Part 2

Printed in the United States of America

10 9 8 7 6 5 4 3 2 1
ISBN: 1-890774-17-0

Contents

Expanded contents

Section 1   CICS programming guidelines

Section 2   CICS command reference

Unit 7   CICS command preview

Unit 8   CICS commands

An alphabetical list of the commands that are commonly used in CICS/COBOL programs, with command syntax, option explanations, exceptional conditions, notes and tips on usage, and coding examples.

Introduction

This goal of this book is to combine all the information you need as a CICS/ COBOL programmer into one handy, easy-to-use source book. That means it gives you information that you would have to dig through the IBM documentation to find otherwise. But it also gives you advice and coding examples that even the manuals don't provide.

How this book can help you

If you check the table of contents, you'll find that this book consists of 14 units, some short, some long. But the focus of each is to provide you with information that will help you work faster and better as you develop CICS/COBOL applications. Some highlights follow.

- Units 1 and 2 summarize the design and programming guidelines that are presented in our introductory book, *Murach's CICS for the COBOL Programmer*. If you adhere to these methods, you will work more productively, your programs will run more efficiently, and your programs will be easier to debug and maintain.

- Units 3 and 4 contain the information you need to compile, test, and debug CICS programs, including how to plan the testing phase, how to use CEDF, and a description of the most common abend codes.

- Unit 5 presents two versions of a model maintenance program. The first one presents traditional design and coding techniques (the ones you're likely to find when you're maintaining programs). The second one presents modular design and coding techniques that separate the user interface from the business logic (these are the ones you may want to implement as you enhance old programs or develop new ones).

- Unit 6 presents model programs for three other types of programs: a menu program, an inquiry program, and an order entry program. When combined with the programs in Unit 5, this gives you a wealth of design and code that you can use as models for your own programs.

- Units 7 and 8 provide detailed reference information for coding CICS commands. Here, you'll find syntax diagrams along with explanations of options, exceptional conditions, and coding considerations for 121 CICS commands. You'll also find lots of coding examples that show you how to use these commands in their proper context.

- Units 9 and 10 give you the same type of reference information for coding BMS mapsets. After Unit 9 gives you syntax, examples, and guidelines for coding BMS mapsets for 3270 displays, Unit 10 shows you how to assemble your BMS mapsets into HTML templates so they can be displayed in a web browser.

- Units 11 through 13 present information that helps you work more effectively in the CICS environment. This includes how to use: Access Method Services to define and manipulate VSAM files, RDO to define resources for an application in a CICS test region, and the master terminal transaction (CEMT) as well as several other CICS-supplied transactions.

- Unit 14 presents reference tables that come in handy during many phases of program development: hexadecimal conversion tables, the EBCDIC character set, and so on.

About *Murach's CICS for the COBOL Programmer*

This reference book assumes that you already know how to develop CICS/COBOL programs. If that isn't true or if you're just getting started as a CICS/COBOL programmer, we recommend that you get our training classic called *Murach's CICS for the COBOL Programmer*. This book has taught CICS to more than 200,000 COBOL programmers, and it presents all of the skills that are essential to effective CICS programming.

In fact, because *CICS for the COBOL Programmer* has a tutorial approach, you'll often find working CICS programmers with both of our CICS books on their desks. Then, when they need to learn new skills, they refer to our tutorial. But when they just need to look something up, they refer to our reference book.

How to download the model programs

If you like using the model programs in Units 5 and 6 of this book as guides for your own programs, you can download them from our web site. Then, you can copy any code that you want to use into your programs and modify it to suit your purposes. To download these programs, just go to www.murach.com, click on the Downloads link at the top of the page, click on the link for *Murach's CICS Desk Reference*, and proceed from there.

Another alternative is to download the model programs for *Murach's CICS for the COBOL Programmer*. This includes all five of the model programs in the *Desk Reference* plus seven others. To download these programs, use the procedure above, but click on the link for *Murach's CICS for the COBOL Programmer*, and proceed from there.

About CICS versions

The focus of this book is on the commands for CICS Transaction Server 1.3 and 2.2 because IBM has dropped or is dropping support for all previous versions including CICS Transaction Server 1.1 and 1.2 as well as CICS MVS/ESA 4.1. If you're maintaining older programs, though, the commands you're most likely to encounter are still included. Also, the commands that have been added in versions of CICS Transaction Server are marked accordingly, so you'll have some perspective on what functions are provided for in the most current releases.

Incidentally, we used Micro Focus Mainframe Express to develop the model programs for our CICS books. In case you're not familiar with it, Mainframe Express is a product that lets you code and test CICS programs on a PC. Then, after we compiled and tested the programs with Mainframe Express, we uploaded them to a mainframe and compiled and tested them using CICS TS 1.3. This is a highly productive way to develop CICS programs, and we thank Micro Focus for letting us experiment with their product.

Please let us know how this book works for you

As far as we know, this book is unique. There are other CICS books, including *Murach's CICS for the COBOL Programmer*, that strive to teach CICS programming to novices. But this is the only book we've seen that's designed specifically to assist the experienced CICS programmer on a daily basis. Now, we hope you'll join with the more than 50,000 programmers who have used previous editions and discover that this is the *one* book you want on your desk as you develop CICS programs.

If you have any comments about this book, we would enjoy hearing from you. We would especially like to know if this book has lived up to your expectations. To respond, please e-mail us at murachbooks@murach.com.

Thanks for buying this book and thanks for using it. We sure hope that it will make all your CICS projects go more smoothly.

Raul Menendez
Author

Mike Murach
Publisher

CICS programming guidelines

Unit 1

CICS program design

Taking the time to design your CICS programs is the key to creating programs that are easier to code, test, debug, and maintain. This unit starts by comparing the two major ways you can design an application program and explains how the theory of pseudo-conversational programming is the basis for both. Then, it gives you a recommended development procedure to follow and describes the various components that make up a complete set of program specifications. After that, it shows you how to use event/response charts and structure charts to plan the processing your programs will do based on user actions. And finally, it shows how a structure listing can be used to document the program design.

Traditional program design vs. modular program design

Today, there are two ways to design and code CICS programs, as shown in figures 1-1 and 1-2. Traditional program design describes the way CICS programs have typically been developed over the years, with the logic for presenting the user interface and the logic for processing user input all in a single program. So if you're maintaining older programs, you're almost certain to work with programs that are designed this way.

You may also use this technique for new program development, depending on your shop standards and the types of programs you're creating. However, more and more programs are being developed using modular program design because that approach makes it possible to separate the business logic from the presentation logic in an application. That, in turn, allows you more flexibility when it comes to providing user interfaces for your applications, including using HTML and GUI front-ends.

Traditional program design

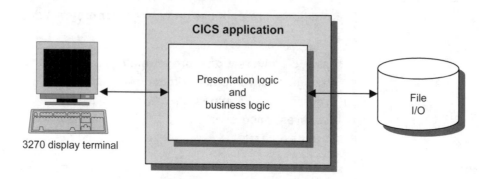

- Traditional CICS programs consist of a single program module that handles both the interaction with the user at a terminal (the *presentation logic*) and the processing of data (the *business logic*).

- Both the presentation logic and the business logic are implemented using COBOL in conjunction with CICS commands, and the user interface is implemented using Basic Mapping Support (BMS).

- Although programs designed using this technique are easy to implement, they can only be run in a CICS environment. In addition, BMS doesn't provide all the features for creating user-friendly interfaces that are available in other languages.

Figure 1-1

Modular program design

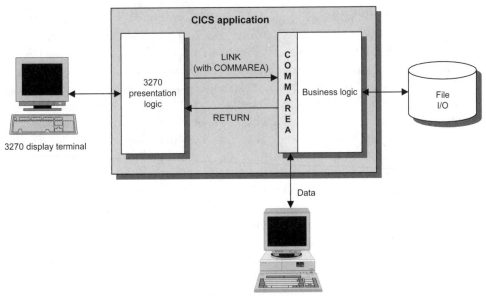

- *Modular CICS programs* separate the presentation logic from the business logic. With this technique, only the presentation logic can perform terminal I/O, and only the business logic can perform file I/O.

- Because the business logic is independent of the presentation logic, it can be used with presentation logic that's written in any language and that can run on any platform. In other words, you don't have to implement the presentation logic using COBOL and CICS and the user interface using BMS. Instead, you can use tools like Java or Visual Basic that allow you to create a user interface that handles the presentation logic itself. You can also create more than one user interface for the same business logic.

- For modular programs to work, the appropriate interface must be provided between the presentation and business logic. If the presentation logic is developed using COBOL/CICS, the interface with the business logic is implemented using a LINK command and the communication area. If the presentation logic is on a different platform or in another language, more sophisticated facilities are required.

- Separating the presentation and business logic facilitates the development of client/server and distributed applications and is critical to the development of web-based applications.

Figure 1-2

Pseudo-conversational programming

Pseudo-conversational programming is a CICS programming technique that you should use for all your interactive programs. In a pseudo-conversational program, every SEND or SEND MAP command must be followed by a RETURN command. In other words, the program must end after it sends data to the terminal. On the RETURN command, the program specifies a trans-id so that when the user presses an attention key (such as the Enter key), the transaction is automatically restarted. Then, the program issues a RECEIVE or RECEIVE MAP command to receive the input data. The program can then process the data, issue another SEND or SEND MAP command, and end again. This is illustrated by the diagram in figure 1-3.

The advantage of pseudo-conversational programming is that the program doesn't sit idle while the user keys in data at the terminal. In contrast, a *conversational program* (one that doesn't terminate itself after it sends data to the terminal) sits idle while it waits for the user to enter input data. And that's inefficient because even though the program is idle, valuable CICS resources (such as main storage) are assigned to it.

The drawback of pseudo-conversational programming is that it requires a different type of design and logic than what you're used to using in COBOL programming. That's because a pseudo-conversational program must be able to figure out what to do each time it's restarted.

A pseudo-conversational program that knows what to do each time it's restarted is one that can interpret the *event* that caused it to restart. It can then process a *response* that's appropriate for that event. For example, suppose a user presses the PF3 key in a program to exit to the main menu. In that case, the event is the user pressing the PF3 key, and the program's response is to issue an XCTL command to transfer control to the menu program. When you design a program using *event-driven program design*, you identify each user input event that can trigger the execution of the pseudo-conversational program, and you design an appropriate response to each event.

Pseudo-conversational processing

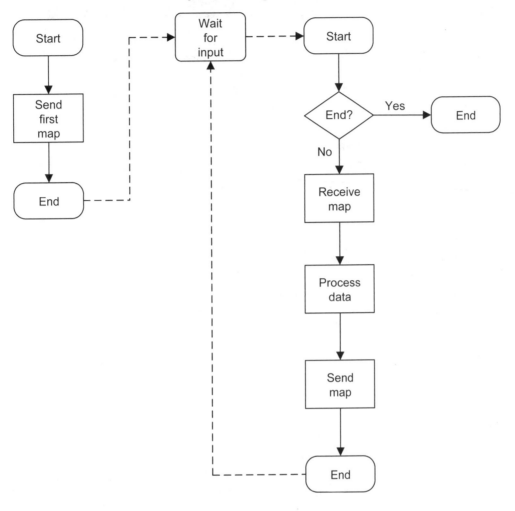

Figure 1-3

A program development procedure

Figure 1-4 shows the preferred sequence for CICS program development. Although practical considerations may force a slightly different development sequence upon you, you should try to follow this sequence as closely as possible. At the least, you should make sure you obtain a complete set of specifications before you design the program, and you should design the program before you code it.

Analysis and design

1. Develop a complete set of program specifications.
2. Design the program using an event/response chart and a structure chart.

Implementation

3. Prepare the BMS mapset.
4. Code the program.
5. Prepare the program for execution.
6. Define the CICS resources needed for the program.
7. Test the program under CICS.

Documentation

8. Document the program.

Figure 1-4

- To define the format of the screens that will be displayed by a program, you code a BMS mapset (see Units 9 and 10).

- To prepare a program for execution, you translate, compile, and link-edit it using IBM-supplied procedures (see Unit 3).

- The CICS resources that must be defined for most programs include the trans-id, the program itself, the mapset, and each file used by the program. To define these resources, you usually use an interactive facility called *Resource Definition Online*, or *RDO* (see Unit 12). At one time, resources like these were always referred to as "table" entries and were defined using special assembler macro instructions. As a result, you'll see terms like "File Control Table" used in the CICS manuals and in some of the explanations of command options and error conditions given in Unit 8 in this book.

- Although coding and testing are shown as separate steps in this procedure, we recommend you use *top-down coding and testing* (or just *top-down testing*) to code and test your programs in phases (see Unit 4).

- The documentation for a program varies from shop to shop, so be sure to follow your shop standards.

Program specifications

The first step in CICS program development is developing a complete set of program specifications. If you forge ahead with design and coding before you have a clear idea of what the program is supposed to do, you'll pay for it later by having to redo your work.

In some cases, you may be given a detailed set of program specifications developed by an analyst. In other cases, the specifications you're given may be quite sketchy. If that's the case, you'll have to fill in the missing details yourself.

At the minimum, your program specifications should include the items shown in figure 1-5:

- a program overview listing the input, output, and processing requirements of the program
- a screen layout for each map used by the program
- a listing of the COPY member for each file used by the program

In addition, the specifications may include decision tables, editing rules, and so on. Try to look beyond the obvious to make sure you have all the information you need to develop your program.

The copy members for the customer maintenance program

The CUSTMAS copy member

```
01  CUSTOMER-MASTER-RECORD.
*
    05  CM-CUSTOMER-NUMBER        PIC X(06).
    05  CM-FIRST-NAME            PIC X(20).
    05  CM-LAST-NAME             PIC X(30).
    05  CM-ADDRESS               PIC X(30).
    05  CM-CITY                  PIC X(20).
    05  CM-STATE                 PIC X(02).
    05  CM-ZIP-CODE              PIC X(10).
*
```

The ERRPARM copy member (required by the SYSERR subprogram)

```
01  ERROR-PARAMETERS.
*
    05  ERR-RESP                 PIC S9(08)  COMP.
    05  ERR-RESP2                PIC S9(08)  COMP.
    05  ERR-TRNID                PIC X(04).
    05  ERR-RSRCE                PIC X(08).
```

Figure 1-5 (part 1 of 3)

The program overview for the customer maintenance program

Program	CUSTMNT2: Customer maintenance program
Trans-id	MNT2
Overview	Maintains customer information in the customer master file by allowing the user to enter new customers, change existing customers, or delete existing customers.
Input/output	CUSTMAS Customer master file MNTMAP1 Customer maintenance key map MNTMAP2 Customer maintenance data map
Processing	1. Control is transferred to this program via XCTL from the menu program INVMENU with no communication area. The user can also start the program by entering the trans-id MNT2. In either case, the program should respond by displaying the key map.
	2. On the key map, the user enters a customer number and selects a processing action (Add, Change, or Delete). Both fields are required. If the user selects Add, the customer number entered must not exist in the file. For Change or Delete, the customer number must exist in the file. If a valid combination isn't entered, an error message should be displayed.
	3. If the user enters a valid combination of action and customer number, the program displays the customer maintenance data map. For an add operation, the user can then enter the customer information. For a change operation, the user can change any of the existing information. For a delete operation, all fields should be set to protected so the user can't enter changes. To complete any of these operations, the user must press the Enter key.
	4. For an add or change, edit the fields to make sure they aren't blank.
	5. If the user presses PF3 from either the key map or the data map, return to the menu program INVMENU by issuing an XCTL command. If the user presses PF12 from the key map, return to the menu program. However, if the user presses PF12 from the data map, redisplay the key map without completing the current operation.
	6. For a change or delete operation, maintain an image of the customer record in the communication area between program executions. If the record is changed in any way between program executions, notify the user and do not complete the operation.
	7. If an unrecoverable error occurs, terminate the program by invoking the SYSERR subprogram with an XCTL command.

Figure 1-5 (part 2 of 3)

The screen layout for the customer maintenance key map

Map name	MNTMAP1	Date	03/12/2001
Program name	CUSTMNT2	Designer	Doug Lowe

```
MNTMAP1              Customer Maintenance                                     XXXX

Type a customer number. Then select an action and press Enter.

Customer number. . . .  XXXXXX

Action . . . . . . . .  X  1. Add a new customer
                           2. Change an existing customer
                           3. Delete an existing customer














XXXXXXXXXXXXXXXXXXXXXXXXXXXXXXXXXXXXXXXXXXXXXXXXXXXXXXXXXXXXXXXXXXXXXXXXXXXXXXXX
F3=Exit      F12=Cancel                                                          X
```

The screen layout for the customer maintenance data map

Map name	MNTMAP2	Date	03/12/2001
Program name	CUSTMNT2	Designer	Doug Lowe

```
MNTMAP2              Customer Maintenance                                     XXXX

XXXXXXXXXXXXXXXXXXXXXXXXXXXXXXXXXXXXXXXXXXXXXXXXXXXXXXXXXXXXXXXXXXXXXXXXXXXXXXXXXX

Customer number. . . . :  XXXXXX

Last name. . . . . . .   XXXXXXXXXXXXXXXXXXXXXXXXXXX
First name . . . . . .   XXXXXXXXXXXXXXXXXXXX
Address. . . . . . . .   XXXXXXXXXXXXXXXXXXXXXXXXXX
City . . . . . . . . .   XXXXXXXXXXXXXXXXXXXX
State. . . . . . . . .   XX
Zip Code . . . . . . .   XXXXXXXXXX










XXXXXXXXXXXXXXXXXXXXXXXXXXXXXXXXXXXXXXXXXXXXXXXXXXXXXXXXXXXXXXXXXXXXXXXXXXXXXXXXXX
F3=Exit      F12=Cancel                                                          X
```

Figure 1-5 (part 3 of 3)

Event/response charts

When you use event-driven program design for a pseudo-conversational program, you identify each user input event that can trigger the execution of the program, and then specify an appropriate program response. In most programs, the appropriate response to a particular event depends on the *context* in which that event occurs. For example, the maintenance program's response to the Enter key depends on whether the key map or the data map is displayed. And if the data map is displayed, the response depends on whether the user is adding, changing, or deleting a customer. Thus, there are four contexts for the customer maintenance program: (1) Get key, (2) Add customer, (3) Change customer, and (4) Delete customer.

To design the program's response to each input event and context, you can create an event/response chart like the one shown in figure 1-6. As you can see, the leftmost column in this chart simply lists each input event that the program must respond to. Then, the second column lists the contexts that are significant for each event. For example, the program must respond differently to the Enter key for each context, but the context doesn't matter for the PF3 key.

The third column summarizes the program's response to each event/context combination. Finally, the fourth column lists the new context that results from each response. For example, this program uses the PF12 key to cancel out of the current operation. So if the user presses PF12 when the context is "Add customer," the program will set the context for the next program execution to "Get key."

Keep in mind that an event/response chart like this is nothing more than a planning tool. As you gain experience developing CICS programs, you'll find it unnecessary to include the amount of detail shown here. Also be aware that this is a design tool; it's not meant to be maintained as part of the documentation for the final version of the program.

An event/response chart for the customer maintenance program

Event	Context	Response	New context
Start the program	n/a	Display the key map.	Get key
PF3	All	Transfer control to the menu program.	n/a
PF12	Get key	Transfer control to the menu program.	n/a
	Add customer Change customer Delete customer	Cancel the operation and display the key map.	Get key
Enter key	Get key	Edit input data. If valid display data map else display an error message.	Add customer, Change customer, or Delete customer Get key
	Add customer	Edit input data. If valid add customer record display key map else display an error message.	Get key Add customer
	Change customer	Edit input data. If valid change customer record display key map else display an error message.	Get key Change customer
	Delete customer	Delete the customer record. Display the key map.	Get key
Clear	Get key	Redisplay the key map without any data.	Unchanged
	Add, Change, or Delete customer	Redisplay the data map with unprotected data erased.	Unchanged
Any PA key	All	Ignore the key.	Unchanged
Any other key	All	Display an appropriate error message.	Unchanged

Figure 1-6

Structure charts

Regardless of whether you're designing a traditional or modular program, you'll use your event/response chart to create a program *structure chart* like the one for the traditional maintenance program shown in figure 1-7. The structure chart, in turn, will serve as a basis for your program code. Each box on the structure chart represents one program module, which can be easily implemented as a single paragraph in your COBOL program. The COBOL paragraph for a module invokes the modules subordinate to it by issuing PERFORM statements.

A general procedure for designing the first two levels of a structure chart

1. Draw the top-level module and give it a name that represents the entire program. It manages the event processing specified in the event/response chart.
2. Decide what event processing should be implemented as separate modules, and draw a box subordinate to the top-level module for each one.

How to determine what modules should make up the second level of a structure chart

*   If the program's response to an event includes receiving data from the terminal, processing it, and sending data back to the terminal, you should create a separate module for the event.

*   If the program's response to an event doesn't include receiving data from the terminal, you should consider creating a separate module only if the response requires more than a few COBOL statements to implement.

*   If the COBOL statements for implementing the top-level module require more than a page or two, you should consider creating additional second-level modules to simplify the coding in the top-level module.

    Note: The design that results from following these guidelines will vary from program to program depending on whether you're designing a traditional or modular program. Some programs will have second-level modules that correspond to the program's contexts. Others will have modules that correspond to particular function keys. Still others will have a combination of the two. Later in this unit, you'll find some additional guidelines for designing modular programs.

The structure chart for the customer maintenance program (traditional design)

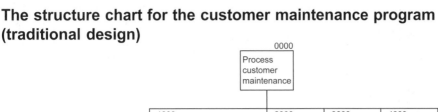

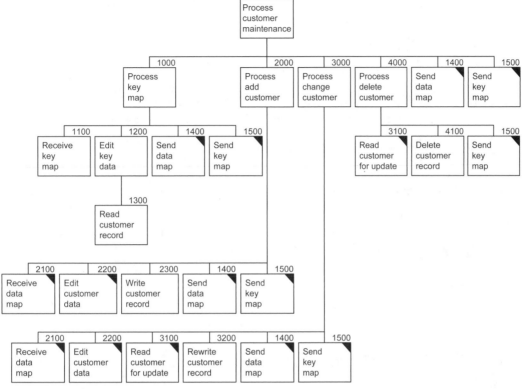

Figure 1-7

A general procedure for designing one leg of a structure chart

1. Draw one subordinate module (or *called module*) for each function that the *control module* (or *calling module*) at the top of the *leg* needs to do. To process the key map, for example, the process-key-map module needs to receive the key map, edit the data in the map, send the customer map if the entry is valid, and resend the key map if the entry is invalid.

2. Use the same thought process for the next level of modules. If any of them require more than one function, draw one subordinate module for each function.

3. Continue this process as needed until each of the lowest-level modules consists of just one function.

Guidelines for designing the legs of a structure chart

- Each module should represent one and only one function.
- The function of a called module must be logically contained in the function of its calling module.
- The code in each module should be manageable.
- Use a generalized send module for each map. Each module will contain one or more SEND MAP commands with various options, such as ERASE, DATAONLY, and ALARM. The send module can decide which SEND MAP command to use by evaluating a flag that's set by the calling module.
- Include a separate module for each file I/O statement so the statements are easy to locate and modify.

How to identify common modules and linked or called programs

- To identify a *common module* that appears more than once in a structure chart, shade its upper right corner. If a common module has subordinate modules, you need to include them only once on the chart.
- To identify a *linked program* that's executed using the LINK command, add a module to the structure chart with a stripe at the top that gives the program name. You can use the same technique to identify a *called program* (a program that's executed using the COBOL Call statement).

How to number the modules in a structure chart

- Use 000 or 0000 for the top-level module.
- Number the modules in the second level from left to right leaving large enough gaps for subordinate modules.
- After the first two levels, number the modules down each leg in appropriate increments.
- When you code the COBOL paragraph for each module later on, the paragraph name will be the module number followed by the module name.

Design variations for modular programs

The specifications for a modular program will show that two programs have to be created: one for the presentation logic and one for the business logic. Keep in mind, though, that the presentation logic may be done in a different language by a different programmer. The specifications will also indicate when the presentation logic links to the business logic.

You don't have to make any changes in the way you develop an event/response chart for a modular program. However, if you want to, you can use some type of notation to clarify which portion of the program should implement the responses. For example, you could include the character *P* after each portion of a response that will be handled by the presentation logic and the character *B* after each portion that will be handled by the business logic.

The main trick in designing a modular program comes in creating the structure chart for each part of the program. At this point, you have to determine which processing belongs in which part. The guidelines that follow will help you with that, and you'll see how they're applied in the structure charts for the modular design of the customer maintenance program.

Design considerations for the presentation logic

The structure chart shown in figure 1-8 illustrates the functions that must be provided for in the presentation logic of a program.

- Because CICS programs are driven by user events, the presentation logic should contain the high-level logic for the program. The presentation logic can be referred to as the *driver program* since it drives the execution of the program.

- The presentation logic must determine what processing is done based on user input and the context in which it's received.

- The presentation logic should handle all screen interactions with the user, so the structure chart will include send and receive modules.

- The presentation logic should handle preliminary editing of the input that's entered by the user. That includes making sure that required entries are made, that entries are numeric when required, and that a valid key has been pressed.

- The presentation logic should link to the business logic whenever business processing is required. This can be shown on the structure chart just like any linked program.

- The presentation logic should maintain a copy of any data it requires between executions in a pseudo-conversational session. It should also maintain a copy of any data that's required by the business logic between its executions. A set module like module 2300 in this figure is often used to set up the communication area so it can be passed to the business logic.

- The presentation logic should *never* include any file I/O statements. That means there are no read, write, rewrite, or delete modules.

The structure chart for the presentation logic of the customer maintenance program

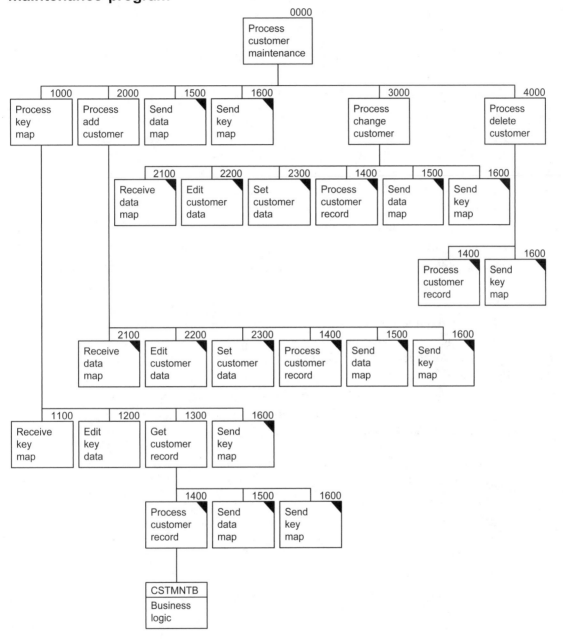

Figure 1-8

Design considerations for the business logic

The structure chart shown in figure 1-9 illustrates the functions that must be provided for in the business logic of a program.

- The processing done by the business logic should be based on information sent to it by the presentation logic.

- The business logic should handle all file processing.

- The business logic should ensure that data integrity is maintained.

- The business logic should handle all editing of data that depends on business rules. That includes checking that a value falls within a particular range, making sure that a record with a corresponding key value does or does not exist, and making sure that related fields have values that agree with one another.

- The business logic should perform all calculations.

- The top-level module of the business logic program should represent the function indicated by the module in the presentation logic program that links to the business logic. In fact, we recommend you use the same name for both modules.

- The modules at the second level should represent the main functions of the business logic. In most cases, these functions will be directly related to the event processing identified by the modules at the second level of the presentation logic.

- A set module is usually used to format the information that needs to be sent back to the presentation logic. If the presentation logic is another CICS program, a standard communication area is most likely used. But if the business logic program is communicating with an application outside of the CICS environment, alternate ways of sending the information may be used. This can include sending HTML and XML data strings back via an HTTP request.

- The business logic should *never* include any terminal I/O statements. That means there are no send or receive modules in the structure chart.

The structure chart for the business logic of the customer maintenance program

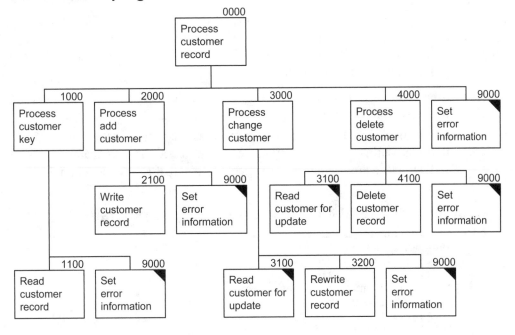

Figure 1-9

Structure listings

If you have a tool that can create a *structure listing* from program source code, use it for final program documentation. That makes it easier to keep the program's documentation up-to-date. The structure listing in figure 1-10 is for the customer maintenance program that uses traditional design.

- A structure listing uses indentation to show the levels of the modules. The letter C in parentheses can be used to identify common modules.

- A structure listing can be used for design as well as for documentation. In fact, you can use the outline feature of any modern word processor to prepare a structure listing as a program design document in place of a structure chart.

A structure listing for the customer maintenance program

```
0000-PROCESS-CUSTOMER-MAINT
    1000-PROCESS-KEY-MAP
        1100-RECEIVE-KEY-MAP
        1200-EDIT-KEY-MAP
            1300-READ-CUSTOMER-RECORD
        1400-SEND-DATA-MAP (C)
        1500-SEND-KEY-MAP (C)
    1400-SEND-DATA-MAP (C)
    1500-SEND-KEY-MAP (C)
    2000-PROCESS-ADD-CUSTOMER
        1400-SEND-DATA-MAP (C)
        1500-SEND-KEY-MAP (C)
        2100-RECEIVE-DATA-MAP (C)
        2200-EDIT-CUSTOMER-DATA (C)
        2300-WRITE-CUSTOMER-RECORD
    3000-PROCESS-CHANGE-CUSTOMER
        1400-SEND-DATA-MAP (C)
        1500-SEND-KEY-MAP (C)
        2100-RECEIVE-DATA-MAP (C)
        2200-EDIT-CUSTOMER-DATA (C)
        3100-READ-CUSTOMER-FOR-UPDATE (C)
        3200-REWRITE-CUSTOMER-RECORD
    4000-PROCESS-DELETE-CUSTOMER
        1500-SEND-KEY-MAP (C)
        3100-READ-CUSTOMER-FOR-UPDATE (C)
        4100-DELETE-CUSTOMER-RECORD
```

Figure 1-10

Unit 2

CICS programming fundamentals

This unit is a review of the fundamentals of coding command-level CICS programs in COBOL. It begins by describing how programs are executed under CICS. Then, it explains how your program can access main storage in various ways. And finally, it explains how to code the Procedure Division of a command-level program.

How programs execute under CICS

To start a program in a CICS environment, you enter a transaction identifier, or trans-id, that's associated with the program. Doing so starts a task that in turn executes the actual program. CICS manages these tasks through a technique called *multitasking*, as shown in figure 2-1.

CICS supports multitasking

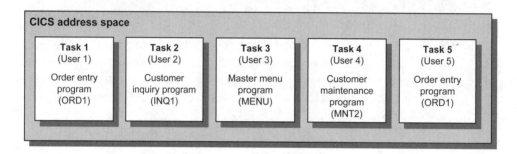

- CICS is a *multitasking system*, which means that it manages the concurrent execution of more than one task.

- A *task* is an execution of one or more programs that function together as a unit called a *transaction*.

- Several users may invoke the same transaction, but each execution of the transaction is treated as a separate task.

Figure 2-1

How CICS invokes an application program

- Each transaction is identified by a unique four-character code called a *transaction identifier*, or just *trans-id*. Most often, a transaction is invoked when an operator enters the transaction's trans-id at a terminal. In that case, the terminal is automatically associated with the resulting task.

- When a transaction is invoked, a specified application program is loaded into storage (if it isn't already in storage), and a task is started. This process is shown in figure 2-2.

- Transactions are defined in the CICS *Program Control Table* (*PCT*). Each trans-id is paired with the name of the program CICS will load and execute when the transaction is invoked.

- The CICS *Processing Program Table* (*PPT*) contains a list of all valid program names and keeps track of which programs are located in storage. CICS uses it to determine whether it will load a new copy of the program when the transaction is invoked.

- Each transaction loads and executes a single program, but that program may issue CICS commands (specifically, LINK or XCTL) to load and execute other programs. And those programs may in turn execute other programs. As a result, even though a task is always the execution of a single transaction, it may result in the execution of more than one program.

Invoking a CICS application program

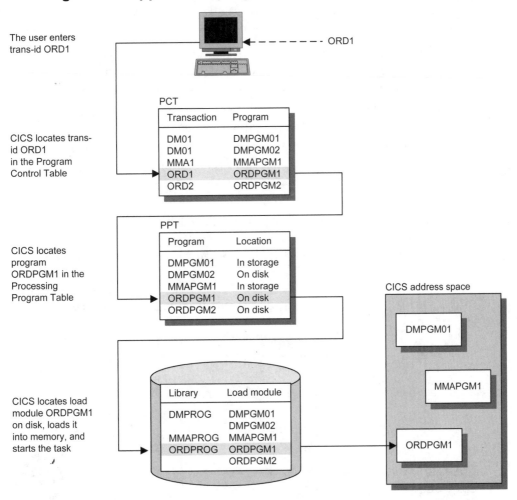

Figure 2-2

Program storage

With few exceptions, all CICS programs need to access main storage in one way or another. In a command-level COBOL program, there are basically two ways you can access main storage: through the Working-Storage Section or through the Linkage Section.

The Working-Storage Section

- When you code a command-level CICS program in COBOL, you can use the Working-Storage Section just as you do in any other COBOL program: for program variables and switches, as well as for data areas for terminal and file I/O.

- When CICS loads your program, it allocates storage for its Working-Storage Section and associates that storage with your program.

- If more than one task is executing the same program, CICS uses *multithreading* to provide each with a separate copy of working storage, as shown in figure 2-3. So you don't have to worry that the fields you've set will be changed by another user's execution of the program.

- Main storage is a more valuable resource under CICS than it is in batch COBOL, so use common sense when dealing with working storage. For example, don't define a 10,000-byte table when a 1,000-byte table will do.

Multithreading provides a separate copy of working storage for each user

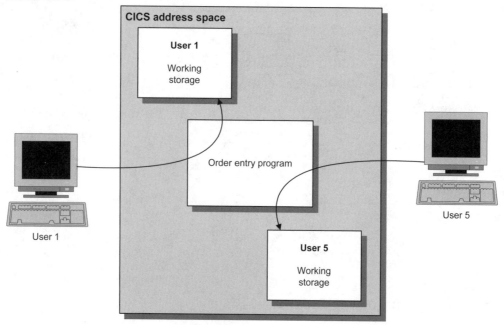

Figure 2-3

The Linkage Section

You'll often need to access storage areas that are *not* associated with your task and, therefore, aren't accessible through your program's Working-Storage Section. You access these areas through entries coded in the Linkage Section.

The communication area

- The *communication area* is an area of main storage that's designed to let programs or tasks communicate with one another.

- In general, you'll use the communication area in one of two ways: (1) to communicate with a program you invoke via a LINK or XCTL command or (2) to communicate with the next task invoked at the same terminal as the current task (this is how pseudo-conversational programming is implemented).

- You provide two definitions for the communication area, as shown in figure 2-4. The working-storage definition, which can have any name, is the source of the data that's passed on to the next program execution. The Linkage Section definition, which must be named DFHCOMMAREA, is used to access the data passed by the previous program execution.

- The communication area can be up to 32K in length, and its contents are up to you. It can contain control totals, file records, flags that indicate the current event context, and so on.

- To send a communication area to a task or program, you specify the name of the area in the COMMAREA option of a LINK, XCTL, or RETURN command. To receive a communication area, you simply code the DFHCOMMAREA field in the Linkage Section.

- Even if you don't need to save data between program executions, you should code a one-byte communication area in working storage and a one-byte DFHCOMMAREA in the Linkage Section. This allows you to detect the first execution of the program in a pseudo-conversational session.

A typical communication area for a master file maintenance program

Entry in the Working-Storage Section

```
01   COMMUNICATION-AREA.
*
     05   CA-CONTEXT-FLAG                    PIC X.
          88   PROCESS-KEY-MAP               VALUE '1'.
          88   PROCESS-ADD-CUSTOMER          VALUE '2'.
          88   PROCESS-CHANGE-CUSTOMER       VALUE '3'.
          88   PROCESS-DELETE-CUSTOMER       VALUE '4'.
     05   CA-CUSTOMER-RECORD.
          10   CA-CUSTOMER-NUMBER            PIC X(6).
          10   FILLER                        PIC X(112).
```

Entry in the Linkage Section

```
01   DFHCOMMAREA                            PIC X(119).
```

Figure 2-4

The Execute Interface Block

- The *Execute Interface Block* (*EIB*) is a CICS area that contains information related to the current task, such as the date and time the task was started and the transaction-id that was used to start it. Figure 2-5 lists some of the fields you'll typically use in a program (Unit 14 of this book contains a complete description of the EIB).

- The definition of the EIB is automatically inserted into the Linkage Section of the program when the program is prepared for execution. You don't have to code it yourself.

- When the user presses an *attention identifer (AID) key*, CICS passes a one-byte value to the program through the EIBAID field in the Execute Interface Block. You can use the value of this field to determine the processing the user has requested.

- The EIBCALEN field contains the length of the data passed to the program through its communication area (DFHCOMMAREA). A length of zero indicates that no data was passed to the program. In a pseudo-conversational program, that means that it's the first execution of the program.

EIB fields that you'll use frequently

Field name	COBOL Picture	Description
EIBAID	X(1)	Most recent AID character (see figure 2-11).
EIBCALEN	S9(4) COMP	Length of DFHCOMMAREA.
EIBCPOSN	S9(4) COMP	Most recent cursor address, given as a displacement value.
EIBDATE	S9(7) COMP-3	Task start date in the format 0CYYDDD (day in year, where *C* identifies the century with 0 for the 1900s, 1 for the 2000s).
EIBDS	X(8)	Most recent data set name.
EIBFN	X(2)	Most recent CICS command code.
EIBRCODE	X(6)	CICS response code.
EIBRESP	S9(8) COMP	Exceptional condition code.
EIBRESP2	S9(8) COMP	Exceptional condition extended code.
EIBRSRCE	X(8)	Most recent resource (map name for a SEND MAP or RECEIVE MAP command, program name for a LINK or XCTL command, file name for a file control command, etc.).
EIBTIME	S9(7) COMP-3	Task starting time in the format 0HHMMSS (hours, minutes, seconds; assumes a 24-hour clock).
EIBTRMID	X(4)	Terminal-id.
EIBTRNID	X(4)	Transaction-id.

Figure 2-5

Other system areas

- The *Common System Area* (*CSA*) is a major CICS control block that contains important system information, including pointers to most of the other CICS control blocks. Access to the information in the CSA is provided through the ASSIGN command.

- The *Common Work Area* (*CWA*) is a storage area that can be accessed by any task in a CICS system. Its format is installation-dependent. It often contains information such as the company name, the current date already converted to the form MM/DD/YYYY, or other application-specific information.

- The *Terminal Control Table User Area* (*TCTUA*) is a user-defined storage area that's unique to the terminal where the current task is attached, and it's maintained even when no task is attached to the terminal. So you may want to keep terminal-related information there.

- The *Transaction Work Area* (*TWA*) is a storage area that's unique to the current task, so you may want to use it to store information about the execution of a transaction. It's deleted when the task ends.

- To access the CWA, TCTUA, or TWA in the Linkage Section, you use the ADDRESS command to establish addressability, as shown in figure 2-6.

Code that accesses the CWA

```
LINKAGE SECTION.
*
 01   DFHCOMMAREA            PIC X.
*
 01   COMMON-WORK-AREA.
*
      05   CWA-CURRENT-DATE    PIC X(8).
      05   CWA-COMPANY-NAME    PIC X(30).
*
 PROCEDURE DIVISON.
*
 0000-PROCESS-CUSTOMER-INQUIRY.
*
        .
      EXEC CICS
          ADDRESS CWA(ADDRESS OF COMMON-WORK-AREA)
      END-EXEC.
      MOVE CWA-COMPANY-NAME TO COMP0.
```

Figure 2-6

User storage

Sometimes, you may want to allocate storage that's not part of your program's Working-Storage Section. To do that, you issue a GETMAIN command or an input command (such as READ or RECEIVE) using the SET option. These commands allocate storage for you and return the address of that storage to your program. Then, you can access that storage via the Linkage Section.

The Procedure Division: Coding basics

How to code program modules

You can improve the readability of your programs by:

- coding each module in the structure chart as a separate COBOL paragraph.
- using the module number followed by the module name from the structure chart to name each paragraph in the program.
- placing the paragraphs in numerical order in the program.

How to code CICS commands

- Each CICS command must begin with the words EXEC CICS and end with the word END-EXEC.
- To make your programs easier to read, we recommend that you separate options with spaces rather than commas and code each option on a separate line. So, your commands should follow this general format:

```
EXEC CICS
    command option-1(value)
            option-2(value)
                .
                .
                .
END-EXEC.
```

How to handle exceptional conditions

- Nearly all CICS commands can result in one or more unusual situations. CICS notifies you of these situations by raising *exceptional conditions*. For most of these conditions, CICS's default action is to terminate the task abnormally.

- Of the more than 70 exceptional conditions listed in the IBM manual, only a handful represent conditions from which your program should be able to recover. To handle these, you use the RESP option.

- The RESP option can be coded on any CICS command. It names a field where CICS places a response code when an exceptional condition occurs. The field must be defined as a binary fullword (PIC S9(8) COMP). Then, you write program code using the DFHRESP keyword to check the response code and override CICS's default error handling, as shown in figure 2-7.

- With response code checking, CICS never takes its default action for exceptional conditions. You have to handle *all* possible responses to the commands that are coded with the RESP option in your program.

- You can also use another option, RESP2, to provide additional error information. Like the RESP option, it names a binary fullword field to record the information. In most cases, though, the RESP option is adequate.

- The response codes returned by RESP and RESP2 are also available in the Execute Interface Block as EIBRESP and EIBRESP2.

- In older programs, the HANDLE CONDITION command was used for exception handling. But using the RESP option is preferred because it's simpler to code and more efficient at run-time.

Response code checking in a read module

```
EXEC CICS
    READ FILE('CUSTMAS')
        INTO(CUSTOMER-MASTER-RECORD)
        RIDFLD(CUSTNOI)
        RESP(RESPONSE-CODE)
END-EXEC.
EVALUATE RESPONSE-CODE
    WHEN DFHRESP(NORMAL)
        MOVE 'Y' TO VALID-DATA-SW
            .
            .
            .
    WHEN DFHRESP(NOTFND)
        MOVE 'N' TO VALID-DATA-SW
        MOVE 'That customer does not exist.' TO MESSAGEO
            .
            .
            .
    WHEN OTHER
        EXEC CICS
            ABEND
        END-EXEC
END-EVALUATE.
```

Figure 2-7

The Procedure Division: Controlling program processing

The guidelines that follow help you implement the design in your event/response charts and structure charts. These guidelines focus on the control logic in a program, so they deal mainly with responding to user events and the contexts in which they occur.

Traditional design: How to code the top-level module of a program

- The coding for the top-level module of a typical pseudo-conversational program using traditional design consists mostly of a single COBOL Evaluate statement that implements the program's event-handling logic, as shown in figure 2-8. Simply put, the Evaluate statement provides a response for each event the program is designed to handle.

- After the Evaluate statement, a RETURN command is used to terminate the program, specifying a trans-id to set up the next pseudo-conversational execution of the program.

- Sometimes you'll need to know the context of an event to determine the appropriate response. To keep track of the program's current context, code a flag field in the communication area, like the one shown in figure 2-9. Then, each time the context changes, the program can set the flag accordingly and on the next execution, it can evaluate the flag as needed.

Traditional design: The top-level module of an inquiry program

```
0000-PROCESS-CUSTOMER-INQUIRY.
*
    EVALUATE TRUE
*
        WHEN EIBCALEN = ZERO
            MOVE LOW-VALUE TO INQMAP1O
            MOVE 'INQ1'    TO TRANIDO
            SET SEND-ERASE TO TRUE
            PERFORM 1400-SEND-CUSTOMER-MAP
*
        WHEN EIBAID = DFHCLEAR
            MOVE LOW-VALUE TO INQMAP1O
            MOVE 'INQ1'    TO TRANIDO
            SET SEND-ERASE TO TRUE
            PERFORM 1400-SEND-CUSTOMER-MAP
*
        WHEN EIBAID = DFHPA1 OR DFHPA2 OR DFHPA3
            CONTINUE
*
        WHEN EIBAID = DFHPF3 OR DFHPF12
            EXEC CICS
                XCTL PROGRAM('INVMENU')
            END-EXEC
*
        WHEN EIBAID = DFHENTER
            PERFORM 1000-PROCESS-CUSTOMER-MAP
*
        WHEN OTHER
            MOVE LOW-VALUE TO INQMAP1O
            MOVE 'Invalid key pressed.' TO MESSAGEO
            SET SEND-DATAONLY-ALARM TO TRUE
            PERFORM 1400-SEND-CUSTOMER-MAP
*
    END-EVALUATE.
*
    EXEC CICS
        RETURN TRANSID('INQ1')
                COMMAREA(COMMUNICATION-AREA)
    END-EXEC.
```

Figure 2-8

A typical context flag that can be checked in an Evaluate statement

```
05  CA-CONTEXT-FLAG              PIC X.
    88  CA-PROCESS-KEY-MAP              VALUE '1'.
    88  CA-PROCESS-ADD-CUSTOMER         VALUE '2'.
    88  CA-PROCESS-CHANGE-CUSTOMER      VALUE '3'.
    88  CA-PROCESS-DELETE-CUSTOMER      VALUE '4'.
```

Figure 2-9

Modular design: How to code the top-level module of the business logic portion

In a modular program, the logic in the top-level module of the presentation portion of the program is almost identical to what it would be in a traditional program. However, the business portion of the program doesn't have to handle user events or send information to the terminal. It just has to handle the data that's passed to it. As a result, there are some differences in how the top-level module is coded, as shown in figure 2-10.

- The top-level module of a business logic program should start by checking that the length of the data that's passed to it is the same as the length of its communication area. If it's not, it should set up the appropriate error processing. If it is, it should move DFHCOMMAREA to the communication area that's defined in working storage.

- The main logic of a business logic program can be coded in an Evaluate statement, just like the main logic of other pseudo-conversational programs. In this case, though, the logic is based on the context flag that's passed to the program through its communication area. It doesn't need to deal with user events.

- After the program does its processing, it should move the communication area in working storage to DFHCOMMAREA so that this data is then available to the presentation logic program. Then, it should issue a RETURN command to return control to the presentation logic program.

Modular design: The top-level module of the business logic portion of a maintenance program

```
      0000-PROCESS-CUSTOMER-RECORD.
  *
          IF EIBCALEN NOT = LENGTH OF DFHCOMMAREA
              SET PROCESS-SEVERE-ERROR TO TRUE
              PERFORM 9000-SET-ERROR-INFO
          ELSE
              MOVE DFHCOMMAREA TO COMMUNICATION-AREA
              EVALUATE TRUE
                  WHEN PROCESS-KEY-MAP
                      PERFORM 1000-PROCESS-CUSTOMER-KEY
                  WHEN PROCESS-ADD-CUSTOMER
                      PERFORM 2000-PROCESS-ADD-CUSTOMER
                  WHEN PROCESS-CHANGE-CUSTOMER
                      PERFORM 3000-PROCESS-CHANGE-CUSTOMER
                  WHEN PROCESS-DELETE-CUSTOMER
                      PERFORM 4000-PROCESS-DELETE-CUSTOMER
              END-EVALUATE
          END-IF.
  *
          MOVE COMMUNICATION-AREA TO DFHCOMMAREA.
          EXEC CICS
              RETURN
          END-EXEC.
```

Figure 2-10

How to detect the use of AID keys

- When a pseudo-conversational program is started, CICS places a value in the Execute Interface Block field EIBAID that indicates which attention key the user pressed.

- To make coding easier and clearer, the EIBAID values are assigned to data names in the IBM-supplied copy member DFHAID, the first part of which is shown in figure 2-11. The highlighted fields are the ones you're likely to use most often.

- You can test the EIBAID field in the top-level module of a program to determine how the program should respond to each attention key, as shown in figure 2-12.

The beginning of the DFHAID copy member

```
01    DFHAID.
      02   DFHNULL    PIC   X   VALUE IS ' '.
      02   DFHENTER   PIC   X   VALUE IS ''''.
      02   DFHCLEAR   PIC   X   VALUE IS '_'.
      02   DFHCLRP    PIC   X   VALUE IS '('.
      02   DFHPEN     PIC   X   VALUE IS '='.
      02   DFHOPID    PIC   X   VALUE IS 'W'.
      02   DFHMSRE    PIC   X   VALUE IS 'X'.
      02   DFHSTRF    PIC   X   VALUE IS 'h'.
      02   DFHTRIG    PIC   X   VALUE IS '''.
      02   DFHPA1     PIC   X   VALUE IS '%'.
      02   DFHPA2     PIC   X   VALUE IS ''.
      02   DFHPA3     PIC   X   VALUE IS ','.
      02   DFHPF1     PIC   X   VALUE IS '1'.
      02   DFHPF2     PIC   X   VALUE IS '2'.
      02   DFHPF3     PIC   X   VALUE IS '3'.
      02   DFHPF4     PIC   X   VALUE IS '4'.
      02   DFHPF5     PIC   X   VALUE IS '5'.
      02   DFHPF6     PIC   X   VALUE IS '6'.
      02   DFHPF7     PIC   X   VALUE IS '7'.
      02   DFHPF8     PIC   X   VALUE IS '8'.
      02   DFHPF9     PIC   X   VALUE IS '9'.
      02   DFHPF10    PIC   X   VALUE IS ':'.
      02   DFHPF11    PIC   X   VALUE IS '#'.
      02   DFHPF12    PIC   X   VALUE IS '@'.
      .
      .
      .
```

Figure 2-11

Using the EIBAID field to manage the event context of a customer maintenance program

```
000-PROCESS-CUSTOMER-MAINT.
    .
    .
    EVALUATE TRUE                                                         ┐
        WHEN EIBCALEN = ZERO                                             │
            .                                                            │
        WHEN EIBAID = DFHPF3                                             │
            .                                                            │
        WHEN EIBAID = DFHPF12                                            │
            IF PROCESS-KEY-MAP                                           │
                .                                                        │
            ELSE                                             Check for all contexts
                .                                            of all valid attention
            END-IF                                           keys (except Enter)
        WHEN EIBAID = DFHCLEAR                                           │
            IF PROCESS-KEY-MAP                                           │
                .                                                        │
            ELSE                                                         │
                .                                                        │
            END-IF                                                       │
        WHEN EIBAID = DFHPA1 OR DFHPA2 OR DFHPA3                         │
            CONTINUE                                                     ┘
        WHEN EIBAID = DFHENTER                                          ┐
            EVALUATE TRUE                                               │
                WHEN PROCESS-KEY-MAP                                     │
                    .                                                    │
                WHEN PROCESS-ADD-CUSTOMER                     Check for all contexts
                    .                                        of the Enter key
                WHEN PROCESS-CHANGE-CUSTOMER                             │
                    .                                                    │
                WHEN PROCESS-DELETE-CUSTOMER                             │
                    .                                                    │
            END-EVALUATE                                                ┘
        WHEN OTHER                                                      ┐
            IF PROCESS-KEY-MAP                                          │
                .                                            Check for all invalid
            ELSE                                             attention keys
                .                                                        │
            END-IF                                                      ┘
    END-EVALUATE.
```

Figure 2-12

How to invoke other programs

If your program needs to invoke another program, there are three ways to do it: (1) invoke another CICS program with a CICS LINK command, (2) invoke another CICS program with a CICS XCTL command, or (3) invoke a subprogram with a COBOL Call statement.

- The LINK command invokes a separate CICS program. When the invoked program ends by issuing a RETURN command, control returns to the invoking program at the point immediately after the LINK command.

- The XCTL command also transfers control to another CICS program. But unlike the LINK command, the XCTL command provides no return mechanism. Instead, the program that issues the XCTL command is terminated and the specified program is invoked.

- The COBOL Call statement invokes a COBOL subprogram that resides on the local system (to invoke a subprogram on a remote system, you use the LINK command). If the subprogram issues CICS commands, the Call statement must pass DFHEIBLK and DFHCOMMAREA as the first two parameters of the Using clause. The CICS translator automatically adds these areas to the Linkage Section of the subprogram and includes them in the Using clause of the Procedure Division statement.

- A subprogram that's invoked by a Call statement can be statically or dynamically linked to the calling program. If the subprogram is statically linked, it must be link-edited with the calling program to form one load module. If it's dynamically linked, a separate load module is created for the subprogram. A statically linked subprogram offers a slight performance advantage over a dynamically linked one, but the difference is negligible.

- One way of thinking of program control within a CICS task is in terms of logical levels, as shown in figure 2-13. CICS is always at the highest logical level. A LINK command transfers control to a program at the next lower logical level. In contrast, the XCTL command and the Call statement pass control to a program at the same level.

- The CICS RETURN command always returns control to the next higher logical level. That's true even if the RETURN command is issued from a subprogram invoked by a Call statement. However, if the subprogram ends with a COBOL Goback statement, control returns to the calling program.

How control is passed from one program to another under CICS

Logical level

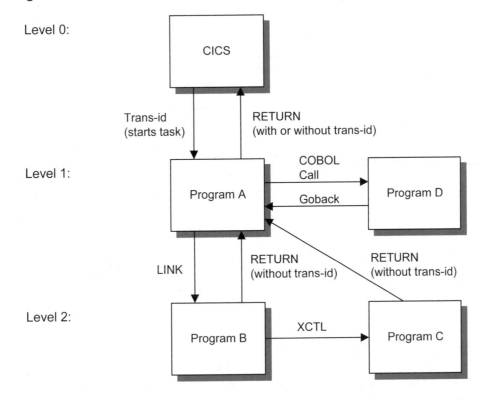

Figure 2-13

The Procedure Division:
User interface and I/O considerations

As in most batch COBOL programs, a lot of the Procedure Division code in a command-level CICS program is written to handle I/O. In the case of a CICS program, however, that I/O handling includes working with the user interface as well as the input the user enters. As for traditional file I/O, there are additional considerations to maintaining file integrity as multiple users access and update the same files on an interactive basis.

How to modify attribute bytes

When you define a BMS map, you specify attributes (such as normal or high intensity and protected or unprotected) for each field on the screen. When you issue a SEND MAP command, however, you can change those attributes by moving a value to the attribute byte field in the field's symbolic map description. For example, if a user enters a field incorrectly, you can change that field's attribute byte to specify high intensity and then send the map (including an appropriate error message) back to the terminal. That way, the error will be more obvious.

- To change an attribute, you can move a hex value that specifies the new attribute to the attribute byte field. But that's difficult to do.

- It's more common to use a copy member like the one in figure 2-14 that assigns names and values to common attribute values. Then, you can use the field names in the copy member to set the attributes.

- IBM supplies a copy member named DFHBMSCA that includes many attribute settings. However, it doesn't include all of the attribute byte values you need to use, and the names assigned to the attributes are cryptic. Instead of DFHBMSCA, then, you should use the copy member that your shop uses or code your own as shown in this figure.

A typical copy member for attribute definitions

```
01  ATTRIBUTE-DEFINITIONS.
*STANDARD ATTRIBUTES*
    05  ATTR-UNPROT                     PIC X    VALUE ' '.
    05  ATTR-UNPROT-MDT                 PIC X    VALUE X'C1'.
    05  ATTR-UNPROT-BRT                 PIC X    VALUE X'C8'.
    05  ATTR-UNPROT-BRT-MDT             PIC X    VALUE X'C9'.
    05  ATTR-UNPROT-DARK                PIC X    VALUE X'4C'.
    05  ATTR-UNPROT-DARK-MDT            PIC X    VALUE X'4D'.
    05  ATTR-UNPROT-NUM                 PIC X    VALUE X'50'.
    05  ATTR-UNPROT-NUM-MDT             PIC X    VALUE X'D1'.
    05  ATTR-UNPROT-NUM-BRT             PIC X    VALUE X'D8'.
    05  ATTR-UNPROT-NUM-BRT-MDT         PIC X    VALUE X'D9'.
    05  ATTR-UNPROT-NUM-DARK            PIC X    VALUE X'5C'.
    05  ATTR-UNPROT-NUM-DARK-MDT        PIC X    VALUE X'5D'.
    05  ATTR-PROT                       PIC X    VALUE X'60'.
    05  ATTR-PROT-MDT                   PIC X    VALUE X'61'.
    05  ATTR-PROT-BRT                   PIC X    VALUE X'E8'.
    05  ATTR-PROT-BRT-MDT               PIC X    VALUE X'E9'.
    05  ATTR-PROT-DARK                  PIC X    VALUE '%'.
    05  ATTR-PROT-DARK-MDT              PIC X    VALUE X'6D'.
    05  ATTR-PROT-SKIP                  PIC X    VALUE X'F0'.
    05  ATTR-PROT-SKIP-MDT              PIC X    VALUE X'F1'.
    05  ATTR-PROT-SKIP-BRT              PIC X    VALUE X'F8'.
    05  ATTR-PROT-SKIP-BRT-MDT          PIC X    VALUE X'F9'.
    05  ATTR-PROT-SKIP-DARK             PIC X    VALUE X'7C'.
    05  ATTR-PROT-SKIP-DARK-MDT         PIC X    VALUE X'7D'.
*EXTENDED HIGHLIGHTING*
    05  ATTR-NO-HIGHLIGHT               PIC X    VALUE X'00'.
    05  ATTR-BLINK                      PIC X    VALUE '1'.
    05  ATTR-REVERSE                    PIC X    VALUE '2'.
    05  ATTR-UNDERSCORE                 PIC X    VALUE '4'.
*EXTENDED COLOR*
    05  ATTR-DEFAULT-COLOR              PIC X    VALUE X'00'.
    05  ATTR-BLUE                       PIC X    VALUE '1'.
    05  ATTR-RED                        PIC X    VALUE '2'.
    05  ATTR-PINK                       PIC X    VALUE '3'.
    05  ATTR-GREEN                      PIC X    VALUE '4'.
    05  ATTR-TURQUOISE                  PIC X    VALUE '5'.
    05  ATTR-YELLOW                     PIC X    VALUE '6'.
    05  ATTR-NEUTRAL                    PIC X    VALUE '7'.
```

COBOL Move statements that change the attributes of two fields

```
MOVE ATTR-UNPROT-BRT TO CUSTNOA.
MOVE ATTR-RED        TO MSGC.
```

Figure 2-14

How to control cursor positioning

Whenever your program issues a SEND MAP command, it should specify in one way or another where the cursor is to be placed on the screen. Listed below are three techniques you can use to position the cursor. Although all three techniques work, you'll find that symbolic cursor positioning offers a flexibility that the other two techniques lack.

The IC option in the DFHMDF macro for a field

- The simplest way to handle cursor positioning is to specify the IC option in one of the fields in the BMS mapset definition. This causes the cursor to be positioned in that field. However, if you need to reposition the cursor on another field, you'll need to specify the CURSOR option on the SEND MAP command.

```
CUSTNO    DFHMDF POS=(2,26),                                            X
                 LENGTH=6,                                              X
                 ATTRB=(NORM,UNPROT,IC),                                X
                 INITIAL='_____'
```

Direct cursor positioning

- In the CURSOR option of the SEND MAP command, you can specify the desired screen position using a value that represents the displacement from the start of the screen:

```
EXEC CICS
    SEND MAP('MNTMAP1')
         MAPSET('MNTSET1')
         FROM(MNTMAP1O)
         CURSOR(346)
END-EXEC.
```

- For a 24x80 screen, the value must be from 0 to 1919, where 0 is row 1/column 1 and 1919 is row 24/column 80. Use this formula to figure the value:

```
(Row-number - 1) x 80 + (Column-number - 1) = Displacement
```

- The drawback of this approach is that it ties your program to specific screen locations. So if you change your mapset, you'll also have to change your SEND MAP commands to indicate the new screen locations.

Symbolic cursor positioning

- For symbolic cursor positioning, you specify which map field will contain the cursor by moving -1 to the map field's length field in the symbolic map. Then, when you issue the SEND MAP command, you specify the CURSOR option without a value. If you move -1 to more than one length field, the cursor is positioned at the first field containing -1.

```
MOVE -1 TO CUSTNO1L.
EXEC CICS
    SEND MAP('MNTMAP1')
         MAPSET('MNTSET1')
         FROM(MNTMAP1O)
         CURSOR
END-EXEC.
```

How to edit terminal input data

- Most CICS programs have to edit data entered by the user to make sure that no fields are missing, that the entries consist of valid data, and that related fields (like state and zip code) have logically related values.

- It's common to edit data entry fields from the bottom of the screen to the top. That way, the error message the program displays relates to the first invalid field on the screen.

- Although there are many ways to edit input data, figure 2-15 shows a general structure you can use. Basically, this module edits each field by using a series of nested IF statements to test for required conditions.

- When you detect an error, you do four things: (1) modify the attribute byte field in the symbolic map so the error is highlighted, (2) move -1 to the length field so the cursor will be positioned in the field, (3) move an error message to the error message field, and (4) set a switch to indicate an input error has been detected.

- An edit module coded according to this figure can be long. You don't have to worry about that if the module's structure is straightforward. However, if some fields require complicated edits (like table or file look-ups), by all means create separate modules for them.

The general structure of an edit module

```
MOVE ATTR-NO-HIGHLIGHT TO extended highlight field for all map fields.

IF error-condition-1 for field-1
    MOVE ATTR-REVERSE  TO extended highlight field for field-1
    MOVE -1            TO length field for field-1
    MOVE error-message TO message field
    MOVE 'N'           TO VALID-DATA-SW
ELSE IF error-condition-2 for field-1
    .
    .
    .
IF error-condition-1 for field-2
    .
    .
    .
IF tests for cross-validation conditions
    .
    .
    .
```

Figure 2-15

How to update file records

Many of the CICS programs you develop will require you to update records in one or more data sets. Although the coding for file updates is relatively straightforward, there are two special considerations to be aware of: (1) avoiding deadlock when updating more than one record and (2) assuring file integrity when updating records in a pseudo-conversational program.

Problem 1: Deadlock

What happens

- *Deadlock* occurs when two tasks are each waiting for a resource that the other is holding. This often happens when two programs are both attempting to update the same two records in two different files, but in a different order. In that case, each program could be holding a record that the other program needs to read for update.

How to handle it

- The easiest way to avoid deadlock is to establish a standard order for updating files. For example, many installations specify that files be updated in alphabetical order, and that file records be updated in key sequence.

Problem 2: File integrity is threatened

What happens

- The UPDATE option of a READ command reserves a record only for the duration of the task. So while a record is displayed at the terminal waiting for the user to enter changes, another program may modify or delete it.

The simplest and most common solution: Detect the problem

- Each pseudo-conversational program that updates a record saves an image of the record between task executions, usually in a temporary storage queue that's uniquely identified by the terminal-id. Then, in the next execution, the program retrieves both the file record and the saved image and compares them. If they're different, it means that the record has been changed by another user, and the update is cancelled.

Another alternative: Prevent the problem

- All the programs in a shop follow a standard way of indicating that a record is being updated. For example, the first byte of a file record could be an "update in progress" switch that's turned on when a program first accesses the record, and turned off when the update is completed. All other programs that update the file must test the switch to see if the record is available.
- A problem with this approach is that the program that initially sets the switch may be unable to reset it. (The program may abend, the system may abend, or the terminal or network may go down.) If that happens, the record will be locked out indefinitely unless a special program is written to clear the switch.

COBOL features you can't use in a command-level CICS program

As you code your command-level programs in COBOL, you must remember that many features of standard COBOL can't be used in a CICS program. Most, but not all, of those features are for functions that are performed using CICS commands instead of standard COBOL statements, as listed in figure 2-16.

- Under CICS, all terminal I/O is handled by the terminal control module, whose services are typically requested by issuing SEND MAP and RECEIVE MAP commands. Because of that, COBOL Accept and Display statements aren't allowed in CICS programs.

- Under CICS, all file I/O is handled by the file control module, whose services are requested by issuing CICS file control commands like READ, WRITE, REWRITE, and DELETE. Because of that, the COBOL statements for file I/O aren't allowed. In addition, Environment Division and File Section statements that pertain to data management should not be coded.

- COBOL statements that invoke operating system functions, like Accept Date and Accept Time, are not allowed. However, COBOL intrinsic functions are allowed.

- Although the COBOL statements for sorting (Sort, Release, and Return) are allowed, their functionality is severely restricted. Because of that, you'll probably never use them. Merge statements are never allowed.

COBOL statements not allowed in CICS programs

Operator communication statements

Accept
Display

File I/O statements

Open
Close
Read
Write
Rewrite
Delete
Start

Other statements

Accept Date/Day/Day-Of-Week/Time
Merge

Figure 2-16

Coding conventions found in older programs

If you're assigned the task of maintaining existing CICS programs, you may come across some coding conventions that haven't been summarized in this section and that don't appear in the model programs in Units 5 and 6. That's particularly true if the programs were written to run under older compilers (typically, the OS/VS COBOL compiler). So figure 2-17 summarizes the coding conventions you're likely to run into in older programs and the way the code is handled in newer programs.

- The HANDLE AID and HANDLE CONDITION commands are described in Unit 8, and you can see an example of each one there.

- The ADDRESS OF special register shown in figure 2-6 was introduced in VS COBOL II. Under OS/VS COBOL, you had to use a coding convention called *Base Locator for Linkage*, or *BLL*, that used pointers to establish addressability to Linkage Section areas like the CWA. (If you need an example of this, please see our book, *Murach's CICS for the COBOL Programmer*.)

- The LENGTH option is still included on many commands, but it's usually optional under VS COBOL II and later compilers. Under OS/VS COBOL, however, it was required in many instances. For example, this option had to be coded on LINK, XCTL, and RETURN commands that included the COMMAREA option to indicate the length of the communication area.

Coding conventions that a maintenance programmer may deal with

Function	Older coding convention	Now done by
Determine what AID key a user pressed to start a program	HANDLE AID command	Checking EIBAID field
Handle exceptional conditions	HANDLE CONDITION command	Response code checking using the RESP option
Access Linkage Section data outside of the communication area and the Execute Interface Block	Base Locator for Linkage (BLL)	Using the COBOL ADDRESS OF special register
Specify the length of I/O areas	LENGTH option of various commands	None

Figure 2-17

Unit 3

JCL procedures for CICS program development

This unit shows you the JCL you need to code to prepare BMS mapsets and command-level COBOL programs for execution on an IBM mainframe under the OS/390 or z/OS operating system. It begins with an overview of the steps involved, followed by the JCL requirements and a brief description of the translator and compiler options you're likely to use. If you don't know much about JCL and would like to have a better understanding of the code that's shown in this unit, please see our book, *Murach's OS/390 and z/OS JCL*.

Preparing a CICS program for execution

Figure 3-1 illustrates the basic process of preparing a CICS program for execution. The left side of this figure shows how BMS mapsets are prepared, while the right side shows how a command-level COBOL program is prepared.

- The source program containing BMS macro instructions is processed by the assembler to produce an object module (the physical map) and a symbolic map. The physical map is then processed by the linkage editor to produce a load module, used by CICS at execution time.

- The source program containing a mixture of standard COBOL statements and CICS commands is processed by the command-level translator, which translates the CICS commands to equivalent COBOL statements. (Each command results in a series of Move statements followed by a Call statement.) Then, the translated program, also in source form, is processed by the COBOL compiler to produce an object module, which is then processed by the linkage editor to produce a load module.

- Besides processing the translated program, the COBOL compiler also processes the symbolic map produced by the assembler.

- Since the translator and compiler execute as separate job steps, you get two sets of source listings and diagnostics. The translator output contains a listing of the source program as you wrote it plus any diagnostic messages related to CICS commands. The compiler output contains a listing of the translated program plus any diagnostics related to standard COBOL statements. As a result, you have to examine both listings to determine if your program was processed without errors.

- Although the translator source listing can be useful at times, you'll probably use the compiler listing most often when testing or debugging your program. That's because the compiler listing contains the expansions of all Copy members included in your program. However, it also contains expansions of all the CICS commands, which can cut down on readability.

The system flowchart for preparing a CICS program for execution

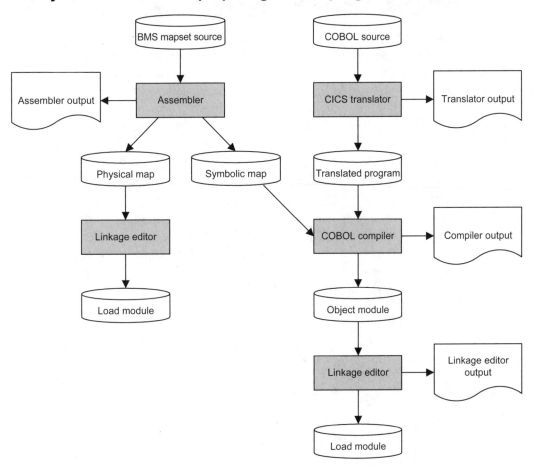

Figure 3-1

How to prepare a BMS mapset

To prepare a BMS mapset, you use the standard cataloged procedure called DFHMAPS, shown in figure 3-2. This procedure processes the BMS mapset source file twice to produce both a symbolic map and a physical map. Many installations have customized the DFHMAPS procedure or have created different procedures altogether. In addition, IBM provides another cataloged procedure that lets you generate an HTML template as well as the physical and symbolic maps from a BMS mapset (for details on this procedure, please see Unit 10). So find out what procedures to use at your shop.

- The DFHMAPS procedure consists of the four job steps shaded in this figure. The COPY step invokes the IEBGENER utility program to copy the BMS source program to a temporary data set that's used as input in the ASMMAP and ASMDSECT job steps. The ASMMAP step invokes the assembler to create a physical map (an object module). The LINKMAP step invokes the linkage editor to process the object module, resulting in a load module that can be used by CICS. And the ASMDSECT step invokes the assembler again, this time creating the symbolic map.

- Both the ASMMAP and the ASMDSECT job steps set the SYSPARM variable to indicate whether the assembler should produce a physical map or a symbolic map. As a result, the DFHMAPS procedure won't work properly unless you specify TYPE=&SYSPARM in the DFHMSD macro instruction in the BMS mapset.

The bottom part of this figure shows how to invoke the DFHMAPS procedure. You specify PROC=DFHMAPS on an EXEC statement along with any required parameters. Then, you supply one or more DD statements to identify data sets required by the procedure.

- There are three symbolic parameters you may need to specify. The MAPLIB parameter specifies the name of the load library that will contain the physical map. The DSCTLIB parameter specifies the name of the source library that will contain the symbolic map. And the MAPNAME parameter specifies the member name to use for the map in both the physical map load library and the symbolic map source library.

- Before processing a BMS mapset with the DFHMAPS procedure, check and see what the default values are for the MAPLIB and DSCTLIB parameters. Often, shops may neglect to specify the correct libraries for both.

- To allocate required data sets, you supply one or more DD statements. At the minimum, you must supply a SYSUT1 DD statement for the COPY step to identify the source program (usually, a member of a partitioned data set or an instream data set). To store the load module in a library other than the procedure's default, you can supply a SYSLMOD DD statement for the LINKMAP step. And to redirect the symbolic map output, you can specify a SYSPUNCH DD statement for the ASMDSECT step.

The IBM procedure for preparing a BMS mapset (DFHMAPS)

```
//DFHMAPS PROC INDEX='CICSTS13.CICS', FOR SDFHMAC
//             MAPLIB='CICSTS13.CICS.SDFHLOAD', TARGET FOR MAP
//             DSCTLIB='CICSTS13.CICS.SDFHMAC', TARGET FOR DSECT
//             MAPNAME=,                          NAME OF MAPSET - REQUIRED
//             A=,                                A=A FOR ALIGNED MAP
//             RMODE=24,                          24/ANY
//             ASMBLR=ASMA90,                     ASSEMBLER PROGRAM NAME
//             REG=2048K,                         REGION FOR ASSEMBLY
//             OUTC=A,                            PRINT SYSOUT CLASS
//             WORK=SYSDA                         WORK FILE UNIT
//COPY     EXEC PGM=IEBGENER
//SYSPRINT DD SYSOUT=&OUTC
//SYSUT2   DD DSN=&&TEMPM,UNIT=&WORK,DISP=(,PASS),
//            DCB=(RECFM=FB,LRECL=80,BLKSIZE=400),
//            SPACE=(400,(50,50))
//SYSIN    DD DUMMY
//* SYSUT1 DD * NEEDED FOR THE MAP SOURCE
//ASMMAP   EXEC PGM=&ASMBLR,REGION=&REG,
//* NOLOAD CHANGED TO NOOBJECT
//  PARM='SYSPARM(&A.MAP),DECK,NOOBJECT'
//SYSPRINT DD SYSOUT=&OUTC
//SYSLIB   DD DSN=&INDEX..SDFHMAC,DISP=SHR
//         DD DSN=SYS1.MACLIB,DISP=SHR
//SYSUT1   DD UNIT=&WORK,SPACE=(CYL,(5,5))
//SYSUT2   DD UNIT=&WORK,SPACE=(CYL,(5,5))
//SYSUT3   DD UNIT=&WORK,SPACE=(CYL,(5,5))
//SYSPUNCH DD DSN=&&MAP,DISP=(,PASS),UNIT=&WORK,
//            DCB=(RECFM=FB,LRECL=80,BLKSIZE=400),
//            SPACE=(400,(50,50))
//SYSIN    DD DSN=&&TEMPM,DISP=(OLD,PASS)
//LINKMAP  EXEC PGM=IEWL,PARM='LIST,LET,XREF,RMODE(&RMODE)'
//SYSPRINT DD SYSOUT=&OUTC
//SYSLMOD  DD DSN=&MAPLIB(&MAPNAME),DISP=SHR
//SYSUT1   DD UNIT=&WORK,SPACE=(1024,(20,20))
//SYSLIN   DD DSN=&&MAP,DISP=(OLD,DELETE)
//* NOLOAD CHANGED TO NOOBJECT
//ASMDSECT EXEC PGM=&ASMBLR,REGION=&REG,
//  PARM='SYSPARM(&A.DSECT),DECK,NOOBJECT'
//SYSPRINT DD SYSOUT=&OUTC
//SYSLIB   DD DSN=&INDEX..SDFHMAC,DISP=SHR
//         DD DSN=SYS1.MACLIB,DISP=SHR
//SYSUT1   DD UNIT=&WORK,SPACE=(CYL,(5,5))
//SYSUT2   DD UNIT=&WORK,SPACE=(CYL,(5,5))
//SYSUT3   DD UNIT=&WORK,SPACE=(CYL,(5,5))
//SYSPUNCH DD DSN=&DSCTLIB(&MAPNAME),DISP=OLD
//SYSIN    DD DSN=&&TEMPM,DISP=(OLD,DELETE)
```

The JCL to invoke this procedure

```
//MM01MAPS JOB  (36512),'R.MENENDEZ',NOTIFY=MM01
//MAPASM   EXEC DFHMAPS,
//             MAPLIB='MM01.CICS.LOADLIB',    TARGET LOADLIB FOR MAP
//             DSCTLIB='MM01.CICS.COPYLIB',   TARGET COPYLIB FOR DSECT
//             MAPNAME=ORDSET1                NAME OF MAPSET (REQUIRED)
//COPY.SYSUT1 DD DSN=MM01.CICS.SOURCE(ORDSET1),DISP=SHR    MAPSET SOURCE
/*
```

Figure 3-2

How to prepare a command-level COBOL program

To prepare a command-level COBOL program for execution, you use the
standard cataloged procedure DFHYITVL, as shown in figure 3-3. This procedure
translates, compiles, and link-edits a command-level program. Like DFHMAPS,
many shops have customized the DFHYITVL procedure or developed their own.
So find out what procedure to use at your installation.

- None of the DFHYITVL symbolic parameters are of general interest to application programmers. However, you can use the PARM parameter on the EXEC
statement that invokes the procedure to specify options for the translator or the
compiler (these options are covered later in this unit). To specify translator
options, specify PARM.TRN on the EXEC statement; to specify compiler
options, specify PARM.COB.

- When you use a PARM parameter, the options you specify override all of the
options set by the procedure. So check the procedure to find out what options
you're overriding, particularly when you're coding PARM.COB. Then, be sure
to include the options you want to keep along with the additional options you
want to specify.

- DFHYITVL has three job steps that are shaded in this figure. The TRN step
translates the source program, producing a translated version of the source
program in a temporary data set. The COB step compiles the translated program produced by the TRN step. And the LKED step link-edits the object
module produced by the COB step.

- When you invoke the procedure, you must supply a SYSIN DD statement for
the TRN step to identify the source program (usually a partitioned data set
member or an instream data set).

- For the COB step, you may need to supply a SYSLIB DD statement to allocate
the source statement libraries your program needs. You code the statement so
the libraries are concatenated to those in the procedure's COB.SYSLIB DD
statement.

- For the LKED step, you must identify the member name for the load module in
one of two ways. If you want the member to be stored in the procedure's
default load library, you can specify a LKED.SYSIN DD statement that includes a NAME statement as instream data. If you want to use a library other
than the procedure's default, however, you can include a LKED.SYSLMOD
DD statement that provides a complete data set and member name.

- If your program calls static subprograms, you also need to code a SYSLIB DD
statement for the LKED step to identify the object library that contains the
subprograms. You concatenate this library with the libraries that are allocated in
the procedure using a statement like this:

```
//LKED.SYSLIB   DD
//              DD
//              DD DSN=MMA2.CICS.OBJLIB,DISP=SHR
```

The IBM translate-compile-and-link procedure for CICS/COBOL (DFHYITVL)

```
//DFHYITVL PROC SUFFIX=1$,            Suffix for translator module
//         INDEX='CICSTS13.CICS', Qualifier(s) for CICS libraries
//         PROGLIB='CICSTS13.CICS.SDFHLOAD', Name of o/p library
//         DSCTLIB='CICSTS13.CICS.SDFHCOB',  Private macro/dsect
//         AD370HLQ='SYS1',          Qualifier(s) for AD/Cycle compiler
//         LE370HLQ='SYS1',          Qualifier(s) for LE/370 libraries
//         OUTC=A,                   Class for print output
//         REG=4M,                   Region size for all steps
//         LNKPARM='LIST,XREF',      Link edit parameters
//         STUB='DFHEILID',          Lked INC. fr DFHELII
//         LIB='SDFHC370',           Library
//         WORK=SYSDA                Unit for work datasets
//TRN      EXEC PGM=DFHECP&SUFFIX,PARM='COBOL3',REGION=&REG
//STEPLIB  DD DSN=&INDEX..SDFHLOAD,DISP=SHR
//SYSPRINT DD SYSOUT=&OUTC
//SYSPUNCH DD DSN=&&SYSCIN,DISP=(,PASS),
//            UNIT=&WORK,DCB=BLKSIZE=400,
//            SPACE=(400,(400,100))
//COB      EXEC PGM=IGYCRCTL,REGION=&REG,
//         PARM='NODYNAM,LIB,OBJECT,RENT,RES,APOST,MAP,XREF'
//STEPLIB  DD DSN=&AD370HLQ..SIGYCOMP,DISP=SHR
//SYSLIB   DD DSN=&DSCTLIB,DISP=SHR
//         DD DSN=&INDEX..SDFHCOB,DISP=SHR
//         DD DSN=&INDEX..SDFHMAC,DISP=SHR
//         DD DSN=&INDEX..SDFHSAMP,DISP=SHR
//SYSPRINT DD SYSOUT=&OUTC
//SYSIN    DD DSN=&&SYSCIN,DISP=(OLD,DELETE)
//SYSLIN   DD DSN=&&LOADSET,DISP=(MOD,PASS),
//            UNIT=&WORK,SPACE=(80,(250,100))
 .
 .
 .
//LKED     EXEC PGM=IEWL,REGION=&REG,
//            PARM='&LNKPARM',COND=(5,LT,COB)
//SYSLIB   DD DSN=&INDEX..SDFHLOAD,DISP=SHR
//         DD DSN=&LE370HLQ..SCEELKED,DISP=SHR
 .
 .
 .
//SYSLIN   DD DSN=&&COPYLINK,DISP=(OLD,DELETE)
//         DD DSN=&&LOADSET,DISP=(OLD,DELETE)
//         DD DDNAME=SYSIN
```

The JCL to invoke this procedure

```
//MM01CMPL    JOB  (36512),'R.MENENDEZ',NOTIFY=MM01
//CICSCMP     EXEC DFHYITVL,
//            PROGLIB='MM01.CICS.LOADLIB'
//TRN.SYSIN   DD   DSN=MM01.CICS.SOURCE(CUSTMNT1),DISP=SHR
//COB.SYSLIB  DD
//            DD   DSN=MM01.CICS.COPYLIB,DISP=SHR
//LKED.SYSIN  DD   *
   NAME CUSTMNT1(R)
/*
```

Figure 3-3

Translator and compiler options

You can influence how the translator and compiler work by passing options to them, like the ones listed in figures 3-4 and 3-5. Options specified for the translator step affect how the COBOL program is interpreted by the translator, while options specified for the compiler step affect how the actual program is compiled. In most cases, though, you'll find that the translator step works just fine using its default options while the compiler step requires additional options.

- Translator and compiler options can be set at three levels. First, the default options are set when the software is installed. Second, the IBM procedures can override the default options. Third, your JCL can override the IBM procedure options or the system defaults.

- To pass options to the translator or compiler, code the options on the PARM parameter of the EXEC statement, as shown in figure 3-6.

- When you use the PARM parameter, the options you set override all of the options set by the procedure you're using. So if you want to retain any options set in the procedure, you must include them in the PARM list.

- To turn an option on in the PARM parameter, you code one of the option names shown in figures 3-4 and 3-5. To turn an option off, you precede the name by NO as in NOXREF (QUOTE and APOST are exceptions).

- To find out what the default settings are for the compiler options, you can code a PARM parameter with no settings so all the procedure options are overridden, like this:

```
PARM.COB=''
```

Then, you can see the default settings by reviewing the compiler listing.

Translator options for CICS

Option	Function
QUOTE	Use the ANSI standard quotation mark (") to delimit literals.
APOST	Use the apostrophe (') to delimit literals.
EDF	The Execution Diagnostics Facility is to apply to the program.
EXCI	The translator is to process EXCI commands (EXCI is an interface that allows a non-CICS program, such as a batch program, to invoke a CICS program).
FLAG	Print the severity of error messages produced by the translator.
VBREF	Print a CICS command cross-reference.
LENGTH	Generate a default length if the LENGTH option is omitted from a CICS command.
OOCOBOL	Accept object-oriented COBOL syntax.
COBOL3	Translate programs compiled by COBOL for OS/390.

Figure 3-4

Compiler options for COBOL

Category	Option	Function
Object module	OBJECT	Write object module output to SYSLIN.
	DECK	Write object module output to SYSPUNCH.
Delimiter	QUOTE	Use the ANSI standard quotation mark (").
	APOST	Use the apostrophe (').
Source library	LIB	Allow Copy statements.
Compiler listing	SOURCE	Print a source listing.
	OFFSET	Print the offset of each Procedure Division verb.
	LIST	Print an assembler listing of the object module.
	MAP	Print the offset of each Data Division field.
	XREF	Print a sorted cross-reference of data and procedure names.
Testing	TEST	Allow interactive debugging.
	FDUMP	Provide a formatted dump at abend.

Figure 3-5

A JCL EXEC statement that turns two compiler options on and one off

```
//STEP1     EXEC PROC=DFHYITVL,PARM.COB='APOST,OBJECT,NOXREF'
```

Figure 3-6

Unit 4

Testing and debugging

This unit contains reference material that you'll use as you test and debug your command-level programs. To begin, it gives some basic information on testing and how it's handled in different installations. Then, it focuses on doing unit tests of your programs, including considerations for top-down testing and for testing modular programs. Next, it gives you instructions for using five IBM-supplied transactions that are helpful during testing and debugging. And finally, it provides a list of commonly encountered transaction abend codes, along with basic techniques for using a transaction dump, to help you with debugging.

Installation-dependent considerations

As a programmer, it's your responsibility to develop programs that work properly. However, the amount of testing you do, the testing procedures you follow, and the testing and debugging tools that are available to you vary from one shop to another. So here are some general considerations to be aware of when you enter the testing phase of program development.

4 common types of testing

Test	Description
Unit test	The program is tested on its own to insure that it works according to the program specifications.
Concurrency test	The program is tested simultaneously at several terminals to make sure that multiple executions of the same program don't interfere with one another.
Integration test	The program is tested in context with other programs in the application.
Regression test	Testing that was originally done against the program is repeated when the program undergoes maintenance.

- A *unit test* is typically done by the programmer who develops the program. During the unit test, the programmer makes sure that the screens are displayed properly, all field edits work as planned, files are updated correctly, and so on.

- A *concurrency test* is done for a program that's run by two or more users at the same time. This test ensures that two or more simultaneous executions of the program don't interfere with one another. For example, suppose a program holds a copy of a record being updated from one execution to the next so it can check that the record hasn't changed before it's updated or deleted. A concurrency test checks to make sure this mechanism works.

- An *integration test* makes sure that a program will work properly with other programs in the same system. Some programming errors aren't detected until the program interacts with other programs. An integration test can also reveal inconsistencies in application design or screen presentation.

- A *regression test* is done whenever a program that was already approved for production is changed. In a regression test, the entire program is retested, not just the portion of the program that was modified. Since more than 70% of all program development is dedicated to maintaining and enhancing existing systems, the need for solid regression testing is clear.

CICS testing environments

Most installations have you test your programs within a CICS testing environment, or *test region*, that's separate from the production environment. That way, you can thoroughly test your programs without fear of affecting the production system. The testing environment consists of a CICS system that's dedicated to testing and test versions of production files.

Some installations maintain several CICS testing environments for various levels of testing. For example, an installation might use one CICS system to let application programmers do unit and concurrency testing. When those tests are complete, the programmer promotes the program to another CICS system, where integration and regression tests are performed by a separate quality assurance group before the program is promoted to the production system. It's also common for installations to create different CICS testing environments for different development projects, to keep the projects separate.

When you're working on a CICS system dedicated to testing, there are a few things you need to find out. The most important of these are listed in figure 4-1.

What you need to know about the testing environment

- Are there one or more testing environments available to you? What testing is done in what environment?

- Do you need to use generic transaction identifiers and program names within the testing environment? These are often assigned to programmers so that the systems programmer doesn't have to define resources for every program that's under development.

- Are there test versions of the files you need to test your program? If not, find out how to create test versions of the files.

- Are testing and debugging aids like the CEMT, CECI, and CEDF transactions available? Are any third-party tools for testing and debugging available? Test systems often provide access to CICS testing and debugging aids, which are usually off-limits to users of production systems.

- Does your shop have a procedure for managing program testing and program versions? Most installations do. Those policies may consist of a simple set of manual procedures for moving programs from the test environment to the production environment. Or they may require the use of change management software that automates the process, doing tasks like keeping track of the status and location of programs, ensuring that a program isn't being changed by more than one programmer at a time, and so on.

Figure 4-1

Developing a unit test plan

A major pitfall in program development is inadequate testing. All too often, a program is put into production without being tested thoroughly enough to be sure all of its routines work. Since many shops rely heavily on the unit test...and since unit testing is your responsibility...it's a good idea to develop a test plan before you begin this phase. Using an organized approach like this is your best defense against production program failures.

A 3-step plan for unit testing

The following is a generalized, 3-step plan that can serve as a starting point for your own unit test plans.

Step 1   Test your BMS map definitions

You should perform this test before you even start coding the program. That way, you can dispense with trivial problems like misspelled words and misaligned data right away.

Step 2   Test your program with valid transactions

After coding your program, test it using a small set of well-chosen input data and verify the results. In essence, test to make sure that your program is doing what it's supposed to do.

Step 3   Give your program a thorough workout

After testing with valid data, test the program's edit routines against every possible combination of errors.

A checklist for program testing

When you test a CICS program, it's often difficult to keep track of all that happens during the test run. As a result, you should use a checklist like this one to make sure you've detected all errors.

What to check for as you examine the appearance of the screen

Are all headings and captions placed correctly?
Are the operator instructions displayed properly?
Is there any garbage on the screen?
Are there any misspellings?
Do all the fields have the correct attributes?
Is the cursor in the correct initial location?
Does the cursor move correctly from field to field?

What to check for as you enter valid data

Are all program screens displayed in the correct sequence?
Do all attention keys work correctly?
Are the user messages always correct?
Are the functions of all attention keys indicated?
Does the program properly acknowledge receipt of valid data?
Are work fields properly cleared after each valid transaction?
Are control totals accumulated properly?
Are files updated properly?

What to check for as you enter invalid data

Does each case of invalid data for each field yield an appropriate error message?
Do lookup routines work properly?
Is the field in error highlighted?
Is the cursor positioned at the field in error?
When you correct the error, do the error message and highlighting go away?
Does the program post transactions even though errors are detected?
Does the program detect all possible cross-validation errors?
Does the program properly detect and highlight multiple entry errors?

Testing a program from the top down

If you're developing a large, complex program, you may save time and frustration by coding and testing it on a top-down basis. In other words, instead of coding the entire program and testing it all at once, you code and test a few modules at a time, starting with the most critical ones. This is referred to as *top-down coding and testing* or just *top-down testing*. Figure 4-2 gives general guidelines for preparing a top-down test plan, while figure 4-3 gives a top-down test plan that could be used for the customer maintenance program that was shown in Unit 1 (its structure chart is in figure 1-7).

- To start implementing a top-down test plan, code the Identification Division and as much of the Data Division as is needed for the first phase of testing. Then, code the Procedure Division modules that are going to be tested.

- When you add new modules to the Procedure Division for the next phase of testing, add any code in the Data Division that's required to support those modules.

- If you include a Perform statement for a module that isn't implemented yet, you can comment out the Perform statement or code a *program stub* for it. You can also comment out other statements you don't want executed.

- If a program stub doesn't have to do anything for the successful completion of a test run, the module can consist of the paragraph name only. Otherwise, it can simulate the function that will be done when the module is fully coded. For example, an input stub can simulate the reading of one or more records.

- The goal of using program stubs is to get the testing done right with a minimum of extra work. If a program stub starts to require a lot of coding, you're usually better off coding the entire module and adding it to that test phase.

- If you want to find out what modules of a program (including program stubs) are executed, you can add code to each module to create a string of the module numbers that are executed. Then, you can move that string to the message area of the map so it's displayed on the screen.

Guidelines for preparing a top-down test plan

*   Test just a few modules at a time, but test all of the processing in each module.
*   Test the critical modules of the program early in the plan, and test the remaining modules in whatever sequence you prefer.
*   Keep the test data to a minimum in the early test phases.

Figure 4-2

A top-down test plan for the customer maintenance program

Phase	Modules	Test
1	0000 (Process customer maintenance) 1500 (Send key map)	Enter all valid and invalid attention keys from the key map to be sure that they're processed properly and that the key map is displayed properly.
2	1000 (Process key map) 1100 (Receive key map) 1200 (Edit key data)	Enter valid and invalid customer numbers and action codes to be sure they're received and edited properly.
3	1300 (Read customer record) 1400 (Send data map)	Enter valid key map entries and all valid and invalid attention keys from the data map to be sure that they're processed properly and that the data map is displayed properly; enter invalid customer numbers to be sure they're handled properly.
4	2000 (Process add customer) 2100 (Receive data map) 2300 (Write customer record)	Enter valid key map and data map entries for an add operation to be sure that the record is written properly.
5	3000 (Process change customer) 3100 (Read customer for update) 3200 (Rewrite customer record)	Enter valid key map and data map entries for a change operation to be sure that the record is rewritten properly.
6	4000 (Process delete customer) 4100 (Delete customer record)	Enter valid key map and data map entries for a delete operation to be sure that the record is deleted.
7	2200 (Edit customer data)	Enter blank fields alone and in various combinations to make sure the editing routine for the add and change operations works properly.

Figure 4-3

Additional considerations for modular programs

When you test a modular program, you have the added burden of making sure that the presentation logic program and the business logic program work together. If both programs are developed using COBOL and CICS and run on the same platform, this process is straightforward. If the presentation logic is written in a different language or runs on another platform, however, you may have to do some extra work.

• The recommended procedure for testing a modular program is to test the presentation logic first, then the interface between the presentation logic and the business logic, then the business logic.

• If the presentation logic and business logic programs are in CICS/COBOL, you must create resource definitions for both of them. However, you only need to define a trans-id for the presentation logic program since the business logic program can't be started with a trans-id.

• If the presentation logic is written in a different language, you may have to test the business logic without the benefit of that program. To do that, you'll probably have to develop a simple CICS program that passes data through the communication area to the business logic just as if it had been entered at a terminal.

• To be sure that the business logic doesn't contain any terminal I/O commands, you should set it to *DPL mode* (*Distributed Program Link* is a CICS intercommunication feature that lets a program running in one CICS system issue a LINK command that invokes a program in another CICS system). In this mode, the program won't be allowed to issue any CICS commands that attempt to access a terminal. To set a program to this mode, you code the program name in a CEMT command like this:

```
CEMT SET PROGRAM(CUSTMNTB) DPLSUBSET
```

CICS service transactions for testing and debugging

CICS provides five service transactions that you may use as you test and debug your programs. You use the first two, CESN and CESF, to sign on and off of CICS. The third one, CEMT, manages the status of CICS resources. The fourth, CECI, allows you to execute CICS commands interactively. And the fifth, CEDF, can help you debug your applications. (If you're not familiar with the syntax conventions used here, they're described in Unit 7.)

CESN: The sign-on transaction

The CESN command signs you on to CICS. Depending on how CICS is set up, you may need to use this command to sign on to CICS before you test your programs.

Syntax

```
CESN [ USER=username ]
     [ PS=password ]
     [ NEWPS=password ]
```

Example

```
CESN USER=RAUL,PS=MMA2000
```

Operation

- You can include the USER and PS parameters on the CESN command to supply your user-id and password. If you omit these parameters, CICS will display a sign-on screen where you can enter them.

- When you enter your password on the sign-on screen, it's displayed as blanks so that no one else can see it. Because of that, we recommend you use this technique if security in your shop is critical.

- You can also include the NEWPS parameter to enter in a new 1- to 8-character password that will replace your existing password.

CESF: The sign-off transaction

The CESF command signs you off of the CICS region you're currently in.

Syntax

```
CESF [ LOGOFF ]
     [ GOODNIGHT ]
```

Example

```
CESF LOGOFF
```

Operation

- If you want to sign off and disconnect your terminal from the CICS region, you can include the LOGOFF or GOODNIGHT parameter on the CESF command.

CEMT: The master terminal transaction

The *master terminal transaction*, more commonly known as *CEMT*, lets you control or inquire about a variety of CICS resources. For example, it can allocate and unallocate files for the CICS region you're working in, or it can refresh the current copy of your program's load module.

Syntax

To force a new copy of a program

```
CEMT SET PROGRAM(name) NEWCOPY
```

To open or close a file

```
CEMT SET FILE(name) { OPEN | CLOSE }
```

To disable or enable a program or transaction

```
CEMT SET PROGRAM(name) { DISABLED | ENABLED }
CEMT SET TRANSACTION(name) { DISABLED | ENABLED }
```

To set a program to DPL mode

```
CEMT SET PROGRAM(name) DPLSUBSET
```

To check on the status of a file, program, or transaction

```
CEMT INQUIRE { FILE(name) | PROGRAM(name) | TRANSACTION(name) }
```

Examples

A command that refreshes CICS's copy of a program named CUSTMNT1

```
CEMT SET PROGRAM(CUSTMNT1) NEWCOPY
```

A command that closes a customer master file

```
CEMT S FI(CUSTMST) CL
```

A command that disables a transaction named MNT1

```
CEMT S TRA(MNT1) D
```

A command that sets a program to run in DPL mode

```
CEMT S PR(CUSTMNTB) DP
```

A command that displays the status of all files that start with the letter C

```
CEMT I FI(C*)
```

Operation

- To use the master terminal transaction, type the CEMT trans-id followed by a CEMT command. The results are displayed on a full-screen panel. You can also enter CEMT without a command and CEMT will help you construct the command.

- The underlined characters in the syntax are the minimum abbreviations CEMT allows.

- After you modify and recompile a program, you should issue the SET PRO-GRAM NEWCOPY command so CICS will refresh its copy of the program from disk.

- To print a file while CICS is running, you must close and disable it first. To do that, you issue the CEMT SET FILE CLOSE command. Before you can use the file again, you must issue the CEMT SET FILE OPEN command to reopen it.

- To end a program that's stuck in a loop, you can use the CEMT SET PRO-GRAM DISABLED or CEMT SET TRANSACTION DISABLED command. These commands must be entered from a terminal other than the one where the task is running.

- To ensure that a business logic program doesn't contain any terminal I/O commands, you can use the CEMT SET PROGRAM DPLSUBSET command to set the program to DPL mode.

- To check on the status of a file, program, or transaction, you can use the CEMT INQUIRE command. You can use the asterisk (*) wildcard to check on the status of all files, programs, or transactions whose names match a specified pattern.

- The CEMT transaction is covered in more detail in Unit 13.

CECI: The command-level interpreter

You can use the *command-level interpreter*, or *CECI*, transaction to issue CICS commands from outside a program. For example, you can use it to issue a SEND MAP command to test a map before you've written the program that processes it. The *CECS* transaction provides a subset of CECI functions.

Syntax

```
{ CECI | CECS } [ CICS-command ]
```

Examples

A CECI command that reads a record from a customer master file
```
CECI READ FILE(CUSTMAS) RIDFLD(123456)
```

A CECI command that displays the map INQMAP1 on the screen
```
CECI SEND MAP(INQMAP1) MAPSET(INQSET1) ERASE
```

Operation

- To invoke the command-level interpreter, enter the CECI trans-id followed by the CICS command you want to execute. If you enter CECI without a CICS command, the command-level interpreter displays a start-up panel with a list of available commands, as shown in figure 4-4. Then, you can enter a command at the top of this panel, like the SEND MAP command shown in this figure.

- CECI checks the syntax of the command you specify and then displays a panel telling you it's about to execute the command. When you press the Enter key, CECI executes the command and displays the results.

- You can also start CECI by entering the CECS trans-id with or without a CICS command. This transaction restricts the functionality of CECI so that it only checks the syntax of the command you specify. It doesn't execute the command.

- When you issue a command from CECI, you don't have to bracket the command with EXEC CICS and END-EXEC, and you don't have to use apostrophes to identify literals.

- You can use the function keys listed at the bottom of the CECI panel to perform functions like displaying help information (PF1), displaying data in hex (PF2), displaying the values of the fields in the Execute Interface Block (PF4), and defining variables for use in the commands you issue (PF5).

The CECI start-up panel

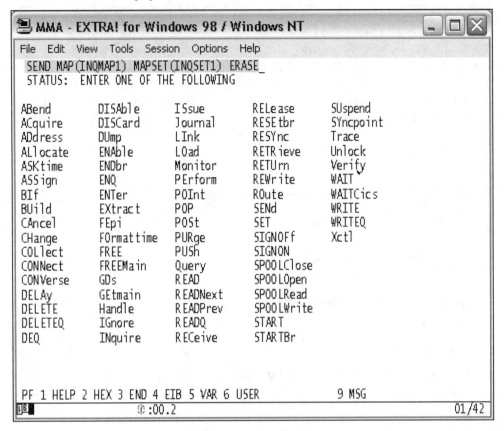

Figure 4-4

CEDF: The Execution Diagnostics Facility

The *Execution Diagnostic Facility*, or *EDF*, is the tool most commonly used to debug CICS programs. Basically, it lets you monitor a command-level program by intercepting all CICS commands the program issues. Although it's not the most powerful online debugging tool available, it has two advantages: (1) programs require no special preparation to work with EDF, and (2) EDF is a standard component of CICS, so all shops have it.

Syntax

```
CEDF [ term-id ]
```

Examples

Starts EDF at the terminal where it's entered (single-screen mode)
```
CEDF
```

Starts EDF at a terminal named H400 (dual-screen mode)
```
CEDF H400
```

Starts EDF for the program with trans-id MNTB running at any terminal
```
CEDX MNTB
```

Operation

- In *single-screen mode*, you run EDF and the program you want to debug at the same terminal. This is the technique you'll use most often.

- In *dual-screen mode*, you run EDF at one terminal and the program you want to debug at the terminal you name when you start EDF. You may want to use this technique to test a program at different types of terminals.

- You can also use EDF to debug a program running at any terminal that's started by the trans-id you specify when you start EDF. You can use this technique to test a program that's not started from a terminal, such as a business logic program whose presentation logic runs outside the CICS environment.

- As a task executes, CICS interrupts it at several key points: before a new program begins to execute, before any CICS command is executed, after any CICS command is executed, before a program ends, before a task ends, whenever an abend occurs, and before a task ends abnormally. At any of these points, you can examine or change the contents of working storage or the Execute Interface Block.

- You can temporarily suspend EDF displays by pressing PF4. Then, EDF won't interrupt your program until an error, an abend, or a normal end-of-task condition occurs. However, you can use PF9 to tell EDF to resume its displays whenever your program issues a particular type of CICS command or whenever a particular exceptional condition occurs.

- To view or change working storage, press PF5. That takes you to a display that's similar to a storage dump.

- When EDF executes a command that ends a program, it displays a task termination screen. In a pseudo-conversational program, you need to enter YES in the REPLY field of this screen in order for EDF to resume when the program restarts.

EDF screen examples

- Once you start EDF and enter the trans-id of the program you want to debug, EDF displays the program initiation screen, which shows information from the Execute Interface Block. To begin program execution, press the Enter key.

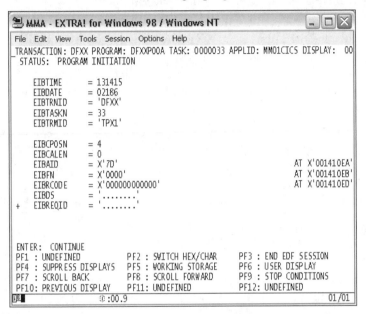

- EDF displays the next command in the program along with its options and their values. To execute the command, press the Enter key. In this case, because the SEND TEXT command produces terminal output, the output will be displayed on the screen.

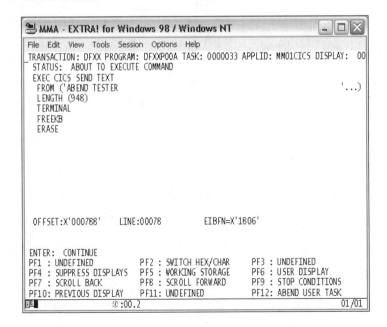

Figure 4-5

CICS abend codes

When a CICS program terminates abnormally, an *abnormal termination message* (or just *abend message*) like this is sent to the terminal:

```
DFH006I TRANSACTION DFXX PROGRAM DFXXP00A  ABEND ASRA AT H400
```

This message indicates that the program DFXXP00A started by transaction DFXX at terminal H400 ended with an *abend code* of ASRA. Almost always, it's the abend code that gives you the information you need to begin debugging your program. Most of the abend codes that occur most often fall into two categories: exceptional condition abends and program check abends.

- An *exceptional condition abend* occurs when a CICS command encounters an unusual situation and the RESP option wasn't included on the command. These abend codes start with AEI or AEY and they indicate which exceptional condition occurred, as shown below. (You'll find brief explanations of many of these conditions in Unit 8, in conjunction with the commands that raise them.)

- A *program check abend* occurs when a program tries to perform an operation that isn't allowed by the hardware. This type of abend always results in an ASRA abend code.

- IBM's *CICS Messages and Codes* manual documents more than 300 possible abend codes. If you encounter an abend code that's not listed in this unit, you can consult that manual for an explanation.

Exceptional condition abends

Code	Condition	Code	Condition	Code	Condition
AEIA	ERROR	AEIV	LENGERR	AEYL	FUNCERR
AEID	EOF	AEIW	QZERO	AEYM	UNEXPIN
AEIE	EIDS	AEIZ	ITEMERR	AEYN	NOPASSBKRD
AEIG	INBFMH	AEI0	PGMIDERR	AEYO	NOPASSBKWR
AEIH	ENDINPT	AEI1	TRANSIDERR	AEYP	SEQIDERR
AEII	NONVAL	AEI2	ENDDATA	AEYQ	SYSIDERR
AEIJ	NOSTART	AEI3	INVTSREQ	AEYR	ISINVREQ
AEIK	TERMIDERR	AEI8	TSIOERR	AEYT	ENVDEFERR
AEIL	DSIDERR	AEI9	MAPFAIL	AEYU	IGREQCD
AEIM	NOTFND	AEYA	INVERRTERM	AEYV	SESSERR
AEIN	DUPREC	AEYB	INVMPSZ	AEYY	NOTALLOC
AEIO	DUPKEY	AEYC	IGREQID	AEYZ	CBIDERR
AEIP	INVREQ	AEYE	INVLDC	AEY0	INVEXITREQ
AEIQ	IOERR	AEYG	JIDERR	AEY1	INVPARTNSET
AEIR	NOSPACE	AEYH	QIDERR	AEY2	INVPARTN
AEIS	NOTOPEN	AEYJ	DSSTAT	AEY3	PARTNFAIL
AEIT	ENDFILE	AEYK	SELNERR	AEY7	NOTAUTH
AEIU	ILLOGIC				

Program check abends (ASRA abend code)

Note: For an ASRA abend, the Program Status Word (PSW) in the storage dump contains a one-byte code identifying the type of program check.

Code	Type	Code	Type
1	Operation exception	9	Fixed-point divide exception
2	Privileged operation	A	Decimal overflow
3	Execute exception	B	Decimal-divide exception
4	Protection exception	C	Exponent overflow
5	Addressing exception	D	Exponent underflow
6	Specification exception	E	Significance exception
7	Data exception	F	Floating-point divide exception
8	Fixed-point overflow		

Other abend codes

Code	Explanation
ABMB	You used the absolute cursor positioning technique and supplied a cursor position that's beyond the limit of the output device.
ABM0	The specified map isn't in the mapset. The map name is misspelled either in the program or in the mapset, or the program specifies the wrong mapset.
AFCV	A request made against a file was unable to acquire a record-level lock. The wait time exceeded the maximum wait time allowed for that request.
AICA	The task exceeded the execution time limit for runaway tasks (the task was looping).
AKCS	The task was canceled because it was suspended for a period longer than the transaction's defined deadlock timeout period. Programming practices that lead to deadlock situations sometimes cause this, but it can also be caused by problems internal to CICS.
AKCT	The task was canceled because it was waiting for terminal input for a period longer than the transaction's defined terminal read timeout period. This happens when an operator starts a conversational program and then leaves the terminal unattended for a long period of time.
AKC3	The task was purged, probably as the result of a master terminal operator issuing the CEMT TASK PURGE command.
APCT	The program could not be found or is disabled.
ASRB	An operating system abend has occurred; CICS was able to abend the transaction and continue processing.
ATCH	The task was purged, probably as the result of a deadlock situation. The task may have been purged automatically when it exceeded the deadlock timeout, or it may have been purged by a master terminal operator issuing the CEMT TASK PURGE command.

Transaction dump debugging

CEDF and other online debugging tools are useful during program testing, but if a production program abends, you'll probably have to use a transaction dump to find out what caused the abend. Here, I'll summarize how to determine the cause of an abend, and how to determine the instruction that caused the abend.

How to determine the cause of an abend

- Locate the correct dump in the dump listing. TASK=xxxx in the dump heading indicates the trans-id for the abending task. DATE= and TIME= in the dump heading indicates the date and time of the abend.
- Note the abend code in the dump heading.
- For ASRA abends, determine the type of program check by looking at the last hex character of the third fullword in the PSW. The PSW program check codes are summarized on the previous page.
- Note the program name that appears at the end of the SYMPTOMS line.

How to determine the instruction that caused the abend

1. Determine the program entry point by locating the program in the module map near the end of the dump.
2. Determine the interrupt address, which is the second fullword of the PSW.
3. Determine the instruction offset by subtracting the program entry point from the interrupt address.
4. Use the Condensed Procedure Listing in the compiler output to determine which COBOL statement caused the abend. Find the statement whose offset is closest to the result of step 3 without exceeding it. (The OFFSET option must be specified at compile time for the Condensed Procedure Listing to be printed.)

Unit 5

A model program using two different designs

This unit presents two versions of a CICS customer maintenance program that allows a user to add, change, or delete records in a customer master file. The first version is done using traditional design, so the presentation logic and the business logic are both coded in a single program. The second version uses modular design, so the presentation and business logic are separated into two programs. These programs illustrate the design and coding guidelines that have been presented throughout this section, and you can use them as starting points for your own maintenance programs.

The customer maintenance program: Traditional design

In the pages that that follow, you'll find the specifications, event/response chart, structure chart, BMS mapset, symbolic map, and CICS source code for the customer maintenance program that's developed in the traditional way, as a single program. If you do much CICS maintenance, you'll often deal with traditional programs that follow the same basic pattern as this one. In addition, depending on your shop standards, you may develop new programs this way as well.

The program overview

Program	CUSTMNT2: Customer maintenance program
Trans-id	MNT2
Overview	Maintains customer information in the customer master file by allowing the user to enter new customers, change existing customers, or delete existing customers.
Input/output	CUSTMAS Customer master file MNTMAP1 Customer maintenance key map MNTMAP2 Customer maintenance data map
Processing	1. Control is transferred to this program via XCTL from the menu program INVMENU with no communication area. The user can also start the program by entering the trans-id MNT2. In either case, the program should respond by displaying the key map.
	2. On the key map, the user enters a customer number and selects a processing action (Add, Change, or Delete). Both the action field and the customer number field must be entered. If the user selects Add, the customer number entered must not exist in the file. For Change or Delete, the customer number must exist in the file. If a valid combination isn't entered, an error message should be displayed.
	3. If the user enters a valid combination of action and customer number, the program displays the customer maintenance data map. For an add operation, the user can then enter the customer information. For a change operation, the user can change any of the existing information. For a delete operation, all fields should be set to protected so the user can't enter changes. To complete any of these operations, the user must press the Enter key.
	4. For an add or change, edit the fields to make sure they aren't blank.
	5. If the user presses PF3 from either the key map or the data map, return to the menu program INVMENU by issuing an XCTL command. If the user presses PF12 from the key map, return to the menu program. However, if the user presses PF12 from the data map, redisplay the key map without completing the current operation.
	6. For a change or delete operation, maintain an image of the customer record in the communication area between program executions. If the record is changed in any way between program executions, notify the user and do not complete the operation.
	7. If an unrecoverable error occurs, terminate the program by invoking the SYSERR subprogram with an XCTL command.

The screen layouts

The screen layout for the customer maintenance key map

Map name _____ MNTMAP1 _____   Date _____ 03/12/2001 _____

Program name _____ CUSTMNT2 _____   Designer _____ Doug Lowe _____

```
MNTMAP1                 Customer Maintenance                                                                  XXXX

Type a customer number.   Then select an action and press Enter.

Customer number. .  .   .   XXXXXX

Action .  .   .   .    .   .   X  1.  Add a new customer
                               2.  Change an existing customer
                               3.  Delete an existing customer









XXXXXXXXXXXXXXXXXXXXXXXXXXXXXXXXXXXXXXXXXXXXXXXXXXXXXXXXXXXXXXXXXXXXXXXXXXXXXXXXX
F3=Exit    F12=Cancel                                                            X
```

The screen layout for the customer maintenance data map

Map name _____ MNTMAP2 _____   Date _____ 03/12/2001 _____

Program name _____ CUSTMNT2 _____   Designer _____ Doug Lowe _____

```
MNTMAP2                 Customer Maintenance                                                                  XXXX

XXXXXXXXXXXXXXXXXXXXXXXXXXXXXXXXXXXXXXXXXXXXXXXXXXXXXXXXXXXXXXXXXXXXXXXXXXXXXXXXXXXXX

Customer number. .  .   :   XXXXXX

Last name.  .   .   .    .   .   XXXXXXXXXXXXXXXXXXXXXXXXXXXXX
First name  .   .    .   .   XXXXXXXXXXXXXXXXXXXX
Address.  .   .   .    .   .   XXXXXXXXXXXXXXXXXXXXXXXXXXXX
City .  .   .    .   .   XXXXXXXXXXXXXXXXXXXXX
State.  .   .    .   .   XX
Zip Code .  .   .    .   .   XXXXXXXXXX









XXXXXXXXXXXXXXXXXXXXXXXXXXXXXXXXXXXXXXXXXXXXXXXXXXXXXXXXXXXXXXXXXXXXXXXXXXXXXXXXX
F3=Exit    F12=Cancel                                                            X
```

The copy members

The CUSTMAS copy member

```
01   CUSTOMER-MASTER-RECORD.
*
     05   CM-CUSTOMER-NUMBER        PIC X(06).
     05   CM-FIRST-NAME            PIC X(20).
     05   CM-LAST-NAME             PIC X(30).
     05   CM-ADDRESS              PIC X(30).
     05   CM-CITY                 PIC X(20).
     05   CM-STATE                PIC X(02).
     05   CM-ZIP-CODE             PIC X(10).
```

The ERRPARM copy member (for the SYSERR program)

```
01   ERROR-PARAMETERS.
*
     05   ERR-RESP                PIC S9(08)   COMP.
     05   ERR-RESP2               PIC S9(08)   COMP.
     05   ERR-TRNID               PIC X(04).
     05   ERR-RSRCE               PIC X(08).
```

The error-handling program (SYSERR)

```
IDENTIFICATION DIVISION.
PROGRAM-ID.  SYSERR.
*
ENVIRONMENT DIVISION.
*
DATA DIVISION.
*
WORKING-STORAGE SECTION.
*
01   ERROR-MESSAGE.
     05   ERROR-LINE-1.
          10   FILLER      PIC X(20)   VALUE 'A serious error has '.
          10   FILLER      PIC X(20)   VALUE 'occurred.  Please co'.
          10   FILLER      PIC X(20)   VALUE 'ntact technical supp'.
          10   FILLER      PIC X(19)   VALUE 'ort.                '.
     05   ERROR-LINE-2     PIC X(79)   VALUE SPACE.
     05   ERROR-LINE-3.
          10   FILLER      PIC X(11)   VALUE 'EIBRESP = '.
          10   EM-RESP     PIC Z(08)9.
          10   FILLER      PIC X(59)   VALUE SPACE.
     05   ERROR-LINE-4.
          10   FILLER      PIC X(11)   VALUE 'EIBRESP2 = '.
          10   EM-RESP2    PIC Z(08)9.
          10   FILLER      PIC X(59)   VALUE SPACE.
     05   ERROR-LINE-5.
          10   FILLER      PIC X(11)   VALUE 'EIBTRNID = '.
          10   EM-TRNID    PIC X(04).
          10   FILLER      PIC X(64)   VALUE SPACE.
     05   ERROR-LINE-6.
          10   FILLER      PIC X(11)   VALUE 'EIBRSRCE = '.
          10   EM-RSRCE    PIC X(08).
          10   FILLER      PIC X(60)   VALUE SPACE.
     05   ERROR-LINE-7     PIC X(79)   VALUE SPACE.
*
COPY ERRPARM.
*
LINKAGE SECTION.
*
01   DFHCOMMAREA          PIC X(20).
*
PROCEDURE DIVISION.
*
0000-DISPLAY-ERROR-MESSAGE.
*
     MOVE DFHCOMMAREA TO ERROR-PARAMETERS.
     MOVE ERR-RESP  TO EM-RESP.
     MOVE ERR-RESP2 TO EM-RESP2.
     MOVE ERR-TRNID TO EM-TRNID.
     MOVE ERR-RSRCE TO EM-RSRCE.
     EXEC CICS
         SEND TEXT FROM(ERROR-MESSAGE)
                   ERASE
                   ALARM
                   FREEKB
     END-EXEC.
     EXEC CICS
         RETURN
     END-EXEC.
```

The event/response chart

Event	Context	Response	New context
Start the program	n/a	Display the key map.	Get key
PF3	All	Transfer control to the menu program.	n/a
PF12	Get key	Transfer control to the menu program.	n/a
	Add customer Change customer Delete customer	Cancel the operation and display the key map.	Get key

Enter key	Get key	Edit input data.
		If valid
		    display data map
		
		else
		    display an error message.
			Add customer,
			Change customer, or
			Delete customer
			
			Get key

	Add customer	Edit input data.
		If valid
		    add customer record
		    display key map
		else
		    display an error message.
			Get key
			
			Add customer

	Change customer	Edit input data.
		If valid
		    change customer record
		    display key map
		else
		    display an error message.
			Get key
			
			Change customer

	Delete customer	Delete the customer record. ˙ Display the key map.	Get key
Clear	Get key	Redisplay the key map without any data.	Unchanged
	Add, Change, or Delete customer	Redisplay the data map with unprotected data erased.	Unchanged
Any PA key	All	Ignore the key.	Unchanged
Any other key	All	Display an appropriate error message.	Unchanged

The structure chart

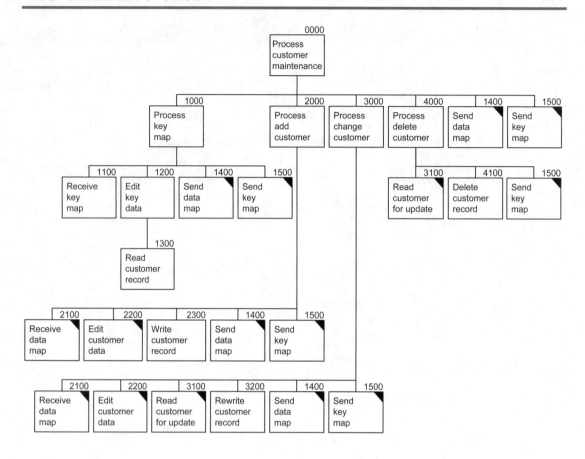

The BMS mapset

```
        PRINT NOGEN
MNTSET2 DFHMSD TYPE=&SYSPARM,                                        X
               LANG=COBOL,                                          X
               MODE=INOUT,                                          X
               TERM=3270-2,                                         X
               CTRL=FREEKB,                                         X
               STORAGE=AUTO,                                        X
               DSATTS=(COLOR,HILIGHT),                              X
               MAPATTS=(COLOR,HILIGHT),                             X
               TIOAPFX=YES
*********************************************************************
MNTMAP1 DFHMDI SIZE=(24,80),                                        X
               LINE=1,                                              X
               COLUMN=1
*********************************************************************
        DFHMDF POS=(1,1),                                           X
               LENGTH=7,                                            X
               ATTRB=(NORM,PROT),                                   X
               COLOR=BLUE,                                          X
               INITIAL='MNTMAP1'
        DFHMDF POS=(1,20),                                          X
               LENGTH=20,                                           X
               ATTRB=(NORM,PROT),                                   X
               COLOR=GREEN,                                         X
               INITIAL='Customer Maintenance'
TRANID1 DFHMDF POS=(1,76),                                          X
               LENGTH=4,                                            X
               ATTRB=(NORM,PROT),                                   X
               COLOR=BLUE,                                          X
               INITIAL='XXXX'
*********************************************************************
        DFHMDF POS=(3,1),                                           X
               LENGTH=63,                                           X
               ATTRB=(NORM,PROT),                                   X
               COLOR=NEUTRAL,                                       X
               INITIAL='Type a customer number.   Then select an action X
               and press Enter.'
        DFHMDF POS=(5,1),                                           X
               LENGTH=24,                                           X
               ATTRB=(NORM,PROT),                                   X
               COLOR=GREEN,                                         X
               INITIAL='Customer number. . . . .'
CUSTNO1 DFHMDF POS=(5,26),                                          X
               LENGTH=6,                                            X
               ATTRB=(NORM,UNPROT,FSET),                            X
               COLOR=TURQUOISE,                                     X
               INITIAL='_____'
        DFHMDF POS=(5,33),                                          X
               LENGTH=1,                                            X
               ATTRB=ASKIP
        DFHMDF POS=(7,1),                                           X
               LENGTH=24,                                           X
               ATTRB=(NORM,PROT),                                   X
               COLOR=GREEN,                                         X
               INITIAL='Action . . . . . . . . .'
```

The BMS mapset: Traditional design (part 1 of 4)

```
ACTION    DFHMDF POS=(7,26),                                          X
                 LENGTH=1,                                            X
                 ATTRB=(NORM,NUM,FSET),                               X
                 COLOR=TURQUOISE,                                     X
                 INITIAL='_'
          DFHMDF POS=(7,28),                                          X
                 LENGTH=21,                                           X
                 ATTRB=(NORM,ASKIP),                                  X
                 COLOR=NEUTRAL,                                       X
                 INITIAL='1. Add a new customer'
          DFHMDF POS=(8,28),                                          X
                 LENGTH=30,                                           X
                 ATTRB=(NORM,ASKIP),                                  X
                 COLOR=NEUTRAL,                                       X
                 INITIAL='2. Change an existing customer'
          DFHMDF POS=(9,28),                                          X
                 LENGTH=21,                                           X
                 ATTRB=(NORM,ASKIP),                                  X
                 COLOR=NEUTRAL,                                       X
                 INITIAL='3. Delete an existing customer'
MSG1      DFHMDF POS=(23,1),                                          X
                 LENGTH=79,                                           X
                 ATTRB=(BRT,PROT),                                    X
                 COLOR=YELLOW
          DFHMDF POS=(24,1),                                          X
                 LENGTH=20,                                           X
                 ATTRB=(NORM,PROT),                                   X
                 COLOR=BLUE,                                          X
                 INITIAL='F3=Exit    F12=Cancel'
DUMMY1    DFHMDF POS=(24,79),                                         X
                 LENGTH=1,                                            X
                 ATTRB=(DRK,PROT,FSET),                               X
                 INITIAL=' '
************************************************************************
MNTMAP2   DFHMDI SIZE=(24,80),                                        X
                 LINE=1,                                              X
                 COLUMN=1
************************************************************************
          DFHMDF POS=(1,1),                                           X
                 LENGTH=7,                                            X
                 ATTRB=(NORM,PROT),                                   X
                 COLOR=BLUE,                                          X
                 INITIAL='MNTMAP2'
          DFHMDF POS=(1,20),                                          X
                 LENGTH=20,                                           X
                 ATTRB=(NORM,PROT),                                   X
                 COLOR=GREEN,                                         X
                 INITIAL='Customer Maintenance'
TRANID2   DFHMDF POS=(1,76),                                          X
                 LENGTH=4,                                            X
                 ATTRB=(NORM,PROT),                                   X
                 COLOR=BLUE,                                          X
                 INITIAL='XXXX'
************************************************************************
```

The BMS mapset: Traditional design (part 2 of 4)

```
INSTR2    DFHMDF POS=(3,1),                                            X
                 LENGTH=79,                                            X
                 ATTRB=(NORM,PROT),                                    X
                 COLOR=NEUTRAL
          DFHMDF POS=(5,1),                                            X
                 LENGTH=24,                                            X
                 ATTRB=(NORM,PROT),                                    X
                 COLOR=GREEN,                                          X
                 INITIAL='Customer number. . . . :'
CUSTNO2   DFHMDF POS=(5,26),                                           X
                 LENGTH=6,                                             X
                 ATTRB=(NORM,PROT,FSET),                               X
                 COLOR=TURQUOISE
*********************************************************************
          DFHMDF POS=(7,1),                                            X
                 LENGTH=24,                                            X
                 ATTRB=(NORM,PROT),                                    X
                 COLOR=GREEN,                                          X
                 INITIAL='Last name. . . . . . . .'
LNAME     DFHMDF POS=(7,26),                                           X
                 LENGTH=30,                                            X
                 ATTRB=(NORM,UNPROT,FSET),                             X
                 COLOR=TURQUOISE
          DFHMDF POS=(7,57),                                           X
                 LENGTH=1,                                             X
                 ATTRB=ASKIP
*********************************************************************
          DFHMDF POS=(8,1),                                            X
                 LENGTH=24,                                            X
                 ATTRB=(NORM,PROT),                                    X
                 COLOR=GREEN,                                          X
                 INITIAL='First name . . . . . . .'
FNAME     DFHMDF POS=(8,26),                                           X
                 LENGTH=20,                                            X
                 ATTRB=(NORM,UNPROT,FSET),                             X
                 COLOR=TURQUOISE
          DFHMDF POS=(8,47),                                           X
                 LENGTH=1,                                             X
                 ATTRB=ASKIP
*********************************************************************
          DFHMDF POS=(9,1),                                            X
                 LENGTH=24,                                            X
                 ATTRB=(NORM,PROT),                                    X
                 COLOR=GREEN,                                          X
                 INITIAL='Address. . . . . . . . .'
ADDR      DFHMDF POS=(9,26),                                           X
                 LENGTH=30,                                            X
                 ATTRB=(NORM,UNPROT,FSET),                             X
                 COLOR=TURQUOISE
          DFHMDF POS=(9,57),                                           X
                 LENGTH=1,                                             X
                 ATTRB=ASKIP
```

The BMS mapset: Traditional design (part 3 of 4)

```
              DFHMDF POS=(10,1),                                         X
                     LENGTH=24,                                          X
                     ATTRB=(NORM,PROT),                                  X
                     COLOR=GREEN,                                        X
                     INITIAL='City . . . . . . . . . .'
   CITY       DFHMDF POS=(10,26),                                        X
                     LENGTH=20,                                          X
                     ATTRB=(NORM,UNPROT,FSET),                           X
                     COLOR=TURQUOISE
              DFHMDF POS=(10,47),                                        X
                     LENGTH=1,                                           X
                     ATTRB=ASKIP
   ****************************************************************************
              DFHMDF POS=(11,1),                                         X
                     LENGTH=24,                                          X
                     ATTRB=(NORM,PROT),                                  X
                     COLOR=GREEN,                                        X
                     INITIAL='State. . . . . . . . . .'
   STATE      DFHMDF POS=(11,26),                                        X
                     LENGTH=2,                                           X
                     ATTRB=(NORM,UNPROT,FSET),                           X
                     COLOR=TURQUOISE
              DFHMDF POS=(11,29),                                        X
                     LENGTH=1,                                           X
                     ATTRB=ASKIP
   ****************************************************************************
              DFHMDF POS=(12,1),                                         X
                     LENGTH=24,                                          X
                     ATTRB=(NORM,PROT),                                  X
                     COLOR=GREEN,                                        X
                     INITIAL='Zip Code . . . . . . . .'
   ZIPCODE    DFHMDF POS=(12,26),                                        X
                     LENGTH=10,                                          X
                     ATTRB=(NORM,UNPROT,FSET),                           X
                     COLOR=TURQUOISE
              DFHMDF POS=(12,37),                                        X
                     LENGTH=1,                                           X
                     ATTRB=ASKIP
   ****************************************************************************
   MSG2       DFHMDF POS=(23,1),                                         X
                     LENGTH=79,                                          X
                     ATTRB=(BRT,PROT),                                   X
                     COLOR=YELLOW
              DFHMDF POS=(24,1),                                         X
                     LENGTH=20,                                          X
                     ATTRB=(NORM,PROT),                                  X
                     COLOR=BLUE,                                         X
                     INITIAL='F3=Exit    F12=Cancel'
   DUMMY2     DFHMDF POS=(24,79),                                        X
                     LENGTH=1,                                           X
                     ATTRB=(DRK,PROT,FSET),                              X
                     INITIAL=' '
   ****************************************************************************
              DFHMSD TYPE=FINAL
              END
```

The BMS mapset: Traditional design (part 4 of 4)

The symbolic map

```
01 MNTMAP1I.
    03 FILLER                          PIC X(12).
    03 TRANID1L                        PIC S9(4) COMP.
    03 TRANID1F                        PIC X.
    03 FILLER REDEFINES TRANID1F.
       05 TRANID1A                      PIC X.
    03 FILLER                          PIC X(2).
    03 TRANID1I                        PIC X(4).
    03 CUSTNO1L                        PIC S9(4) COMP.
    03 CUSTNO1F                        PIC X.
    03 FILLER REDEFINES CUSTNO1F.
       05 CUSTNO1A                      PIC X.
    03 FILLER                          PIC X(2).
    03 CUSTNO1I                        PIC X(6).
    03 ACTIONL                         PIC S9(4) COMP.
    03 ACTIONF                         PIC X.
    03 FILLER REDEFINES ACTIONF.
       05 ACTIONA                       PIC X.
    03 FILLER                          PIC X(2).
    03 ACTIONI                         PIC X(1).
    03 MSG1L                           PIC S9(4) COMP.
    03 MSG1F                           PIC X.
    03 FILLER REDEFINES MSG1F.
       05 MSG1A                         PIC X.
    03 FILLER                          PIC X(2).
    03 MSG1I                           PIC X(79).
    03 DUMMY1L                         PIC S9(4) COMP.
    03 DUMMY1F                         PIC X.
    03 FILLER REDEFINES DUMMY1F.
       05 DUMMY1A                       PIC X.
    03 FILLER                          PIC X(2).
    03 DUMMY1I                         PIC X(1).
01 MNTMAP1O REDEFINES MNTMAP1I.
    03 FILLER                          PIC X(12).
    03 FILLER                          PIC X(3).
    03 TRANID1C                        PIC X.
    03 TRANID1H                        PIC X.
    03 TRANID1O                        PIC X(4).
    03 FILLER                          PIC X(3).
    03 CUSTNO1C                        PIC X.
    03 CUSTNO1H                        PIC X.
    03 CUSTNO1O                        PIC X(6).
    03 FILLER                          PIC X(3).
    03 ACTIONC                         PIC X.
    03 ACTIONH                         PIC X.
    03 ACTIONO                         PIC X(1).
    03 FILLER                          PIC X(3).
    03 MSG1C                           PIC X.
    03 MSG1H                           PIC X.
    03 MSG1O                           PIC X(79).
    03 FILLER                          PIC X(3).
    03 DUMMY1C                         PIC X.
    03 DUMMY1H                         PIC X.
    03 DUMMY1O                         PIC X(1).
```

The symbolic map: Traditional design (part 1 of 3)

```
01  MNTMAP2I.
    03  FILLER                              PIC X(12).
    03  TRANID2L                            PIC S9(4) COMP.
    03  TRANID2F                            PIC X.
    03  FILLER REDEFINES TRANID2F.
        05  TRANID2A                        PIC X.
    03  FILLER                              PIC X(2).
    03  TRANID2I                            PIC X(4).
    03  INSTR2L                             PIC S9(4) COMP.
    03  INSTR2F                             PIC X.
    03  FILLER REDEFINES INSTR2F.
        05  INSTR2A                         PIC X.
    03  FILLER                              PIC X(2).
    03  INSTR2I                             PIC X(79).
    03  CUSTNO2L                            PIC S9(4) COMP.
    03  CUSTNO2F                            PIC X.
    03  FILLER REDEFINES CUSTNO2F.
        05  CUSTNO2A                        PIC X.
    03  FILLER                              PIC X(2).
    03  CUSTNO2I                            PIC X(6).
    03  LNAMEL                              PIC S9(4) COMP.
    03  LNAMEF                              PIC X.
    03  FILLER REDEFINES LNAMEF.
        05  LNAMEA                          PIC X.
    03  FILLER                              PIC X(2).
    03  LNAMEI                              PIC X(30).
    03  FNAMEL                              PIC S9(4) COMP.
    03  FNAMEF                              PIC X.
    03  FILLER REDEFINES FNAMEF.
        05  FNAMEA                          PIC X.
    03  FILLER                              PIC X(2).
    03  FNAMEI                              PIC X(20).
    03  ADDRL                               PIC S9(4) COMP.
    03  ADDRF                               PIC X.
    03  FILLER REDEFINES ADDRF.
        05  ADDRA                           PIC X.
    03  FILLER                              PIC X(2).
    03  ADDRI                               PIC X(30).
    03  CITYL                               PIC S9(4) COMP.
    03  CITYF                               PIC X.
    03  FILLER REDEFINES CITYF.
        05  CITYA                           PIC X.
    03  FILLER                              PIC X(2).
    03  CITYI                               PIC X(20).
    03  STATEL                              PIC S9(4) COMP.
    03  STATEF                              PIC X.
    03  FILLER REDEFINES STATEF.
        05  STATEA                          PIC X.
    03  FILLER                              PIC X(2).
    03  STATEI                              PIC X(2).
    03  ZIPCODEL                            PIC S9(4) COMP.
    03  ZIPCODEF                            PIC X.
    03  FILLER REDEFINES ZIPCODEF.
        05  ZIPCODEA                        PIC X.
    03  FILLER                              PIC X(2).
    03  ZIPCODEI                            PIC X(10).
    03  MSG2L                               PIC S9(4) COMP.
```

The symbolic map: Traditional design (part 2 of 3)

```
    03  MSG2F                         PIC X.
    03  FILLER REDEFINES MSG2F.
        05  MSG2A                        PIC X.
    03  FILLER                        PIC X(2).
    03  MSG2I                         PIC X(79).
    03  DUMMY2L                       PIC S9(4) COMP.
    03  DUMMY2F                       PIC X.
    03  FILLER REDEFINES DUMMY2F.
        05  DUMMY2A                      PIC X.
    03  FILLER                        PIC X(2).
    03  DUMMY2I                       PIC X(1).
01  MNTMAP2O REDEFINES MNTMAP2I.
    03  FILLER                        PIC X(12).
    03  FILLER                        PIC X(3).
    03  TRANID2C                      PIC X.
    03  TRANID2H                      PIC X.
    03  TRANID2O                      PIC X(4).
    03  FILLER                        PIC X(3).
    03  INSTR2C                       PIC X.
    03  INSTR2H                       PIC X.
    03  INSTR2O                       PIC X(79).
    03  FILLER                        PIC X(3).
    03  CUSTNO2C                      PIC X.
    03  CUSTNO2H                      PIC X.
    03  CUSTNO2O                      PIC X(6).
    03  FILLER                        PIC X(3).
    03  LNAMEC                        PIC X.
    03  LNAMEH                        PIC X.
    03  LNAMEO                        PIC X(30).
    03  FILLER                        PIC X(3).
    03  FNAMEC                        PIC X.
    03  FNAMEH                        PIC X.
    03  FNAMEO                        PIC X(20).
    03  FILLER                        PIC X(3).
    03  ADDRC                         PIC X.
    03  ADDRH                         PIC X.
    03  ADDRO                         PIC X(30).
    03  FILLER                        PIC X(3).
    03  CITYC                         PIC X.
    03  CITYH                         PIC X.
    03  CITYO                         PIC X(20).
    03  FILLER                        PIC X(3).
    03  STATEC                        PIC X.
    03  STATEH                        PIC X.
    03  STATEO                        PIC X(2).
    03  FILLER                        PIC X(3).
    03  ZIPCODEC                      PIC X.
    03  ZIPCODEH                      PIC X.
    03  ZIPCODEO                      PIC X(10).
    03  FILLER                        PIC X(3).
    03  MSG2C                         PIC X.
    03  MSG2H                         PIC X.
    03  MSG2O                         PIC X(79).
    03  FILLER                        PIC X(3).
    03  DUMMY2C                       PIC X.
    03  DUMMY2H                       PIC X.
    03  DUMMY2O                       PIC X(1).
```

The symbolic map: Traditional design (part 3 of 3)

The customer maintenance program: CUSTMNT2

```
      IDENTIFICATION DIVISION.
      PROGRAM-ID.  CUSTMNT2.
*
      ENVIRONMENT DIVISION.
*
      DATA DIVISION.
*
      WORKING-STORAGE SECTION.
*
      01   SWITCHES.
           05   VALID-DATA-SW              PIC X(01) VALUE 'Y'.
                88   VALID-DATA                      VALUE 'Y'.
*
      01   FLAGS.
           05   SEND-FLAG                  PIC X(01).
                88   SEND-ERASE                      VALUE '1'.
                88   SEND-ERASE-ALARM                VALUE '2'.
                88   SEND-DATAONLY                   VALUE '3'.
                88   SEND-DATAONLY-ALARM             VALUE '4'.
*
      01   WORK-FIELDS.
           05   RESPONSE-CODE              PIC S9(08) COMP.
*
      01   USER-INSTRUCTIONS.
           05   ADD-INSTRUCTION            PIC X(79) VALUE
                'Type information for new customer.  Then Press Enter.'.
           05   CHANGE-INSTRUCTION         PIC X(79) VALUE
                'Type changes.  Then press Enter.'.
           05   DELETE-INSTRUCTION         PIC X(79) VALUE
                'Press Enter to delete this customer or press F12 to canc
-               'el.'.
*
      01   COMMUNICATION-AREA.
           05   CA-CONTEXT-FLAG            PIC X(01).
                88   PROCESS-KEY-MAP                 VALUE '1'.
                88   PROCESS-ADD-CUSTOMER            VALUE '2'.
                88   PROCESS-CHANGE-CUSTOMER         VALUE '3'.
                88   PROCESS-DELETE-CUSTOMER         VALUE '4'.
           05   CA-CUSTOMER-RECORD.
                10   CA-CUSTOMER-NUMBER    PIC X(06).
                10   FILLER                PIC X(112).
*
      COPY CUSTMAS.
*
      COPY MNTSET2.
*
      COPY DFHAID.
*
      COPY ATTR.
*
      COPY ERRPARM.
*
      LINKAGE SECTION.
*
      01   DFHCOMMAREA                     PIC X(119).
```

The CUSTMNT2 program (part 1 of 11)

```
*
 PROCEDURE DIVISION.
*
 0000-PROCESS-CUSTOMER-MAINT.
*
     IF EIBCALEN > ZERO
         MOVE DFHCOMMAREA TO COMMUNICATION-AREA
     END-IF.
*
     EVALUATE TRUE
         WHEN EIBCALEN = ZERO
             MOVE LOW-VALUE TO MNTMAP1O
             MOVE -1 TO CUSTNO1L
             SET SEND-ERASE TO TRUE
             PERFORM 1500-SEND-KEY-MAP
             SET PROCESS-KEY-MAP TO TRUE
*
         WHEN EIBAID = DFHPF3
             EXEC CICS
                 XCTL PROGRAM('INVMENU')
             END-EXEC
*
         WHEN EIBAID = DFHPF12
             IF PROCESS-KEY-MAP
                 EXEC CICS
                     XCTL PROGRAM('INVMENU')
                 END-EXEC
             ELSE
                 MOVE LOW-VALUE TO MNTMAP1O
                 MOVE -1 TO CUSTNO1L
                 SET SEND-ERASE TO TRUE
                 PERFORM 1500-SEND-KEY-MAP
                 SET PROCESS-KEY-MAP TO TRUE
             END-IF
*
         WHEN EIBAID = DFHCLEAR
             IF PROCESS-KEY-MAP
                 MOVE LOW-VALUE TO MNTMAP1O
                 MOVE -1 TO CUSTNO1L
                 SET SEND-ERASE TO TRUE
                 PERFORM 1500-SEND-KEY-MAP
             ELSE
                 MOVE LOW-VALUE TO MNTMAP2O
                 MOVE CA-CUSTOMER-NUMBER TO CUSTNO2O
                 EVALUATE TRUE
                     WHEN PROCESS-ADD-CUSTOMER
                         MOVE ADD-INSTRUCTION     TO INSTR2O
                     WHEN PROCESS-CHANGE-CUSTOMER
                         MOVE CHANGE-INSTRUCTION TO INSTR2O
                     WHEN PROCESS-DELETE-CUSTOMER
                         MOVE DELETE-INSTRUCTION TO INSTR2O
                 END-EVALUATE
                 MOVE -1 TO LNAMEL
                 SET SEND-ERASE TO TRUE
                 PERFORM 1400-SEND-DATA-MAP
             END-IF
*
```

The CUSTMNT2 program (part 2 of 11)

```
                      WHEN EIBAID = DFHPA1 OR DFHPA2 OR DFHPA3
                          CONTINUE
         *
                      WHEN EIBAID = DFHENTER
                          EVALUATE TRUE
                              WHEN PROCESS-KEY-MAP
                                  PERFORM 1000-PROCESS-KEY-MAP
                              WHEN PROCESS-ADD-CUSTOMER
                                  PERFORM 2000-PROCESS-ADD-CUSTOMER
                              WHEN PROCESS-CHANGE-CUSTOMER
                                  PERFORM 3000-PROCESS-CHANGE-CUSTOMER
                              WHEN PROCESS-DELETE-CUSTOMER
                                  PERFORM 4000-PROCESS-DELETE-CUSTOMER
                          END-EVALUATE
         *
                      WHEN OTHER
                          IF PROCESS-KEY-MAP
                              MOVE LOW-VALUE TO MNTMAP1O
                              MOVE 'That key is unassigned.' TO MSG1O
                              MOVE -1 TO CUSTNO1L
                              SET SEND-DATAONLY-ALARM TO TRUE
                              PERFORM 1500-SEND-KEY-MAP
                          ELSE
                              MOVE LOW-VALUE TO MNTMAP2O
                              MOVE 'That key is unassigned.' TO MSG2O
                              MOVE -1 TO LNAMEL
                              SET SEND-DATAONLY-ALARM TO TRUE
                              PERFORM 1400-SEND-DATA-MAP
                          END-IF
                  END-EVALUATE.
         *
                  EXEC CICS
                      RETURN TRANSID('MNT2')
                              COMMAREA(COMMUNICATION-AREA)
                  END-EXEC.
         *
          1000-PROCESS-KEY-MAP.
         *
                  PERFORM 1100-RECEIVE-KEY-MAP.
                  PERFORM 1200-EDIT-KEY-DATA.
                  IF VALID-DATA
                      IF NOT PROCESS-DELETE-CUSTOMER
                          INSPECT CUSTOMER-MASTER-RECORD
                              REPLACING ALL SPACE BY '_'
                      END-IF
                      MOVE CUSTNO1I       TO CUSTNO2O
                      MOVE CM-LAST-NAME   TO LNAMEO
                      MOVE CM-FIRST-NAME  TO FNAMEO
                      MOVE CM-ADDRESS     TO ADDRO
                      MOVE CM-CITY        TO CITYO
                      MOVE CM-STATE       TO STATEO
                      MOVE CM-ZIP-CODE    TO ZIPCODEO
                      MOVE -1 TO LNAMEL
                      SET SEND-ERASE TO TRUE
                      PERFORM 1400-SEND-DATA-MAP
```

The CUSTMNT2 program (part 3 of 11)

```
            ELSE
                MOVE LOW-VALUE TO CUSTNO1O
                                 ACTIONO
                SET SEND-DATAONLY-ALARM TO TRUE
                PERFORM 1500-SEND-KEY-MAP
            END-IF.
*
     1100-RECEIVE-KEY-MAP.
*
            EXEC CICS
                RECEIVE MAP('MNTMAP1')
                        MAPSET('MNTSET2')
                        INTO(MNTMAP1I)
            END-EXEC.
            INSPECT MNTMAP1I
                REPLACING ALL '_' BY SPACE.
*
     1200-EDIT-KEY-DATA.
*
            MOVE ATTR-NO-HIGHLIGHT TO ACTIONH
                                     CUSTNO1H.
*
            IF ACTIONI NOT = '1' AND '2' AND '3'
                MOVE ATTR-REVERSE TO ACTIONH
                MOVE -1 TO ACTIONL
                MOVE 'Action must be 1, 2, or 3.' TO MSG1O
                MOVE 'N' TO VALID-DATA-SW
            END-IF.
            IF      CUSTNO1L = ZERO
                OR CUSTNO1I = SPACE
                MOVE ATTR-REVERSE TO CUSTNO1H
                MOVE -1 TO CUSTNO1L
                MOVE 'You must enter a customer number.' TO MSG1O
                MOVE 'N' TO VALID-DATA-SW
            END-IF.
*
            IF VALID-DATA
                MOVE LOW-VALUE TO MNTMAP2O
                EVALUATE ACTIONI
                    WHEN '1'
                        PERFORM 1300-READ-CUSTOMER-RECORD
                        IF RESPONSE-CODE = DFHRESP(NOTFND)
                            MOVE ADD-INSTRUCTION TO INSTR2O
                            SET PROCESS-ADD-CUSTOMER TO TRUE
                            MOVE SPACE TO CUSTOMER-MASTER-RECORD
                        ELSE
                            IF RESPONSE-CODE = DFHRESP(NORMAL)
                                MOVE 'That customer already exists.'
                                    TO MSG1O
                                MOVE 'N' TO VALID-DATA-SW
                            END-IF
                        END-IF
```

The CUSTMNT2 program (part 4 of 11)

```
              WHEN '2'
                  PERFORM 1300-READ-CUSTOMER-RECORD
                  IF RESPONSE-CODE = DFHRESP(NORMAL)
                      MOVE CUSTOMER-MASTER-RECORD TO
                          CA-CUSTOMER-RECORD
                      MOVE CHANGE-INSTRUCTION TO INSTR2O
                      SET PROCESS-CHANGE-CUSTOMER TO TRUE
                  ELSE
                      IF RESPONSE-CODE = DFHRESP(NOTFND)
                          MOVE 'That customer does not exist.' TO
                              MSG1O
                          MOVE 'N' TO VALID-DATA-SW
                      END-IF
                  END-IF
              WHEN '3'
                  PERFORM 1300-READ-CUSTOMER-RECORD
                  IF RESPONSE-CODE = DFHRESP(NORMAL)
                      MOVE CUSTOMER-MASTER-RECORD TO
                          CA-CUSTOMER-RECORD
                      MOVE DELETE-INSTRUCTION TO INSTR2O
                      SET PROCESS-DELETE-CUSTOMER TO TRUE
                      MOVE ATTR-PROT TO LNAMEA
                                       FNAMEA
                                       ADDRA
                                       CITYA
                                       STATEA
                                       ZIPCODEA
                  ELSE
                      IF RESPONSE-CODE = DFHRESP(NOTFND)
                          MOVE 'That customer does not exist.' TO
                              MSG1O
                          MOVE 'N' TO VALID-DATA-SW
                      END-IF
                  END-IF
          END-EVALUATE.
 *
  1300-READ-CUSTOMER-RECORD.
 *
      EXEC CICS
          READ FILE('CUSTMAS')
              INTO(CUSTOMER-MASTER-RECORD)
              RIDFLD(CUSTNO1I)
              RESP(RESPONSE-CODE)
      END-EXEC.
      IF      RESPONSE-CODE NOT = DFHRESP(NORMAL)
          AND RESPONSE-CODE NOT = DFHRESP(NOTFND)
          PERFORM 9999-TERMINATE-PROGRAM
      END-IF.
 *
  1400-SEND-DATA-MAP.
 *
      MOVE 'MNT2' TO TRANID2O.
 *
```

The CUSTMNT2 program (part 5 of 11)

```
        EVALUATE TRUE
            WHEN SEND-ERASE
                EXEC CICS
                    SEND MAP('MNTMAP2')
                        MAPSET('MNTSET2')
                        FROM(MNTMAP2O)
                        ERASE
                        CURSOR
                END-EXEC
            WHEN SEND-DATAONLY-ALARM
                EXEC CICS
                    SEND MAP('MNTMAP2')
                        MAPSET('MNTSET2')
                        FROM(MNTMAP2O)
                        DATAONLY
                        ALARM
                        CURSOR
                END-EXEC
        END-EVALUATE.
*
 1500-SEND-KEY-MAP.
*
    MOVE 'MNT2' TO TRANID1O.
*
    EVALUATE TRUE
        WHEN SEND-ERASE
            EXEC CICS
                SEND MAP('MNTMAP1')
                    MAPSET('MNTSET2')
                    FROM(MNTMAP1O)
                    ERASE
                    CURSOR
            END-EXEC
        WHEN SEND-ERASE-ALARM
            EXEC CICS
                SEND MAP('MNTMAP1')
                    MAPSET('MNTSET2')
                    FROM(MNTMAP1O)
                    ERASE
                    ALARM
                    CURSOR
            END-EXEC
        WHEN SEND-DATAONLY-ALARM
            EXEC CICS
                SEND MAP('MNTMAP1')
                    MAPSET('MNTSET2')
                    FROM(MNTMAP1O)
                    DATAONLY
                    ALARM
                    CURSOR
            END-EXEC
    END-EVALUATE.
*
```

The CUSTMNT2 program (part 6 of 11)

```
        2000-PROCESS-ADD-CUSTOMER.
*
            PERFORM 2100-RECEIVE-DATA-MAP.
            PERFORM 2200-EDIT-CUSTOMER-DATA.
            IF VALID-DATA
                PERFORM 2300-WRITE-CUSTOMER-RECORD
                IF RESPONSE-CODE = DFHRESP(NORMAL)
                    MOVE 'Customer record added.' TO MSG1O
                    SET SEND-ERASE TO TRUE
                ELSE
                    IF RESPONSE-CODE = DFHRESP(DUPREC)
                        MOVE 'Another user has added a record with that c
-                           'ustomer number.' TO MSG1O
                        SET SEND-ERASE-ALARM TO TRUE
                    END-IF
                END-IF
                MOVE -1 TO CUSTNO1L
                PERFORM 1500-SEND-KEY-MAP
                SET PROCESS-KEY-MAP TO TRUE
            ELSE
                MOVE LOW-VALUE TO LNAMEO
                                  FNAMEO
                                  ADDRO
                                  CITYO
                                  STATEO
                                  ZIPCODEO
                SET SEND-DATAONLY-ALARM TO TRUE
                PERFORM 1400-SEND-DATA-MAP
            END-IF.
*
        2100-RECEIVE-DATA-MAP.
*
            EXEC CICS
                RECEIVE MAP('MNTMAP2')
                        MAPSET('MNTSET2')
                        INTO(MNTMAP2I)
            END-EXEC.
            INSPECT MNTMAP2I
                REPLACING ALL '_' BY SPACE.
*
        2200-EDIT-CUSTOMER-DATA.
*
            MOVE ATTR-NO-HIGHLIGHT TO ZIPCODEH
                                      STATEH
                                      CITYH
                                      ADDRH
                                      FNAMEH
                                      LNAMEH.
*
            IF       ZIPCODEI = SPACE
                  OR ZIPCODEL = ZERO
                MOVE ATTR-REVERSE TO ZIPCODEH
                MOVE -1 TO ZIPCODEL
                MOVE 'You must enter a zip code.' TO MSG2O
                MOVE 'N' TO VALID-DATA-SW
            END-IF.
```

The CUSTMNT2 program (part 7 of 11)

```
*
      IF       STATEI = SPACE
         OR STATEL = ZERO
         MOVE ATTR-REVERSE TO STATEH
         MOVE -1 TO STATEL
         MOVE 'You must enter a state.' TO MSG2O
         MOVE 'N' TO VALID-DATA-SW
      END-IF.
*
      IF       CITYI = SPACE
         OR CITYL = ZERO
         MOVE ATTR-REVERSE TO CITYH
         MOVE -1 TO CITYL
         MOVE 'You must enter a city.' TO MSG2O
         MOVE 'N' TO VALID-DATA-SW
      END-IF.
*
      IF       ADDRI = SPACE
         OR ADDRL = ZERO
         MOVE ATTR-REVERSE TO ADDRH
         MOVE -1 TO ADDRL
         MOVE 'You must enter an address.' TO MSG2O
         MOVE 'N' TO VALID-DATA-SW
      END-IF.
*
      IF       FNAMEI = SPACE
         OR FNAMEL = ZERO
         MOVE ATTR-REVERSE TO FNAMEH
         MOVE -1 TO FNAMEL
         MOVE 'You must enter a first name.' TO MSG2O
         MOVE 'N' TO VALID-DATA-SW
      END-IF.
*
      IF       LNAMEI = SPACE
         OR LNAMEL = ZERO
         MOVE ATTR-REVERSE TO LNAMEH
         MOVE -1 TO LNAMEL
         MOVE 'You must enter a last name.' TO MSG2O
         MOVE 'N' TO VALID-DATA-SW
      END-IF.
*
 2300-WRITE-CUSTOMER-RECORD.
*
      MOVE CUSTNO2I TO CM-CUSTOMER-NUMBER.
      MOVE LNAMEI    TO CM-LAST-NAME.
      MOVE FNAMEI    TO CM-FIRST-NAME.
      MOVE ADDRI     TO CM-ADDRESS.
      MOVE CITYI     TO CM-CITY.
      MOVE STATEI    TO CM-STATE.
      MOVE ZIPCODEI TO CM-ZIP-CODE.
      EXEC CICS
         WRITE FILE('CUSTMAS')
               FROM(CUSTOMER-MASTER-RECORD)
               RIDFLD(CM-CUSTOMER-NUMBER)
               RESP(RESPONSE-CODE)
      END-EXEC.
```

The CUSTMNT2 program (part 8 of 11)

```
        IF      RESPONSE-CODE NOT = DFHRESP(NORMAL)
            AND RESPONSE-CODE NOT = DFHRESP(DUPREC)
                PERFORM 9999-TERMINATE-PROGRAM
        END-IF.
*
    3000-PROCESS-CHANGE-CUSTOMER.
*
        PERFORM 2100-RECEIVE-DATA-MAP.
        PERFORM 2200-EDIT-CUSTOMER-DATA.
        IF VALID-DATA
            MOVE CUSTNO2I TO CM-CUSTOMER-NUMBER
            PERFORM 3100-READ-CUSTOMER-FOR-UPDATE
            IF RESPONSE-CODE = DFHRESP(NORMAL)
                IF CUSTOMER-MASTER-RECORD = CA-CUSTOMER-RECORD
                    PERFORM 3200-REWRITE-CUSTOMER-RECORD
                    MOVE 'Customer record updated.' TO MSG1O
                    SET SEND-ERASE TO TRUE
                ELSE
                    MOVE 'Another user has updated the record.  Try a
-                        'gain.' TO MSG1O
                    SET SEND-ERASE-ALARM TO TRUE
                END-IF
            ELSE
                IF RESPONSE-CODE = DFHRESP(NOTFND)
                    MOVE 'Another user has deleted the record.' TO
                        MSG1O
                    SET SEND-ERASE-ALARM TO TRUE
                END-IF
            END-IF
            MOVE -1 TO CUSTNO1L
            PERFORM 1500-SEND-KEY-MAP
            SET PROCESS-KEY-MAP TO TRUE
        ELSE
            MOVE LOW-VALUE TO LNAMEO
                            FNAMEO
                            ADDRO
                            CITYO
                            STATEO
                            ZIPCODEO
            SET SEND-DATAONLY-ALARM TO TRUE
            PERFORM 1400-SEND-DATA-MAP
        END-IF.
*
    3100-READ-CUSTOMER-FOR-UPDATE.
*
        EXEC CICS
            READ FILE('CUSTMAS')
                INTO(CUSTOMER-MASTER-RECORD)
                RIDFLD(CM-CUSTOMER-NUMBER)
                UPDATE
                RESP(RESPONSE-CODE)
        END-EXEC.
        IF      RESPONSE-CODE NOT = DFHRESP(NORMAL)
            AND RESPONSE-CODE NOT = DFHRESP(NOTFND)
                PERFORM 9999-TERMINATE-PROGRAM
        END-IF.
```

The CUSTMNT2 program (part 9 of 11)

```
*
 3200-REWRITE-CUSTOMER-RECORD.
*
     MOVE LNAMEI     TO CM-LAST-NAME.
     MOVE FNAMEI     TO CM-FIRST-NAME.
     MOVE ADDRI      TO CM-ADDRESS.
     MOVE CITYI      TO CM-CITY.
     MOVE STATEI     TO CM-STATE.
     MOVE ZIPCODEI TO CM-ZIP-CODE.
     EXEC CICS
         REWRITE FILE('CUSTMAS')
                 FROM(CUSTOMER-MASTER-RECORD)
                 RESP(RESPONSE-CODE)
     END-EXEC.
     IF RESPONSE-CODE NOT = DFHRESP(NORMAL)
         PERFORM 9999-TERMINATE-PROGRAM
     END-IF.
*
 4000-PROCESS-DELETE-CUSTOMER.
*
     MOVE CA-CUSTOMER-NUMBER TO CM-CUSTOMER-NUMBER.
     PERFORM 3100-READ-CUSTOMER-FOR-UPDATE.
     IF RESPONSE-CODE = DFHRESP(NORMAL)
         IF CUSTOMER-MASTER-RECORD = CA-CUSTOMER-RECORD
             PERFORM 4100-DELETE-CUSTOMER-RECORD
             MOVE 'Customer deleted.' TO MSG1O
             SET SEND-ERASE TO TRUE
         ELSE
             MOVE 'Another user has updated the record.  Try again
-              '.' TO MSG1O
             SET SEND-ERASE-ALARM TO TRUE
         END-IF
     ELSE
         IF RESPONSE-CODE = DFHRESP(NOTFND)
             MOVE 'Another user has deleted the record.' TO
                 MSG1O
             SET SEND-ERASE-ALARM TO TRUE
         END-IF
     END-IF.
     MOVE -1 TO CUSTNO1L.
     PERFORM 1500-SEND-KEY-MAP.
     SET PROCESS-KEY-MAP TO TRUE.
*
 4100-DELETE-CUSTOMER-RECORD.
*
     EXEC CICS
         DELETE FILE('CUSTMAS')
                RESP(RESPONSE-CODE)
     END-EXEC.
     IF  RESPONSE-CODE NOT = DFHRESP(NORMAL)
         PERFORM 9999-TERMINATE-PROGRAM
     END-IF.
*
```

The CUSTMNT2 program (part 10 of 11)

```
      9999-TERMINATE-PROGRAM.
*
          MOVE EIBRESP  TO ERR-RESP.
          MOVE EIBRESP2 TO ERR-RESP2.
          MOVE EIBTRNID TO ERR-TRNID.
          MOVE EIBRSRCE TO ERR-RSRCE.
          EXEC CICS
              XCTL PROGRAM('SYSERR')
                   COMMAREA(ERROR-PARAMETERS)
          END-EXEC.
```

The CUSTMNT2 program (part 11 of 11)

The customer maintenance program: Modular design

In the pages that that follow, you'll find the specifications, event/response chart, structure chart, BMS mapset, symbolic map, and CICS source code for the customer maintenance program that's developed using modular design, with the presentation logic and the business logic separated into two programs. Many shops are developing new CICS programs using this approach because it allows you to use alternate user interfaces, including HTML pages over the Internet or a local intranet.

The program overview

Program	CSTMNTP: Customer maintenance program (presentation logic) CSTMNTB: Customer maintenance program (business logic)
Trans-id	CMNT
Overview	Lets the user enter new customer records, change existing customer records, or delete existing customer records.
Input/output	CUSTMAS Customer master file CMNTMP1 Customer maintenance key map CMNTMP2 Customer maintenance data map

Processing

1. Control is transferred to the presentation logic portion of this program (CSTMNTP) via XCTL from the menu program INVMENU with no communication area. The user can also start the program by entering the trans-id CMNT. In either case, the program should respond by displaying the key map.

2. On the key map, the user enters a customer number and selects a processing action (Add, Change, or Delete). Both fields must be entered. If they are, the program should link to CSTMNTB to make sure the customer doesn't exist for an add, but does exist for a change or delete. If a valid combination of customer number and action isn't entered, an error message should be displayed.

3. If the user enters a valid combination of action and customer number, display the data map. For an add operation, the user can then enter the customer information. For a change operation, the user can change any of the existing information. For a delete operation, all fields should be set to protected so the user can't enter changes. To complete any of these operations, the user must press the Enter key.

4. For an add or change, edit the fields to make sure they aren't blank, then link to CUSTMNTB and write or rewrite the record; for a delete, link to CUSTMNTB and delete the record.

5. If the user presses PF3 from either the key map or the data map, return to the menu program INVMENU by issuing an XCTL command. If the user presses PF12 from the key map, return to the menu program. However, if the user presses PF12 from the data map, redisplay the key map without completing the current operation.

6. For a change or delete operation, maintain an image of the customer record in the communication area between program executions. If the record is changed in any way between program executions, notify the user and do not complete the operation.

7. If an unrecoverable error occurs, terminate the program from CSTMNTP by invoking the SYSERR subprogram.

The screen layouts

The screen layout for the customer maintenance key map

Map name	CMNTMP1	Date	03/12/2001
Program name	CSTMNTP	Designer	Doug Lowe

```
CMNTMP1                 Customer Maintenance                                      XXXX

Type a customer number.  Then select an action and press Enter.

Customer number.  .   .   .   XXXXXX

Action  .   .   .   .   .   .   X  1.  Add a new customer
                                   2.  Change an existing customer
                                   3.  Delete an existing customer












XXXXXXXXXXXXXXXXXXXXXXXXXXXXXXXXXXXXXXXXXXXXXXXXXXXXXXXXXXXXXXXXXXXXXXXXXXXXXXXXXX
F3=Exit     F12=Cancel                                                             X
```

The screen layout for the customer maintenance data map

Map name	CMNTMP2	Date	03/12/2001
Program name	CSTMNTP	Designer	Doug Lowe

```
CMNTMP2                 Customer Maintenance                                      XXXX

XXXXXXXXXXXXXXXXXXXXXXXXXXXXXXXXXXXXXXXXXXXXXXXXXXXXXXXXXXXXXXXXXXXXXXXXXXXXXXXXXXXX

Customer number.  .   .   .   :  XXXXXX

Last  name.   .   .   .   .   .  XXXXXXXXXXXXXXXXXXXXXXXXXXXXXX
First name.   .   .   .   .   .  XXXXXXXXXXXXXXXXXXXX
Address.  .   .   .   .   .   .  XXXXXXXXXXXXXXXXXXXXXXXXXXXXXX
City  .   .   .   .   .   .   .  XXXXXXXXXXXXXXXXXXXXX
State.    .   .   .   .   .   .  XX
Zip Code  .   .   .   .   .   .  XXXXXXXXXX











XXXXXXXXXXXXXXXXXXXXXXXXXXXXXXXXXXXXXXXXXXXXXXXXXXXXXXXXXXXXXXXXXXXXXXXXXXXXXXXXXXXX
F3=Exit     F12=Cancel                                                             X
```

The copy members

The CUSTMAS copy member

```
01   CUSTOMER-MASTER-RECORD.
*
       05   CM-CUSTOMER-NUMBER          PIC X(06).
       05   CM-FIRST-NAME               PIC X(20).
       05   CM-LAST-NAME                PIC X(30).
       05   CM-ADDRESS                  PIC X(30).
       05   CM-CITY                     PIC X(20).
       05   CM-STATE                    PIC X(02).
       05   CM-ZIP-CODE                 PIC X(10).
```

The ERRPARM copy member (for the SYSERR program)

```
01   ERROR-PARAMETERS.
*
       05   ERR-RESP                    PIC S9(08)   COMP.
       05   ERR-RESP2                   PIC S9(08)   COMP.
       05   ERR-TRNID                   PIC X(04).
       05   ERR-RSRCE                   PIC X(08).
```

The error-handling program (SYSERR)

```
IDENTIFICATION DIVISION.
PROGRAM-ID.  SYSERR.
*
ENVIRONMENT DIVISION.
*
DATA DIVISION.
*
WORKING-STORAGE SECTION.
*
01  ERROR-MESSAGE.
    05  ERROR-LINE-1.
        10  FILLER      PIC X(20)  VALUE 'A serious error has '.
        10  FILLER      PIC X(20)  VALUE 'occurred.  Please co'.
        10  FILLER      PIC X(20)  VALUE 'ntact technical supp'.
        10  FILLER      PIC X(19)  VALUE 'ort.               '.
    05  ERROR-LINE-2    PIC X(79)  VALUE SPACE.
    05  ERROR-LINE-3.
        10  FILLER      PIC X(11)  VALUE 'EIBRESP  = '.
        10  EM-RESP     PIC Z(08)9.
        10  FILLER      PIC X(59)  VALUE SPACE.
    05  ERROR-LINE-4.
        10  FILLER      PIC X(11)  VALUE 'EIBRESP2 = '.
        10  EM-RESP2    PIC Z(08)9.
        10  FILLER      PIC X(59)  VALUE SPACE.
    05  ERROR-LINE-5.
        10  FILLER      PIC X(11)  VALUE 'EIBTRNID = '.
        10  EM-TRNID    PIC X(04).
        10  FILLER      PIC X(64)  VALUE SPACE.
    05  ERROR-LINE-6.
        10  FILLER      PIC X(11)  VALUE 'EIBRSRCE = '.
        10  EM-RSRCE    PIC X(08).
        10  FILLER      PIC X(60)  VALUE SPACE.
    05  ERROR-LINE-7    PIC X(79)  VALUE SPACE.
*
COPY ERRPARM.
*
LINKAGE SECTION.
*
01  DFHCOMMAREA        PIC X(20).
*
PROCEDURE DIVISION.
*
0000-DISPLAY-ERROR-MESSAGE.
*
    MOVE DFHCOMMAREA TO ERROR-PARAMETERS.
    MOVE ERR-RESP  TO EM-RESP.
    MOVE ERR-RESP2 TO EM-RESP2.
    MOVE ERR-TRNID TO EM-TRNID.
    MOVE ERR-RSRCE TO EM-RSRCE.
    EXEC CICS
        SEND TEXT FROM(ERROR-MESSAGE)
                  ERASE
                  ALARM
                  FREEKB
    END-EXEC.
    EXEC CICS
        RETURN
    END-EXEC.
```

The event/response chart

Event	Context	Response	New context
Start the program	n/a	Display the key map.	Get key
PF3	All	Transfer control to the menu program.	n/a
PF12	Get key	Transfer control to the menu program.	n/a
	Add customer Change customer Delete customer	Cancel the operation and display the key map.	Get key

Enter key	Get key	Edit input data.
		If valid
		   display data map
		
		else
		   display an error message.
			Add customer,
			Change customer, or
			Delete customer
			
			Get key

	Add customer	Edit input data.
		If valid
		   add customer record
		   display key map
		else
		   display an error message.
			Get key
			
			Add customer

	Change customer	Edit input data.
		If valid
		   change customer record
		   display key map
		else
		   display an error message.
			Get key
			
			Change customer

	Delete customer	Delete the customer record. Display the key map.	Get key
Clear	Get key	Redisplay the key map without any data.	Unchanged
	Add, Change, or Delete customer	Redisplay the data map with unprotected data erased.	Unchanged
Any PA key	All	Ignore the key.	Unchanged
Any other key	All	Display an appropriate error message.	Unchanged

The structure chart for the presentation logic

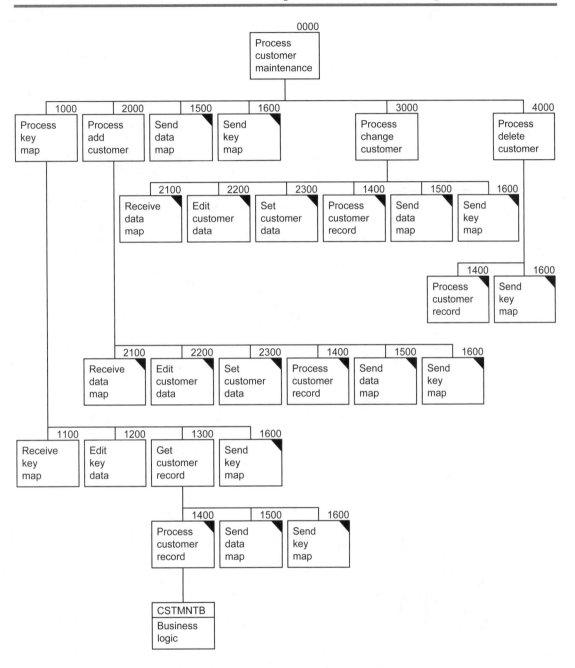

The structure chart for the business logic

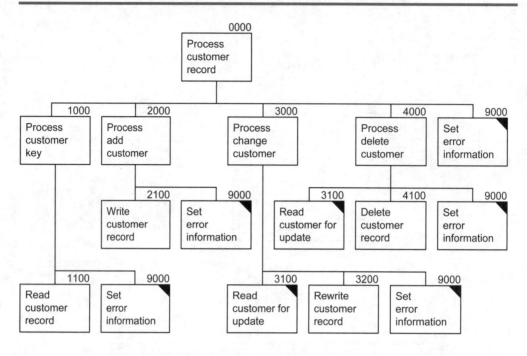

The BMS mapset for the presentation logic

```
          PRINT NOGEN
CMNTSET   DFHMSD TYPE=&SYSPARM,                                        X
                 LANG=COBOL,                                          X
                 MODE=INOUT,                                          X
                 TERM=3270-2,                                         X
                 CTRL=FREEKB,                                         X
                 STORAGE=AUTO,                                        X
                 DSATTS=(COLOR,HILIGHT),                              X
                 MAPATTS=(COLOR,HILIGHT),                             X
                 TIOAPFX=YES
*******************************************************************
CMNTMP1   DFHMDI SIZE=(24,80),                                        X
                 LINE=1,                                              X
                 COLUMN=1
*******************************************************************
          DFHMDF POS=(1,1),                                           X
                 LENGTH=7,                                            X
                 ATTRB=(NORM,PROT),                                   X
                 COLOR=BLUE,                                          X
                 INITIAL='MNTMAP1'
          DFHMDF POS=(1,20),                                          X
                 LENGTH=20,                                           X
                 ATTRB=(NORM,PROT),                                   X
                 COLOR=GREEN,                                         X
                 INITIAL='Customer Maintenance'
TRANID1   DFHMDF POS=(1,76),                                          X
                 LENGTH=4,                                            X
                 ATTRB=(NORM,PROT),                                   X
                 COLOR=BLUE,                                          X
                 INITIAL='XXXX'
*******************************************************************
          DFHMDF POS=(3,1),                                           X
                 LENGTH=63,                                           X
                 ATTRB=(NORM,PROT),                                   X
                 COLOR=NEUTRAL,                                       X
                 INITIAL='Type a customer number.  Then select an action X
                 and press Enter.'
          DFHMDF POS=(5,1),                                           X
                 LENGTH=24,                                           X
                 ATTRB=(NORM,PROT),                                   X
                 COLOR=GREEN,                                         X
                 INITIAL='Customer number. . . . .'
CUSTNO1   DFHMDF POS=(5,26),                                          X
                 LENGTH=6,                                            X
                 ATTRB=(NORM,UNPROT,FSET),                            X
                 COLOR=TURQUOISE,                                     X
                 INITIAL='_____'
          DFHMDF POS=(5,33),                                          X
                 LENGTH=1,                                            X
                 ATTRB=ASKIP
          DFHMDF POS=(7,1),                                           X
                 LENGTH=24,                                           X
                 ATTRB=(NORM,PROT),                                   X
                 COLOR=GREEN,                                         X
                 INITIAL='Action . . . . . . . . . .'
```

The BMS mapset for the presentation logic (part 1 of 4)

```
ACTION    DFHMDF POS=(7,26),                                              X
                 LENGTH=1,                                                X
                 ATTRB=(NORM,NUM,FSET),                                   X
                 COLOR=TURQUOISE,                                         X
                 INITIAL='_'
          DFHMDF POS=(7,28),                                             X
                 LENGTH=21,                                               X
                 ATTRB=(NORM,ASKIP),                                      X
                 COLOR=NEUTRAL,                                           X
                 INITIAL='1. Add a new customer'
          DFHMDF POS=(8,28),                                             X
                 LENGTH=30,                                               X
                 ATTRB=(NORM,ASKIP),                                      X
                 COLOR=NEUTRAL,                                           X
                 INITIAL='2. Change an existing customer'
          DFHMDF POS=(9,28),                                             X
                 LENGTH=21,                                               X
                 ATTRB=(NORM,ASKIP),                                      X
                 COLOR=NEUTRAL,                                           X
                 INITIAL='3. Delete an existing customer'
MSG1      DFHMDF POS=(23,1),                                             X
                 LENGTH=79,                                               X
                 ATTRB=(BRT,PROT),                                        X
                 COLOR=YELLOW
          DFHMDF POS=(24,1),                                             X
                 LENGTH=20,                                               X
                 ATTRB=(NORM,PROT),                                       X
                 COLOR=BLUE,                                              X
                 INITIAL='F3=Exit    F12=Cancel'
DUMMY1    DFHMDF POS=(24,79),                                            X
                 LENGTH=1,                                                X
                 ATTRB=(DRK,PROT,FSET),                                   X
                 INITIAL=' '
*********************************************************************
CMNTMP2   DFHMDI SIZE=(24,80),                                          X
                 LINE=1,                                                  X
                 COLUMN=1
*********************************************************************
          DFHMDF POS=(1,1),                                             X
                 LENGTH=7,                                                X
                 ATTRB=(NORM,PROT),                                       X
                 COLOR=BLUE,                                              X
                 INITIAL='MNTMAP2'
          DFHMDF POS=(1,20),                                            X
                 LENGTH=20,                                               X
                 ATTRB=(NORM,PROT),                                       X
                 COLOR=GREEN,                                             X
                 INITIAL='Customer Maintenance'
TRANID2   DFHMDF POS=(1,76),                                            X
                 LENGTH=4,                                                X
                 ATTRB=(NORM,PROT),                                       X
                 COLOR=BLUE,                                              X
                 INITIAL='XXXX'
*********************************************************************
```

The BMS mapset for the presentation logic (part 2 of 4)

```
INSTR2   DFHMDF POS=(3,1),                                              X
                LENGTH=79,                                              X
                ATTRB=(NORM,PROT),                                      X
                COLOR=NEUTRAL
         DFHMDF POS=(5,1),                                              X
                LENGTH=24,                                              X
                ATTRB=(NORM,PROT),                                      X
                COLOR=GREEN,                                            X
                INITIAL='Customer number. . . . :'
CUSTNO2  DFHMDF POS=(5,26),                                             X
                LENGTH=6,                                               X
                ATTRB=(NORM,PROT,FSET),                                 X
                COLOR=TURQUOISE
**********************************************************************
         DFHMDF POS=(7,1),                                              X
                LENGTH=24,                                              X
                ATTRB=(NORM,PROT),                                      X
                COLOR=GREEN,                                            X
                INITIAL='Last name. . . . . . . .'
LNAME    DFHMDF POS=(7,26),                                             X
                LENGTH=30,                                              X
                ATTRB=(NORM,UNPROT,FSET),                               X
                COLOR=TURQUOISE
         DFHMDF POS=(7,57),                                             X
                LENGTH=1,                                               X
                ATTRB=ASKIP
**********************************************************************
         DFHMDF POS=(8,1),                                              X
                LENGTH=24,                                              X
                ATTRB=(NORM,PROT),                                      X
                COLOR=GREEN,                                            X
                INITIAL='First name . . . . . . .'
FNAME    DFHMDF POS=(8,26),                                             X
                LENGTH=20,                                              X
                ATTRB=(NORM,UNPROT,FSET),                               X
                COLOR=TURQUOISE
         DFHMDF POS=(8,47),                                             X
                LENGTH=1,                                               X
                ATTRB=ASKIP
**********************************************************************
         DFHMDF POS=(9,1),                                              X
                LENGTH=24,                                              X
                ATTRB=(NORM,PROT),                                      X
                COLOR=GREEN,                                            X
                INITIAL='Address. . . . . . . . .'
ADDR     DFHMDF POS=(9,26),                                             X
                LENGTH=30,                                              X
                ATTRB=(NORM,UNPROT,FSET),                               X
                COLOR=TURQUOISE
         DFHMDF POS=(9,57),                                             X
                LENGTH=1,                                               X
                ATTRB=ASKIP
**********************************************************************
```

The BMS mapset for the presentation logic (part 3 of 4)

```
              DFHMDF POS=(10,1),                                          X
                     LENGTH=24,                                           X
                     ATTRB=(NORM,PROT),                                   X
                     COLOR=GREEN,                                         X
                     INITIAL='City . . . . . . . . . .'
CITY          DFHMDF POS=(10,26),                                         X
                     LENGTH=20,                                           X
                     ATTRB=(NORM,UNPROT,FSET),                            X
                     COLOR=TURQUOISE
              DFHMDF POS=(10,47),                                         X
                     LENGTH=1,                                            X
                     ATTRB=ASKIP
**********************************************************************
              DFHMDF POS=(11,1),                                          X
                     LENGTH=24,                                           X
                     ATTRB=(NORM,PROT),                                   X
                     COLOR=GREEN,                                         X
                     INITIAL='State. . . . . . . . . .'
STATE         DFHMDF POS=(11,26),                                         X
                     LENGTH=2,                                            X
                     ATTRB=(NORM,UNPROT,FSET),                            X
                     COLOR=TURQUOISE
              DFHMDF POS=(11,29),                                         X
                     LENGTH=1,                                            X
                     ATTRB=ASKIP
**********************************************************************
              DFHMDF POS=(12,1),                                          X
                     LENGTH=24,                                           X
                     ATTRB=(NORM,PROT),                                   X
                     COLOR=GREEN,                                         X
                     INITIAL='Zip Code . . . . . . . .'
ZIPCODE       DFHMDF POS=(12,26),                                         X
                     LENGTH=10,                                           X
                     ATTRB=(NORM,UNPROT,FSET),                            X
                     COLOR=TURQUOISE
              DFHMDF POS=(12,37),                                         X
                     LENGTH=1,                                            X
                     ATTRB=ASKIP
**********************************************************************
MSG2          DFHMDF POS=(23,1),                                          X
                     LENGTH=79,                                           X
                     ATTRB=(BRT,PROT),                                    X
                     COLOR=YELLOW
              DFHMDF POS=(24,1),                                          X
                     LENGTH=20,                                           X
                     ATTRB=(NORM,PROT),                                   X
                     COLOR=BLUE,                                          X
                     INITIAL='F3=Exit    F12=Cancel'
DUMMY2        DFHMDF POS=(24,79),                                         X
                     LENGTH=1,                                            X
                     ATTRB=(DRK,PROT,FSET),                               X
                     INITIAL=' '
**********************************************************************
              DFHMSD TYPE=FINAL
              END
```

The BMS mapset for the presentation logic (part 4 of 4)

The symbolic map for the presentation logic

```
01  CMNTMP1I.
    03  FILLER                           PIC X(12).
    03  TRANID1L                         PIC S9(4) COMP.
    03  TRANID1F                         PIC X.
    03  FILLER REDEFINES TRANID1F.
        05  TRANID1A                     PIC X.
    03  FILLER                           PIC X(2).
    03  TRANID1I                         PIC X(4).
    03  CUSTNO1L                         PIC S9(4) COMP.
    03  CUSTNO1F                         PIC X.
    03  FILLER REDEFINES CUSTNO1F.
        05  CUSTNO1A                     PIC X.
    03  FILLER                           PIC X(2).
    03  CUSTNO1I                         PIC X(6).
    03  ACTIONL                          PIC S9(4) COMP.
    03  ACTIONF                          PIC X.
    03  FILLER REDEFINES ACTIONF.
        05  ACTIONA                      PIC X.
    03  FILLER                           PIC X(2).
    03  ACTIONI                          PIC X(1).
    03  MSG1L                            PIC S9(4) COMP.
    03  MSG1F                            PIC X.
    03  FILLER REDEFINES MSG1F.
        05  MSG1A                        PIC X.
    03  FILLER                           PIC X(2).
    03  MSG1I                            PIC X(79).
    03  DUMMY1L                          PIC S9(4) COMP.
    03  DUMMY1F                          PIC X.
    03  FILLER REDEFINES DUMMY1F.
        05  DUMMY1A                      PIC X.
    03  FILLER                           PIC X(2).
    03  DUMMY1I                          PIC X(1).
01  CMNTMP1O REDEFINES CMNTMP1I.
    03  FILLER                           PIC X(12).
    03  FILLER                           PIC X(3).
    03  TRANID1C                         PIC X.
    03  TRANID1H                         PIC X.
    03  TRANID1O                         PIC X(4).
    03  FILLER                           PIC X(3).
    03  CUSTNO1C                         PIC X.
    03  CUSTNO1H                         PIC X.
    03  CUSTNO1O                         PIC X(6).
    03  FILLER                           PIC X(3).
    03  ACTIONC                          PIC X.
    03  ACTIONH                          PIC X.
    03  ACTIONO                          PIC X(1).
    03  FILLER                           PIC X(3).
    03  MSG1C                            PIC X.
    03  MSG1H                            PIC X.
    03  MSG1O                            PIC X(79).
    03  FILLER                           PIC X(3).
    03  DUMMY1C                          PIC X.
    03  DUMMY1H                          PIC X.
    03  DUMMY1O                          PIC X(1).
```

The symbolic map for the presentation logic (part 1 of 3)

```
01 CMNTMP2I.
    03 FILLER                               PIC X(12).
    03 TRANID2L                             PIC S9(4) COMP.
    03 TRANID2F                             PIC X.
    03 FILLER REDEFINES TRANID2F.
        05 TRANID2A                         PIC X.
    03 FILLER                               PIC X(2).
    03 TRANID2I                             PIC X(4).
    03 INSTR2L                              PIC S9(4) COMP.
    03 INSTR2F                              PIC X.
    03 FILLER REDEFINES INSTR2F.
        05 INSTR2A                          PIC X.
    03 FILLER                               PIC X(2).
    03 INSTR2I                              PIC X(79).
    03 CUSTNO2L                             PIC S9(4) COMP.
    03 CUSTNO2F                             PIC X.
    03 FILLER REDEFINES CUSTNO2F.
        05 CUSTNO2A                         PIC X.
    03 FILLER                               PIC X(2).
    03 CUSTNO2I                             PIC X(6).
    03 LNAMEL                               PIC S9(4) COMP.
    03 LNAMEF                               PIC X.
    03 FILLER REDEFINES LNAMEF.
        05 LNAMEA                           PIC X.
    03 FILLER                               PIC X(2).
    03 LNAMEI                               PIC X(30).
    03 FNAMEL                               PIC S9(4) COMP.
    03 FNAMEF                               PIC X.
    03 FILLER REDEFINES FNAMEF.
        05 FNAMEA                           PIC X.
    03 FILLER                               PIC X(2).
    03 FNAMEI                               PIC X(20).
    03 ADDRL                                PIC S9(4) COMP.
    03 ADDRF                                PIC X.
    03 FILLER REDEFINES ADDRF.
        05 ADDRA                            PIC X.
    03 FILLER                               PIC X(2).
    03 ADDRI                                PIC X(30).
    03 CITYL                                PIC S9(4) COMP.
    03 CITYF                                PIC X.
    03 FILLER REDEFINES CITYF.
        05 CITYA                            PIC X.
    03 FILLER                               PIC X(2).
    03 CITYI                                PIC X(20).
    03 STATEL                               PIC S9(4) COMP.
    03 STATEF                               PIC X.
    03 FILLER REDEFINES STATEF.
        05 STATEA                           PIC X.
    03 FILLER                               PIC X(2).
    03 STATEI                               PIC X(2).
    03 ZIPCODEL                             PIC S9(4) COMP.
    03 ZIPCODEF                             PIC X.
    03 FILLER REDEFINES ZIPCODEF.
        05 ZIPCODEA                         PIC X.
    03 FILLER                               PIC X(2).
    03 ZIPCODEI                             PIC X(10).
    03 MSG2L                                PIC S9(4) COMP.
    03 MSG2F                                PIC X.
```

The symbolic map for the presentation logic (part 2 of 3)

```
    03 FILLER REDEFINES MSG2F.
       05 MSG2A                        PIC X.
    03 FILLER                      PIC X(2).
    03 MSG2I                       PIC X(79).
    03 DUMMY2L                     PIC S9(4) COMP.
    03 DUMMY2F                     PIC X.
    03 FILLER REDEFINES DUMMY2F.
       05 DUMMY2A                     PIC X.
    03 FILLER                      PIC X(2).
    03 DUMMY2I                     PIC X(1).
01 CMNTMP2O REDEFINES CMNTMP2I.
    03 FILLER                      PIC X(12).
    03 FILLER                      PIC X(3).
    03 TRANID2C                    PIC X.
    03 TRANID2H                    PIC X.
    03 TRANID2O                    PIC X(4).
    03 FILLER                      PIC X(3).
    03 INSTR2C                     PIC X.
    03 INSTR2H                     PIC X.
    03 INSTR2O                     PIC X(79).
    03 FILLER                      PIC X(3).
    03 CUSTNO2C                    PIC X.
    03 CUSTNO2H                    PIC X.
    03 CUSTNO2O                    PIC X(6).
    03 FILLER                      PIC X(3).
    03 LNAMEC                      PIC X.
    03 LNAMEH                      PIC X.
    03 LNAMEO                      PIC X(30).
    03 FILLER                      PIC X(3).
    03 FNAMEC                      PIC X.
    03 FNAMEH                      PIC X.
    03 FNAMEO                      PIC X(20).
    03 FILLER                      PIC X(3).
    03 ADDRC                       PIC X.
    03 ADDRH                       PIC X.
    03 ADDRO                       PIC X(30).
    03 FILLER                      PIC X(3).
    03 CITYC                       PIC X.
    03 CITYH                       PIC X.
    03 CITYO                       PIC X(20).
    03 FILLER                      PIC X(3).
    03 STATEC                      PIC X.
    03 STATEH                      PIC X.
    03 STATEO                      PIC X(2).
    03 FILLER                      PIC X(3).
    03 ZIPCODEC                    PIC X.
    03 ZIPCODEH                    PIC X.
    03 ZIPCODEO                    PIC X(10).
    03 FILLER                      PIC X(3).
    03 MSG2C                       PIC X.
    03 MSG2H                       PIC X.
    03 MSG2O                       PIC X(79).
    03 FILLER                      PIC X(3).
    03 DUMMY2C                     PIC X.
    03 DUMMY2H                     PIC X.
    03 DUMMY2O                     PIC X(1).
```

The symbolic map for the presentation logic (part 3 of 3)

The presentation logic program: CSTMNTP

```
         IDENTIFICATION DIVISION.
         PROGRAM-ID.  CSTMNTP.
       *
         ENVIRONMENT DIVISION.
       *
         DATA DIVISION.
       *
         WORKING-STORAGE SECTION.
       *
         01   SWITCHES.
              05   VALID-DATA-SW              PIC X(01)    VALUE 'Y'.
                   88   VALID-DATA                         VALUE 'Y'.
       *
         01   FLAGS.
              05   SEND-FLAG                  PIC X(01).
                   88   SEND-ERASE                         VALUE '1'.
                   88   SEND-ERASE-ALARM                   VALUE '2'.
                   88   SEND-DATAONLY                      VALUE '3'.
                   88   SEND-DATAONLY-ALARM                VALUE '4'.
       *
         01   USER-INSTRUCTIONS.
              05   ADD-INSTRUCTION            PIC X(79)    VALUE
                   'Type information for new customer.  Then Press Enter.'.
              05   CHANGE-INSTRUCTION         PIC X(79)    VALUE
                   'Type changes.  Then press Enter.'.
              05   DELETE-INSTRUCTION         PIC X(79)    VALUE
                   'Press Enter to delete this customer or press F12 to canc
       -         'el.'.
       *
         01   COMMUNICATION-AREA.
              05   CA-CONTEXT-FLAG            PIC X(01).
                   88   PROCESS-KEY-MAP                    VALUE '1'.
                   88   PROCESS-ADD-CUSTOMER               VALUE '2'.
                   88   PROCESS-CHANGE-CUSTOMER            VALUE '3'.
                   88   PROCESS-DELETE-CUSTOMER            VALUE '4'.
              05   CA-ACTION-FLAG             PIC X(01).
                   88   ADD-REQUEST                        VALUE '1'.
                   88   CHANGE-REQUEST                     VALUE '2'.
                   88   DELETE-REQUEST                     VALUE '3'.
              05   CA-CUSTOMER-RECORD.
                   10   CA-CUSTOMER-NUMBER    PIC X(06).
                   10   CA-FIRST-NAME         PIC X(20).
                   10   CA-LAST-NAME          PIC X(30).
                   10   CA-ADDRESS            PIC X(30).
                   10   CA-CITY               PIC X(20).
                   10   CA-STATE              PIC X(02).
                   10   CA-ZIP-CODE           PIC X(10).
              05   CA-SAVE-CUSTOMER-MASTER    PIC X(118).
              05   CA-RETURN-CONDITION        PIC X(01).
                   88   PROCESS-OK                         VALUE '1'.
                   88   PROCESS-ERROR                      VALUE '2'.
                   88   PROCESS-SEVERE-ERROR               VALUE '3'.
              05   CA-RETURN-MESSAGE          PIC X(79).
```

The CSTMNTP program (part 1 of 9)

```
        05  CA-ERROR-PARAMETERS.
            10  CA-ERR-RESP                 PIC S9(08)  COMP.
            10  CA-ERR-RESP2                PIC S9(08)  COMP.
            10  CA-ERR-RSRCE                PIC X(08).
*
 COPY CMNTSET.
*
 COPY DFHAID.
*
 COPY ATTR.
*
 COPY ERRPARM.
*
 LINKAGE SECTION.
*
 01  DFHCOMMAREA                           PIC X(334).
*
 PROCEDURE DIVISION.
*
 0000-PROCESS-CUSTOMER-MAINT.
*
     IF EIBCALEN > ZERO
         MOVE DFHCOMMAREA TO COMMUNICATION-AREA
     END-IF.
*
     EVALUATE TRUE
*
         WHEN EIBCALEN = ZERO
             MOVE LOW-VALUE TO CMNTMP1O
             MOVE -1 TO CUSTNO1L
             SET SEND-ERASE TO TRUE
             PERFORM 1600-SEND-KEY-MAP
             SET PROCESS-KEY-MAP TO TRUE
*
         WHEN EIBAID = DFHPF3
             EXEC CICS
                 XCTL PROGRAM('INVMENU')
             END-EXEC
*
         WHEN EIBAID = DFHPF12
             IF PROCESS-KEY-MAP
                 EXEC CICS
                     XCTL PROGRAM('INVMENU')
                 END-EXEC
             ELSE
                 MOVE LOW-VALUE TO CMNTMP1O
                 MOVE -1 TO CUSTNO1L
                 SET SEND-ERASE TO TRUE
                 PERFORM 1600-SEND-KEY-MAP
                 SET PROCESS-KEY-MAP TO TRUE
             END-IF
*
         WHEN EIBAID = DFHCLEAR
             IF PROCESS-KEY-MAP
                 MOVE LOW-VALUE TO CMNTMP1O
```

The CSTMNTP program (part 2 of 9)

```
                            MOVE -1 TO CUSTNO1L
                            SET SEND-ERASE TO TRUE
                            PERFORM 1600-SEND-KEY-MAP
                        ELSE
                            MOVE LOW-VALUE TO CMNTMP2O
                            MOVE CA-CUSTOMER-NUMBER TO CUSTNO2O
                            EVALUATE TRUE
                                WHEN PROCESS-ADD-CUSTOMER
                                    MOVE ADD-INSTRUCTION      TO INSTR2O
                                WHEN PROCESS-CHANGE-CUSTOMER
                                    MOVE CHANGE-INSTRUCTION TO INSTR2O
                                WHEN PROCESS-DELETE-CUSTOMER
                                    MOVE DELETE-INSTRUCTION TO INSTR2O
                            END-EVALUATE
                            MOVE -1 TO LNAMEL
                            SET SEND-ERASE TO TRUE
                            PERFORM 1500-SEND-DATA-MAP
                        END-IF
*
                WHEN EIBAID = DFHPA1 OR DFHPA2 OR DFHPA3
                    CONTINUE
*
                WHEN EIBAID = DFHENTER
                    EVALUATE TRUE
                        WHEN PROCESS-KEY-MAP
                            PERFORM 1000-PROCESS-KEY-MAP
                        WHEN PROCESS-ADD-CUSTOMER
                            PERFORM 2000-PROCESS-ADD-CUSTOMER
                        WHEN PROCESS-CHANGE-CUSTOMER
                            PERFORM 3000-PROCESS-CHANGE-CUSTOMER
                        WHEN PROCESS-DELETE-CUSTOMER
                            PERFORM 4000-PROCESS-DELETE-CUSTOMER
                    END-EVALUATE
*
                WHEN OTHER
                    IF PROCESS-KEY-MAP
                        MOVE LOW-VALUE TO CMNTMP1O
                        MOVE 'That key is unassigned.' TO MSG1O
                        MOVE -1 TO CUSTNO1L
                        SET SEND-DATAONLY-ALARM TO TRUE
                        PERFORM 1600-SEND-KEY-MAP
                    ELSE
                        MOVE LOW-VALUE TO CMNTMP2O
                        MOVE 'That key is unassigned.' TO MSG2O
                        MOVE -1 TO LNAMEL
                        SET SEND-DATAONLY-ALARM TO TRUE
                        PERFORM 1500-SEND-DATA-MAP
                    END-IF
*
            END-EVALUATE.
*
            EXEC CICS
                RETURN TRANSID('CMNT')
                       COMMAREA(COMMUNICATION-AREA)
            END-EXEC.
```

The CSTMNTP program (part 3 of 9)

```
*
 1000-PROCESS-KEY-MAP.
*
     MOVE LOW-VALUE TO CA-CUSTOMER-RECORD.
     PERFORM 1100-RECEIVE-KEY-MAP.
     PERFORM 1200-EDIT-KEY-DATA.
     IF VALID-DATA
         PERFORM 1300-GET-CUSTOMER-RECORD
     ELSE
         MOVE LOW-VALUE TO CUSTNO1O
                          ACTIONO
         SET SEND-DATAONLY-ALARM TO TRUE
         PERFORM 1600-SEND-KEY-MAP
     END-IF.
*
 1100-RECEIVE-KEY-MAP.
*
     EXEC CICS
         RECEIVE MAP('CMNTMP1')
                 MAPSET('CMNTSET')
                 INTO(CMNTMP1I)
     END-EXEC.
     INSPECT CMNTMP1I
         REPLACING ALL '_' BY SPACE.
*
 1200-EDIT-KEY-DATA.
*
     MOVE ATTR-NO-HIGHLIGHT TO ACTIONH
                              CUSTNO1H.

     IF ACTIONI NOT = '1' AND '2' AND '3'
         MOVE ATTR-REVERSE TO ACTIONH
         MOVE -1 TO ACTIONL
         MOVE 'Action must be 1, 2, or 3.' TO MSG1O
         MOVE 'N' TO VALID-DATA-SW
     END-IF.
*
     IF    CUSTNO1L = ZERO
        OR CUSTNO1I = SPACE
         MOVE ATTR-REVERSE TO CUSTNO1H
         MOVE -1 TO CUSTNO1L
         MOVE 'You must enter a customer number.' TO MSG1O
         MOVE 'N' TO VALID-DATA-SW
     END-IF.
*
 1300-GET-CUSTOMER-RECORD.
*
     MOVE CUSTNO1I TO CA-CUSTOMER-NUMBER.
     MOVE ACTIONI  TO CA-ACTION-FLAG.
     PERFORM 1400-PROCESS-CUSTOMER-RECORD.
     IF PROCESS-OK
         EVALUATE ACTIONI
             WHEN '1'
                 MOVE ADD-INSTRUCTION TO INSTR2O
                 SET PROCESS-ADD-CUSTOMER TO TRUE
```

The CSTMNTP program (part 4 of 9)

```
                        WHEN '2'
                            MOVE CHANGE-INSTRUCTION TO INSTR2O
                            SET PROCESS-CHANGE-CUSTOMER TO TRUE
                        WHEN '3'
                            MOVE DELETE-INSTRUCTION TO INSTR2O
                            SET PROCESS-DELETE-CUSTOMER TO TRUE
                            MOVE ATTR-PROT TO LNAMEA
                                            FNAMEA
                                            ADDRA
                                            CITYA
                                            STATEA
                                            ZIPCODEA
                    END-EVALUATE
                    IF NOT PROCESS-DELETE-CUSTOMER
                        INSPECT CA-CUSTOMER-RECORD
                            REPLACING ALL SPACE BY '_'
                    END-IF
                    MOVE CUSTNO1I        TO CUSTNO2O
                    MOVE CA-LAST-NAME    TO LNAMEO
                    MOVE CA-FIRST-NAME   TO FNAMEO
                    MOVE CA-ADDRESS      TO ADDRO
                    MOVE CA-CITY         TO CITYO
                    MOVE CA-STATE        TO STATEO
                    MOVE CA-ZIP-CODE     TO ZIPCODEO
                    MOVE -1              TO LNAMEL
                    SET SEND-ERASE TO TRUE
                    PERFORM 1500-SEND-DATA-MAP
                ELSE
                    MOVE LOW-VALUE TO CUSTNO1O
                                      ACTIONO
                    SET SEND-DATAONLY-ALARM TO TRUE
                    MOVE -1 TO CUSTNO1L
                    PERFORM 1600-SEND-KEY-MAP
                END-IF.
        *
         1400-PROCESS-CUSTOMER-RECORD.
        *
            EXEC CICS
                LINK PROGRAM('CSTMNTB')
                COMMAREA(COMMUNICATION-AREA)
            END-EXEC.
        *
            IF PROCESS-SEVERE-ERROR
                PERFORM 9999-TERMINATE-PROGRAM
            ELSE
                MOVE CA-RETURN-MESSAGE TO MSG1O
            END-IF.
        *
```

The CSTMNTP program (part 5 of 9)

```
    1500-SEND-DATA-MAP.
*
        MOVE 'CMNT' TO TRANID2O.
        EVALUATE TRUE
            WHEN SEND-ERASE
                EXEC CICS
                    SEND MAP('CMNTMP2')
                         MAPSET('CMNTSET')
                         FROM(CMNTMP2O)
                         ERASE
                         CURSOR
                END-EXEC
            WHEN SEND-DATAONLY-ALARM
                EXEC CICS
                    SEND MAP('CMNTMP2')
                         MAPSET('CMNTSET')
                         FROM(CMNTMP2O)
                         DATAONLY
                         ALARM
                         CURSOR
            END-EXEC
        END-EVALUATE.
*
    1600-SEND-KEY-MAP.
*
        MOVE 'CMNT' TO TRANID1O.
        EVALUATE TRUE
            WHEN SEND-ERASE
                EXEC CICS
                    SEND MAP('CMNTMP1')
                         MAPSET('CMNTSET')
                         FROM(CMNTMP1O)
                         ERASE
                         CURSOR
                END-EXEC
            WHEN SEND-ERASE-ALARM
                EXEC CICS
                    SEND MAP('CMNTMP1')
                         MAPSET('CMNTSET')
                         FROM(CMNTMP1O)
                         ERASE
                         ALARM
                         CURSOR
                END-EXEC
            WHEN SEND-DATAONLY-ALARM
                EXEC CICS
                    SEND MAP('CMNTMP1')
                         MAPSET('CMNTSET')
                         FROM(CMNTMP1O)
                         DATAONLY
                         ALARM
                         CURSOR
                END-EXEC
        END-EVALUATE.
*
```

The CSTMNTP program (part 6 of 9)

```
2000-PROCESS-ADD-CUSTOMER.
*
    PERFORM 2100-RECEIVE-DATA-MAP.
    PERFORM 2200-EDIT-CUSTOMER-DATA.
    IF VALID-DATA
        PERFORM 2300-SET-CUSTOMER-DATA
        PERFORM 1400-PROCESS-CUSTOMER-RECORD
        IF PROCESS-OK
            SET SEND-ERASE TO TRUE
        ELSE
            SET SEND-ERASE-ALARM TO TRUE
        END-IF
        MOVE -1 TO CUSTNO1L
        PERFORM 1600-SEND-KEY-MAP
        SET PROCESS-KEY-MAP TO TRUE
    ELSE
        MOVE LOW-VALUE TO LNAMEO
                         FNAMEO
                         ADDRO
                         CITYO
                         STATEO
                         ZIPCODEO
        SET SEND-DATAONLY-ALARM TO TRUE
        PERFORM 1500-SEND-DATA-MAP
    END-IF.
*
2100-RECEIVE-DATA-MAP.
*
    EXEC CICS
        RECEIVE MAP('CMNTMP2')
                MAPSET('CMNTSET')
                INTO(CMNTMP2I)
    END-EXEC.
    INSPECT CMNTMP2I
        REPLACING ALL '_' BY SPACE.
*
2200-EDIT-CUSTOMER-DATA.
*
    MOVE ATTR-NO-HIGHLIGHT TO ZIPCODEH
                            STATEH
                            CITYH
                            ADDRH
                            FNAMEH
                            LNAMEH.
*
    IF    ZIPCODEI = SPACE
       OR ZIPCODEL = ZERO
          MOVE ATTR-REVERSE TO ZIPCODEH
          MOVE -1 TO ZIPCODEL
          MOVE 'You must enter a zip code.' TO MSG2O
          MOVE 'N' TO VALID-DATA-SW
    END-IF.
*
```

The CSTMNTP program (part 7 of 9)

```
        IF     STATEI = SPACE
           OR STATEL = ZERO
             MOVE ATTR-REVERSE TO STATEH
             MOVE -1 TO STATEL
             MOVE 'You must enter a state.' TO MSG2O
             MOVE 'N' TO VALID-DATA-SW
        END-IF.
*
        IF     CITYI = SPACE
           OR CITYL = ZERO
             MOVE ATTR-REVERSE TO CITYH
             MOVE -1 TO CITYL
             MOVE 'You must enter a city.' TO MSG2O
             MOVE 'N' TO VALID-DATA-SW
        END-IF.
*
        IF     ADDRI = SPACE
           OR ADDRL = ZERO
             MOVE ATTR-REVERSE TO ADDRH
             MOVE -1 TO ADDRL
             MOVE 'You must enter an address.' TO MSG2O
             MOVE 'N' TO VALID-DATA-SW
        END-IF.
*
        IF     FNAMEI = SPACE
           OR FNAMEL = ZERO
             MOVE ATTR-REVERSE TO FNAMEH
             MOVE -1 TO FNAMEL
             MOVE 'You must enter a first name.' TO MSG2O
             MOVE 'N' TO VALID-DATA-SW
        END-IF.
*
        IF     LNAMEI = SPACE
           OR LNAMEL = ZERO
             MOVE ATTR-REVERSE TO LNAMEH
             MOVE -1 TO LNAMEL
             MOVE 'You must enter a last name.' TO MSG2O
             MOVE 'N' TO VALID-DATA-SW
        END-IF.
*
 2300-SET-CUSTOMER-DATA.
*
        MOVE CUSTNO2I TO CA-CUSTOMER-NUMBER.
        MOVE LNAMEI   TO CA-LAST-NAME.
        MOVE FNAMEI   TO CA-FIRST-NAME.
        MOVE ADDRI    TO CA-ADDRESS.
        MOVE CITYI    TO CA-CITY.
        MOVE STATEI   TO CA-STATE.
        MOVE ZIPCODEI TO CA-ZIP-CODE.
*
```

The CSTMNTP program (part 8 of 9)

```
      3000-PROCESS-CHANGE-CUSTOMER.
*
          PERFORM 2100-RECEIVE-DATA-MAP.
          PERFORM 2200-EDIT-CUSTOMER-DATA.
          IF VALID-DATA
              PERFORM 2300-SET-CUSTOMER-DATA
              PERFORM 1400-PROCESS-CUSTOMER-RECORD
              IF PROCESS-OK
                  SET SEND-ERASE TO TRUE
              ELSE
                  SET SEND-ERASE-ALARM TO TRUE
              END-IF
              MOVE -1 TO CUSTNO1L
              PERFORM 1600-SEND-KEY-MAP
              SET PROCESS-KEY-MAP TO TRUE
          ELSE
              MOVE LOW-VALUE TO LNAMEO
                               FNAMEO
                               ADDRO
                               CITYO
                               STATEO
                               ZIPCODEO
              SET SEND-DATAONLY-ALARM TO TRUE
              PERFORM 1500-SEND-DATA-MAP
          END-IF.
*
      4000-PROCESS-DELETE-CUSTOMER.
*
          PERFORM 1400-PROCESS-CUSTOMER-RECORD.
          IF PROCESS-OK
              SET SEND-ERASE TO TRUE
          ELSE
              SET SEND-ERASE-ALARM TO TRUE
          END-IF.
          MOVE -1 TO CUSTNO1L.
          PERFORM 1600-SEND-KEY-MAP.
          SET PROCESS-KEY-MAP TO TRUE.
*
      9999-TERMINATE-PROGRAM.
*
          MOVE CA-ERR-RESP  TO ERR-RESP.
          MOVE CA-ERR-RESP2 TO ERR-RESP2.
          MOVE EIBTRNID        TO ERR-TRNID.
          MOVE CA-ERR-RSRCE TO ERR-RSRCE.
*
          EXEC CICS
              XCTL PROGRAM('SYSERR')
                   COMMAREA(ERROR-PARAMETERS)
          END-EXEC.
```

The CSTMNTP program (part 9 of 9)

The business logic program: CSTMNTB

```
IDENTIFICATION DIVISION.
*
PROGRAM-ID.   CSTMNTB.
*
ENVIRONMENT DIVISION.
*
DATA DIVISION.
*
WORKING-STORAGE SECTION.
*
01   WORK-FIELDS.
*
     05   RESPONSE-CODE                    PIC S9(08)  COMP.
*
01   COMMUNICATION-AREA.
*
     05   CA-CONTEXT-FLAG                  PIC X(01).
          88   PROCESS-KEY-MAP                         VALUE '1'.
          88   PROCESS-ADD-CUSTOMER                    VALUE '2'.
          88   PROCESS-CHANGE-CUSTOMER                 VALUE '3'.
          88   PROCESS-DELETE-CUSTOMER                 VALUE '4'.
     05   CA-ACTION-FLAG                   PIC X(01).
          88   ADD-REQUEST                             VALUE '1'.
          88   CHANGE-REQUEST                          VALUE '2'.
          88   DELETE-REQUEST                          VALUE '3'.
     05   CA-CUSTOMER-RECORD.
          10   CA-CUSTOMER-NUMBER          PIC X(06).
          10   CA-FIRST-NAME               PIC X(20).
          10   CA-LAST-NAME                PIC X(30).
          10   CA-ADDRESS                  PIC X(30).
          10   CA-CITY                     PIC X(20).
          10   CA-STATE                    PIC X(02).
          10   CA-ZIP-CODE                 PIC X(10).
     05   CA-SAVE-CUSTOMER-MASTER          PIC X(118).
     05   CA-RETURN-CONDITION              PIC X(01).
          88   PROCESS-OK                              VALUE '1'.
          88   PROCESS-ERROR                           VALUE '2'.
          88   PROCESS-SEVERE-ERROR                    VALUE '3'.
     05   CA-RETURN-MESSAGE                PIC X(79).
     05   CA-ERROR-PARAMETERS.
          10   CA-ERR-RESP                 PIC S9(08)  COMP.
          10   CA-ERR-RESP2                PIC S9(08)  COMP.
          10   CA-ERR-RSRCE                PIC X(08).
*
COPY CUSTMAS.
*
LINKAGE SECTION.
*
01   DFHCOMMAREA                          PIC X(334).
*
```

The CSTMNTB program (part 1 of 5)

```
        PROCEDURE DIVISION.
      *
        0000-PROCESS-CUSTOMER-RECORD.
      *
            IF EIBCALEN NOT = LENGTH OF DFHCOMMAREA
                SET PROCESS-SEVERE-ERROR TO TRUE
                PERFORM 9000-SET-ERROR-INFO
            ELSE
                MOVE DFHCOMMAREA TO COMMUNICATION-AREA
                EVALUATE TRUE
                    WHEN PROCESS-KEY-MAP
                        PERFORM 1000-PROCESS-CUSTOMER-KEY
                    WHEN PROCESS-ADD-CUSTOMER
                        PERFORM 2000-PROCESS-ADD-CUSTOMER
                    WHEN PROCESS-CHANGE-CUSTOMER
                        PERFORM 3000-PROCESS-CHANGE-CUSTOMER
                    WHEN PROCESS-DELETE-CUSTOMER
                        PERFORM 4000-PROCESS-DELETE-CUSTOMER
                END-EVALUATE
            END-IF.
      *
            MOVE COMMUNICATION-AREA TO DFHCOMMAREA.
            EXEC CICS
                RETURN
            END-EXEC.
      *
        1000-PROCESS-CUSTOMER-KEY.
      *
            PERFORM 1100-READ-CUSTOMER-RECORD.
            EVALUATE RESPONSE-CODE
                WHEN DFHRESP(NORMAL)
                    IF ADD-REQUEST
                        SET PROCESS-ERROR TO TRUE
                        MOVE 'That customer already exists.' TO
                            CA-RETURN-MESSAGE
                    ELSE
                        SET PROCESS-OK TO TRUE
                        MOVE CUSTOMER-MASTER-RECORD TO CA-CUSTOMER-RECORD
                        MOVE CUSTOMER-MASTER-RECORD TO
                            CA-SAVE-CUSTOMER-MASTER
                        MOVE SPACE TO CA-RETURN-MESSAGE
                    END-IF
                WHEN DFHRESP(NOTFND)
                    IF ADD-REQUEST
                        SET PROCESS-OK TO TRUE
                    ELSE
                        SET PROCESS-ERROR TO TRUE
                        MOVE 'That customer does not exist.' TO
                            CA-RETURN-MESSAGE
                    END-IF
                WHEN OTHER
                    SET PROCESS-SEVERE-ERROR TO TRUE
                    PERFORM 9000-SET-ERROR-INFO
            END-EVALUATE.
      *
```

The CSTMNTB program (part 2 of 5)

```
    1100-READ-CUSTOMER-RECORD.
*
        EXEC CICS
            READ FILE('CUSTMAS')
                INTO(CUSTOMER-MASTER-RECORD)
                RIDFLD(CA-CUSTOMER-NUMBER)
                RESP(RESPONSE-CODE)
        END-EXEC.
*
    2000-PROCESS-ADD-CUSTOMER.
*
        MOVE CA-CUSTOMER-RECORD TO CUSTOMER-MASTER-RECORD.
        PERFORM 2100-WRITE-CUSTOMER-RECORD.
        EVALUATE RESPONSE-CODE
            WHEN DFHRESP(NORMAL)
                SET PROCESS-OK TO TRUE
                MOVE 'Customer record added.' TO CA-RETURN-MESSAGE
            WHEN DFHRESP(DUPREC)
                SET PROCESS-ERROR TO TRUE
                MOVE 'Another user has added a record with that custo
-               'mer number.' TO CA-RETURN-MESSAGE
            WHEN OTHER
                SET PROCESS-SEVERE-ERROR TO TRUE
                PERFORM 9000-SET-ERROR-INFO
        END-EVALUATE.
*
    2100-WRITE-CUSTOMER-RECORD.
*
        EXEC CICS
            WRITE FILE('CUSTMAS')
                FROM(CUSTOMER-MASTER-RECORD)
                RIDFLD(CM-CUSTOMER-NUMBER)
                RESP(RESPONSE-CODE)
        END-EXEC.
*
```

The CSTMNTB program (part 3 of 5)

```
     3000-PROCESS-CHANGE-CUSTOMER.
*
         PERFORM 3100-READ-CUSTOMER-FOR-UPDATE.
         EVALUATE RESPONSE-CODE
             WHEN DFHRESP(NORMAL)
                 IF CUSTOMER-MASTER-RECORD = CA-SAVE-CUSTOMER-MASTER
                     MOVE CA-CUSTOMER-RECORD TO
                         CUSTOMER-MASTER-RECORD
                     PERFORM 3200-REWRITE-CUSTOMER-RECORD
                     IF RESPONSE-CODE NOT = DFHRESP(NORMAL)
                         SET PROCESS-SEVERE-ERROR TO TRUE
                         PERFORM 9000-SET-ERROR-INFO
                     ELSE
                         SET PROCESS-OK TO TRUE
                         MOVE 'Customer record updated.' TO
                             CA-RETURN-MESSAGE
                     END-IF
                 ELSE
                     SET PROCESS-ERROR TO TRUE
                     MOVE 'Another user has updated the record. Try ag
-                        'ain.' TO CA-RETURN-MESSAGE
                 END-IF
             WHEN DFHRESP(NOTFND)
                 SET PROCESS-ERROR TO TRUE
                 MOVE 'Another user has deleted the record.'
                     TO CA-RETURN-MESSAGE
             WHEN OTHER
                 SET PROCESS-SEVERE-ERROR TO TRUE
                 PERFORM 9000-SET-ERROR-INFO
         END-EVALUATE.
*
     3100-READ-CUSTOMER-FOR-UPDATE.
*
         EXEC CICS
             READ FILE('CUSTMAS')
                 INTO(CUSTOMER-MASTER-RECORD)
                 RIDFLD(CA-CUSTOMER-NUMBER)
                 UPDATE
                 RESP(RESPONSE-CODE)
         END-EXEC.
*
     3200-REWRITE-CUSTOMER-RECORD.
*
         EXEC CICS
             REWRITE FILE('CUSTMAS')
                 FROM(CUSTOMER-MASTER-RECORD)
                 RESP(RESPONSE-CODE)
         END-EXEC.
*
```

The CSTMNTB program (part 4 of 5)

```
  4000-PROCESS-DELETE-CUSTOMER.
*
      PERFORM 3100-READ-CUSTOMER-FOR-UPDATE.
      EVALUATE RESPONSE-CODE
          WHEN DFHRESP(NORMAL)
              IF CUSTOMER-MASTER-RECORD = CA-SAVE-CUSTOMER-MASTER
                  PERFORM 4100-DELETE-CUSTOMER-RECORD
                  IF RESPONSE-CODE NOT = DFHRESP(NORMAL)
                      SET PROCESS-SEVERE-ERROR TO TRUE
                      PERFORM 9000-SET-ERROR-INFO
                  ELSE
                      SET PROCESS-OK TO TRUE
                      MOVE 'Customer record deleted.' TO
                          CA-RETURN-MESSAGE
                  END-IF
              ELSE
                  SET PROCESS-ERROR TO TRUE
                  MOVE 'Another user has updated the record.  Try a
-                      'gain.' TO CA-RETURN-MESSAGE
              END-IF
          WHEN DFHRESP(NOTFND)
              SET PROCESS-ERROR TO TRUE
              MOVE 'Another user has deleted the record.'
                  TO CA-RETURN-MESSAGE
          WHEN OTHER
              SET PROCESS-SEVERE-ERROR TO TRUE
              PERFORM 9000-SET-ERROR-INFO
      END-EVALUATE.
*
  4100-DELETE-CUSTOMER-RECORD.
*
      EXEC CICS
          DELETE FILE('CUSTMAS')
                 RESP(RESPONSE-CODE)
      END-EXEC.
*
  9000-SET-ERROR-INFO.
*
      MOVE EIBRESP  TO CA-ERR-RESP.
      MOVE EIBRESP2 TO CA-ERR-RESP2.
      MOVE EIBRSRCE TO CA-ERR-RSRCE.
```

The CSTMNTB program (part 5 of 5)

Unit 6

3 more model programs

This unit presents 3 more complete CICS programs, all using traditional design, that you can use as guides as you develop and maintain your own programs:

1. A menu program for a customer service system.

2. A customer inquiry program that uses browse commands to move through a VSAM customer file.

3. An order entry program that writes records to a VSAM file. This program uses a programmer-generated symbolic map.

All 3 programs are presented in *Murach's CICS for the COBOL Programmer*, where you'll find complete descriptions of the code. To get electronic versions of these or other programs in *Murach's CICS*, please go to our web site at www.murach.com, and click on the Downloads link at the top of the page.

The menu program

The program overview

Program	INVMENU: Invoice menu program
Trans-id	MENU
Overview	Displays a menu and lets the user select which program to run: customer inquiry, customer maintenance, or order entry.
Input/output	MENMAP1 Menu map
Processing	1. The menu program is invoked when the user enters the trans-id MENU, when another program transfers control to it via an XCTL command with no communication area, or when another program transfers control to it via a RETURN command with the MENU trans-id. The program should respond by displaying the menu map.
	2. On the menu map, the user enters an action code. If the action code is valid (1, 2, or 3), the program should XCTL to the inquiry program, the maintenance program, or the order entry program. If the action code is not valid, the program should display an error message.
	3. If the user presses PF3 or PF12, the program should display the message "Session ended" and terminate by issuing a RETURN command without a trans-id.

The screen layout

Map name _____ **MENMAP1** _____   Date _____ 03/07/2001 _____

Program name _____ **INVMENU** _____   Designer _____ Doug Lowe _____

```
        1234567890123456789012345678901234567890123456789012345678901234567890123456789012345678
 1  MENMAP1              Master Menu                                                        XXXX
 2
 3  Select an action.    Then press Enter.
 4
 5  Action . . . . X  1.  Display customer information
 6                    2.  Maintain customer information
 7                    3.  Enter orders
 8
 9
10
11
12
13
14
15
16
17
18
19
20
21
22
23  XXXXXXXXXXXXXXXXXXXXXXXXXXXXXXXXXXXXXXXXXXXXXXXXXXXXXXXXXXXXXXXXXXXXXXXXXXXXXXXXXX
24  F3=Exit    F12=Cancel                                                                     X
```

The event/response chart

Event	Response
Start the program	Display the menu map.
PF3 or PF12	Display a termination message and end.
Enter key	If the action code is 1, XCTL to the inquiry program.
	If the action code is 2, XCTL to the maintenance program.
	If the action code is 3, XCTL to the order entry program.
	Otherwise, display an error message.
Clear key	Redisplay the menu map.
Any PA key	Ignore the key.
Any other key	Display an appropriate error message.

The structure chart

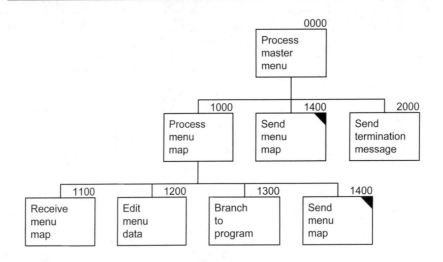

The BMS mapset

```
        PRINT NOGEN
MENSET1 DFHMSD TYPE=&SYSPARM,                                        X
            LANG=COBOL,                                              X
            MODE=INOUT,                                              X
            TERM=3270-2,                                             X
            CTRL=FREEKB,                                             X
            STORAGE=AUTO,                                            X
            DSATTS=(COLOR,HILIGHT),                                  X
            MAPATTS=(COLOR,HILIGHT),                                 X
            TIOAPFX=YES
****************************************************************
MENMAP1 DFHMDI SIZE=(24,80),                                        X
            LINE=1,                                                 X
            COLUMN=1
****************************************************************
        DFHMDF POS=(1,1),                                           X
            LENGTH=7,                                               X
            ATTRB=(NORM,PROT),                                      X
            COLOR=BLUE,                                             X
            INITIAL='MENMAP1'
        DFHMDF POS=(1,20),                                          X
            LENGTH=11,                                              X
            ATTRB=(NORM,PROT),                                      X
            COLOR=GREEN,                                            X
            INITIAL='Master Menu'
TRANID  DFHMDF POS=(1,76),                                          X
            LENGTH=4,                                               X
            ATTRB=(NORM,PROT),                                      X
            COLOR=BLUE,                                             X
            INITIAL='XXXX'
****************************************************************
        DFHMDF POS=(3,1),                                           X
            LENGTH=36,                                              X
            ATTRB=(NORM,PROT),                                      X
            COLOR=NEUTRAL,                                          X
            INITIAL='Select an action.  Then press Enter.'
        DFHMDF POS=(5,1),                                           X
            LENGTH=14,                                              X
            ATTRB=(NORM,PROT),                                      X
            COLOR=GREEN,                                            X
            INITIAL='Action . . . .'
ACTION  DFHMDF POS=(5,16),                                          X
            LENGTH=1,                                               X
            ATTRB=(NORM,NUM,IC),                                    X
            COLOR=TURQUOISE,                                        X
            INITIAL='_'
        DFHMDF POS=(5,18),                                          X
            LENGTH=32,                                              X
            ATTRB=(NORM,ASKIP),                                     X
            COLOR=NEUTRAL,                                          X
            INITIAL='1.  Display customer information'
```

The BMS mapset for the menu program (part 1 of 2)

```
          DFHMDF POS=(6,18),                                               X
                 LENGTH=33,                                                X
                 ATTRB=(NORM,PROT),                                        X
                 COLOR=NEUTRAL,                                            X
                 INITIAL='2.  Maintain customer information'
          DFHMDF POS=(7,18),                                               X
                 LENGTH=16,                                                X
                 ATTRB=(NORM,PROT),                                        X
                 COLOR=NEUTRAL,                                            X
                 INITIAL='3.  Enter orders'
***********************************************************************
MESSAGE   DFHMDF POS=(23,1),                                              X
                 LENGTH=79,                                                X
                 ATTRB=(BRT,PROT),                                         X
                 COLOR=YELLOW
          DFHMDF POS=(24,1),                                               X
                 LENGTH=20,                                                X
                 ATTRB=(NORM,PROT),                                        X
                 COLOR=BLUE,                                               X
                 INITIAL='F3=Exit    F12=Cancel'
DUMMY     DFHMDF POS=(24,79),                                              X
                 LENGTH=1,                                                 X
                 ATTRB=(DRK,PROT,FSET),                                    X
                 INITIAL=' '
***********************************************************************
          DFHMSD TYPE=FINAL
          END
```

The BMS mapset for the menu program (part 2 of 2)

The symbolic map

```
01 MENMAP1I.
    03 FILLER                       PIC X(12).
    03 TRANIDL                      PIC S9(4) COMP.
    03 TRANIDF                      PIC X.
    03 FILLER REDEFINES TRANIDF.
        05 TRANIDA                  PIC X.
    03 FILLER                       PIC X(2).
    03 TRANIDI                      PIC X(4).
    03 ACTIONL                      PIC S9(4) COMP.
    03 ACTIONF                      PIC X.
    03 FILLER REDEFINES ACTIONF.
        05 ACTIONA                  PIC X.
    03 FILLER                       PIC X(2).
    03 ACTIONI                      PIC X(1).
    03 MESSAGEL                     PIC S9(4) COMP.
    03 MESSAGEF                     PIC X.
    03 FILLER REDEFINES MESSAGEF.
        05 MESSAGEA                 PIC X.
    03 FILLER                       PIC X(2).
    03 MESSAGEI                     PIC X(79).
    03 DUMMYL                       PIC S9(4) COMP.
    03 DUMMYF                       PIC X.
    03 FILLER REDEFINES DUMMYF.
        05 DUMMYA                   PIC X.
    03 FILLER                       PIC X(2).
    03 DUMMYI                       PIC X(1).
01 MENMAP1O REDEFINES MENMAP1I.
    03 FILLER                       PIC X(12).
    03 FILLER                       PIC X(3).
    03 TRANIDC                      PIC X.
    03 TRANIDH                      PIC X.
    03 TRANIDO                      PIC X(4).
    03 FILLER                       PIC X(3).
    03 ACTIONC                      PIC X.
    03 ACTIONH                      PIC X.
    03 ACTIONO                      PIC X(1).
    03 FILLER                       PIC X(3).
    03 MESSAGEC                     PIC X.
    03 MESSAGEH                     PIC X.
    03 MESSAGEO                     PIC X(79).
    03 FILLER                       PIC X(3).
    03 DUMMYC                       PIC X.
    03 DUMMYH                       PIC X.
    03 DUMMYO                       PIC X(1).
```

The menu program: INVMENU

```
        IDENTIFICATION  DIVISION.
  *
        PROGRAM-ID.  INVMENU.
  *
        ENVIRONMENT DIVISION.
  *
        DATA DIVISION.
  *
        WORKING-STORAGE SECTION.
  *
        01   SWITCHES.
  *
             05   VALID-DATA-SW          PIC X(01) VALUE 'Y'.
                  88   VALID-DATA                  VALUE 'Y'.
  *
        01   FLAGS.
  *
             05   SEND-FLAG              PIC X(01).
                  88   SEND-ERASE                  VALUE '1'.
                  88   SEND-DATAONLY               VALUE '2'.
                  88   SEND-DATAONLY-ALARM         VALUE '3'.
  *
        01   PROGRAM-TABLE.
  *
             05   PROGRAM-LIST.
                  10   PROGRAM-1         PIC X(08) VALUE 'CUSTINQ1'.
                  10   PROGRAM-2         PIC X(08) VALUE 'CUSTMNT2'.
                  10   PROGRAM-3         PIC X(08) VALUE 'ORDRENT '.
             05   PROGRAM-NAME           REDEFINES PROGRAM-LIST
                                         OCCURS 3 TIMES
                                         PIC X(08).
  *
        01   SUBSCRIPTS.
  *
             05   ACTION-SUB            PIC 9(01).
  *
        01   END-OF-SESSION-MESSAGE     PIC X(13) VALUE 'Session ended'.
  *
        01   RESPONSE-CODE             PIC S9(08) COMP.
  *
        01   COMMUNICATION-AREA         PIC X(01).
  *
        COPY MENSET1.
  *
        COPY DFHAID.
  *
        COPY ATTR.
  *
        LINKAGE SECTION.
  *
        01   DFHCOMMAREA                PIC X(01).
```

The INVMENU program (part 1 of 3)

```
           PROCEDURE DIVISION.
          *
           0000-PROCESS-MASTER-MENU.
          *
               EVALUATE TRUE
          *
                   WHEN EIBCALEN = ZERO
                       MOVE LOW-VALUE TO MENMAP1O
                       SET SEND-ERASE TO TRUE
                       PERFORM 1400-SEND-MENU-MAP
          *
                   WHEN EIBAID = DFHCLEAR
                       MOVE LOW-VALUE TO MENMAP1O
                       SET SEND-ERASE TO TRUE
                       PERFORM 1400-SEND-MENU-MAP
          *
                   WHEN EIBAID = DFHPA1 OR DFHPA2 OR DFHPA3
                       CONTINUE
          *
                   WHEN EIBAID = DFHPF3 OR DFHPF12
                       PERFORM 2000-SEND-TERMINATION-MESSAGE
                       EXEC CICS
                           RETURN
                       END-EXEC
          *
                   WHEN EIBAID = DFHENTER
                       PERFORM 1000-PROCESS-MENU-MAP
          *
                   WHEN OTHER
                       MOVE 'Invalid key pressed.' TO MESSAGEO
                       SET SEND-DATAONLY-ALARM TO TRUE
                       PERFORM 1400-SEND-MENU-MAP
          *
               END-EVALUATE.
          *
               EXEC CICS
                   RETURN TRANSID('MENU')
                           COMMAREA(COMMUNICATION-AREA)
               END-EXEC.
          *
           1000-PROCESS-MENU-MAP.
          *
               PERFORM 1100-RECEIVE-MENU-MAP.
               PERFORM 1200-EDIT-MENU-DATA.
               IF VALID-DATA
                   MOVE ACTIONI TO ACTION-SUB
                   PERFORM 1300-BRANCH-TO-PROGRAM
               END-IF.
               SET SEND-DATAONLY-ALARM TO TRUE.
               PERFORM 1400-SEND-MENU-MAP.
          *
           1100-RECEIVE-MENU-MAP.
          *
               EXEC CICS
                   RECEIVE MAP('MENMAP1')
                           MAPSET('MENSET1')
                           INTO(MENMAP1I)
               END-EXEC.
```

The INVMENU program (part 2 of 3)

```
 1200-EDIT-MENU-DATA.
*
     IF ACTIONI NOT = '1' AND '2' AND '3'
         MOVE ATTR-REVERSE TO ACTIONH
         MOVE 'You must enter 1, 2, or 3.' TO MESSAGEO
         MOVE 'N' TO VALID-DATA-SW
     END-IF.
*
 1300-BRANCH-TO-PROGRAM.
*
     EXEC CICS
         XCTL PROGRAM(PROGRAM-NAME(ACTION-SUB))
         RESP(RESPONSE-CODE)
     END-EXEC.
*
     MOVE 'That program is not available.' TO MESSAGEO.
*
 1400-SEND-MENU-MAP.
*
     MOVE 'MENU' TO TRANIDO.
     EVALUATE TRUE
         WHEN SEND-ERASE
             EXEC CICS
                 SEND MAP('MENMAP1')
                      MAPSET('MENSET1')
                      FROM(MENMAP1O)
                      ERASE
             END-EXEC
         WHEN SEND-DATAONLY
             EXEC CICS
                 SEND MAP('MENMAP1')
                      MAPSET('MENSET1')
                      FROM(MENMAP1O)
                      DATAONLY
             END-EXEC
         WHEN SEND-DATAONLY-ALARM
             EXEC CICS
                 SEND MAP('MENMAP1')
                      MAPSET('MENSET1')
                      FROM(MENMAP1O)
                      DATAONLY
                      ALARM
             END-EXEC
     END-EVALUATE.
*
 2000-SEND-TERMINATION-MESSAGE.
*
     EXEC CICS
         SEND TEXT FROM(END-OF-SESSION-MESSAGE)
                   ERASE
                   FREEKB
     END-EXEC.
```

The INVMENU program (part 3 of 3)

The customer inquiry program

The program overview

Program	CUSTINQ2: Customer inquiry
Trans-id	INQ2
Overview	Displays records from the customer file, allowing the user to scroll forwards or backwards using PF keys.
Input/output	INQMAP2 Customer inquiry map CUSTMAS Customer master file (the copy member is shown in Unit 5)
Processing	1. Control is transferred to this program via XCTL from the menu program INVMENU with no communication area. The user can also start the program by entering the trans-id INQ2. In either case, the program should respond by displaying the customer inquiry map.

2. The user selects a customer record display by pressing an attention key, as follows:

Enter	Display the customer indicated by the entry in the customer number field.
PF5	Display the first customer in the file.
PF6	Display the last customer in the file.
PF7	Display the previous customer.
PF8	Display the next customer.

The program then reads and displays the appropriate customer record.

3. Use the pseudo-conversational programming technique. To restart the browse at the correct record during the next program execution, save the key of the customer currently displayed in the communication area.

4. If the user presses PF3 or PF12, return to the menu program INVMENU by issuing an XCTL command.

5. If an unrecoverable error occurs, terminate the program by invoking the SYSERR subprogram with an XCTL command.

The screen layout

Map name	INQMAP2	Date	04/03/2001
Program name	CUSTINQ2	Designer	Doug Lowe

```
 1 INQMAP2                   Customer  Inquiry                                                        XXXX
 2
 3 To start a new browse, type a customer number.   Then press Enter.
 4
 5 Customer number. .  .  .   XXXXXX
 6
 7 Name and address .  .  . : XXXXXXXXXXXXXXXXXXXXXXXXXXXXXX
 8                            XXXXXXXXXXXXXXXXXXXXX
 9                            XXXXXXXXXXXXXXXXXXXXXXXXXXXXX
10                            XXXXXXXXXXXXXXXXXX  XX  XXXXXXXXXX
11
12
13
14
15
16
17
18
19
20
21
22
23 XXXXXXXXXXXXXXXXXXXXXXXXXXXXXXXXXXXXXXXXXXXXXXXXXXXXXXXXXXXXXXXXXXXXXXXXXXXXXXXXX
24 F3=Exit    F5=First   F6=Last   F7=Prev   F8=Next   F12=Cancel                              X
```

The event/response chart

Event	Response
Start the program	Display the inquiry map.
PF3 or PF12	Transfer control to the menu program.
Enter key	Read and display the customer record for the customer number entered by the user using this sequence of commands: RECEIVE MAP READ SEND MAP
PF5	Read and display the first record in the file using this sequence of commands: STARTBR RIDFLD(low-values) READNEXT ENDBR SEND MAP
PF6	Read and display the last record in the file using this sequence of commands: STARTBR RIDFLD(high-values) READPREV ENDBR SEND MAP
PF7	Read and display the previous record using this sequence of commands: STARTBR RIDFLD(commarea key) READNEXT READPREV READPREV ENDBR SEND MAP
PF8	Read and display the next record using this sequence of commands: STARTBR RIDFLD(commarea key) READNEXT READNEXT ENDBR SEND MAP
Clear key	Redisplay the current map without any data.
Any PA key	Ignore the key.
Any other key	Display an error message.

The structure chart

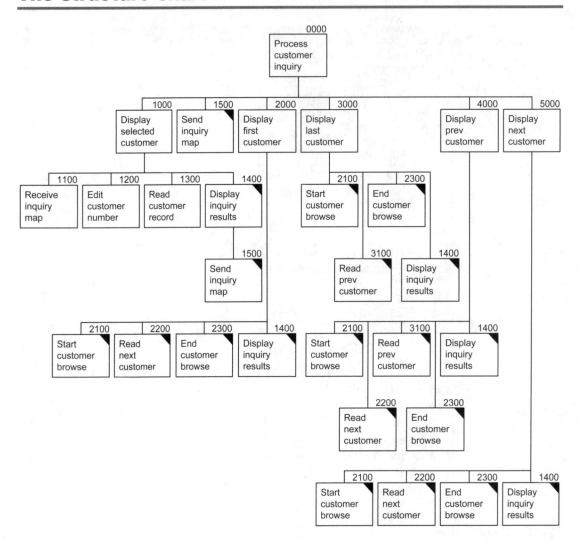

The BMS mapset

```
           PRINT NOGEN
INQSET2    DFHMSD TYPE=&SYSPARM,                                          X
                  LANG=COBOL,                                            X
                  MODE=INOUT,                                            X
                  TERM=3270-2,                                           X
                  CTRL=FREEKB,                                           X
                  STORAGE=AUTO,                                          X
                  TIOAPFX=YES
***************************************************************************
INQMAP2    DFHMDI SIZE=(24,80),                                          X
                  LINE=1,                                                X
                  COLUMN=1
***************************************************************************
           DFHMDF POS=(1,1),                                            X
                  LENGTH=8,                                              X
                  ATTRB=(NORM,PROT),                                     X
                  COLOR=BLUE,                                            X
                  INITIAL='INQMAP2'
           DFHMDF POS=(1,20),                                           X
                  LENGTH=16,                                             X
                  ATTRB=(NORM,PROT),                                     X
                  COLOR=GREEN,                                           X
                  INITIAL='Customer Inquiry'
TRANID     DFHMDF POS=(1,76),                                           X
                  LENGTH=4,                                              X
                  ATTRB=(NORM,PROT),                                     X
                  COLOR=BLUE,                                            X
                  INITIAL='XXXX'
***************************************************************************
           DFHMDF POS=(3,1),                                            X
                  LENGTH=65,                                             X
                  ATTRB=(NORM,PROT),                                     X
                  COLOR=NEUTRAL,                                         X
                  INITIAL='To start a new browse, type a customer number. X
                   Then press Enter.'
           DFHMDF POS=(5,1),                                            X
                  LENGTH=24,                                             X
                  ATTRB=(NORM,PROT),                                     X
                  COLOR=GREEN,                                           X
                  INITIAL='Customer number. . . . .'
CUSTNO     DFHMDF POS=(5,26),                                           X
                  LENGTH=6,                                              X
                  ATTRB=(NORM,UNPROT),                                   X
                  COLOR=TURQUOISE,                                       X
                  INITIAL='_____'
           DFHMDF POS=(5,33),                                           X
                  LENGTH=1,                                              X
                  ATTRB=ASKIP
***************************************************************************
           DFHMDF POS=(7,1),                                            X
                  LENGTH=24,                                             X
                  ATTRB=(NORM,PROT),                                     X
                  COLOR=GREEN,                                           X
                  INITIAL='Name and address . . . :'
```

The BMS mapset for the customer inquiry program (part 1 of 2)

```
LNAME      DFHMDF POS=(7,26),                                               X
                  LENGTH=30,                                                X
                  COLOR=TURQUOISE,                                          X
                  ATTRB=(NORM,PROT)
FNAME      DFHMDF POS=(8,26),                                               X
                  LENGTH=20,                                                X
                  COLOR=TURQUOISE,                                          X
                  ATTRB=(NORM,PROT)
ADDR       DFHMDF POS=(9,26),                                               X
                  LENGTH=30,                                                X
                  COLOR=TURQUOISE,                                          X
                  ATTRB=(NORM,PROT)
CITY       DFHMDF POS=(10,26),                                              X
                  LENGTH=20,                                                X
                  COLOR=TURQUOISE,                                          X
                  ATTRB=(NORM,PROT)
STATE      DFHMDF POS=(10,47),                                              X
                  LENGTH=2,                                                 X
                  COLOR=TURQUOISE,                                          X
                  ATTRB=(NORM,PROT)
ZIPCODE    DFHMDF POS=(10,50),                                             X
                  LENGTH=10,                                                X
                  COLOR=TURQUOISE,                                          X
                  ATTRB=(NORM,PROT)
***************************************************************************
MESSAGE    DFHMDF POS=(23,1),                                              X
                  LENGTH=79,                                                X
                  ATTRB=(BRT,PROT),                                         X
                  COLOR=YELLOW
           DFHMDF POS=(24,1),                                              X
                  LENGTH=35,                                                X
                  ATTRB=(NORM,PROT),                                        X
                  COLOR=BLUE,                                               X
                  INITIAL='F3=Exit  F5=First  F6=Last  F7=Prev'
           DFHMDF POS=(24,38),                                             X
                  LENGTH=19,                                                X
                  ATTRB=(NORM,PROT),                                        X
                  COLOR=BLUE,                                               X
                  INITIAL='F8=Next  F12=Cancel'
DUMMY      DFHMDF POS=(24,79),                                             X
                  LENGTH=1,                                                 X
                  ATTRB=(DRK,PROT,FSET),                                    X
                  INITIAL=' '
***************************************************************************
           DFHMSD TYPE=FINAL
           END
```

The BMS mapset for the customer inquiry program (part 2 of 2)

The symbolic map

```
01  INQMAP2I.
     03  FILLER                          PIC X(12).
     03  TRANIDL                         PIC S9(4) COMP.
     03  TRANIDF                         PIC X.
     03  FILLER REDEFINES TRANIDF.
         05  TRANIDA                     PIC X.
     03  TRANIDI                         PIC X(4).
     03  CUSTNOL                         PIC S9(4) COMP.
     03  CUSTNOF                         PIC X.
     03  FILLER REDEFINES CUSTNOF.
         05  CUSTNOA                     PIC X.
     03  CUSTNOI                         PIC X(6).
     03  LNAMEL                          PIC S9(4) COMP.
     03  LNAMEF                          PIC X.
     03  FILLER REDEFINES LNAMEF.
         05  LNAMEA                      PIC X.
     03  LNAMEI                          PIC X(30).
     03  FNAMEL                          PIC S9(4) COMP.
     03  FNAMEF                          PIC X.
     03  FILLER REDEFINES FNAMEF.
         05  FNAMEA                      PIC X.
     03  FNAMEI                          PIC X(20).
     03  ADDRL                           PIC S9(4) COMP.
     03  ADDRF                           PIC X.
     03  FILLER REDEFINES ADDRF.
         05  ADDRA                       PIC X.
     03  ADDRI                           PIC X(30).
     03  CITYL                           PIC S9(4) COMP.
     03  CITYF                           PIC X.
     03  FILLER REDEFINES CITYF.
         05  CITYA                       PIC X.
     03  CITYI                           PIC X(20).
     03  STATEL                          PIC S9(4) COMP.
     03  STATEF                          PIC X.
     03  FILLER REDEFINES STATEF.
         05  STATEA                      PIC X.
     03  STATEI                          PIC X(2).
     03  ZIPCODEL                        PIC S9(4) COMP.
     03  ZIPCODEF                        PIC X.
     03  FILLER REDEFINES ZIPCODEF.
         05  ZIPCODEA                    PIC X.
     03  ZIPCODEI                        PIC X(10).
     03  MESSAGEL                        PIC S9(4) COMP.
     03  MESSAGEF                        PIC X.
     03  FILLER REDEFINES MESSAGEF.
         05  MESSAGEA                    PIC X.
     03  MESSAGEI                        PIC X(79).
     03  DUMMYL                          PIC S9(4) COMP.
     03  DUMMYF                          PIC X.
     03  FILLER REDEFINES DUMMYF.
         05  DUMMYA                      PIC X.
     03  DUMMYI                          PIC X(1).
```

The symbolic map for the customer inquiry program (part 1 of 2)

```
01 INQMAP2O REDEFINES INQMAP2I.
   03 FILLER                        PIC X(12).
   03 FILLER                        PIC X(3).
   03 TRANIDO                       PIC X(4).
   03 FILLER                        PIC X(3).
   03 CUSTNOO                       PIC X(6).
   03 FILLER                        PIC X(3).
   03 LNAMEO                        PIC X(30).
   03 FILLER                        PIC X(3).
   03 FNAMEO                        PIC X(20).
   03 FILLER                        PIC X(3).
   03 ADDRO                         PIC X(30).
   03 FILLER                        PIC X(3).
   03 CITYO                         PIC X(20).
   03 FILLER                        PIC X(3).
   03 STATEO                        PIC X(2).
   03 FILLER                        PIC X(3).
   03 ZIPCODEO                      PIC X(10).
   03 FILLER                        PIC X(3).
   03 MESSAGEO                      PIC X(79).
   03 FILLER                        PIC X(3).
   03 DUMMYO                        PIC X(1).
```

The symbolic map for the customer inquiry program (part 2 of 2)

The customer inquiry program: CUSTINQ2

```
      IDENTIFICATION DIVISION.
*
      PROGRAM-ID.  CUSTINQ2.
*
      ENVIRONMENT DIVISION.
*
      DATA DIVISION.
*
      WORKING-STORAGE SECTION.
*
      01  SWITCHES.
*
          05  VALID-DATA-SW              PIC X(01)   VALUE 'Y'.
              88  VALID-DATA                         VALUE 'Y'.
          05  CUSTOMER-FOUND-SW          PIC X(01)   VALUE 'Y'.
              88  CUSTOMER-FOUND                     VALUE 'Y'.
*
      01  FLAGS.
*
          05  DISPLAY-FLAG               PIC X(01).
              88  DISPLAY-NEW-CUSTOMER               VALUE '1'.
              88  DISPLAY-SPACES                     VALUE '2'.
              88  DISPLAY-LOW-VALUES                 VALUE '3'.
          05  SEND-FLAG                  PIC X(01).
              88  SEND-ERASE                         VALUE '1'.
              88  SEND-DATAONLY                      VALUE '2'.
              88  SEND-DATAONLY-ALARM                VALUE '3'.
*
      01  COMMUNICATION-AREA.
*
          05  CA-CUSTOMER-NUMBER         PIC X(06).
*
      01  RESPONSE-CODE                  PIC S9(08) COMP.
*
      COPY CUSTMAS.
*
      COPY INQSET2.
*
      COPY DFHAID.
*
      COPY ERRPARM.
*
      LINKAGE SECTION.
*
      01  DFHCOMMAREA                    PIC X(06).
*
```

The CUSTINQ2 program (part 1 of 7)

```
      PROCEDURE DIVISION.
 *
      0000-PROCESS-CUSTOMER-INQUIRY.
 *
          IF EIBCALEN > ZERO
              MOVE DFHCOMMAREA TO COMMUNICATION-AREA
          END-IF.
 *
          EVALUATE TRUE
 *
              WHEN EIBCALEN = ZERO
                  MOVE LOW-VALUE TO CA-CUSTOMER-NUMBER
                  MOVE LOW-VALUE TO INQMAP2O
                  SET SEND-ERASE TO TRUE
                  PERFORM 1500-SEND-INQUIRY-MAP
 *
              WHEN EIBAID = DFHCLEAR
                  MOVE LOW-VALUE TO CA-CUSTOMER-NUMBER
                  MOVE LOW-VALUE TO INQMAP2O
                  SET SEND-ERASE TO TRUE
                  PERFORM 1500-SEND-INQUIRY-MAP
 *
              WHEN EIBAID = DFHPA1 OR DFHPA2 OR DFHPA3
                  CONTINUE
 *
              WHEN EIBAID = DFHPF3 OR DFHPF12
                  EXEC CICS
                      XCTL PROGRAM('INVMENU')
                  END-EXEC
 *
              WHEN EIBAID = DFHENTER
                  PERFORM 1000-DISPLAY-SELECTED-CUSTOMER
 *
              WHEN EIBAID = DFHPF5
                  PERFORM 2000-DISPLAY-FIRST-CUSTOMER
 *
              WHEN EIBAID = DFHPF6
                  PERFORM 3000-DISPLAY-LAST-CUSTOMER
 *
              WHEN EIBAID = DFHPF7
                  PERFORM 4000-DISPLAY-PREV-CUSTOMER
 *
              WHEN EIBAID = DFHPF8
                  PERFORM 5000-DISPLAY-NEXT-CUSTOMER
 *
              WHEN OTHER
                  MOVE LOW-VALUE TO INQMAP2O
                  MOVE 'Invalid key pressed.' TO MESSAGEO
                  SET SEND-DATAONLY-ALARM TO TRUE
                  PERFORM 1500-SEND-INQUIRY-MAP
 *
          END-EVALUATE.
 *
          EXEC CICS
              RETURN TRANSID('INQ2')
                      COMMAREA(COMMUNICATION-AREA)
          END-EXEC.
 *
```

The CUSTINQ2 program (part 2 of 7)

```
 1000-DISPLAY-SELECTED-CUSTOMER.
*
     PERFORM 1100-RECEIVE-INQUIRY-MAP.
     PERFORM 1200-EDIT-CUSTOMER-NUMBER.
     IF VALID-DATA
         PERFORM 1300-READ-CUSTOMER-RECORD
         IF CUSTOMER-FOUND
             SET DISPLAY-NEW-CUSTOMER TO TRUE
             PERFORM 1400-DISPLAY-INQUIRY-RESULTS
             MOVE CM-CUSTOMER-NUMBER TO CA-CUSTOMER-NUMBER
         ELSE
             SET DISPLAY-SPACES TO TRUE
             PERFORM 1400-DISPLAY-INQUIRY-RESULTS
         END-IF
     ELSE
         SET DISPLAY-LOW-VALUES TO TRUE
         PERFORM 1400-DISPLAY-INQUIRY-RESULTS
     END-IF.
*
 1100-RECEIVE-INQUIRY-MAP.
*
     EXEC CICS
         RECEIVE MAP('INQMAP2')
                 MAPSET('INQSET2')
                 INTO(INQMAP2I)
     END-EXEC.
*
     INSPECT INQMAP2I
         REPLACING ALL '_' BY SPACE.
*
 1200-EDIT-CUSTOMER-NUMBER.
*
     IF      CUSTNOL = ZERO
          OR CUSTNOI = SPACE
         MOVE 'N' TO VALID-DATA-SW
         MOVE 'You must enter a customer number.' TO MESSAGEO
     END-IF.
*
 1300-READ-CUSTOMER-RECORD.
*
     EXEC CICS
         READ FILE('CUSTMAS')
              INTO(CUSTOMER-MASTER-RECORD)
              RIDFLD(CUSTNOI)
              RESP(RESPONSE-CODE)
     END-EXEC.
*
     IF RESPONSE-CODE = DFHRESP(NOTFND)
         MOVE 'N' TO CUSTOMER-FOUND-SW
         MOVE 'That customer does not exist.' TO MESSAGEO
     ELSE
         IF RESPONSE-CODE NOT = DFHRESP(NORMAL)
             PERFORM 9999-TERMINATE-PROGRAM
         END-IF
     END-IF.
*
```

The CUSTINQ2 program (part 3 of 7)

```
1400-DISPLAY-INQUIRY-RESULTS.
*
    IF DISPLAY-NEW-CUSTOMER
        MOVE CM-CUSTOMER-NUMBER TO CUSTNOO
        MOVE CM-LAST-NAME       TO LNAMEO
        MOVE CM-FIRST-NAME      TO FNAMEO
        MOVE CM-ADDRESS         TO ADDRO
        MOVE CM-CITY            TO CITYO
        MOVE CM-STATE           TO STATEO
        MOVE CM-ZIP-CODE        TO ZIPCODEO
        MOVE SPACE              TO MESSAGEO
        SET SEND-DATAONLY       TO TRUE
    ELSE
        IF DISPLAY-SPACES
            MOVE LOW-VALUE TO CUSTNOO
            MOVE SPACE     TO LNAMEO
                              FNAMEO
                              ADDRO
                              CITYO
                              STATEO
                              ZIPCODEO
            SET SEND-DATAONLY-ALARM TO TRUE
        ELSE
            IF DISPLAY-LOW-VALUES
                SET SEND-DATAONLY-ALARM TO TRUE
            END-IF
        END-IF
    END-IF.
*
    PERFORM 1500-SEND-INQUIRY-MAP.
*
 1500-SEND-INQUIRY-MAP.
*
    MOVE 'INQ2' TO TRANIDO.
    EVALUATE TRUE
        WHEN SEND-ERASE
            EXEC CICS
                SEND MAP('INQMAP2')
                     MAPSET('INQSET2')
                     FROM(INQMAP2O)
                     ERASE
            END-EXEC
        WHEN SEND-DATAONLY
            EXEC CICS
                SEND MAP('INQMAP2')
                     MAPSET('INQSET2')
                     FROM(INQMAP2O)
                     DATAONLY
            END-EXEC
        WHEN SEND-DATAONLY-ALARM
            EXEC CICS
                SEND MAP('INQMAP2')
                     MAPSET('INQSET2')
                     FROM(INQMAP2O)
                     DATAONLY
                     ALARM
            END-EXEC
    END-EVALUATE.
```

The CUSTINQ2 program (part 4 of 7)

```
*
 2000-DISPLAY-FIRST-CUSTOMER.
*
     MOVE LOW-VALUE TO CM-CUSTOMER-NUMBER
                      INQMAP2O.
     PERFORM 2100-START-CUSTOMER-BROWSE.
     IF CUSTOMER-FOUND
         PERFORM 2200-READ-NEXT-CUSTOMER
     END-IF.
     PERFORM 2300-END-CUSTOMER-BROWSE.
     IF CUSTOMER-FOUND
         SET DISPLAY-NEW-CUSTOMER TO TRUE
         PERFORM 1400-DISPLAY-INQUIRY-RESULTS
         MOVE CM-CUSTOMER-NUMBER TO CA-CUSTOMER-NUMBER
     ELSE
         SET DISPLAY-SPACES TO TRUE
         PERFORM 1400-DISPLAY-INQUIRY-RESULTS
     END-IF.
*
 2100-START-CUSTOMER-BROWSE.
*
     EXEC CICS
         STARTBR FILE('CUSTMAS')
                 RIDFLD(CM-CUSTOMER-NUMBER)
                 RESP(RESPONSE-CODE)
     END-EXEC.
     IF RESPONSE-CODE = DFHRESP(NORMAL)
         MOVE 'Y' TO CUSTOMER-FOUND-SW
         MOVE SPACE TO MESSAGEO
     ELSE
         IF RESPONSE-CODE = DFHRESP(NOTFND)
             MOVE 'N' TO CUSTOMER-FOUND-SW
             MOVE 'There are no customers in the file.'
                 TO MESSAGEO
         ELSE
             PERFORM 9999-TERMINATE-PROGRAM
         END-IF
     END-IF.
*
 2200-READ-NEXT-CUSTOMER.
*
     EXEC CICS
         READNEXT FILE('CUSTMAS')
                  INTO(CUSTOMER-MASTER-RECORD)
                  RIDFLD(CM-CUSTOMER-NUMBER)
                  RESP(RESPONSE-CODE)
     END-EXEC.
     EVALUATE RESPONSE-CODE
         WHEN DFHRESP(NORMAL)
             MOVE 'Y' TO CUSTOMER-FOUND-SW
         WHEN DFHRESP(ENDFILE)
             MOVE 'N' TO CUSTOMER-FOUND-SW
             MOVE 'There are no more records in the file.'
                 TO MESSAGEO
         WHEN OTHER
             PERFORM 9999-TERMINATE-PROGRAM
     END-EVALUATE.
*
```

The CUSTINQ2 program (part 5 of 7)

```
    2300-END-CUSTOMER-BROWSE.
*
        EXEC CICS
            ENDBR FILE('CUSTMAS')
                  RESP(RESPONSE-CODE)
        END-EXEC.
        IF RESPONSE-CODE NOT = DFHRESP(NORMAL)
            PERFORM 9999-TERMINATE-PROGRAM
        END-IF.
*
    3000-DISPLAY-LAST-CUSTOMER.
*
        MOVE HIGH-VALUE TO CM-CUSTOMER-NUMBER.
        MOVE LOW-VALUE  TO INQMAP2O.
        PERFORM 2100-START-CUSTOMER-BROWSE.
        IF CUSTOMER-FOUND
            PERFORM 3100-READ-PREV-CUSTOMER
        END-IF.
        PERFORM 2300-END-CUSTOMER-BROWSE.
        IF CUSTOMER-FOUND
            SET DISPLAY-NEW-CUSTOMER TO TRUE
            PERFORM 1400-DISPLAY-INQUIRY-RESULTS
            MOVE CM-CUSTOMER-NUMBER TO CA-CUSTOMER-NUMBER
        ELSE
            SET DISPLAY-SPACES TO TRUE
            PERFORM 1400-DISPLAY-INQUIRY-RESULTS
        END-IF.
*
    3100-READ-PREV-CUSTOMER.
*
        EXEC CICS
            READPREV FILE('CUSTMAS')
                     INTO(CUSTOMER-MASTER-RECORD)
                     RIDFLD(CM-CUSTOMER-NUMBER)
                     RESP(RESPONSE-CODE)
        END-EXEC.
        EVALUATE RESPONSE-CODE
            WHEN DFHRESP(NORMAL)
                MOVE 'Y' TO CUSTOMER-FOUND-SW
            WHEN DFHRESP(ENDFILE)
                MOVE 'N' TO CUSTOMER-FOUND-SW
                MOVE 'There are no more records in the file.'
                    TO MESSAGEO
            WHEN OTHER
                PERFORM 9999-TERMINATE-PROGRAM
        END-EVALUATE.
*
```

The CUSTINQ2 program (part 6 of 7)

```
 4000-DISPLAY-PREV-CUSTOMER.
*
     MOVE CA-CUSTOMER-NUMBER TO CM-CUSTOMER-NUMBER.
     MOVE LOW-VALUE          TO INQMAP2O.
     PERFORM 2100-START-CUSTOMER-BROWSE.
     IF CUSTOMER-FOUND
         PERFORM 2200-READ-NEXT-CUSTOMER
         PERFORM 3100-READ-PREV-CUSTOMER
         PERFORM 3100-READ-PREV-CUSTOMER
     END-IF.
     PERFORM 2300-END-CUSTOMER-BROWSE.
     IF CUSTOMER-FOUND
         SET DISPLAY-NEW-CUSTOMER TO TRUE
         PERFORM 1400-DISPLAY-INQUIRY-RESULTS
         MOVE CM-CUSTOMER-NUMBER TO CA-CUSTOMER-NUMBER
     ELSE
         SET DISPLAY-LOW-VALUES TO TRUE
         PERFORM 1400-DISPLAY-INQUIRY-RESULTS
     END-IF.
*
 5000-DISPLAY-NEXT-CUSTOMER.
*
     MOVE CA-CUSTOMER-NUMBER TO CM-CUSTOMER-NUMBER.
     MOVE LOW-VALUE          TO INQMAP2O.
     PERFORM 2100-START-CUSTOMER-BROWSE.
     IF CUSTOMER-FOUND
         PERFORM 2200-READ-NEXT-CUSTOMER
         PERFORM 2200-READ-NEXT-CUSTOMER
     END-IF.
     PERFORM 2300-END-CUSTOMER-BROWSE.
     IF CUSTOMER-FOUND
         SET DISPLAY-NEW-CUSTOMER TO TRUE
         PERFORM 1400-DISPLAY-INQUIRY-RESULTS
         MOVE CM-CUSTOMER-NUMBER TO CA-CUSTOMER-NUMBER
     ELSE
         SET DISPLAY-LOW-VALUES TO TRUE
         PERFORM 1400-DISPLAY-INQUIRY-RESULTS
     END-IF.
*
 9999-TERMINATE-PROGRAM.
*
     MOVE EIBRESP  TO ERR-RESP.
     MOVE EIBRESP2 TO ERR-RESP2.
     MOVE EIBTRNID TO ERR-TRNID.
     MOVE EIBRSRCE TO ERR-RSRCE.
*
     EXEC CICS
         XCTL PROGRAM('SYSERR')
              COMMAREA(ERROR-PARAMETERS)
     END-EXEC.
```

The CUSTINQ2 program (part 7 of 7)

The order entry program

The program overview

Program	ORDRENT: Order entry program
Trans-id	ORD1
Overview	Writes orders to an invoice file based on data entered by the user.
Input/output	INVOICE Invoice file
	CUSTMAS Customer master file (the copy member is shown in Unit 5)
	PRODUCT Product (inventory) file
	ORDMAP1 Order entry map

Processing

1. Control is transferred to this program via XCTL from the menu program INVMENU with no communication area. The user can also start the program by entering the trans-id ORD1. In either case, the program should respond by displaying the order entry map.

2. On the order entry map, the user enters a customer number, a PO number, and data for up to 10 line items. The program edits the data according to the rules listed in step 3. If the data is valid, the program redisplays the map with all fields protected. Then, the user can post the order by pressing the Enter key or make additional changes by pressing PF4. If the user presses PF4, the program should unprotect the entry fields and let the user enter changes. If the user presses PF12, the program should cancel the order and redisplay the entry screen with blank fields. The user ends the program by pressing PF3.

3. Order data should be edited according to the following rules:

Customer number	Must be in the customer file
Product code	Must be in the product file
Quantity	Must be a valid integer (use the INTEDIT subprogram)
Net price	Must be a valid decimal number (use the NUMEDIT subprogram)

   In addition, the following cross-validation requirements must be checked:

   a. If the user enters a product code, a quantity for that line item is required;

   b. The user cannot enter a quantity or net price on a line without a product code;

   c. The user must enter at least one line item.

4. If the user does not enter a net price, use the list price from the appropriate product record.

5. To obtain the invoice number, invoke the GETINV subprogram with a LINK command.

6. Use the ASKTIME and FORMATTIME commands to get the current date for the invoices and format it as MMDDYYYY.

7. When the user exits the program, display the total number of orders entered before returning to the menu.

8. If an unrecoverable error occurs, terminate the program by invoking the SYSERR subprogram with an XCTL command.

The screen layout

Map name	ORDMAP1	Date	03/19/2001
Program name	ORDRENT	Designer	Doug Lowe

```
    ORDMAP1                  Order Entry                                                                          XXXX
    XXXXXXXXXXXXXXXXXXXXXXXXXXXXXXXXXXXXXXXXXXXXXXXXXXXXXXXXXXXXXXXXXXXXXXXXXXXXXXXXXX
    Customer number  .  .  . XXXXX       Customer: XXXXXXXXXXXXXXXXXXXXXXXXXXXXXX
    P.O. number  .  .  .  .  . XXXXXXXXXX            XXXXXXXXXXXXXXXXXXXXX
                                                     XXXXXXXXXXXXXXXXXXXXXXXXXXX
                                                     XXXXXXXXXXXXXXXXXXX  XX  XXXXXXXXXX
    Prod code       Qty   Description                      List           Net        Amount
    XXXXXXXXXX  XXXXX  XXXXXXXXXXXXXXXXXXXXX  Z,ZZZ,ZZ9.99  XXXXXXXXXX  Z,ZZZ,ZZ9.99
    XXXXXXXXXX  XXXXX  XXXXXXXXXXXXXXXXXXXXX  Z,ZZZ,ZZ9.99  XXXXXXXXXX  Z,ZZZ,ZZ9.99
    XXXXXXXXXX  XXXXX  XXXXXXXXXXXXXXXXXXXXX  Z,ZZZ,ZZ9.99  XXXXXXXXXX  Z,ZZZ,ZZ9.99
    XXXXXXXXXX  XXXXX  XXXXXXXXXXXXXXXXXXXXX  Z,ZZZ,ZZ9.99  XXXXXXXXXX  Z,ZZZ,ZZ9.99
    XXXXXXXXXX  XXXXX  XXXXXXXXXXXXXXXXXXXXX  Z,ZZZ,ZZ9.99  XXXXXXXXXX  Z,ZZZ,ZZ9.99
    XXXXXXXXXX  XXXXX  XXXXXXXXXXXXXXXXXXXXX  Z,ZZZ,ZZ9.99  XXXXXXXXXX  Z,ZZZ,ZZ9.99
    XXXXXXXXXX  XXXXX  XXXXXXXXXXXXXXXXXXXXX  Z,ZZZ,ZZ9.99  XXXXXXXXXX  Z,ZZZ,ZZ9.99
    XXXXXXXXXX  XXXXX  XXXXXXXXXXXXXXXXXXXXX  Z,ZZZ,ZZ9.99  XXXXXXXXXX  Z,ZZZ,ZZ9.99
    XXXXXXXXXX  XXXXX  XXXXXXXXXXXXXXXXXXXXX  Z,ZZZ,ZZ9.99  XXXXXXXXXX  Z,ZZZ,ZZ9.99
    XXXXXXXXXX  XXXXX  XXXXXXXXXXXXXXXXXXXXX  Z,ZZZ,ZZ9.99  XXXXXXXXXX  Z,ZZZ,ZZ9.99

                                                Invoice total:            Z,ZZZ,ZZ9.99
    XXXXXXXXXXXXXXXXXXXXXXXXXXXXXXXXXXXXXXXXXXXXXXXXXXXXXXXXXXXXXXXXXXXXXXXXXXXXXXXXXX
    XXXXXXXXXXXXXXXXXXXXXXXXXXXXXXXXXXXXXXX                                          X
```

The copy members

The PRODUCT copy member

```
01  PRODUCT-MASTER-RECORD.
*
    05  PRM-PRODUCT-CODE            PIC X(10).
    05  PRM-PRODUCT-DESCRIPTION     PIC X(20).
    05  PRM-UNIT-PRICE              PIC S9(7)V99    COMP-3.
    05  PRM-QUANTITY-ON-HAND        PIC S9(7)       COMP-3.
```

The INVOICE copy member

```
01  INVOICE-RECORD.
*
    05  INV-INVOICE-NUMBER          PIC 9(6).
    05  INV-INVOICE-DATE            PIC 9(8).
    05  INV-CUSTOMER-NUMBER         PIC X(6).
    05  INV-PO-NUMBER               PIC X(10).
    05  INV-LINE-ITEM               OCCURS 10.
        10  INV-PRODUCT-CODE        PIC X(10).
        10  INV-QUANTITY            PIC S9(7)       COMP-3.
        10  INV-UNIT-PRICE          PIC S9(7)V99    COMP-3.
        10  INV-AMOUNT              PIC S9(7)V99    COMP-3.
    05  INV-INVOICE-TOTAL           PIC S9(7)V99    COMP-3.
```

The INVCTL copy member

```
01  INVCTL-RECORD.
*
    05  INVCTL-RECORD-KEY           PIC X.
    05  INVCTL-NEXT-INVOICE-NUMBER  PIC 9(6).
```

The event/response chart

Event	Context	Response	New context
Start the program	n/a	Display the order map.	Process entry
PF3	All	Transfer control to the menu program.	n/a
PF12	Process entry	Transfer control to the menu program.	n/a
	Process verify	Cancel the order and redisplay the order map with entry fields unprotected.	Process entry

Enter key	Process entry	Edit input data.
		If valid
		    protect all fields
		    display confirmation message.
		If not valid
		    display error message.
			Process verify
			
			Process entry

	Process verify	Get the invoice number. Write the invoice record. Redisplay the order map with entry fields unprotected.	Process entry
PF4	Process entry	Display an "invalid key pressed" message.	Unchanged
	Process verify	Redisplay the order map with entry fields unprotected.	Process entry
Clear key	All	Redisplay the map.	Process entry
Any PA key	All	Ignore the key.	Unchanged
Any other key	All	Display an appropriate error message.	Unchanged

The structure chart

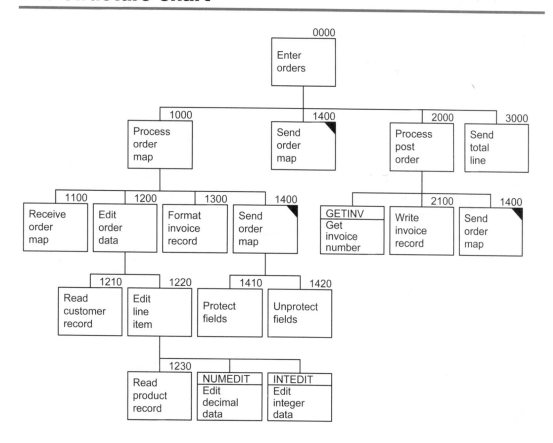

The BMS mapset

```
          PRINT NOGEN
ORDSET1   DFHMSD TYPE=&SYSPARM,                                         X
                 LANG=COBOL,                                            X
                 MODE=INOUT,                                            X
                 TERM=3270-2,                                           X
                 CTRL=FREEKB,                                           X
                 STORAGE=AUTO,                                          X
                 DSATTS=(COLOR,HILIGHT),                                X
                 MAPATTS=(COLOR,HILIGHT),                               X
                 TIOAPFX=YES
**********************************************************************
ORDMAP1   DFHMDI SIZE=(24,80),                                         X
                 LINE=1,                                               X
                 COLUMN=1
**********************************************************************
          DFHMDF POS=(1,1),                                            X
                 LENGTH=7,                                             X
                 ATTRB=(NORM,PROT),                                    X
                 COLOR=BLUE,                                           X
                 INITIAL='ORDMAP1'
          DFHMDF POS=(1,20),                                           X
                 LENGTH=11,                                            X
                 ATTRB=(NORM,PROT),                                    X
                 COLOR=GREEN,                                          X
                 INITIAL='Order Entry'
TRANID    DFHMDF POS=(1,76),                                           X
                 LENGTH=4,                                             X
                 ATTRB=(NORM,PROT),                                    X
                 COLOR=BLUE,                                           X
                 INITIAL='XXXX'
**********************************************************************
INSTR     DFHMDF POS=(3,1),                                            X
                 LENGTH=79,                                            X
                 ATTRB=(NORM,PROT),                                    X
                 COLOR=NEUTRAL
          DFHMDF POS=(5,1),                                            X
                 LENGTH=21,                                            X
                 ATTRB=(NORM,PROT),                                    X
                 COLOR=GREEN,                                          X
                 INITIAL='Customer number . . .'
CUSTNO    DFHMDF POS=(5,23),                                           X
                 LENGTH=6,                                             X
                 ATTRB=(NORM,UNPROT),                                  X
                 COLOR=TURQUOISE,                                      X
                 INITIAL='_____'
          DFHMDF POS=(5,30),                                           X
                 LENGTH=1,                                             X
                 ATTRB=ASKIP
          DFHMDF POS=(5,36),                                           X
                 LENGTH=9,                                             X
                 ATTRB=(NORM,PROT),                                    X
                 COLOR=GREEN,                                          X
                 INITIAL='Customer:'
```

The BMS mapset for the order entry program (part 1 of 3)

```
LNAME      DFHMDF POS=(5,46),                                              X
                  LENGTH=30,                                               X
                  ATTRB=(NORM,PROT),                                       X
                  COLOR=TURQUOISE
           DFHMDF POS=(6,1),                                               X
                  LENGTH=21,                                               X
                  ATTRB=(NORM,PROT),                                       X
                  COLOR=GREEN,                                             X
                  INITIAL='P.O. number . . . . .'
PO         DFHMDF POS=(6,23),                                              X
                  LENGTH=10,                                               X
                  ATTRB=(NORM,UNPROT),                                     X
                  COLOR=TURQUOISE,                                         X
                  INITIAL='_____'
           DFHMDF POS=(6,34),                                             X
                  LENGTH=1,                                                X
                  ATTRB=ASKIP
FNAME      DFHMDF POS=(6,46),                                              X
                  LENGTH=20,                                               X
                  ATTRB=(NORM,PROT),                                       X
                  COLOR=TURQUOISE
ADDR       DFHMDF POS=(7,46),                                             X
                  LENGTH=30,                                               X
                  ATTRB=(NORM,PROT),                                       X
                  COLOR=TURQUOISE
CITY       DFHMDF POS=(8,46),                                             X
                  LENGTH=20,                                               X
                  ATTRB=(NORM,PROT),                                       X
                  COLOR=TURQUOISE
STATE      DFHMDF POS=(8,67),                                             X
                  LENGTH=2,                                                X
                  ATTRB=(NORM,PROT),                                       X
                  COLOR=TURQUOISE
ZIPCODE    DFHMDF POS=(8,70),                                             X
                  LENGTH=10,                                               X
                  ATTRB=(NORM,PROT),                                       X
                  COLOR=TURQUOISE
           DFHMDF POS=(10,1),                                             X
                  LENGTH=30,                                               X
                  ATTRB=(NORM,PROT),                                       X
                  COLOR=BLUE,                                              X
                  INITIAL='Prod code    Qty  Description'
           DFHMDF POS=(10,49),                                            X
                  LENGTH=29,                                               X
                  ATTRB=(NORM,PROT),                                       X
                  COLOR=BLUE,                                              X
                  INITIAL='List          Net       Amount'
***********************************************************************
*          LINE PCODE 1                                               *
***********************************************************************
PCODE1     DFHMDF POS=(11,1),                                             X
                  LENGTH=10,                                               X
                  ATTRB=(NORM,UNPROT),                                     X
                  COLOR=TURQUOISE,                                         X
                  INITIAL='_____'
           DFHMDF POS=(11,12),                                           X
                  LENGTH=1,                                               X
                  ATTRB=ASKIP
```

The BMS mapset for the order entry program (part 2 of 3)

```
QTY1      DFHMDF POS=(11,13),                                                X
                 LENGTH=5,                                                   X
                 ATTRB=(NORM,NUM),                                           X
                 COLOR=TURQUOISE,                                            X
                 INITIAL='_____'
          DFHMDF POS=(11,19),                                                X
                 LENGTH=1,                                                   X
                 ATTRB=ASKIP
DESC1     DFHMDF POS=(11,20),                                                X
                 LENGTH=20,                                                  X
                 ATTRB=(NORM,PROT),                                          X
                 COLOR=TURQUOISE
LIST1     DFHMDF POS=(11,41),                                                X
                 LENGTH=12,                                                  X
                 ATTRB=(NORM,PROT),                                          X
                 COLOR=TURQUOISE,                                            X
                 PICOUT='Z,ZZZ,ZZ9.99'
NET1      DFHMDF POS=(11,55),                                                X
                 LENGTH=10,                                                  X
                 ATTRB=(NORM,NUM),                                           X
                 COLOR=TURQUOISE,                                            X
                 PICOUT='ZZZZZ9.99',                                         X
                 INITIAL='_____'
AMT1      DFHMDF POS=(11,66),                                                X
                 LENGTH=12,                                                  X
                 ATTRB=(NORM,PROT),                                          X
                 COLOR=TURQUOISE,                                            X
                 PICOUT='Z,ZZZ,ZZ9.99'
*****************************************************************************
.         The BMS macros that define line items 2 through 10
.         are similar to those that define line item 1.
*****************************************************************************
          DFHMDF POS=(22,44),                                                X
                 LENGTH=14,                                                  X
                 ATTRB=(NORM,PROT),                                          X
                 COLOR=GREEN,                                                X
                 INITIAL='Invoice total:'
TOTAL     DFHMDF POS=(22,66),                                                X
                 LENGTH=12,                                                  X
                 ATTRB=(NORM,PROT),                                          X
                 COLOR=TURQUOISE,                                            X
                 PICOUT='Z,ZZZ,ZZ9.99'
*****************************************************************************
MSG       DFHMDF POS=(23,1),                                                 X
                 LENGTH=79,                                                  X
                 ATTRB=(BRT,PROT),                                           X
                 COLOR=YELLOW
FKEY      DFHMDF POS=(24,1),                                                 X
                 LENGTH=40,                                                  X
                 ATTRB=(NORM,PROT),                                          X
                 COLOR=BLUE
DUMMY     DFHMDF POS=(24,79),                                                X
                 LENGTH=1,                                                   X
                 ATTRB=(DRK,PROT,FSET),                                      X
                 INITIAL=' '
*****************************************************************************
          DFHMSD TYPE=FINAL
          END
```

The BMS mapset for the order entry program (part 3 of 3)

The programmer-generated symbolic map

```
01  ORDMAP1.
*
    05  FILLLER               PIC X(12).
*
    05  ORD-L-TRANID          PIC S9(04)  COMP.
    05  ORD-A-TRANID          PIC X(01).
    05  ORD-C-TRANID          PIC X(01).
    05  ORD-H-TRANID          PIC X(01).
    05  ORD-D-TRANID          PIC X(04).
*
    05  ORD-L-INSTR           PIC S9(04)  COMP.
    05  ORD-A-INSTR           PIC X(01).
    05  ORD-C-INSTR           PIC X(01).
    05  ORD-H-INSTR           PIC X(01).
    05  ORD-D-INSTR           PIC X(79).
*
    05  ORD-L-CUSTNO          PIC S9(04)  COMP.
    05  ORD-A-CUSTNO          PIC X(01).
    05  ORD-C-CUSTNO          PIC X(01).
    05  ORD-H-CUSTNO          PIC X(01).
    05  ORD-D-CUSTNO          PIC X(06).
*
    05  ORD-L-LNAME           PIC S9(04)  COMP.
    05  ORD-A-LNAME           PIC X(01).
    05  ORD-C-LNAME           PIC X(01).
    05  ORD-H-LNAME           PIC X(01).
    05  ORD-D-LNAME           PIC X(30).
*
    05  ORD-L-PO              PIC S9(04)  COMP.
    05  ORD-A-PO              PIC X(01).
    05  ORD-C-PO              PIC X(01).
    05  ORD-H-PO              PIC X(01).
    05  ORD-D-PO              PIC X(10).
*
    05  ORD-L-FNAME           PIC S9(04)  COMP.
    05  ORD-A-FNAME           PIC X(01).
    05  ORD-C-FNAME           PIC X(01).
    05  ORD-H-FNAME           PIC X(01).
    05  ORD-D-FNAME           PIC X(20).
*
    05  ORD-L-ADDR            PIC S9(04)  COMP.
    05  ORD-A-ADDR            PIC X(01).
    05  ORD-C-ADDR            PIC X(01).
    05  ORD-H-ADDR            PIC X(01).
    05  ORD-D-ADDR            PIC X(30).
*
    05  ORD-L-CITY            PIC S9(04)  COMP.
    05  ORD-A-CITY            PIC X(01).
    05  ORD-C-CITY            PIC X(01).
    05  ORD-H-CITY            PIC X(01).
    05  ORD-D-CITY            PIC X(20).
*
```

The programmer-generated symbolic map for the order entry program (part 1 of 3)

```
05   ORD-L-STATE              PIC S9(04)   COMP.
05   ORD-A-STATE              PIC X(01).
05   ORD-C-STATE              PIC X(01).
05   ORD-H-STATE              PIC X(01).
05   ORD-D-STATE              PIC X(02).
*
05   ORD-L-ZIPCODE            PIC S9(04)   COMP.
05   ORD-A-ZIPCODE            PIC X(01).
05   ORD-C-ZIPCODE            PIC X(01).
05   ORD-H-ZIPCODE            PIC X(01).
05   ORD-D-ZIPCODE            PIC X(10).
*
05   ORD-LINE-ITEM            OCCURS 10 TIMES.
*
     10   ORD-L-PCODE          PIC S9(04)   COMP.
     10   ORD-A-PCODE          PIC X(01).
     10   ORD-C-PCODE          PIC X(01).
     10   ORD-H-PCODE          PIC X(01).
     10   ORD-D-PCODE          PIC X(10).
*
     10   ORD-L-QTY            PIC S9(04)   COMP.
     10   ORD-A-QTY            PIC X(01).
     10   ORD-C-QTY            PIC X(01).
     10   ORD-H-QTY            PIC X(01).
     10   ORD-D-QTY            PIC ZZZZ9
                              BLANK WHEN ZERO.
     10   ORD-D-QTY-ALPHA      REDEFINES ORD-D-QTY
                              PIC X(05).
*
     10   ORD-L-DESC           PIC S9(04)   COMP.
     10   ORD-A-DESC           PIC X(01).
     10   ORD-C-DESC           PIC X(01).
     10   ORD-H-DESC           PIC X(01).
     10   ORD-D-DESC           PIC X(20).
*
     10   ORD-L-LIST           PIC S9(04)   COMP.
     10   ORD-A-LIST           PIC X(01).
     10   ORD-C-LIST           PIC X(01).
     10   ORD-H-LIST           PIC X(01).
     10   ORD-D-LIST           PIC Z,ZZZ,ZZ9.99
                              BLANK WHEN ZERO.
*
     10   ORD-L-NET            PIC S9(04)   COMP.
     10   ORD-A-NET            PIC X(01).
     10   ORD-C-NET            PIC X(01).
     10   ORD-H-NET            PIC X(01).
     10   ORD-D-NET            PIC ZZZZZZ9.99
                              BLANK WHEN ZERO.
     10   ORD-D-NET-ALPHA      REDEFINES ORD-D-NET
                              PIC X(10).
*
     10   ORD-L-AMOUNT         PIC S9(04)   COMP.
     10   ORD-A-AMOUNT         PIC X(01).
     10   ORD-C-AMOUNT         PIC X(01).
     10   ORD-H-AMOUNT         PIC X(01).
     10   ORD-D-AMOUNT         PIC Z,ZZZ,ZZ9.99
                              BLANK WHEN ZERO.
*
```

The programmer-generated symbolic map for the order entry program (part 2 of 3)

```
    05   ORD-L-TOTAL              PIC S9(04)   COMP.
    05   ORD-A-TOTAL              PIC X(01).
    05   ORD-C-TOTAL              PIC X(01).
    05   ORD-H-TOTAL              PIC X(01).
    05   ORD-D-TOTAL              PIC Z,ZZZ,ZZ9.99
                                  BLANK WHEN ZERO.
*
    05   ORD-L-MESSAGE            PIC S9(04)   COMP.
    05   ORD-A-MESSAGE            PIC X(01).
    05   ORD-C-MESSAGE            PIC X(01).
    05   ORD-H-MESSAGE            PIC X(01).
    05   ORD-D-MESSAGE            PIC X(79).
*
    05   ORD-L-FKEY               PIC S9(04)   COMP.
    05   ORD-A-FKEY               PIC X(01).
    05   ORD-C-FKEY               PIC X(01).
    05   ORD-H-FKEY               PIC X(01).
    05   ORD-D-FKEY               PIC X(40).
*
    05   ORD-L-DUMMY              PIC S9(04)   COMP.
    05   ORD-A-DUMMY              PIC X(01).
    05   ORD-C-DUMMY              PIC X(01).
    05   ORD-H-DUMMY              PIC X(01).
    05   ORD-D-DUMMY              PIC X(01).
*
```

The programmer-generated symbolic map for the order entry program (part 3 of 3)

The order entry program: ORDRENT

```
IDENTIFICATION DIVISION.
*
PROGRAM-ID.  ORDRENT.
*
ENVIRONMENT DIVISION.
*
DATA DIVISION.
*
WORKING-STORAGE SECTION.
*
01  SWITCHES.
*
    05  VALID-DATA-SW               PIC X(01)    VALUE 'Y'.
        88  VALID-DATA                           VALUE 'Y'.
    05  CUSTOMER-FOUND-SW           PIC X(01)    VALUE 'Y'.
        88  CUSTOMER-FOUND                       VALUE 'Y'.
    05  PRODUCT-FOUND-SW            PIC X(01)    VALUE 'Y'.
        88  PRODUCT-FOUND                        VALUE 'Y'.
    05  VALID-QUANTITY-SW           PIC X(01)    VALUE 'Y'.
        88  VALID-QUANTITY                       VALUE 'Y'.
    05  VALID-NET-SW               PIC X(01)    VALUE 'Y'.
        88  VALID-NET                            VALUE 'Y'.
*
01  FLAGS.
*
    05  SEND-FLAG                  PIC X(01).
        88  SEND-ERASE                           VALUE '1'.
        88  SEND-DATAONLY                        VALUE '2'.
        88  SEND-DATAONLY-ALARM                  VALUE '3'.
    05  FIELD-PROTECTION-FLAG      PIC X(01).
        88  PROTECT-FIELDS                       VALUE '1'.
        88  UNPROTECT-FIELDS                     VALUE '2'.
*
01  WORK-FIELDS.
*
    05  ITEM-SUB          PIC S9(03)  COMP-3  VALUE ZERO.
    05  LINE-ITEM-COUNT   PIC S9(03)  COMP-3  VALUE ZERO.
    05  NET-NUMERIC       PIC 9(07)V99.
    05  QTY-NUMERIC       PIC 9(05).
    05  ABSOLUTE-TIME     PIC S9(15)  COMP-3.
*
01  RESPONSE-CODE                  PIC S9(08)  COMP.
*
01  COMMUNICATION-AREA.
*
    05  CA-CONTEXT-FLAG            PIC X(01).
        88  PROCESS-ENTRY                        VALUE '1'.
        88  PROCESS-VERIFY                       VALUE '2'.
    05  CA-TOTAL-ORDERS           PIC S9(03)  COMP-3.
    05  CA-INVOICE-RECORD         PIC X(318).
    05  CA-FIELDS-ENTERED.
        10  CA-PO-ENTERED-SW      PIC X(01).
            88  CA-PO-ENTERED                    VALUE 'Y'.
```

The ORDRENT program (part 1 of 12)

```
            10   CA-LINE-ITEM                  OCCURS 10.
                 15   CA-PCODE-ENTERED-SW      PIC X(01).
                      88   CA-PCODE-ENTERED              VALUE 'Y'.
                 15   CA-QTY-ENTERED-SW        PIC X(01).
                      88   CA-QTY-ENTERED                VALUE 'Y'.
                 15   CA-NET-ENTERED-SW        PIC X(01).
                      88   CA-NET-ENTERED                VALUE 'Y'.
*
 01   TOTAL-LINE.
*
     05   TL-TOTAL-ORDERS    PIC ZZ9.
     05   FILLER             PIC X(20) VALUE ' Orders entered.  Pr'.
     05   FILLER             PIC X(20) VALUE 'ess Enter to continu'.
     05   FILLER             PIC X(02) VALUE 'e.'.
*
 COPY INVOICE.
*
 COPY CUSTMAS.
*
 COPY PRODUCT.
*
 COPY INVCTL.
*
 COPY ORDSET1.
*
 COPY DFHAID.
*
 COPY ATTR.
*
 COPY ERRPARM.
*
 LINKAGE SECTION.
*
 01   DFHCOMMAREA           PIC X(352).
*
 PROCEDURE DIVISION.
*
 0000-ENTER-ORDERS.
*
     IF EIBCALEN > ZERO
         MOVE DFHCOMMAREA TO COMMUNICATION-AREA
     END-IF.
*
     EVALUATE TRUE
*
         WHEN EIBCALEN = ZERO
             MOVE LOW-VALUE TO ORDMAP1
             MOVE LOW-VALUE TO COMMUNICATION-AREA
             MOVE ZERO        TO CA-TOTAL-ORDERS
             MOVE 'Type order details.  Then press Enter.'
                 TO ORD-D-INSTR
             MOVE 'F3=Exit    F12=Cancel' TO ORD-D-FKEY
             MOVE -1 TO ORD-L-CUSTNO
             SET SEND-ERASE TO TRUE
             PERFORM 1400-SEND-ORDER-MAP
             SET PROCESS-ENTRY TO TRUE
*
```

The ORDRENT program (part 2 of 12)

```
              WHEN EIBAID = DFHCLEAR
                  MOVE LOW-VALUE TO ORDMAP1
                  MOVE LOW-VALUE TO CA-INVOICE-RECORD
                                    CA-FIELDS-ENTERED
                  MOVE 'Type order details.  Then press Enter.'
                      TO ORD-D-INSTR
                  MOVE 'F3=Exit   F12=Cancel' TO ORD-D-FKEY
                  MOVE -1 TO ORD-L-CUSTNO
                  SET SEND-ERASE TO TRUE
                  PERFORM 1400-SEND-ORDER-MAP
                  SET PROCESS-ENTRY TO TRUE
*
              WHEN EIBAID = DFHPA1 OR DFHPA2 OR DFHPA3
                  CONTINUE
*
              WHEN EIBAID = DFHPF3
                  PERFORM 3000-SEND-TOTAL-LINE
                  EXEC CICS
                      RETURN TRANSID('MENU')
                  END-EXEC
*
              WHEN EIBAID = DFHPF12
                  IF PROCESS-VERIFY
                      MOVE LOW-VALUE TO ORDMAP1
                      MOVE LOW-VALUE TO CA-INVOICE-RECORD
                                        CA-FIELDS-ENTERED
                      MOVE 'Type order details.  Then press Enter.'
                          TO ORD-D-INSTR
                      MOVE 'F3=Exit   F12=Cancel' TO ORD-D-FKEY
                      MOVE -1 TO ORD-L-CUSTNO
                      SET SEND-ERASE TO TRUE
                      PERFORM 1400-SEND-ORDER-MAP
                      SET PROCESS-ENTRY TO TRUE
                  ELSE
                      IF PROCESS-ENTRY
                          PERFORM 3000-SEND-TOTAL-LINE
                          EXEC CICS
                              RETURN TRANSID('MENU')
                          END-EXEC
                      END-IF
                  END-IF
*
              WHEN EIBAID = DFHENTER
                  IF PROCESS-ENTRY
                      PERFORM 1000-PROCESS-ORDER-MAP
                  ELSE
                      IF PROCESS-VERIFY
                          PERFORM 2000-PROCESS-POST-ORDER
                          SET PROCESS-ENTRY TO TRUE
                      END-IF
                  END-IF
*
```

The ORDRENT program (part 3 of 12)

```
                WHEN EIBAID = DFHPF4
                    IF PROCESS-VERIFY
                        MOVE LOW-VALUE TO ORDMAP1
                        MOVE 'Type corrections.  Then press Enter.'
                            TO ORD-D-INSTR
                        MOVE 'F3=Exit   F12=Cancel' TO ORD-D-FKEY
                        MOVE -1 TO ORD-L-CUSTNO
                        SET UNPROTECT-FIELDS TO TRUE
                        SET SEND-DATAONLY TO TRUE
                        PERFORM 1400-SEND-ORDER-MAP
                        SET PROCESS-ENTRY TO TRUE
                    ELSE
                        IF PROCESS-ENTRY
                            MOVE LOW-VALUE TO ORDMAP1
                            MOVE 'Invalid key pressed.' TO ORD-D-MESSAGE
                            MOVE -1 TO ORD-L-CUSTNO
                            SET SEND-DATAONLY-ALARM TO TRUE
                            PERFORM 1400-SEND-ORDER-MAP
                        END-IF
                    END-IF
*
                WHEN OTHER
                    MOVE LOW-VALUE TO ORDMAP1
                    MOVE 'Invalid key pressed.' TO ORD-D-MESSAGE
                    MOVE -1 TO ORD-L-CUSTNO
                    SET SEND-DATAONLY-ALARM TO TRUE
                    PERFORM 1400-SEND-ORDER-MAP
*
            END-EVALUATE.
*
            EXEC CICS
                RETURN TRANSID('ORD1')
                       COMMAREA(COMMUNICATION-AREA)
            END-EXEC.
*
 1000-PROCESS-ORDER-MAP.
*
            PERFORM 1100-RECEIVE-ORDER-MAP.
            PERFORM 1200-EDIT-ORDER-DATA.
*
            IF VALID-DATA
                PERFORM 1300-FORMAT-INVOICE-RECORD
                MOVE 'Press Enter to post this order.  Or press F4 to ent
-                   'er corrections.' TO ORD-D-INSTR
                MOVE 'F3=Exit   F4=Change   F12=Cancel' TO ORD-D-FKEY
                MOVE SPACE TO ORD-D-MESSAGE
                SET SEND-DATAONLY TO TRUE
                SET PROTECT-FIELDS TO TRUE
                PERFORM 1400-SEND-ORDER-MAP
                SET PROCESS-VERIFY TO TRUE
            ELSE
                MOVE 'Type corrections.  Then press Enter.'
                    TO ORD-D-INSTR
                MOVE 'F3=Exit   F12=Cancel' TO ORD-D-FKEY
                SET SEND-DATAONLY-ALARM TO TRUE
                PERFORM 1400-SEND-ORDER-MAP
            END-IF.
```

The ORDRENT program (part 4 of 12)

```
*
 1100-RECEIVE-ORDER-MAP.
*
     EXEC CICS
         RECEIVE MAP('ORDMAP1')
                 MAPSET('ORDSET1')
                 INTO(ORDMAP1)
     END-EXEC.
*
     INSPECT ORDMAP1
         REPLACING ALL '_' BY SPACE.
*
 1200-EDIT-ORDER-DATA.
*
     MOVE ATTR-NO-HIGHLIGHT TO ORD-H-CUSTNO
                               ORD-H-PO.
     MOVE ZERO TO LINE-ITEM-COUNT
                  INV-INVOICE-TOTAL.
*
     PERFORM 1220-EDIT-LINE-ITEM
         VARYING ITEM-SUB FROM 10 BY -1
           UNTIL ITEM-SUB < 1.
*
     MOVE INV-INVOICE-TOTAL TO ORD-D-TOTAL.
     IF       LINE-ITEM-COUNT = ZERO
         AND VALID-DATA
         MOVE ATTR-REVERSE TO ORD-H-PCODE(1)
         MOVE -1 TO ORD-L-PCODE(1)
         MOVE 'You must enter at least one line item.'
            TO ORD-D-MESSAGE
         MOVE 'N' TO VALID-DATA-SW
     END-IF.
*
     IF       ORD-L-PO = ZERO
         OR ORD-D-PO = SPACE
         MOVE 'N' TO CA-PO-ENTERED-SW
     ELSE
         MOVE 'Y' TO CA-PO-ENTERED-SW
     END-IF.
*
     IF       ORD-L-CUSTNO = ZERO
         OR ORD-D-CUSTNO = SPACE
         MOVE ATTR-REVERSE TO ORD-H-CUSTNO
         MOVE -1 TO ORD-L-CUSTNO
         MOVE 'You must enter a customer number.'
            TO ORD-D-MESSAGE
         MOVE 'N' TO VALID-DATA-SW
     ELSE
         PERFORM 1210-READ-CUSTOMER-RECORD
         IF CUSTOMER-FOUND
             MOVE CM-LAST-NAME  TO ORD-D-LNAME
             MOVE CM-FIRST-NAME TO ORD-D-FNAME
             MOVE CM-ADDRESS    TO ORD-D-ADDR
             MOVE CM-CITY       TO ORD-D-CITY
             MOVE CM-STATE      TO ORD-D-STATE
             MOVE CM-ZIP-CODE   TO ORD-D-ZIPCODE
         ELSE
```

The ORDRENT program (part 5 of 12)

```
                    MOVE SPACE TO ORD-D-LNAME
                                 ORD-D-FNAME
                                 ORD-D-ADDR
                                 ORD-D-CITY
                                 ORD-D-STATE
                                 ORD-D-ZIPCODE
                MOVE ATTR-REVERSE TO ORD-H-CUSTNO
                MOVE -1 TO ORD-L-CUSTNO
                MOVE 'That customer does not exist.'
                     TO ORD-D-MESSAGE
                MOVE 'N' TO VALID-DATA-SW
            END-IF
        END-IF.
*
        IF VALID-DATA
            MOVE -1 TO ORD-L-CUSTNO
        END-IF.
*
 1210-READ-CUSTOMER-RECORD.
*
        EXEC CICS
            READ FILE('CUSTMAS')
                 INTO(CUSTOMER-MASTER-RECORD)
                 RIDFLD(ORD-D-CUSTNO)
                 RESP(RESPONSE-CODE)
        END-EXEC.
*
        IF RESPONSE-CODE = DFHRESP(NORMAL)
            MOVE 'Y' TO CUSTOMER-FOUND-SW
        ELSE
            IF RESPONSE-CODE = DFHRESP(NOTFND)
                MOVE 'N' TO CUSTOMER-FOUND-SW
            ELSE
                PERFORM 9999-TERMINATE-PROGRAM
            END-IF
        END-IF.
*
 1220-EDIT-LINE-ITEM.
*
        MOVE ATTR-NO-HIGHLIGHT TO ORD-H-PCODE(ITEM-SUB)
                                  ORD-H-QTY(ITEM-SUB)
                                  ORD-H-NET(ITEM-SUB).
        MOVE 'N' TO PRODUCT-FOUND-SW.
        MOVE 'N' TO VALID-QUANTITY-SW.
*
        IF          ORD-L-PCODE(ITEM-SUB) > ZERO
            AND ORD-D-PCODE(ITEM-SUB) NOT = SPACE
            MOVE 'Y' TO CA-PCODE-ENTERED-SW(ITEM-SUB)
        ELSE
            MOVE 'N' TO CA-PCODE-ENTERED-SW(ITEM-SUB)
        END-IF.
*
        IF          ORD-L-QTY(ITEM-SUB) > ZERO
            AND ORD-D-QTY-ALPHA(ITEM-SUB) NOT = SPACE
            MOVE 'Y' TO CA-QTY-ENTERED-SW(ITEM-SUB)
        ELSE
            MOVE 'N' TO CA-QTY-ENTERED-SW(ITEM-SUB)
        END-IF.
```

The ORDRENT program (part 6 of 12)

```
        IF        ORD-L-NET(ITEM-SUB) > ZERO
              AND ORD-D-NET-ALPHA(ITEM-SUB) NOT = SPACE
            MOVE 'Y' TO CA-NET-ENTERED-SW(ITEM-SUB)
        ELSE
            MOVE 'N' TO CA-NET-ENTERED-SW(ITEM-SUB)
        END-IF.
*
        IF            CA-NET-ENTERED(ITEM-SUB)
              AND NOT CA-PCODE-ENTERED(ITEM-SUB)
            MOVE ATTR-REVERSE TO ORD-H-PCODE(ITEM-SUB)
            MOVE -1 TO ORD-L-PCODE(ITEM-SUB)
            MOVE 'You cannot enter a net price without a product code
-           '.' TO ORD-D-MESSAGE
            MOVE 'N' TO VALID-DATA-SW
        END-IF.
*
        IF CA-NET-ENTERED(ITEM-SUB)
            CALL 'NUMEDIT' USING ORD-D-NET-ALPHA(ITEM-SUB)
                                 NET-NUMERIC
                                 VALID-NET-SW
            IF VALID-NET
                MOVE NET-NUMERIC TO ORD-D-NET(ITEM-SUB)
            ELSE
                MOVE ATTR-REVERSE TO ORD-H-NET(ITEM-SUB)
                MOVE -1 TO ORD-L-NET(ITEM-SUB)
                MOVE 'Net price must be numeric.' TO ORD-D-MESSAGE
                MOVE 'N' TO VALID-DATA-SW
                MOVE 'N' TO VALID-QUANTITY-SW
            END-IF
        END-IF.
*
        IF            CA-QTY-ENTERED(ITEM-SUB)
              AND NOT CA-PCODE-ENTERED(ITEM-SUB)
            MOVE ATTR-REVERSE TO ORD-H-PCODE(ITEM-SUB)
            MOVE -1 TO ORD-L-PCODE(ITEM-SUB)
            MOVE 'You cannot enter a quantity without a product code.
            ' ' TO ORD-D-MESSAGE
            MOVE 'N' TO VALID-DATA-SW
        END-IF.
*
        IF CA-QTY-ENTERED(ITEM-SUB)
            CALL 'INTEDIT' USING ORD-D-QTY-ALPHA(ITEM-SUB)
                                 QTY-NUMERIC
                                 VALID-QUANTITY-SW
            IF VALID-QUANTITY
                IF QTY-NUMERIC > ZERO
                    MOVE QTY-NUMERIC TO ORD-D-QTY(ITEM-SUB)
                ELSE
                    MOVE ATTR-REVERSE TO ORD-H-QTY(ITEM-SUB)
                    MOVE -1 TO ORD-L-QTY(ITEM-SUB)
                    MOVE 'Quantity must be greater than zero.'
                        TO ORD-D-MESSAGE
                    MOVE 'N' TO VALID-DATA-SW
                    MOVE 'N' TO VALID-QUANTITY-SW
                END-IF
```

The ORDRENT program (part 7 of 12)

```
            ELSE
                MOVE ATTR-REVERSE TO ORD-H-QTY(ITEM-SUB)
                MOVE -1 TO ORD-L-QTY(ITEM-SUB)
                MOVE 'Quantity must be numeric.' TO ORD-D-MESSAGE
                MOVE 'N' TO VALID-DATA-SW
                MOVE 'N' TO VALID-QUANTITY-SW
            END-IF
        END-IF.
*
        IF            CA-PCODE-ENTERED(ITEM-SUB)
            AND NOT CA-QTY-ENTERED(ITEM-SUB)
            MOVE ATTR-REVERSE TO ORD-H-QTY(ITEM-SUB)
            MOVE -1 TO ORD-L-QTY(ITEM-SUB)
            MOVE 'You must enter a quantity.' TO ORD-D-MESSAGE
            MOVE 'N' TO VALID-DATA-SW
        END-IF.
*
        IF NOT CA-PCODE-ENTERED(ITEM-SUB)
            MOVE SPACE TO ORD-D-DESC(ITEM-SUB)
            MOVE ZERO  TO ORD-D-LIST(ITEM-SUB)
                          ORD-D-AMOUNT(ITEM-SUB)
        ELSE
            ADD 1 TO LINE-ITEM-COUNT
            PERFORM 1230-READ-PRODUCT-RECORD
            IF PRODUCT-FOUND
                MOVE PRM-PRODUCT-DESCRIPTION
                                    TO ORD-D-DESC(ITEM-SUB)
                MOVE PRM-UNIT-PRICE TO ORD-D-LIST(ITEM-SUB)
                IF NOT CA-NET-ENTERED(ITEM-SUB)
                    MOVE PRM-UNIT-PRICE TO ORD-D-NET(ITEM-SUB)
                                           NET-NUMERIC
                END-IF
                IF VALID-QUANTITY AND VALID-NET
                    MULTIPLY NET-NUMERIC BY QTY-NUMERIC
                        GIVING ORD-D-AMOUNT(ITEM-SUB)
                               INV-AMOUNT(ITEM-SUB)
                        ON SIZE ERROR
                            MOVE ATTR-REVERSE TO ORD-H-QTY(ITEM-SUB)
                            MOVE -1 TO ORD-L-QTY(ITEM-SUB)
                            MOVE 'Line item amount is too large.'
                                TO ORD-D-MESSAGE
                            MOVE 'N' TO VALID-DATA-SW
                            MOVE ZERO TO ORD-D-AMOUNT(ITEM-SUB)
                                         INV-AMOUNT(ITEM-SUB)
                    END-MULTIPLY
                    ADD INV-AMOUNT(ITEM-SUB) TO INV-INVOICE-TOTAL
                        ON SIZE ERROR
                            MOVE ATTR-REVERSE TO ORD-H-QTY(ITEM-SUB)
                            MOVE -1 TO ORD-L-QTY(ITEM-SUB)
                            MOVE 'Invoice total is too large.'
                                TO ORD-D-MESSAGE
                            MOVE 'N' TO VALID-DATA-SW
                            MOVE ZERO TO INV-INVOICE-TOTAL
                    END-ADD
                END-IF
            ELSE
```

The ORDRENT program (part 8 of 12)

```
                               MOVE SPACE TO ORD-D-DESC(ITEM-SUB)
                               MOVE ZERO  TO ORD-D-LIST(ITEM-SUB)
                                             ORD-D-AMOUNT(ITEM-SUB)
                               MOVE ATTR-REVERSE TO ORD-H-PCODE(ITEM-SUB)
                               MOVE -1     TO ORD-L-PCODE(ITEM-SUB)
                               MOVE 'That product does not exist.'
                                          TO ORD-D-MESSAGE
                               MOVE 'N'    TO VALID-DATA-SW
                           END-IF
                       END-IF.
  *
    1230-READ-PRODUCT-RECORD.
  *
           EXEC CICS
               READ FILE('PRODUCT')
                     INTO(PRODUCT-MASTER-RECORD)
                     RIDFLD(ORD-D-PCODE(ITEM-SUB))
                     RESP(RESPONSE-CODE)
           END-EXEC.
  *
           IF RESPONSE-CODE = DFHRESP(NORMAL)
               MOVE 'Y' TO PRODUCT-FOUND-SW
           ELSE
               IF RESPONSE-CODE = DFHRESP(NOTFND)
                   MOVE 'N' TO PRODUCT-FOUND-SW
               ELSE
                   PERFORM 9999-TERMINATE-PROGRAM
               END-IF
           END-IF.
  *
    1300-FORMAT-INVOICE-RECORD.
  *
           EXEC CICS
               ASKTIME ABSTIME(ABSOLUTE-TIME)
           END-EXEC.
           EXEC CICS
               FORMATTIME ABSTIME(ABSOLUTE-TIME)
                   MMDDYYYY(INV-INVOICE-DATE)
           END-EXEC.
           MOVE ORD-D-CUSTNO TO INV-CUSTOMER-NUMBER.
           MOVE ORD-D-PO      TO INV-PO-NUMBER.
           PERFORM VARYING ITEM-SUB FROM 1 BY 1
                   UNTIL ITEM-SUB > 10
               IF CA-PCODE-ENTERED(ITEM-SUB)
                   MOVE ORD-D-PCODE(ITEM-SUB)
                             TO INV-PRODUCT-CODE(ITEM-SUB)
                   MOVE ORD-D-QTY(ITEM-SUB)
                             TO INV-QUANTITY(ITEM-SUB)
                   MOVE ORD-D-NET(ITEM-SUB)
                             TO INV-UNIT-PRICE(ITEM-SUB)
               ELSE
                   MOVE SPACE TO INV-PRODUCT-CODE(ITEM-SUB)
                   MOVE ZERO   TO INV-QUANTITY(ITEM-SUB)
                             INV-UNIT-PRICE(ITEM-SUB)
                             INV-AMOUNT(ITEM-SUB)
               END-IF
           END-PERFORM.
           MOVE INVOICE-RECORD TO CA-INVOICE-RECORD.
```

The ORDRENT program (part 9 of 12)

```
     1400-SEND-ORDER-MAP.
*
         MOVE 'ORD1' TO ORD-D-TRANID.
*
         IF PROTECT-FIELDS
             PERFORM 1410-PROTECT-FIELDS
         ELSE
             IF UNPROTECT-FIELDS
                 PERFORM 1420-UNPROTECT-FIELDS
             END-IF
         END-IF.
*
         EVALUATE TRUE
             WHEN SEND-ERASE
                 EXEC CICS
                     SEND MAP('ORDMAP1')
                         MAPSET('ORDSET1')
                         FROM(ORDMAP1)
                         CURSOR
                         ERASE
                 END-EXEC
             WHEN SEND-DATAONLY
                 EXEC CICS
                     SEND MAP('ORDMAP1')
                         MAPSET('ORDSET1')
                         FROM(ORDMAP1)
                         CURSOR
                         DATAONLY
                 END-EXEC
             WHEN SEND-DATAONLY-ALARM
                 EXEC CICS
                     SEND MAP('ORDMAP1')
                         MAPSET('ORDSET1')
                         FROM(ORDMAP1)
                         CURSOR
                         DATAONLY
                         ALARM
                 END-EXEC
         END-EVALUATE.
*
     1410-PROTECT-FIELDS.
*
         MOVE ATTR-PROT TO ORD-A-CUSTNO.
         IF CA-PO-ENTERED
             MOVE ATTR-PROT TO ORD-A-PO
         ELSE
             MOVE ATTR-PROT-DARK TO ORD-A-PO
         END-IF.
*
```

The ORDRENT program (part 10 of 12)

```
              PERFORM VARYING ITEM-SUB FROM 1 BY 1
                      UNTIL ITEM-SUB > 10
                  IF CA-PCODE-ENTERED(ITEM-SUB)
                      MOVE ATTR-PROT TO ORD-A-PCODE(ITEM-SUB)
                  ELSE
                      MOVE ATTR-PROT-DARK TO ORD-A-PCODE(ITEM-SUB)
                  END-IF
                  IF CA-QTY-ENTERED(ITEM-SUB)
                      MOVE ATTR-PROT TO ORD-A-QTY(ITEM-SUB)
                  ELSE
                      MOVE ATTR-PROT-DARK TO ORD-A-QTY(ITEM-SUB)
                  END-IF
                  IF      CA-NET-ENTERED(ITEM-SUB)
                      OR  CA-PCODE-ENTERED(ITEM-SUB)
                      MOVE ATTR-PROT TO ORD-A-NET(ITEM-SUB)
                  ELSE
                      MOVE ATTR-PROT-DARK TO ORD-A-NET(ITEM-SUB)
                  END-IF
              END-PERFORM.
     *
      1420-UNPROTECT-FIELDS.
     *
              MOVE ATTR-UNPROT-MDT TO ORD-A-CUSTNO.
              IF CA-PO-ENTERED
                  MOVE ATTR-UNPROT-MDT TO ORD-A-PO
              ELSE
                  MOVE ATTR-UNPROT     TO ORD-A-PO
              END-IF.
     *
              MOVE ATTR-TURQUOISE TO ORD-C-CUSTNO
                                     ORD-C-PO.
     *
              PERFORM VARYING ITEM-SUB FROM 1 BY 1
                      UNTIL ITEM-SUB > 10
                  IF CA-PCODE-ENTERED(ITEM-SUB)
                      MOVE ATTR-UNPROT-MDT TO ORD-A-PCODE(ITEM-SUB)
                  ELSE
                      MOVE ATTR-UNPROT     TO ORD-A-PCODE(ITEM-SUB)
                  END-IF
                  IF CA-QTY-ENTERED(ITEM-SUB)
                      MOVE ATTR-UNPROT-MDT TO ORD-A-QTY(ITEM-SUB)
                  ELSE
                      MOVE ATTR-UNPROT     TO ORD-A-QTY(ITEM-SUB)
                  END-IF
                  IF CA-NET-ENTERED(ITEM-SUB)
                      MOVE ATTR-UNPROT-MDT TO ORD-A-NET(ITEM-SUB)
                  ELSE
                      MOVE ATTR-UNPROT     TO ORD-A-NET(ITEM-SUB)
                  END-IF
                  MOVE ATTR-TURQUOISE TO ORD-C-PCODE(ITEM-SUB)
                                         ORD-C-QTY(ITEM-SUB)
                                         ORD-C-NET(ITEM-SUB)
              END-PERFORM.
     *
```

The ORDRENT program (part 11 of 12)

```
 2000-PROCESS-POST-ORDER.
*
     MOVE CA-INVOICE-RECORD TO INVOICE-RECORD.
*
     EXEC CICS
         LINK PROGRAM('GETINV')
             COMMAREA(INV-INVOICE-NUMBER)
     END-EXEC.
*
     PERFORM 2100-WRITE-INVOICE-RECORD.
     ADD 1 TO CA-TOTAL-ORDERS.
     MOVE 'Type order details.  Then press Enter.'
         TO ORD-D-INSTR.
     MOVE 'Order posted.' TO ORD-D-MESSAGE.
     MOVE 'F3=Exit   F12=Cancel' TO ORD-D-FKEY.
     MOVE -1 TO ORD-L-CUSTNO.
     SET SEND-ERASE TO TRUE.
     PERFORM 1400-SEND-ORDER-MAP.
*
 2100-WRITE-INVOICE-RECORD.
*
     EXEC CICS
         WRITE FILE('INVOICE')
             FROM(INVOICE-RECORD)
             RIDFLD(INV-INVOICE-NUMBER)
     END-EXEC.
*
 3000-SEND-TOTAL-LINE.
*
     MOVE CA-TOTAL-ORDERS TO TL-TOTAL-ORDERS.
*
     EXEC CICS
         SEND TEXT FROM(TOTAL-LINE)
                   ERASE
                   FREEKB
     END-EXEC.
*
 9999-TERMINATE-PROGRAM.
*
     MOVE EIBRESP  TO ERR-RESP.
     MOVE EIBRESP2 TO ERR-RESP2.
     MOVE EIBTRNID TO ERR-TRNID.
     MOVE EIBRSRCE TO ERR-RSRCE.
*
     EXEC CICS
         XCTL PROGRAM('SYSERR')
             COMMAREA(ERROR-PARAMETERS)
     END-EXEC.
```

The ORDRENT program (part 12 of 12)

The GETINV subprogram

```
IDENTIFICATION DIVISION.
*
PROGRAM-ID.  GETINV.
*
ENVIRONMENT DIVISION.
*
DATA DIVISION.
*
WORKING-STORAGE SECTION.
*
COPY INVCTL.
*
LINKAGE SECTION.
*
01  DFHCOMMAREA   PIC 9(06).
*
PROCEDURE DIVISION.
*
0000-GET-INVOICE-NUMBER.
*
    MOVE ZERO TO INVCTL-RECORD-KEY.
    EXEC CICS
        READ FILE('INVCTL')
             INTO(INVCTL-RECORD)
             RIDFLD(INVCTL-RECORD-KEY)
             UPDATE
    END-EXEC.
    MOVE INVCTL-NEXT-INVOICE-NUMBER TO DFHCOMMAREA.
    ADD 1 TO INVCTL-NEXT-INVOICE-NUMBER.
    EXEC CICS
        REWRITE FILE('INVCTL')
                FROM(INVCTL-RECORD)
    END-EXEC.
    EXEC CICS
        RETURN
    END-EXEC.
```

The INTEDIT subprogram

```
 IDENTIFICATION DIVISION.
*
 PROGRAM-ID.   INTEDIT.
*
 ENVIRONMENT DIVISION.
*
 DATA DIVISION.
*
 WORKING-STORAGE SECTION.
*
 01   WORK-FIELDS.
*
      05   INTEGER-PART        PIC 9(05).
      05   INTEGER-LENGTH      PIC S9(03)  COMP-3.
*
 LINKAGE SECTION.
*
 01   UNEDITED-NUMBER          PIC X(05).
*
 01   EDITED-NUMBER            PIC 9(05).
*
 01   VALID-NUMBER-SW          PIC X(01).
      88   VALID-NUMBER        VALUE 'Y'.
*
 PROCEDURE DIVISION USING  UNEDITED-NUMBER
                           EDITED-NUMBER
                           VALID-NUMBER-SW.
*
 0000-EDIT-NUMBER.
*
      MOVE ZERO TO INTEGER-LENGTH.
      INSPECT UNEDITED-NUMBER
          REPLACING LEADING SPACE BY ZERO.
      INSPECT UNEDITED-NUMBER
          TALLYING INTEGER-LENGTH FOR CHARACTERS
              BEFORE INITIAL SPACE.
      IF UNEDITED-NUMBER(1:INTEGER-LENGTH) NUMERIC
          MOVE UNEDITED-NUMBER(1:INTEGER-LENGTH)
              TO EDITED-NUMBER
          MOVE 'Y' TO VALID-NUMBER-SW
      ELSE
          MOVE 'N' TO VALID-NUMBER-SW
      END-IF.
*
 0000-EXIT.
*
      EXIT PROGRAM.
```

The NUMEDIT subprogram

```
IDENTIFICATION DIVISION.
PROGRAM-ID.  NUMEDIT.
*
ENVIRONMENT DIVISION.
*
DATA DIVISION.
*
WORKING-STORAGE SECTION.
*
01   WORK-FIELDS.
     05   INTEGER-PART        PIC 9(10).
     05   INTEGER-PART-X      REDEFINES   INTEGER-PART.
          10   INTEGER-CHAR   PIC X(01)   OCCURS 10.
     05   DECIMAL-PART        PIC V9(10).
     05   DECIMAL-PART-X      REDEFINES   DECIMAL-PART.
          10   DECIMAL-CHAR   PIC X(01)   OCCURS 10.
     05   DECIMAL-POS         PIC S9(03)  COMP-3.
     05   INTEGER-LENGTH      PIC S9(03)  COMP-3.
     05   INTEGER-SUB         PIC S9(03)  COMP-3.
     05   DECIMAL-SUB         PIC S9(03)  COMP-3.
     05   UNEDIT-SUB          PIC S9(03)  COMP-3.
*
LINKAGE SECTION.
*
01   UNEDITED-NUMBER.
     05   UNEDITED-CHAR       OCCURS 10   PIC X.
*
01   EDITED-NUMBER           PIC 9(07)V99.
*
01   VALID-NUMBER-SW         PIC X(01).
     88   VALID-NUMBER       VALUE 'Y'.
*
PROCEDURE DIVISION USING UNEDITED-NUMBER
                         EDITED-NUMBER
                         VALID-NUMBER-SW.
*
0000-EDIT-NUMBER.
*
     MOVE 'Y' TO VALID-NUMBER-SW.
     MOVE ZERO TO INTEGER-PART
                  DECIMAL-PART
                  DECIMAL-POS.
     INSPECT UNEDITED-NUMBER
         TALLYING DECIMAL-POS FOR CHARACTERS
             BEFORE INITIAL '.'.
     IF DECIMAL-POS < 10
         PERFORM 1000-EDIT-DECIMAL-NUMBER
     ELSE
         PERFORM 2000-EDIT-INTEGER
     END-IF.
     IF VALID-NUMBER
         COMPUTE EDITED-NUMBER = INTEGER-PART + DECIMAL-PART
     END-IF.
*
```

The NUMEDIT subprogram (part 1 of 2)

```
    0000-EXIT.
*
    EXIT PROGRAM.
*
 1000-EDIT-DECIMAL-NUMBER.
*
    MOVE 10 TO INTEGER-SUB.
    PERFORM 1100-EDIT-INTEGER-PART
        VARYING UNEDIT-SUB FROM DECIMAL-POS BY -1
          UNTIL UNEDIT-SUB < 1.
    MOVE 1 TO DECIMAL-SUB.
    ADD 2 TO DECIMAL-POS.
    PERFORM 1200-EDIT-DECIMAL-PART
        VARYING UNEDIT-SUB FROM DECIMAL-POS BY 1
          UNTIL UNEDIT-SUB > 10.
*
 1100-EDIT-INTEGER-PART.
*
    IF UNEDITED-CHAR(UNEDIT-SUB) NUMERIC
        MOVE UNEDITED-CHAR(UNEDIT-SUB)
            TO INTEGER-CHAR(INTEGER-SUB)
        SUBTRACT 1 FROM INTEGER-SUB
    ELSE IF UNEDITED-CHAR(UNEDIT-SUB) NOT = SPACE
        MOVE 'N' TO VALID-NUMBER-SW
    END-IF.
*
 1200-EDIT-DECIMAL-PART.
*
    IF UNEDITED-CHAR(UNEDIT-SUB) NUMERIC
        MOVE UNEDITED-CHAR(UNEDIT-SUB)
            TO DECIMAL-CHAR(DECIMAL-SUB)
        ADD 1 TO DECIMAL-SUB
    ELSE IF UNEDITED-CHAR(UNEDIT-SUB) NOT = SPACE
        MOVE 'N' TO VALID-NUMBER-SW
    END-IF.
*
 2000-EDIT-INTEGER.
*
    INSPECT UNEDITED-NUMBER
        REPLACING LEADING SPACE BY ZERO.
    MOVE ZERO TO INTEGER-LENGTH.
    INSPECT UNEDITED-NUMBER
        TALLYING INTEGER-LENGTH FOR CHARACTERS
            BEFORE INITIAL SPACE.
    MOVE 10 TO INTEGER-SUB.
    PERFORM 1100-EDIT-INTEGER-PART
        VARYING UNEDIT-SUB FROM INTEGER-LENGTH BY -1
          UNTIL UNEDIT-SUB < 1.
    MOVE ZERO TO DECIMAL-PART.
```

The NUMEDIT subprogram (part 2 of 2)

CICS command reference

Unit 7

CICS command preview

This unit presents information that will help you use the CICS command reference material in Unit 8. First, it gives you a summary of the syntax conventions that are used for all the CICS commands. Second, it presents two error-handling options—RESP and RESP2—that can be coded on any CICS command. And finally, it lists the commands in Unit 8 by function. So if you're not sure which command you're looking for, you can check here before going to the alphabetical list in Unit 8.

Syntax conventions

Syntax notation

Unit 8 presents the syntax for each of the CICS commands as well as an explanation of what each command does. In order to accurately represent each command, the following syntax methods are used:

UPPERCASE	Indicates CICS code that must be entered as shown.
option	Indicates an option that must be coded.
[option]	Indicates an option that may be coded but that is not required in order for the command to successfully execute.
{ option | option }	Indicates a set of alternative options, one of which must be coded.
[option | option]	Indicates a set of alternative options, one of which may be coded.
{ option } { option }	Indicates a set of alternative options, one of which must be coded.
[{ option } { option }]	Indicates a set of alternative options, one of which may be coded.
<u>option</u>	Indicates the default option.
option-1 option-2	Indicates that option-2 is coded only in conjunction with option-1.
...	Indicates that the preceding option may be repeated multiple times.

Argument values

Most CICS commands require you to code one or more options. And most of the options require you to supply a value, or argument, in parentheses. The command syntax specifies which of these types of values you can code for each option:

data-value	A COBOL data name coded in the Working-Storage or Linkage Section or a literal. The option may require a binary halfword, a binary fullword, an unsigned binary doubleword, or a character string.
data-area	A COBOL data name coded in the Working-Storage or Linkage Section. The option may require a binary halfword, a binary fullword, an unsigned binary doubleword, or a character string.
cvda	A CICS-value data area defined in the Working-Storage or Linkage Section as a binary fullword. The value typically describes the state of a particular resource. You can use the DFHVALUE keyword to work with cvda values.

pointer-ref	The name of a BLL cell coded in the Linkage Section. A pointer-ref must be a binary fullword. Use the COBOL ADDRESS OF special register to set the reference.
pointer-value	The name of a BLL cell coded in the Linkage Section or the name of a Working-Storage Section field that contains a BLL cell value. A pointer-value must be a binary fullword. Use the COBOL ADDRESS OF special register to set the value.
name	An alphanumeric literal or the name of a Working-Storage or Linkage Section field that contains the value to be used.
filename	An alphanumeric literal or a Working-Storage or Linkage Section field that specifies the name of a file.
systemname	An alphanumeric literal or a Working-Storage or Linkage Section field that specifies a remote system ID.
label	The name of a paragraph or section.
hhmmss	A numeric literal or the name of a seven-digit packed-decimal field (PIC S9(7) COMP-3) defined in the Working-Storage or Linkage Section. *hh* represents hours, *mm* represents minutes, and *ss* represents seconds.
hh	A numeric literal or the name of a binary fullword defined in the Working-Storage or Linkage Section that represents hours.
mins	A numeric literal or the name of a binary fullword defined in the Working-Storage or Linkage Section that represents minutes.
secs	A numeric literal or the name of a binary fullword defined in the Working-Storage or Linkage Section that represents seconds.

Data types

The value or data field you specify for an argument must match the data type required by the option. Usually, one of four specific types is required:

binary halfword	PIC S9(4) COMP or PIC X(2)
binary fullword	PIC S9(8) COMP or PIC X(4)
binary doubleword	PIC 9(18) COMP or PIC X(9)
character string	PIC X(n)

For binary halfwords, fullwords, and doublewords, don't use PIC X(2), PIC X(4), or PIC X(9) if you need to perform arithmetic on the values the fields contain. If an option doesn't specify a particular data type, you can use any group or elementary item.

RESP and RESP2 options

You can use the RESP and RESP2 options on any CICS command to test if any exceptional conditions were raised during the execution of the command. The RESP option holds the condition raised and the RESP2 option can help determine why the condition was raised. Unit 8 includes the RESP conditions that can be raised for each command, but I didn't include any of the RESP2 conditions because they aren't used very often. For a full listing of the RESP2 codes available for each CICS command, see the IBM *CICS Application Programming Reference* manual.

Syntax

```
[ RESP(data-value) [ RESP2(data-value) ] ]
```

Explanation

RESP   A binary fullword (PIC S9(8) COMP) field that receives any exceptional condition that's raised during the execution of a CICS command. You should include this parameter in most of the CICS commands you code. To test the condition, use the keyword DFHRESP.

RESP2   A binary fullword (PIC S9(8) COMP) field that further describes the condition raised in the RESP parameter. Unlike the RESP option, RESP2 values have no associated symbolic names, and you can't use the DFHRESP keyword to test the value.

Coding example

```
EXEC CICS
    READ FILE('ACCOUNT')
         INTO(ACCOUNT-RECORD)
         RIDFLD(ACCOUNT-NUMBER)
         RESP(RESPONSE-CODE)
END-EXEC.

IF RESPONSE-CODE = DFHRESP(NORMAL)
    MOVE 'Y' TO RECORD-FOUND-SW
ELSE
    IF RESPONSE-CODE = DFHRESP(NOTFND)
        MOVE 'N' TO RECORD-FOUND-SW
    ELSE
        PERFORM 9999-TERMINATE-PROGRAM
    END-IF
END-IF.
```

Commands by function

Unit 8 presents the CICS commands in alphabetical order because that's the easiest way to look up a specific command. Occasionally, though, you may want to view the CICS commands that are related by function. So the following lists all of the CICS commands in Unit 8 by function group.

Abend support

ABEND
HANDLE ABEND

APPC mapped conversation

ALLOCATE
CONNECT PROCESS
CONVERSE
EXTRACT ATTRIBUTES
EXTRACT PROCESS
FREE
ISSUE ABEND
ISSUE CONFIRMATION
ISSUE ERROR
ISSUE PREPARE
ISSUE SIGNAL
RECEIVE
SEND
WAIT CONVID

Authentication

CHANGE PASSWORD
SIGNOFF
SIGNON
VERIFY PASSWORD

BMS

PURGE MESSAGE
RECEIVE MAP
ROUTE
SEND CONTROL
SEND MAP
SEND PAGE
SEND TEXT
SEND TEXT NOEDIT

Built-in functions

BIF DEEDIT

Console support

WRITE OPERATOR

Diagnostic services

DUMP TRANSACTION
ENTER TRACENUM

Document services

DOCUMENT CREATE
DOCUMENT INSERT
DOCUMENT RETRIEVE
DOCUMENT SET

Environment services

ADDRESS
ADDRESS SET
ASSIGN

Exception support

HANDLE CONDITION
IGNORE CONDITION
POP HANDLE
PUSH HANDLE

File control

DELETE
ENDBR
READ
READNEXT
READPREV
RESETBR
REWRITE
STARTBR
UNLOCK
WRITE

Interval control

ASKTIME
CANCEL
DELAY
FORMATTIME
POST
RETRIEVE
START
WAIT EVENT

Journaling

JOURNAL
WAIT JOURNALNAME
WAIT JOURNALNUM
WRITE JOURNALNAME
WRITE JOURNALNUM

Named counter server

DEFINE COUNTER/DCOUNTER
DELETE COUNTER/DCOUNTER
GET COUNTER/DCOUNTER
QUERY COUNTER/DCOUNTER
REWIND COUNTER/DCOUNTER
UPDATE COUNTER/DCOUNTER

Program control

LINK
LOAD
RELEASE
RETURN
XCTL

Scheduling

START ATTACH
START BREXIT

Security

QUERY SECURITY

Storage control

FREEMAIN
GETMAIN

Syncpoint

SYNCPOINT

Task control

CHANGE TASK
DEQ
ENQ
SUSPEND

TCP/IP services

EXTRACT CERTIFICATE
EXTRACT TCPIP

Temporary storage control

DELETEQ TS
READQ TS
WRITEQ TS

Terminal control

ALLOCATE
BUILD ATTACH
CONVERSE
EXTRACT ATTACH
EXTRACT ATTRIBUTES
FREE
HANDLE AID
ISSUE COPY
ISSUE DISCONNECT
ISSUE ERASEAUP
ISSUE PRINT
RECEIVE
SEND

Transient data

DELETEQ TD
READQ TD
WRITEQ TD

Web services

WEB ENDBROWSE FORMFIELD
WEB ENDBROWSE HTTPHEADER
WEB EXTRACT
WEB READ FORMFIELD
WEB READ HTTPHEADER
WEB READNEXT FORMFIELD
WEB READNEXT HTTPHEADER
WEB RECEIVE
WEB RETRIEVE
WEB SEND
WEB STARTBROWSE FORMFIELD
WEB STARTBROWSE HTTPHEADER
WEB WRITE HTTPHEADER

Unit 8

CICS commands

This unit provides a complete reference to all of the CICS commands you're likely to use in a command-level program. The commands are listed in alphabetical order to make each entry easy to locate. For each command, you'll find:

- a brief statement of the command's function
- the command's syntax
- an explanation of each of the command's options
- a listing and explanation of the exceptional conditions that can be raised by the command
- notes and tips that will help you better understand how the command works or help you use the command more effectively
- one or more real-life examples of how to use the command

Note that for any CICS command, you can code the RESP and RESP2 options to handle any exceptional conditions that arise. If you're maintaining older programs, you may also encounter the HANDLE CONDITION command being used for exception handling. However, using the RESP options results in code that's simpler, easier to manage, and more efficient at run-time, so that's the approach that's recommended today. An overview of exception handling using RESP and RESP2 is given in Unit 2, and the syntax details are given in Unit 7.

A second option that can be coded on any command is the NOHANDLE option. It tells CICS to ignore any HANDLE CONDITION command in effect and to skip the default action if an exceptional condition is raised. Because RESP, RESP2, and NOHANDLE can be coded for any CICS command, they aren't listed in the command syntax in this unit.

The ABEND command

Function

Abend support. The ABEND command forces the current task to terminate abnormally. If a HANDLE ABEND command is in effect, control will be transferred to the routine it specifies. Otherwise, control is returned to CICS. An optional storage dump can be produced.

Syntax

```
EXEC CICS
    ABEND [ ABCODE(name) ]
          [ CANCEL ]
          [ NODUMP ]
END-EXEC.
```

Options

ABCODE   Specifies that a storage dump should be produced. The name supplied is used to identify the dump, and it should be a 4-character value with no leading spaces. If you omit the name, the dump is identified by ????. If you omit ABCODE, a dump is not produced.

CANCEL   Specifies that any active abend exit set up by a HANDLE ABEND command should be ignored.

NODUMP   Specifies that a dump should not be produced. Since this is the default if ABCODE isn't coded, you'll rarely use the NODUMP option.

Exceptional conditions

No exceptional conditions are raised as a result of the ABEND command.

Notes and tips

- Don't start an ABCODE name with the letter A because abend codes starting with A are reserved by CICS.
- Storage dumps are written to the CICS dump data sets. You'll have to determine your installation's procedures for printing dumps.
- Because the ABEND command causes your task to abend, dynamic transaction backout is invoked. As a result, any changes your task made to recoverable resources will be reversed.

Coding example

This example shows how to issue an ABEND command, producing a storage dump identified by the abend code R100.

```
9000-ABEND-PROGRAM.
*
    EXEC CICS
        ABEND ABCODE('R100')
    END-EXEC.
```

The ADDRESS command

Function

Environment services. The ADDRESS command lets you access CICS storage areas that are maintained outside of your program.

Syntax

```
EXEC CICS
    ADDRESS [ ACEE(pointer-ref) ]
            [ COMMAREA(pointer-ref) ]
            [ CWA(pointer-ref) ]
            [ EIB(pointer-ref) ]
            [ TCTUA(pointer-ref) ]
            [ TWA(pointer-ref) ]
END-EXEC.
```

Options

ACEE	Establishes addressability to the Access Control Environment Element, a control block that provides an interface to an external security manager (ESM). If no ACEE exists, the pointer is set to the null value (hex FF000000).
COMMAREA	Establishes addressability to the Communication Area. The ADDRESS COMMAREA command is used only in C programs, because COBOL automatically establishes addressability to the communication area. If the COMMAREA doesn't exist, the pointer is set to the null value (hex FF000000).
CWA	Establishes addressability to the Common Work Area, a user-defined storage area common to all tasks in a single CICS system. If a CWA doesn't exist, the pointer is set to the null value (hex FF000000).
EIB	Establishes addressability to the Execute Interface Block. Normally, this addressability is automatically established when your program is entered. However, if a called subprogram or a C routine needs to access information in the EIB, it must issue an ADDRESS EIB command.
TCTUA	Establishes addressability to the Terminal Control Table User Area, a user-defined storage area that's unique to the terminal to which the current task is attached. If a TCTUA doesn't exist, the pointer is set to the null value (hex FF000000).
TWA	Establishes addressability to the Transaction Work Area, a user-defined storage area that's unique to the current task. The TWA is deleted when the current task ends. If a TWA doesn't exist, the pointer is set to the null value (X'FF000000').

Exceptional condition

No exceptional conditions are raised as a result of the ADDRESS command.

Notes and tips

- The ADDRESS command simply returns the address of one or more system areas. You must provide the linkage to access those areas by using the ADDRESS OF special register. If the program was written for the OS/VS COBOL compiler, you code BLL cells in the Linkage Section instead.
- The format of the CWA is installation-dependent. It often contains useful information, such as the company name, the current date already converted to the form MM/DD/YYYY, and application-specific information.
- The TCTUA and TWA don't have much use in command-level programming; they're leftovers from the days of macro-level programming. In a command-level application, the function of both has been replaced by the communication area. The TCTUA was usually used to pass information from task to task in a pseudo-conversational application (that function is now done using the COMMAREA option on a RETURN command), and the TWA was used to pass information among programs within a task (that function is now done using the COMMAREA option on a LINK or XCTL command).
- The use of any of these options opens your program to the possibility of corrupting storage that's outside of your program's storage. And that can lead to serious problems. As a result, the ADDRESS command should be avoided whenever possible.

Coding example

This example shows how to access the Common Work Area.The ADDRESS OF special register is used to provide linkage to the COMMON-WORK-AREA field, which defines the CWA.

```
    LINKAGE SECTION.
*
 01  COMMON-WORK-AREA.
     05  CWA-CURRENT-DATE  PIC X(10).
     05  CWA-COMPANY-NAME  PIC X(30).
     .
     .
*
 PROCEDURE DIVISION.
*
     .
     .
     EXEC CICS
         ADDRESS CWA(ADDRESS OF COMMON-WORK-AREA)
     END-EXEC.
```

The ADDRESS SET command

Function

Environment services. The ADDRESS SET command lets you set the address of a working-storage structure or pointer. Doing so allows you to reference the same allocation of memory in more than one way.

Syntax

```
EXEC CICS
    ADDRESS { SET(data-area) USING(pointer-ref) }
            { SET(pointer-ref) USING(data-area) }
END-EXEC.
```

Options

SET   Sets a pointer reference.

USING   Supplies a pointer value.

Exceptional conditions

No exceptional conditions are raised as a result of the ADDRESS SET command.

Notes and tips

*   The value you specify in the USING option is used to set the reference in the SET option. You use the ADDRESS OF special register to provide the linkage to the data area specified in either the SET or USING option.

Coding example

The following command could be used in a program that accesses a DL/I database. It establishes addressability to a set of pointers for a Linkage Section area called the PCB that contains information about the database. A field in a Linkage Section area called the UIB (User Interface Block) supplies the address of the PCB pointers.

```
EXEC CICS
    ADDRESS SET(ADDRESS OF PCB-PTRS)
            USING(UIBPCBAL)
END-EXEC.
```

The ALLOCATE command

Function

APPC mapped conversation/Terminal control. Establishes a distributed processing session with an MRO session, a remote APPC logical unit, or a remote LUTYPE6.1 logical unit.

Syntax

MRO

```
EXEC CICS
    ALLOCATE   SYSID(systemname)
               [ NOQUEUE ]
               [ STATE(cvda) ]
END-EXEC.
```

APPC

```
EXEC CICS
    ALLOCATE { SYSID(systemname) [ PROFILE(name) ] | PARTNER(name) }
             [ NOQUEUE ]
             [ STATE(cvda) ]
END-EXEC.
```

LUTYPE6.1

```
EXEC CICS
    ALLOCATE { SYSID(systemname) | SESSION(name) }
             [ PROFILE(name) ]
             [ NOQUEUE ]
END-EXEC.
```

Options

SYSID	Specifies the 1- to 4-character name of the system with which a session is to be established.
PROFILE	Specifies the 1- to 8-character name of a set of session-processing options. If omitted, the default profile (DFHCICSA) is used.
PARTNER	(APPC only) Specifies the 1- to 8-character name for a set of definitions that includes the name of the logical unit NETNAME. This option can be used as an alternative to the SYSID and PROFILE options.
SESSION	(LUTYPE6.1 only) Specifies a 1- to 4-character session name.
NOQUEUE	Specifies that if a session is not immediately available, control should return to the program. If omitted, the program will be suspended until a session is available. The NOSUSPEND option that was used in earlier versions of CICS is still supported as an alternative to NOQUEUE.
STATE	Specifies a binary fullword (PIC S9(8) COMP) where CICS places state information.

Exceptional conditions

Note: The default action for all of these conditions except for EOC, SYSBUSY, and SESSBUSY is to terminate the task. The default action for EOC and SESSBUSY is to ignore the ALLOCATE command. The default action for the SYSBUSY condition is to suspend the task until a session becomes available.

CBIDERR	The profile cannot be located.
INVREQ	The request is not allowed.
EOC	(LUTYPE6.1 only) The request is received with the end-of-chain indicator set. Field EIBEOC also contains this indicator.
NETNAMEIDERR	(APPC only) The NETNAME specified through the PARTNER option is invalid.
PARTNERIDERR	(APPC only) The name specified through the PARTNER option is invalid.
SYSBUSY	A session is not available.
SESSBUSY	(LUTYPE6.1 only) The specified session is not available.
SYSIDERR	The SYSID is invalid, or CICS is unable to establish a session.
SESSIONERR	(LUTYPE6.1 only) The SESSION is invalid, or CICS is unable to establish a specific session.

Notes and tips

- If the session is successfully allocated, the conversation-id is returned in the Execute Interface Block field EIBRSRCE. Be sure to move this value to a working-storage field so you can specify it in subsequent commands.

- SYSBUSY is one of the few exceptional conditions that does not cause your task to be terminated. Instead, its action depends on whether you handle the condition (using the RESP option or a HANDLE CONDITION command) and whether you specify NOQUEUE on the ALLOCATE command. If you do neither, SYSBUSY simply causes your task to be suspended until the session becomes available; then, control returns to your program at the first statement following the ALLOCATE command. If your program handles the SYSBUSY condition, the specified error processing is done, and the program must issue the ALLOCATE command again to establish the session. If you specify NOQUEUE, control is returned to the statement following the ALLOCATE command if the session is unavailable; again, you'll have to issue another ALLOCATE command to establish the session later.

- The STATE option returns a value that indicates the current state of the conversation. For a successful ALLOCATE command, the STATE value is always ALLOCATED. The value of the STATE field can be tested using the CICS keyword DFHVALUE, in much the same way as you use DFHRESP to test the response code returned in the RESP field:

```
IF CONVERSATION-STATE = DFHVALUE(ALLOCATED)
```

Coding example

The following example establishes a session with a system named SDOA.

```
1000-INITIATE-CONVERSATION.
*
    EXEC CICS
        ALLOCATE SYSID('SDOA')
                 RESP(RESPONSE-CODE)
    END-EXEC.

    IF RESPONSE-CODE = DFHRESP(NORMAL)
        MOVE EIBRSRCE TO CONVERSATION-ID
    ELSE
        PERFORM 9999-TERMINATE-PROGRAM
    END-IF.
```

The ASKTIME command

Function

Interval control. The ASKTIME command lets you obtain the current time and date. This information is stored in two Execute Interface Block fields: EIBTIME and EIBDATE. When a task is started, those fields are set to reflect the starting time and date for the task. ASKTIME simply updates those fields. You can also use the ABSTIME option to specify a field where CICS places an *absolute time*. You can then use this field in a FORMATTIME command to format the time in one of several ways.

Syntax

```
EXEC CICS
    ASKTIME [ ABSTIME(data-area) ]
END-EXEC.
```

Option

ABSTIME   Specifies a 15-digit packed-decimal field (PIC S9(15) COMP-3). The value returned represents the number of milliseconds that have elapsed since midnight, January 1, 1900. The value is suitable for timing operations or for conversion (using FORMATTIME) to other formats.

Exceptional conditions

No exceptional conditions are raised as a result of the ASKTIME command.

Notes and tips

- The time values stored in EIBTIME and EIBDATE are precise enough for most uses, such as time-stamping data or displaying the current time and date on the terminal screen. So use the ASKTIME command only when you need an absolutely precise time value.

- EIBDATE is a 7-digit packed-decimal field (PIC S9(7) COMP-3). The date is stored in the form *0cyyddd*, where *c* identifies the century (0 = 1900's, 1 = 2000's), *yy* is the last two digits of the year, and *ddd* is the current date's number within the year. January 1, 1990 is 0090001; December 31, 2001 is 0101365.

- EIBTIME is also a 7-digit packed-decimal field (PIC S9(7) COMP-3). The time is stored in the form *0hhmmss*, where *hh* represents hours (24-hour clock), *mm* represents minutes, and *ss* represents seconds. Midnight is stored as 0000000; one second before midnight is 0235959.

Coding example

This example shows how to obtain an absolute time and, using a FORMATTIME command, get the current day-of-week. ABSOLUTE-TIME is a 15-digit packed-decimal field (PIC S9(15) COMP-3), and DAY-OF-WEEK is a binary fullword (PIC S9(8) COMP).

```
    0500-GET-DAY-OF-WEEK.
*
      EXEC CICS
          ASKTIME ABSTIME(ABSOLUTE-TIME)
      END-EXEC.
      EXEC CICS
          FORMATTIME ABSTIME(ABSOLUTE-TIME)
                     DAYOFWEEK(DAY-OF-WEEK)
      END-EXEC.
```

The ASSIGN command

Function

Environment services. The ASSIGN command lets you obtain information from various system control areas. Although business applications don't usually need to use any of this run-time information, it can be useful at times.

Syntax

```
EXEC CICS
    ASSIGN option(data-area)...
END-EXEC.
```

Options

Note: You can specify up to 16 of the following options on a single ASSIGN command. Each must specify a data area, but the format of the data area depends on the option you specify.

ABCODE	4-byte alphanumeric field. Returns the abend code if an abend has occurred; otherwise, returns spaces.
ABDUMP	1-byte alphanumeric field. Returns HIGH-VALUE (hex FF) if a dump has been produced and ABCODE contains an abend code; otherwise, returns LOW-VALUE (hex 00).
ABPROGRAM	8-byte alphanumeric field. Returns the name of the most recently abended program.
ACTIVITY	16-byte alphanumeric field. Returns the name of a CICS Business Transaction Services (BTS) activity if this program is executing on behalf of the BTS activity.
ACTIVITYID	52-byte alphanumeric field. Returns the CICS-assigned identifier of a BTS activity-instance if this program is executing on behalf of the BTS activity.
ALTSCRNHT	Binary halfword (PIC S9(4) COMP). Returns the alternate height in lines of the display terminal.
ALTSCRNWD	Binary halfword (PIC S9(4) COMP). Returns the alternate width in columns of the display terminal.
APLKYBD	1-byte alphanumeric field. Returns HIGH-VALUE (hex FF) if the terminal supports the APL keyboard feature; otherwise, returns LOW-VALUE (hex 00).
APLTEXT	1-byte alphanumeric field. Returns HIGH-VALUE (hex FF) if the terminal supports the APL text feature; otherwise, returns LOW-VALUE (hex 00).
APPLID	8-byte alphanumeric field. Returns the name used to identify the CICS system to other CICS systems or to a batch system.

ASRAINTRPT	8-byte alphanumeric field. Returns the PSW interrupt information for the most recent ASRA, ASRB, ASRD, or AICA abend. If these abends do not occur during the current task, LOW-VALUE (hex zeros) is returned.
ASRAKEY	Binary fullword (PIC S9(8) COMP). Returns the execution key for the most recent ASRA, ASRB, AICA, or AEYD abend. The values that can be returned are CICSEXECKEY, USEREXECKEY, NONCICS, and NOTAPPLIC (if none of these abends has occurred). You can test for these values using the CICS keyword DFHVALUE.
ASRAPSW	8-byte alphanumeric field. Returns the PSW for the most recent ASRA, ASRB, ASRD, or AICA abend. If these abends do not occur during the current task, LOW-VALUE (hex zeros) is returned.
ASRAREGS	64-byte alphanumeric field. Returns the contents of the general registers for the most recent ASRA, ASRB, ASRD, or AICA abend. If these abends do not occur during the current task, LOW-VALUE (hex zeros) is returned.
ASRASPC	Binary fullword (PIC S9(8) COMP). Returns the type of space in control at the time of the last ASRA, ASRB, ASRD, or AICA abend. The values that can be returned are SUBSPACE, BASESPACE, and NOTAPPLIC (if none of these abends has occurred). You can test for these values using the CICS keyword DFHVALUE.
ASRASTG	Binary fullword (PIC S9(8) COMP). Returns the type of storage being addressed at the time of the last ASRA or AEYD abend. The values that can be returned are CICS, USER, READONLY, and NOTAPPLIC (if none of these abends has occurred). You can test for these values using the CICS keyword DFHVALUE.
BRIDGE	(TS 1.2 and later) 4-byte alphanumeric field. Returns the TRANSID of the bridge monitor that issued a START BREXIT TRANSID command.
BTRANS	1-byte alphanumeric field. Returns HIGH-VALUE (hex FF) if the terminal supports background transparency; otherwise, returns LOW-VALUE (hex 00).
CMDSEC	1-byte alphanumeric field. Returns the letter X if command security checking is enabled for the current task; otherwise, returns a space.
COLOR	1-byte alphanumeric field. Returns HIGH-VALUE (hex FF) if the terminal supports extended color; otherwise, returns LOW- VALUE (hex 00).
CWALENG	Binary halfword (PIC S9(4) COMP). Returns the length of the Common Work Area (CWA).
DEFSCRNHT	Binary halfword (PIC S9(4) COMP). Returns the default height in lines of the display terminal. If the task is not initiated from a terminal, an INVREQ condition occurs.
DEFSCRNWD	Binary halfword (PIC S9(4) COMP). Returns the default width in columns of the display terminal. If the task is not initiated from a terminal, an INVREQ condition occurs.
DELIMITER	1-byte alphanumeric field. Returns the data link control character received from an IBM 3600 terminal. Hex values are:

80	End-of-text (ETX)	10	Start of header (SOH)
40	End-of-block (ETB)	08	Transparent input
20	Inter-record separator (IRS)		

If the task is not initiated from a terminal, an INVREQ condition occurs.

DESTCOUNT	Binary halfword (PIC S9(4) COMP). Used with BMS overflow processing: following a ROUTE command, returns the number of different terminal types specified in the route list; during BMS overflow processing, returns a number indicating which type of terminal caused the overflow.
DESTID	8-byte alphanumeric field. Returns the destination identifier when batch data interchange is used.
DESTIDLENG	Binary halfword (PIC S9(4) COMP). Returns the length of the DESTID field.
DSSCS	1-byte alphanumeric field. Returns HIGH-VALUE (hex FF) if the terminal is an SCS device; otherwise, returns LOW-VALUE (hex 00).
DS3270	1-byte alphanumeric field. Returns HIGH-VALUE (hex FF) if the terminal is a 3270 device; otherwise, returns LOW-VALUE (hex 00).
EWASUPP	1-byte alphanumeric field. Returns HIGH-VALUE (hex FF) if the terminal supports Erase Write Alternative (EWA); otherwise, returns LOW-VALUE (hex 00).
EXTDS	1-byte alphanumeric field. Returns HIGH-VALUE (hex FF) if the terminal supports 3270 extended data streams; otherwise, returns LOW-VALUE (hex 00).
FACILITY	4-byte alphanumeric field. Returns the identifier of the facility, such as a terminal or destination, that initiated the task.
FCI	1-byte alphanumeric field. Returns a hex value that indicates the type of facility that initiated the task. Some of the values are: 01 A terminal 04 Interval control 08 A destination
GCHARS	Binary halfword (PIC S9(4) COMP). Returns the global identifier of the graphic character set used by the terminal. The numeric value can be from 1 to 65534.
GCODES	Binary halfword (PIC S9(4) COMP). Returns a number representing the code page used by the terminal. The numeric value can be from 1 to 65534.
GMMI	1-byte alphanumeric field. Returns HIGH-VALUE (hex FF) if the CICS "Good morning" message should be displayed at the terminal; otherwise, returns LOW-VALUE (hex 00).
HILIGHT	1-byte alphanumeric field. Returns HIGH-VALUE (hex FF) if the terminal supports extended highlighting; otherwise, returns LOW-VALUE (hex 00).
INITPARM	60-byte alphanumeric field. Returns a data area containing any initialization parameters specified for the program in the INITPARM system initialization parameter; otherwise, returns LOW-VALUE (hex 00).
INITPARMLEN	Binary halfword (PIC S9(4) COMP). Returns the length of the INITPARM field if one exists; otherwise, returns zero.
INPARTN	2-byte alphanumeric field. Returns the name of the most recent input partition.
INVOKINGPROG	8-byte alphanumeric field. Returns the name of the application program that used the LINK or XCTL command to link to or transfer control to the current program. If the current program is at the highest level, spaces are returned.

KATAKANA	1-byte alphanumeric field. Returns HIGH-VALUE (hex FF) if the terminal supports Katakana (a DBCS for Japanese characters); otherwise, returns LOW-VALUE (hex 00).
LANGINUSE	3-byte alphanumeric field. Returns a mnemonic code showing the current language in use. Some of the values available are:

ENU	US English	DEU	German
ENG	UK English	ITA	Italian
CHS	Simplified Chinese	NLD	Dutch
FRA	French		

LDCMNEM	2-byte alphanumeric field. Returns the logical device code (LDC) mnemonic for the device that has encountered BMS overflow.
LDCNUM	1-byte numeric field. Returns the LDC numeric value for the device that has encountered BMS overflow.
MAPCOLUMN	Binary halfword (PIC S9(4) COMP). Returns the number of the column where the current output map is positioned.
MAPHEIGHT	Binary halfword (PIC S9(4) COMP). Returns the height (in lines) of the current output map.
MAPLINE	Binary halfword (PIC S9(4) COMP). Returns the number of the line where the current output map is positioned.
MAPWIDTH	Binary halfword (PIC S9(4) COMP). Returns the width (in columns) of the current output map.
MSRCONTROL	1-byte alphanumeric field. Returns HIGH-VALUE (hex FF) if the terminal has a magnetic slot reader (MSR); otherwise, returns LOW-VALUE (hex 00).
NATLANGINUSE	1-byte alphanumeric field. Returns a mnemonic code that indicates the national language in use. Some of the values available are:

E	US English	G	German
A	UK English	I	Italian
C	Simplified Chinese	9	Dutch
F	French		

NETNAME	8-byte alphanumeric field. Returns the name of the VTAM logical unit that originated the task.
NEXTTRANSID	4-byte alphanumeric field. Returns the trans-id of the next transaction to be executed, specified either by a RETURN TRANSID command or a SET NEXTTRANSID command.
NUMTAB	1-byte alphanumeric field. Used for 2980 terminals to position the passbook printer.
OPCLASS	3-byte alphanumeric field. Returns the operator's class.
OPERKEYS	8-byte alphanumeric field. Returns a null string. This command is retained for compatibility with previous releases of CICS.
OPID	3-byte alphanumeric field. Returns the operator's ID number.
OPSECURITY	3-byte alphanumeric field. Returns a null string. This command is retained for compatibility with previous releases of CICS.
ORGABCODE	4-byte alphanumeric field. Returns the original abend code when repeated abends are encountered.

OUTLINE	1-byte alphanumeric field. Returns HIGH-VALUE (hex FF) if the terminal supports outlining; otherwise, returns LOW-VALUE (hex 00).
PAGENUM	Binary halfword (PIC S9(4) COMP). Used for BMS overflow processing; returns the current page number for the destination that caused the overflow.
PARTNPAGE	2-byte alphanumeric field. Returns the name of the most recent input partition that caused page overflow.
PARTNS	1-byte alphanumeric field. Returns HIGH-VALUE (hex FF) if the terminal supports partitions; otherwise, returns LOW-VALUE (hex 00).
PARTNSET	6-byte alphanumeric field. Returns the name of the partition set in use. If no partition set is in use, returns spaces.
PRINSYSID	4-byte alphanumeric field. Returns the local name of the principal facility in an APPC, MRO, or LU6.1 connection.
PROCESS	36-byte alphanumeric field. Returns the name of a CICS Business Transaction Services (BTS) process if this program is executing on behalf of the BTS activity.
PROCESSTYPE	8-byte alphanumeric field. Returns the process type of the BTS process if this program is executing on behalf of the BTS activity.
PROGRAM	8-byte alphanumeric field. Returns the name of the current program.
PS	1-byte alphanumeric field. Returns HIGH-VALUE (hex FF) if the terminal supports programmed symbols; otherwise, returns LOW-VALUE (hex 00).
QNAME	4-byte alphanumeric field. Returns the name of the transient data destination that caused the task to be initiated.
RESSEC	1-byte alphanumeric field. Returns the letter X if resource security checking is enabled for the current task; otherwise, returns a space.
RESTART	1-byte alphanumeric field. Returns HIGH-VALUE (hex FF) if a task has been restarted; otherwise, returns LOW-VALUE (hex 00).
RETURNPROG	8-byte alphanumeric field. Returns the name of the program that control will be returned to when the current program has finished executing. If the current program is at the highest level, spaces are returned.
SCRNHT	Binary halfword (PIC S9(4) COMP). Returns the height in lines of the 3270 terminal.
SCRNWD	Binary halfword (PIC S9(4) COMP). Returns the width in columns of the 3270 terminal.
SIGDATA	Binary halfword (PIC S9(4) COMP). Returns the signal data received from a logical unit.
SOSI	1-byte alphanumeric field. Returns HIGH-VALUE (hex FF) if the terminal supports DBCS fields; otherwise, returns LOW-VALUE (hex 00).

STARTCODE	2-byte alphanumeric field. Returns a code that indicates how the current task was started. Possible codes are:
	D Distributed program link (DPL) without the SYNCONRETURN option
	DS Distributed program link (DPL) with the SYNCONRETURN option
	QD Transient data ATI
	S Interval control START command without data
	SD Interval control START command with data
	SZ Interval control FEPI START command
	TD Terminal input
	U Other task attached by user
STATIONID	1-byte alphanumeric field. Returns the station identifier for a 2980 terminal.
SYSID	4-byte alphanumeric field. Returns the name of the local CICS system.
TASKPRIORITY	Binary halfword (PIC S9(4) COMP). Returns the current task's priority (0 to 255).
TCTUALENG	Binary halfword (PIC S9(4) COMP). Returns the length of the Terminal Control Table User Area (TCTUA).
TELLERID	1-byte alphanumeric field. Returns the teller identifier for a 2980 terminal.
TERMCODE	2-byte alphanumeric field. Returns a code indicating the terminal type and model.
TERMPRIORITY	Binary halfword (PIC S9(4) COMP). Returns the current terminal's priority (0 to 255).
TEXTKYBD	1-byte alphanumeric field. Returns HIGH-VALUE (hex FF) if the terminal supports TEXTKYBD; otherwise, returns LOW-VALUE (hex 00).
TEXTPRINT	1-byte alphanumeric field. Returns HIGH-VALUE (hex FF) if the terminal supports TEXTPRINT; otherwise, returns LOW-VALUE (hex 00).
TRANPRIORITY	Binary halfword (PIC S9(4) COMP). Returns the current transaction's priority (0 to 255).
TWALENG	Binary halfword (PIC S9(4) COMP). Returns the length of the Transaction Work Area (TWA).
UNATTEND	1-byte alphanumeric field. Returns HIGH-VALUE (hex FF) if the terminal is unattended; otherwise, returns LOW-VALUE (hex 00).
USERID	8-byte alphanumeric field. Returns the user-id of the currently signed-on user.
USERNAME	20-byte alphanumeric field. Returns the name of the currently signed-on user.
USERPRIORITY	Binary halfword (PIC S9(4) COMP). Returns the current user's priority (0 to 255).
VALIDATION	1-byte alphanumeric field. Returns HIGH-VALUE (hex FF) if the terminal supports field validation; otherwise, returns LOW-VALUE (hex 00).

Exceptional condition

INVREQ   The request is not allowed. The default action for this condition is to terminate the task.

Notes and tips

- The following ASSIGN command options are useful for programs that need to use advanced capabilities of 3270 devices:

BTRANS	HILIGHT	SCRNHT
COLOR	OUTLINE	SCRNWD
EXTDS	PS	VALIDATION

- The following ASSIGN command options are useful for programs that need to use advanced BMS facilities:

DESTCOUNT	MAPLINE
MAPCOLUMN	MAPWIDTH
MAPHEIGHT	PAGENUM

Coding example

This example shows how to obtain four terminal characteristics: screen height, screen width, color support, and field outlining support. This information can then be used to determine how data should be sent to the terminal.

```
EXEC CICS
    ASSIGN SCRNHT(SCREEN-HEIGHT)
           SCRNWD(SCREEN-WIDTH)
           COLOR(TERMINAL-COLOR-SW)
           OUTLINE(TERMINAL-OUTLINE-SW)
END-EXEC.
```

The BIF DEEDIT command

Function

Built-in functions. The BIF DEEDIT command formats alphanumeric data into numeric data. Non-numeric characters are removed, and the remaining data is right-justified and padded on the left with zeros.

Syntax

```
EXEC CICS
    BIF DEEDIT   FIELD(data-area)
               [ LENGTH(data-value) ]
END-EXEC.
```

Options

FIELD   Specifies the data area that contains the data to be de-edited.

LENGTH   Specifies a binary halfword (PIC S9(4) COMP) or literal value that indicates the length of the data area specified in the FIELD option.

Exceptional conditions

No exceptional conditions are raised as a result of the BIF DEEDIT command.

Notes and tips

- The BIF DEEDIT command doesn't really provide all the functions needed to properly process free-form input data. For example, decimal points are removed so 10.00 yields 1000.

Coding example

This example shows how to de-edit a 10-byte field. The LENGTH parameter is optional.

```
EXEC CICS
    BIF DEEDIT FIELD(NUMERIC-TEXT-ENTRY-FIELD)
               LENGTH(10)
END-EXEC.
```

The BUILD ATTACH command

Function

Terminal control. The BUILD ATTACH command creates an ATTACH Function Management Header (FMH) that can be used to initiate a background transaction in an LU6.1 or MRO session.

Syntax

```
EXEC CICS
    BUILD ATTACH    ATTACHID(name)
                  [ PROCESS(name) ]
                  [ RESOURCE(name) ]
                  [ RPROCESS(name) ]
                  [ RRESOURCE(name) ]
                  [ QUEUE(name) ]
                  [ IUTYPE(data-value) ]
                  [ DATASTR(data-value) ]
                  [ RECFM(data-value) ]
    END-EXEC.
```

Options

ATTACHID	Specifies a 1- to 8-character name for the ATTACH FMH. This name is later specified in the ATTACHID option of a SEND command to send the ATTACH FMH to the remote system.
PROCESS	Specifies the name of the process to be started on the remote system. If the remote system is a CICS system, this option names the trans-id of the transaction to be started.
RESOURCE	Specifies a value for the resource name field in the ATTACH FMH. Not used if the remote system is a CICS system.
RPROCESS	Specifies a value for the return process name field in the ATTACH FMH. Not used if the remote system is a CICS system.
RRESOURCE	Specifies a value for the resource field in the ATTACH FMH. Not used if the remote system is a CICS system.
QUEUE	Specifies a value for the queue name field in the ATTACH FMH. Not used if the remote system is a CICS system.
IUTYPE	Specifies a value for the interchange unit field in the ATTACH FMH as a binary halfword (PIC S9(4) COMP) or literal value. Not used if the remote system is a CICS system.
DATASTR	Specifies a value for the data stream profile field in the ATTACH FMH as a binary halfword (PIC S9(4) COMP) or literal value. Not used if the remote system is a CICS system.
RECFM	Specifies a value for the deblocking algorithm field in the ATTACH FMH as a binary halfword (PIC S9(4) COMP) or literal value. Not used if the remote system is a CICS system.

Exceptional conditions

No exceptional conditions are raised as a result of the BUILD ATTACH command.

Notes and tips

- The BUILD ATTACH command creates an ATTACH Function Management Header (FMH) that can be used to start a back-end transaction. If the remote system is a CICS system, you'll probably code only the ATTACHID and PROCESS options. The other options may or may not be required when the other system is non-CICS.

- An alternative way to start a back-end transaction on a remote CICS system is to place the trans-id in the first 4 characters of the first data sent to the remote system via a SEND command.

Coding example

The following example shows how to create an ATTACH FMH that specifies BAK1 as back-end trans-id. The ATTACHID value ('BAKFMH1') can then be specified in a SEND command to send the FMH to the remote system.

```
EXEC CICS
    BUILD ATTACH ATTACHID('BAKFMH1')
                 PROCESS('BAK1')
END-EXEC.
```

The CANCEL command

Function

Interval control. The CANCEL command cancels the effect of a DELAY, POST, or START command.

Syntax

```
EXEC CICS
    CANCEL [ REQID(name)
                [ SYSID(systemname) ]
                [ TRANSID(name) ] ]
END-EXEC.
```

Options

REQID	Specifies an 8-character request-id that was associated with the command you want cancelled. The only case where REQID isn't required is when you're cancelling a POST command you issued earlier from within the same task. In that case, don't code any options on the CANCEL command. REQID is required if you code TRANSID or SYSID.
SYSID	Specifies the 1- to 4-character name of a remote system where a DELAY, POST, or START command is to be cancelled.
TRANSID	Specifies a 4-character transaction identifier for the transaction you want cancelled. TRANSID isn't normally used, since REQID is required to uniquely identify the START command, and thus the transaction, to be cancelled.

Exceptional conditions

Note: The default action for these conditions is to terminate the task.

ISCINVREQ	An undeterminable error occurred on the remote system specified in the SYSID option.
NOTAUTH	The transaction entry specified that resource security checking should be done, and the operator is not authorized to cancel the requested interval control function.
NOTFND	There is no unexpired interval control command associated with the request identifier you specified.
SYSIDERR	The system identified by SYSID could not be located or accessed.

Notes and tips

- To cancel an interval control request, you must usually supply the request-id of the command you want to cancel. There are two ways to get the request-id. The first is to retrieve it from EIBREQID immediately after the DELAY, POST, or START command and store it in a variable for later use. The second is to assign your own request-id by coding the REQID option on the DELAY, POST, or START command. Usually, it's easier to let CICS assign the request-id and just move it from EIBREQID if you need to use it later.

- The CANCEL command won't work if the interval control command you want to cancel has already expired. For example, if you issue a START command to start a task in 10 minutes, you can't cancel it with a CANCEL command once the 10-minute period has elapsed and the task has started. If you issue a CANCEL command for an interval control command that has expired, the NOTFND condition is raised.

Coding example

This example shows how to cancel a command whose request-id is stored in a field named START-REQUEST-ID.

```
EXEC CICS
    CANCEL REQID(START-REQUEST-ID)
END-EXEC.
```

The CHANGE PASSWORD command

Function

Authentication. The CHANGE PASSWORD command lets you change a user's password. The password is recorded in an external security manager (ESM) like RACF.

Syntax

```
EXEC CICS
    CHANGE    PASSWORD(data-value)
              NEWPASSWORD(data-value)
              USERID(data-value)
            [ ESMREASON(data-area) ]
            [ ESMRESP(data-area) ]
    END-EXEC.
```

Options

PASSWORD	Specifies the current 8-character password for the specified user.
NEWPASSWORD	Specifies the new 8-character password that's to replace the current password for the user. The user's password is changed only if the PASSWORD option specifies a valid current password.
USERID	Specifies the 8-character user-id as it appears in the ESM.
ESMREASON	Specifies a binary fullword (PIC S9(8) COMP) field that returns a reason condition from the external security manager.
ESMRESP	Specifies a binary fullword (PIC S9(8) COMP) field that returns a response code from the external security manager.

Exceptional conditions

Note: The default action for these conditions is to terminate the task.

INVREQ	Either the external security manager is not responding or there is an unknown return code in ESMRESP.
NOAUTH	The operator is not authorized to change the password for the specified user-id, the supplied password is wrong, or the new password specified is not acceptable.
USERIDERR	The user-id specified in the USERID option is not known to the external security manager.

Notes and tips

- There aren't many occasions for using the CHANGE PASSWORD command unless your application is in charge of maintaining user accounts. If that's the case, having the ability to change someone's password without having to directly access an external security manager like RACF can come in handy.

- Don't confuse the ESMRESP option with the normal RESP option for this command. ESMRESP will only return condition codes from the external security manager. However, if CHANGE PASSWORD encounters an exceptional condition, the condition code will be returned in RESP.

- Remember to clear the password fields as soon as you can. That's because these fields can potentially be revealed in a transaction or system dump should the transaction abend.

Coding example

The following code shows how the CHANGE PASSWORD command can be used to change a user's password.

```
EXEC CICS
    CHANGE  PASSWORD(OLD-PASSWORD)
            NEWPASSWORD(NEW-PASSWORD)
            USERID(CURRENT-USERID)
            ESMRESP(RACF-RESPONSE-CODE)
    END-EXEC.
```

The CHANGE TASK command

Function

Task control. The CHANGE TASK command changes the priority of the current task.

Syntax

```
EXEC CICS
    CHANGE TASK [ PRIORITY(data-value) ]
END-EXEC.
```

Option

PRIORITY   Specifies a binary fullword (PIC S9(8) COMP) or literal value that indicates the new dispatching priority for the task. The value must be in the range of 0 to 255.

Exceptional condition

INVREQ   The PRIORITY value is not in the range of 0 to 255. The default action for this condition is to terminate the task.

Notes and tips

• It's unlikely that you'll need to change your task's priority. If you do, keep in mind that when you issue the CHANGE TASK command, your program gives control back to the CICS task dispatcher. As a result, other pending tasks with higher priority may be dispatched before control returns to your program.

• You can use the ASSIGN TASKPRIORITY command to determine a task's current dispatching priority.

Coding example

The following example changes the dispatching priority of the current task to 100.

```
EXEC CICS
    CHANGE TASK PRIORITY(100)
END-EXEC.
```

The CONNECT PROCESS command

Function

APPC mapped conversation. The CONNECT PROCESS command initiates an application program on a remote system once a session has been established with an ALLOCATE command.

Syntax

```
EXEC CICS
    CONNECT PROCESS { CONVID(name) | SESSION(name) }
                    { PROCNAME(data-area)
                          PROCLENGTH(data-value) }
                    { PARTNER(name) }
                      SYNCLEVEL(data-value)
                    [ PIPLIST(data-area)
                         [ PIPLENGTH(data-value) ] ]
                    [ STATE(cvda) ]
    END-EXEC.
```

Options

CONVID	Specifies the 4-character conversation-id obtained from the Execute Interface Block field EIBRSRCE following a successful ALLOCATE command.
SESSION	A synonym for CONVID provided for compatibility with earlier releases. CONVID is preferred.
PROCNAME	Specifies the name of the process to be started on the remote system. If the remote system is another CICS system, PROCNAME specifies a 1- to 4-character transaction identifier. If the remote system is not a CICS system, the PROCNAME can be up to 64 characters in length.
PROCLENGTH	Specifies the length of the PROCNAME field as a binary halfword (PIC S9(4) COMP) or literal value.
PARTNER	Specifies the 8-character name of a set of definitions that includes the name of a remote partner transaction. This option can be used as an alternative to PROCNAME and PROCLENGTH.
SYNCLEVEL	Specifies the number 0, 1, or 2 to indicate the degree of synchronization required between the programs. SYNCLEVEL 0 (None) indicates that no synchronization is required. SYNCLEVEL 1 (Confirm) provides the low-level support required for applications to perform their own synchronization. SYNCLEVEL 2 (Syncpoint) automatically coordinates SYNCPOINT and SYNCPOINT ROLLBACK commands.
PIPLIST	Specifies an area that contains a list of Process Initialization Parameters (PIP) that is passed to the remote program.
PIPLENGTH	Specifies a binary halfword (PIC S9(4) COMP) or literal value that indicates the length of the PIPLIST area.

STATE   Specifies a binary fullword (PIC S9(8) COMP) where CICS places state
               information. The values returned are:

ALLOCATED	RECEIVE
CONFFREE	ROLLBACK
CONFRECEIVE	SEND
CONFSEND	SYNCFREE
FREE	SYNCRECEIVE
PENDFREE	SYNCSEND
PENDRECEIVE	

Exceptional conditions

Note: The default action for these conditions is to terminate the task.

INVREQ	The request is not allowed.
LENGERR	A length error has occurred.
NOTALLOC	The conversation has not been properly allocated.
PARTNERIDERR	The name specified in the PARTNER option is not recognized by CICS.
TERMERR	A session error has occurred.

Notes and tips

- The STATE option returns a value that indicates the current state of the conversation. For a successful CONNECT PROCESS command, the STATE field is
set to SEND. The value of the STATE field can be tested using the CICS
keyword DFHVALUE, in much the same way as you use DFHRESP to test the
response code returned in the RESP field:

```
IF CONVERSATION-STATE = DFHVALUE(SEND)
```

- CICS doesn't use the data in the PIPLIST field, so you can use it to pass data to
the started program. The PIPLIST consists of one or more PIPs. Each PIP
consists of a binary halfword length field, a binary halfword field set to zero,
and a variable-length data area. The length field should be set to the length of
the data area plus 4. For example, here's a PIPLIST with two PIPs:

```
01  PIP-LIST.
    05  PIP-1.
        10  FILLER      PIC S9(04)  COMP  VALUE 54.
        10  FILLER      PIC S9(04)  COMP  VALUE ZERO.
        10  PIP1-DATA   PIC X(50).
    05  PIP-2.
        10  FILLER      PIC S9(04)  COMP  VALUE 20.
        10  FILLER      PIC S9(04)  COMP  VALUE ZERO.
        10  PIP2-DATA   PIC X(16).
```

The PIPLENGTH option should specify the complete length of the PIPLIST
field (74 in this case).

Coding example

The following example shows how the ALLOCATE and CONNECT PROCESS
commands are used together to initiate a conversation with a transaction named
RMT1 on a remote system named SDOA.

```
    1000-INITIATE-CONVERSATION.
*
    EXEC CICS
        ALLOCATE SYSID('SDOA')
                 RESP(RESPONSE-CODE)
    END-EXEC.

    IF RESPONSE-CODE = DFHRESP(NORMAL)
        MOVE EIBRSRCE TO CONVERSATION-ID
    ELSE
        PERFORM 9999-TERMINATE-PROGRAM
    END-IF.

    EXEC CICS
        CONNECT PROCESS CONVID(CONVERSATION-ID)
                        PROCNAME('RMT1')
                        PROCLENGTH(4)
                        SYNCLEVEL(2)
                        RESP(RESPONSE-CODE)
    END-EXEC.

    IF RESPONSE-CODE NOT = DFHRESP(NORMAL)
        PERFORM 9999-TERMINATE-PROGRAM
    END-IF.
```

The CONVERSE command

Function

APPC mapped conversation/Terminal control. The CONVERSE command sends
data to a remote process and receives a response. It combines the functions of a
SEND and a RECEIVE command.

Syntax

```
EXEC CICS
    CONVERSE [ CONVID(name) | SESSION(name) ]
             [ ATTACHID(name) ]
               FROM(data-area)
             { FROMLENGTH(data-value)   }
             { FROMFLENGTH(data-value)  }
             { INTO(data-area)   }
             { SET(pointer-ref) }
             { TOLENGTH(data-area)   }
             { TOFLENGTH(data-area) }
             [ { MAXLENGTH(data-value)   }
               { MAXFLENGTH(data-value) } ]
             [ NOTRUNCATE ]
             [ STATE(cvda) ]
    END-EXEC.
```

Options

CONVID	Specifies the 4-character conversation-id obtained from the Execute Interface Block field EIBRSRCE following a successful ALLOCATE command.
SESSION	A synonym for CONVID provided for compatibility with earlier releases. CONVID is preferred.
ATTACHID	Specifies the 1- to 8-character name for the ATTACH FMH that was specified on the BUILD ATTACH command.
FROM	Specifies the data area to be sent to the remote program.
FROMLENGTH	Specifies a binary halfword (PIC S9(4) COMP) or literal value that indicates the length of the FROM area.
FROMFLENGTH	Specifies a binary fullword (PIC S9(8) COMP) or literal value that indicates the length of the FROM area. A fullword alternative to FROMLENGTH.
INTO	Specifies the area where data received from the remote program is to be placed.
SET	Specifies a binary fullword (PIC S9(8) COMP) where the address of the received data is placed.

TOLENGTH	Specifies a binary halfword (PIC S9(4) COMP) where CICS places the length of the received data. If you specify INTO but not MAXLENGTH, the initial value of the TOLENGTH field is used to determine the maximum length of the data that can be received.
TOFLENGTH	Specifies a binary fullword (PIC S9(4) COMP) where CICS places the length of the received data. If you specify INTO but not MAXLENGTH, the initial value of the TOLENGTH field is used to determine the maximum length of the data that can be received. A fullword alternative to TOLENGTH.
MAXLENGTH	Specifies a binary halfword (PIC S9(4) COMP) or literal value that indicates the maximum length of the data that can be received.
MAXFLENGTH	Specifies a binary fullword (PIC S9(8) COMP) or literal value that indicates the maximum length of the data that can be received. A fullword alternative to MAXLENGTH.
NOTRUNCATE	Specifies that if the length of the received data is greater than the maximum specified, the excess data should not be discarded. Instead, it should be saved and used to fulfill subsequent RECEIVE commands. If NOTRUNCATE is omitted, excess data is discarded.
STATE	Specifies a binary fullword (PIC S9(8) COMP) where CICS places state information. The values that can be returned are:

ALLOCATED	RECEIVE
CONFFREE	ROLLBACK
CONFRECEIVE	SEND
CONFSEND	SYNCFREE
FREE	SYNCRECEIVE
PENDFREE	SYNCSEND
PENDRECEIVE	

Exceptional conditions

Note: The default action for all of these conditions except EOC and SIGNAL is to terminate the task. The default action for the EOC and SIGNAL conditions is to ignore the condition.

EOC	The end of the message chain has been received. This is the normal response code for CONVERSE.
INVREQ	The request is not allowed.
LENGERR	The data received from the remote process is longer than the maximum specified, or the specification for the maximum length is invalid.
NOTALLOC	The conversation has not been properly allocated.
SIGNAL	The remote program has executed an ISSUE SIGNAL command.
TERMERR	A session error has occurred.

Notes and tips

- The STATE option returns a value that indicates the current state of the conversation. If both the SEND and RECEIVE are successful, the STATE field will be set to SEND. The value of the STATE field can be tested using the CICS keyword DFHVALUE, in much the same way as you use DFHRESP to test the response code returned in the RESP field:

```
IF CONVERSATION-STATE = DFHVALUE(SEND)
```

- If your conversation is designed to allow the partner program to use the ISSUE SIGNAL command, you should test for the SIGNAL condition. When you do, remember that EOC is a normal response for the CONVERSE command.

Coding example

The following example shows a CONVERSE command that instructs a back-end transaction to return data for a particular customer. In this example, the customer data is stored in three distinct files. Rather than issue three distributed READ commands, the front-end program just sends a customer number to the back-end program, which reads the three files and returns the combined information to the front-end program.

```
    WORKING-STORAGE SECTION.
    .
    .
    01  SEND-MESSAGE.
        05   SM-CUSTOMER-NUMBER      PIC X(06).
    01  RECEIVE-MESSAGE.
        05   RM-CUSTOMER-FOUND-SW    PIC X(01).
             88   RM-CUSTOMER-FOUND       VALUE 'Y'.
        05   RM-CUST-DATA-1          PIC X(520).
        05   RM-CUST-DATA-2          PIC X(300).
        05   RM-CUST-DATA-3          PIC X(255).
    01  RECEIVE-MESSAGE-LENGTH       PIC S9(4) COMP  VALUE '1076'.
    .
    .
    PROCEDURE DIVISION.
    .
    .
    2300-GET-CUSTOMER-DATA.
*
        MOVE CUSTNOI TO SM-CUSTOMER-NUMBER.
        EXEC CICS
            CONVERSE CONVID(CONVERSATION-ID)
                     FROM(SEND-MESSAGE)
                     FROMLENGTH(6)
                     INTO(RECEIVE-MESSAGE)
                     TOLENGTH(RECEIVE-MESSAGE-LENGTH)
        END-EXEC.
        IF RM-CUSTOMER-FOUND
            MOVE RM-CUST-DATA-1 TO CUSTOMER-MASTER-RECORD
            MOVE RM-CUST-DATA-2 TO ACCOUNT-MASTER-RECORD
            MOVE RM-CUST-DATA-3 TO CUSTOMER-HISTORY-RECORD
        END-IF.
```

The DEFINE COUNTER command

Function

Named counter server. The DEFINE COUNTER command lets you define a new named counter in a named counter pool of the coupling facility.

Syntax

```
EXEC CICS
    DEFINE  { COUNTER(name) | DCOUNTER(name) }
            [ POOL(name) ]
            [ VALUE(data-value) ]
            [ MINIMUM(data-value) ]
            [ MAXIMUM(data-value) ]
    END-EXEC.
```

Options

COUNTER	Specifies the 16-character name of the named counter to be created. All the value fields for this counter will then be handled as signed binary fullwords (PIC S9(8) COMP).
DCOUNTER	Specifies the 16-character name of the named counter to be created. All the value fields for this counter will then be handled as unsigned binary doublewords (PIC 9(18) COMP).
POOL	Specifies the 8-character name of the pool in which the named counter is to be created. If there's no matching entry in the DFHNCOPT options table, the default named counter pool on the NCPLDFT system initialization parameter is used.
VALUE	Specifies a signed binary fullword (PIC S9(8) COMP), unsigned binary doubleword (PIC 9(18) COMP), or literal value that indicates the starting value for the counter. You can specify a number that is equal to, or greater than, the minimum value specified and up to the maximum value plus 1. If you omit this option and the MINIMUM option, the counter is created with an initial value of zero.
MINIMUM	Specifies a signed binary fullword (PIC S9(8) COMP), unsigned binary doubleword (PIC 9(18) COMP), or literal value that indicates the minimum value for the counter. The counter is reset to this value after a REWIND COUNTER command. If MINIMUM is omitted, the default counter minimum is set to LOW-VALUE (hex zeros). However, if MINIMUM is coded, the VALUE option must also be coded or the CICS translator will issue an error.
MAXIMUM	Specifies a signed binary fullword (PIC S9(8) COMP), unsigned binary doubleword (PIC 9(18) COMP), or literal value that indicates the maximum value for the counter. Once the counter reaches this number, it must be reset by the REWIND COUNTER command. If MAXIMUM is omitted, the default counter maximum is set to HIGH-VALUE (hex FF).

Exceptional conditions

INVREQ   The statement was coded improperly or there was a problem defining the named counter in the coupling facility. The default action for this condition is to terminate the task.

Notes and tips

- You use the DEFINE COUNTER command to create a named counter that generates unique sequence numbers. You can then use these values for functions such as assigning control numbers (like customer, account, or invoice numbers) by using the GET COUNTER command.

- The named counter facility is designed to run in a Parallel Sysplex environment. That means that the facility is controlled by a named counter server, allowing multiple regions (CICS or non-CICS) to draw from the same counter.

- Before the named counter facility was available, in order to share a set of sequence numbers in a CICS application, you had to use either a shared CICS data table or a CICS common work area (CWA) to store a number that was updated by each application. The problem with the shared CICS data table is that all of the CICS regions have to reside on the same MVS image. And the problem with the CWA is that it can only be used within the same CICS region.

- If you use a field, not a literal value, to assign a COUNTER or DCOUNTER name, make sure that the field is padded with trailing spaces if the name is less than 16 characters long.

Coding example

The following example shows a DEFINE COUNTER command that defines a counter named ORDERINV that's used to assign invoice numbers. The counter is created in a pool area named MMA, and its initial value is 100 with a maximum value of 999999.

```
EXEC CICS
    DEFINE COUNTER('ORDERINV')
           POOL('MMA')
           VALUE(100)
           MINIMUM(100)
           MAXIMUM(999999)
END-EXEC.
```

The DELAY command

Function

Interval control. The DELAY command lets you suspend your task until a specified time interval has elapsed or a specified time of day has arrived.

Syntax

```
EXEC CICS
    DELAY [ { INTERVAL(hhmmss) }
            { TIME(hhmmss) }
            { FOR [HOURS(hh)] [MINUTES(mins)] [SECONDS(secs)] }
            { UNTIL [HOURS(hh)] [MINUTES(mins)] [SECONDS(secs)] } ]
          [ REQID(name) ]
    END-EXEC.
```

Options

Note: If INTERVAL, TIME, FOR, and UNTIL are all omitted, INTERVAL(0) is assumed.

INTERVAL   Specifies a duration for the delay. You can code a literal in the form *hhmmss*; leading zeros can be omitted. Or, you can code the data name for a 7-digit packed-decimal field (PIC S9(7) COMP-3) with a value in the form *0hhmmss*.

TIME   Specifies the time of day when the delay will end. You can code a literal in the form *hhmmss*; leading zeros can be omitted. Or, you can code the data name for a 7-digit packed-decimal field (PIC S9(7) COMP-3) with a value in the form *0hhmmss*.

FOR   Specifies that the HOURS, MINUTES, and SECONDS options indicate a duration for the delay.

UNTIL   Specifies that the HOURS, MINUTES, and SECONDS options indicate a time of day when the delay will end.

HOURS   Specifies a binary fullword (PIC S9(8) COMP) in the range of 0 to 99.

MINUTES   Specifies a binary fullword (PIC S9(8) COMP) in the range of 0 to 59 when HOURS or SECONDS is also specified, or 0 to 5999 when only MINUTES is specified.

SECONDS   Specifies a binary fullword (PIC S9(8) COMP) in the range of 0 to 59 when HOURS or MINUTES is also specified, or 0 to 359999 when only SECONDS is specified.

REQID   Specifies a 1- to 8-character request identifier that's associated with the DELAY command.

Exceptional conditions

EXPIRED   The time specified in the TIME or UNTIL option has already expired. The default action for this condition is to return control immediately to your program.

INVREQ   The command is not valid, or the specified hours, minutes, or seconds are out of range. The default action for this condition is to terminate the task.

Notes and tips

- There aren't many good uses for the DELAY command; most installations are more concerned with speeding up CICS response time than with delaying it. For some projects, it might be appropriate to force a minimum response time on terminal transactions. To do that with a DELAY command, get the time from EIBTIME or ASKTIME when the task first starts. Add a fixed amount to this time, and then, just before issuing the SEND MAP command, issue a DELAY command specifying the calculated time in the TIME or UNTIL option. A better alternative, however, is to use the POST and WAIT EVENT commands.

- One possible use for the DELAY command is when your program needs to retry an operation after a failure, allowing time for an operator to correct the problem that caused the failure. In this case, you might delay your task 15 seconds before retrying the operation. Be sure, though, to limit the number of retries so that your task doesn't wait indefinitely.

- There are two ways to use the HOURS, MINUTES, and SECONDS options following FOR. If you use them in combination, the ranges are 0 to 99 for HOURS, 0 to 59 for MINUTES, and 0 to 59 for SECONDS. However, if you specify only one option, you can use the larger ranges: 0 to 99 for HOURS, 0 to 5999 for MINUTES, or 0 to 359999 for SECONDS. For example, you could specify FOR MINUTES(1) SECONDS(30), or you could specify FOR SECONDS(90). Both have the same effect.

- If you use the REQID option, be sure to pass the request identifier value to other programs so that they can cancel the DELAY request if necessary. To do this, you can store the value in a TS queue or in the TWA.

Coding examples

These examples show two ways to delay a task for 15 seconds.

```
EXEC CICS
    DELAY INTERVAL(15)
END-EXEC.

EXEC CICS
    DELAY FOR SECONDS(15)
END-EXEC.
```

The DELETE command

Function

File control. The DELETE command removes a record from a file. The record may have been previously read by a READ command with the UPDATE option, or the record may be retrieved and deleted in a single operation by the DELETE command. In addition, you can specify a generic key to delete more than one record. The file can be a VSAM KSDS or RRDS, a path, or a data table, but not an ESDS.

Syntax

```
EXEC CICS
    DELETE   FILE(filename)
        [ { RIDFLD(data-area)
              [ KEYLENGTH(data-value)
                  [ GENERIC
                       [ NUMREC(data-area) ] ] ] }
          { TOKEN(data-area) } ]
        [ RBA | RRN ]
        [ NOSUSPEND ]
        [ SYSID(systemname) ]
    END-EXEC.
```

Options

FILE	Specifies the 1- to 8-character name of the data set that contains the record to be deleted. If SYSID is also specified, the data set named is assumed to be on a remote system regardless of whether or not the name is also defined in the File Control Table (FCT).
RIDFLD	Specifies a data area that identifies the record to be deleted. If omitted, the record must have been previously retrieved using a READ command with the UPDATE option. The contents of the RIDFLD field depends on whether RBA or RRN is specified; if neither is specified, the RIDFLD field contains a key for a VSAM KSDS or path. For a generic delete (see the KEYLENGTH and GENERIC options below), the RIDFLD must still be as long as the file's defined key length.
TOKEN	Specifies a binary fullword (PIC S9(8) COMP) that represents a unique identifier for this DELETE request. Use this option to associate this DELETE request with a previous READ, READNEXT, or READPREV for UPDATE request.
KEYLENGTH	Specifies a binary halfword (PIC S9(4) COMP) or literal value that indicates the length of the key. Used for a generic delete along with the GENERIC option; must be less than the file's defined key length. Also used when the SYSID option is specified. Not valid if RBA or RRN is specified.

GENERIC	Specifies that only a part of the key in the RIDFLD field should be used, as indicated by the KEYLENGTH option. All records with a key whose leftmost character positions (as specified by KEYLENGTH) match the RIDFLD field are deleted.
NUMREC	Specifies a binary halfword (PIC S9(4) COMP) or literal value that CICS sets to the number of records deleted by a generic delete. Valid only when GENERIC and KEYLENGTH are specified.
RBA	Specifies that the RIDFLD field is a relative byte address (RBA) for a VSAM KSDS. An RBA is a binary fullword (PIC S9(8) COMP). This option can't be used for data tables, files opened in RLS mode, or KSDS files that can hold more than 4GB of data.
RRN	Specifies that the RIDFLD is a relative record number (RRN) for a VSAM RRDS. An RRN is a binary fullword (PIC S9(8) COMP). The RRN of the first record in an RRDS is 1.
NOSUSPEND	(RLS only) Specifies that the DELETE request is not to wait if the VSAM file has an active lock against the record. This includes records locked as a result of a deadlock.
SYSID	Specifies the 1- to 4-character name of a remote system that contains the file.

Exceptional conditions

Note: The default action for these conditions is to terminate the task.

CHANGED	A delete request was issued for a record in a data table defined in the coupling facility that has since been changed.
DISABLED	The data set is disabled, probably as a result of the master terminal operator explicitly disabling the file using CEMT SET DISABLE.
DUPKEY	Occurs only when deleting via an alternate index path that allows duplicate keys; indicates that more than one record with the specified key exists. The DELETE command deletes only the first.
FILENOTFOUND	The file named in the FILE option can't be found in the file resource definition.
ILLOGIC	An error occurred that doesn't fall within any of the other response conditions listed.
INVREQ	The delete request is prohibited by the file's FCT entry. Can also occur if the record was not previously retrieved by a READ command with the UPDATE option and the DELETE command doesn't specify RIDFLD or if a READ UPDATE command was issued for the file and the DELETE command does specify RIDFLD.
IOERR	An I/O error occurred.
ISCINVREQ	An undeterminable error occurred on the remote system specified in the SYSID option.
LOADING	A delete request was issued to a user-maintained table while it was loading.
LOCKED	An attempt was made to delete a record specifying the RIDFLD option but a retained lock exists against this key.

NOTAUTH	A resource security check has failed on the file because the operator is not authorized to access the data set.
NOTFND	The specified record could not be located.
NOTOPEN	The file is not open.
RECORDBUSY	The record is currently locked by a VSAM active lock. This only occurs if the NOSUSPEND option is used in the DELETE command.
SYSIDERR	The system identified by SYSID could not be located or accessed.

Notes and tips

- For recoverable files, the DELETE command causes your task to hold the control interval that contains the record until your task ends. While it is held, no other task can update any of the records in that CI.

- To prevent deadlock situations, follow two rules: (1) update files in alphabetical order and (2) update records in ascending key sequence.

- The only exceptional condition you normally need to anticipate for the DELETE command is NOTFND. If you're deleting records via a path that allows non-unique keys, you should also provide for DUPKEY.

- When the DELETE command is used to delete records from a CICS-maintained data table, the records are deleted from both the in-memory and the VSAM KSDS data tables.

- When the DELETE command is used to delete records from a user-maintained data table, the records are only deleted from the in-memory table.

- The RBA and NOSUSPEND options are affected by whether the file being accessed is in RLS (record level sharing) mode. VSAM files in RLS mode can be shared and updated by multiple CICS regions.

Coding example (READ UPDATE and DELETE)

This example retrieves and deletes a VSAM KSDS record. Two separate program modules are involved. After module 3500 is invoked to read the record, the program determines if module 3600 should be invoked to delete the record. (If the read and delete operations are always performed together, it would be better to combine them as in the next example.)

```
        PERFORM 3500-READ-ACCOUNT-RECORD.
        IF RECORD-FOUND
            PERFORM 3600-DELETE-ACCOUNT-RECORD
        END-IF.
            .
            .
    *
     3500-READ-ACCOUNT-RECORD.
    *
        EXEC CICS
            READ FILE('ACCOUNT')
                INTO(ACCOUNT-RECORD)
                RIDFLD(AR-ACCOUNT-NUMBER)
                UPDATE
                RESP(RESPONSE-CODE)
        END-EXEC.

        EVALUATE RESPONSE-CODE
            WHEN DFHRESP(NORMAL)
                MOVE 'Y' TO RECORD-FOUND-SW
            WHEN DFHRESP(NOTFND)
                MOVE 'N' TO RECORD-FOUND-SW
            WHEN OTHER
                PERFORM 9999-TERMINATE-PROGRAM
        END-PERFORM.
    *
     3600-DELETE-ACCOUNT-RECORD.
    *
        EXEC CICS
            DELETE FILE('ACCOUNT')
        END-EXEC.
```

Coding example (DELETE only)

This example retrieves and deletes a VSAM KSDS record with a single DELETE command; no READ UPDATE command is involved. The NOTFND condition is provided for in case the record to be deleted doesn't exist.

```
3500-DELETE-ACCOUNT-RECORD.
*
      EXEC CICS
          DELETE FILE('ACCOUNT')
                 RIDFLD(AR-ACCOUNT-NUMBER)
                 RESP(RESPONSE-CODE)
      END-EXEC.

      EVALUATE RESPONSE-CODE
         WHEN DFHRESP(NORMAL)
            MOVE 'Y' TO RECORD-FOUND-SW
         WHEN DFHRESP(NOTFND)
            MOVE 'N' TO RECORD-FOUND-SW
         WHEN OTHER
            PERFORM 9999-TERMINATE-PROGRAM
      END-PERFORM.
```

The DELETE COUNTER command

Function

Named counter server. The DELETE COUNTER command lets you delete a named counter from a specified pool.

Syntax

```
EXEC CICS
    DELETE   { COUNTER(name) | DCOUNTER(name) }
             [ POOL(name) ]
END-EXEC.
```

Options

COUNTER   Specifies the 16-character name of the fullword counter to be deleted.

DCOUNTER   Specifies the 16-character name of the doubleword counter to be deleted.

POOL   Specifies the 8-character name of the pool in which the named counter is to be deleted. If there's no matching entry in the DFHNCOPT options table, the default named counter pool on the NCPLDFT system initialization parameter is used.

Exceptional condition

INVREQ   The statement was coded improperly or there was a problem finding the named counter in the coupling facility. The default action for this condition is to terminate the task.

Notes and tips

- The named counter facility is designed to run in a Parallel Sysplex environment. That means that the facility is controlled by a named counter server, allowing multiple regions to draw from the same counter.
- If you use a field, not a literal value, to assign a COUNTER or DCOUNTER name, make sure that the field is padded with trailing spaces if the name is less than 16 characters long.

Coding example

The following example shows a DELETE COUNTER command that deletes a counter named ORDERINV in a pool area named MMA.

```
EXEC CICS
    DELETE COUNTER('ORDERINV')
           POOL('MMA')
END-EXEC.
```

The DELETEQ TD command

Function

Transient data. The DELETEQ TD command deletes the records in an intra-partition transient data queue, reclaiming the space occupied by its records and removing any records that haven't been read.

Syntax

```
EXEC CICS
    DELETEQ TD   QUEUE(name)
                 [ SYSID(systemname) ]
END-EXEC.
```

Options

QUEUE	Specifies the 1- to 4-character name of the destination to be deleted.
SYSID	Specifies the 1- to 4-character name of a remote system that contains the queue.

Exceptional conditions

Note: The default action for these conditions is to terminate the task.

DISABLED	The queue has been disabled.
INVREQ	The QUEUE option species an extrapartition queue.
ISCINVREQ	An undeterminable error occurred on the remote system specified in the SYSID option.
LOCKED	The request can't be performed because use of the queue has been restricted. This can happen to any request for a logically-recoverable queue defined with WAIT(YES) and WAITACTION(REJECT) in the TDQUEUE resource definition.
NOTAUTH	A resource security check has failed on the specified queue because the user is not authorized to access the destination.
QIDERR	The destination specified in the QUEUE option isn't defined to CICS in the Destination Control Table (DCT).
SYSIDERR	The system identified by SYSID could not be located or accessed.

Notes and tips

- You should always delete an transient data queue once its records have been processed. Although you can't retrieve records once they've been processed, the space they occupy is still allocated to the destination. So unless you issue a DELETEQ TD command, that space isn't available for other uses.

- It's important to realize that the DELETEQ TD command deletes the records in a destination but doesn't delete the destination itself. Destinations must be defined separately to CICS, so they can't be created or deleted while CICS is running.

- You can issue a DELETEQ TD command only against an intrapartition transient data queue. If you specify an extrapartition queue, the INVREQ condition will be raised. (An intrapartition transient data queue can be accessed only from within CICS, while an extrapartition transient data queue can also be accessed by batch programs running outside of CICS.)

Coding example

This example shows how to issue a DELETEQ TD command to delete a transient data queue. No exceptional conditions are handled. The name of the destination is stored in the 4-character alphanumeric field named DESTINATION-ID.

```
    5400-DELETE-TRANSIENT-DATA.
*
    EXEC CICS
        DELETEQ TD QUEUE(DESTINATION-ID)
    END-EXEC.
```

The DELETEQ TS command

Function

Temporary storage control. The DELETEQ TS command deletes a temporary storage queue, deleting any records remaining in the queue and reclaiming the space used by the queue.

Syntax

```
EXEC CICS
    DELETEQ TS { QUEUE(name) | QNAME(name) }
              [ SYSID(systemname) ]
END-EXEC.
```

Options

QUEUE	Specifies the 1- to 8-character name of the temporary storage queue to be deleted.
QNAME	(TS 1.3 and later) Specifies the 1- to 16-character name of the temporary storage queue to be deleted. An alternative to the QUEUE option.
SYSID	Specifies the 1- to 4-character name of a remote system that contains the queue.

Exceptional conditions

Note: The default action for these conditions is to terminate the task.

INVREQ	The queue was created for internal use by CICS and therefore can't be deleted by a user program or the queue name specified consists of only binary zeros.
ISCINVREQ	An undeterminable error occurred on the remote system specified in the SYSID option.
LOCKED	The request can't be performed because use of the queue has been restricted.
NOTAUTH	A resource security check has failed on the specified queue because the user is not authorized to access the destination.
QIDERR	The queue specified in the QUEUE/QNAME option doesn't exist.
SYSIDERR	The system identified by SYSID could not be located or accessed.

Notes and tips

- Temporary storage queues are created dynamically. In other words, whenever a program writes a record to a queue that doesn't exist, the queue is created. Once created, however, a queue must be explicitly deleted. No special resource definitions are required for temporary storage queues, unless they are to be made recoverable.

- There are two ways to delete a temporary storage queue. An application program can issue a DELETEQ TS command, or an operator with the proper authority can invoke the CEBR transaction and issue a PURGE command. (CEBR is the temporary storage browse transaction, and it's described briefly in Unit 13.) Because a queue can be deleted at any time, you should check the QIDERR condition whenever you issue a DELETEQ TS command.

Coding example

This example shows how to issue a DELETEQ TS command to delete a temporary storage queue. The QIDERR condition is ignored so that if the queue does not exist, the task won't be terminated. The temporary storage queue name is stored in a field named TS-QUEUE-ID.

```
5500-DELETE-TEMPORARY-STORAGE.
*
    EXEC CICS
        DELETEQ TS QUEUE(TS-QUEUE-ID)
                   RESP(RESPONSE-CODE)
    END-EXEC.

    IF      RESPONSE-CODE NOT = DFHRESP(NORMAL)
        AND RESPONSE-CODE NOT = DFHRESP(QIDERR)
        PERFORM 9999-TERMINATE-PROGRAM
    END-IF.
```

The DEQ command

Function

Task control. The DEQ command releases a user-defined resource that was reserved for exclusive use by an ENQ command issued by your task. Then, the next
task that has issued an ENQ command for the same resource will be allowed to
continue.

Syntax

```
EXEC CICS
    DEQ   RESOURCE(data-area)
          [ LENGTH(data-value) ]
          [ UOW | TASK | MAXLIFETIME(data-area) ]
END-EXEC.
```

Options

RESOURCE	Identifies the resource to be released. If LENGTH is also specified, the character string (up to 255 bytes) contained in the data area is used to identify the resource; if LENGTH is omitted, the address of the data area identifies the resource.
LENGTH	Specifies a binary halfword (PIC S9(4) COMP) or literal value that indicates the length (up to 255 bytes) of the character string specified in the RESOURCE option.
UOW	Specifies that the enqueue was acquired with UOW (unit of work) specified as the duration. This is the default. For compatibility with previous releases of CICS/ESA, LUW can also be used.
TASK	Specifies that the enqueue was acquired with TASK specified as the duration.
MAXLIFETIME	Specifies a binary fullword (PIC S9(8) COMP) that indicates the duration of the enqueued resource. The field's value can be set to either DFHVALUE(UOW) or DFHVALUE(TASK).

Exceptional conditions

Note: The default action for these conditions is to terminate the task.

INVREQ	The MAXLIFETIME value is incorrect.
LENGERR	The LENGTH value is not in the range of 1 to 255.

Notes and tips

- The ENQ/DEQ facility is useful for single threading access to resources that you don't want to be shared: printers, destinations, temporary storage queues, etc.

- The ENQ/DEQ facility will work properly only if all tasks that use a particular resource issue ENQ commands and identify the resource in the same way. The ENQ/DEQ facility does nothing to prevent programs that don't issue an ENQ command from accessing the resource.

- If multiple tasks have enqueued the same resource, the highest priority task waiting for the resource will proceed when a DEQ command is issued. The remaining tasks will continue to be enqueued.

- If no DEQ command is issued, a resource is automatically dequeued when a syncpoint is taken or the task ends.

- Most installations have a standard that specifies how resources are named. Find out what that standard is and be sure to follow it.

Coding example

This example shows how to issue a DEQ command to release a printer that was reserved by an ENQ command so the program could send output to it. The printer's terminal-id is used as the character string in the RESOURCE option.

```
    01  PRINTER-ID        PIC X(4)      VALUE 'L86P'.
*
         .
         .
*
     PROCEDURE DIVISION.
*
     0000-PRODUCE-INVENTORY-LISTING.
*
         .
         .
        EXEC CICS
            ENQ RESOURCE(PRINTER-ID)
                LENGTH(4)
        END-EXEC.

        PERFORM 2000-PRINT-INVENTORY-LINE
            UNTIL END-OF-REPORT.

        PERFORM 3000-PRINT-TOTAL-LINE.

        EXEC CICS
            DEQ RESOURCE(PRINTER-ID)
                LENGTH(4)
        END-EXEC.
         .
         .
```

The DOCUMENT CREATE command

Function

Document services. (TS 1.3 and later) The DOCUMENT CREATE command is typically used to create HTML documents and special forms. The document created can be empty or its contents can be based on an existing document.

Syntax

```
EXEC CICS
    DOCUMENT CREATE     DOCTOKEN(data-area)
                        [ { FROM(data-area) LENGTH(data-value) }
                          { TEXT(data-area) LENGTH(data-value) }
                          { BINARY(data-area) LENGTH(data-value) }
                          { FROMDOC(data-area) }
                          { TEMPLATE(name) } ]
                        [ SYMBOLLIST(data-area) LISTLENGTH(data-value)
                            [ DELIMITER(data-value) ]
                            [ UNESCAPED ] ]
                        [ DOCSIZE(data-area) ]
                        [ HOSTCODEPAGE(name) ]
    END-EXEC.
```

Options

DOCTOKEN	Specifies the 16-character symbolic name of the document to be created. CICS generates this name when the document is created. Other DOCU-MENT commands can then refer to the document by this name.
FROM	Specifies the data area that's to be used to create the document. This data area can be a template or an existing document that's been retrieved.
TEXT	Specifies a character string data area that's used to create the document. No attempt is made to parse the data for symbol substitution.
BINARY	Specifies a binary data area that's used to create the document. This option lets you insert a block of data that won't be converted to the client's code page when the data is sent, allowing embedded code to be passed to the new document.
LENGTH	Specifies a binary fullword (PIC S9(8) COMP) that contains the length of the data area used by the FROM, TEXT, or BINARY options to create the document.
FROMDOC	Specifies the DOCTOKEN name of another document whose contents are to be copied to the new document being created.
TEMPLATE	Specifies the 48-character name of a template defined to CICS through the RDO facility. The contents of the template is copied to the new document being created.

SYMBOLLIST	Specifies a field that contains a symbol list. A symbol list is a character string that consists of one or more symbol definitions separated by ampersands. Each symbol definition consists of a name, an equals sign, and a value. Example: tranid=INV1&user=MM01&orderno=123456. During document creation, the values in the symbol list are substituted for the corresponding names (symbols) in the document contents.
LISTLENGTH	Specifies a binary fullword (PIC S9(8) COMP) that contains the length of the SYMBOLLIST.
DELIMITER	(TS 2.1 and later) Specifies a 1-character field or literal value used to delimit symbol definitions in the SYMBOLLIST. If not specified, the value defaults to an ampersand.
UNESCAPED	(TS 2.1 and later) Prevents CICS from escaping symbol values contained in the SYMBOLLIST. If used, plus signs are not converted to spaces, and sequences in the format *%nn* are not converted to single character values (where *nn* is the ASCII value for the character).
DOCSIZE	Specifies a binary fullword (PIC S9(8) COMP) that's updated with the current size of the document in bytes.
HOSTCODEPAGE	Specifies the 8-character name of the host codepage to be used for the data being added to the document. HOSTCODEPAGE can only be used with the TEXT, TEMPLATE, and SYMBOLLIST options.

Exceptional conditions

Note: The default action for these conditions is to terminate the task.

INVREQ	The document or template specified in the FROM option is not in a valid format.
NOTFND	The document or template specified in the FROMDOC or TEMPLATE option can't be found or is named incorrectly.
SYMBOLERR	A symbol specified in the symbol list doesn't conform to the naming rules for symbols.
TEMPLATERR	An invalid #set, #include, or #echo command was encountered while processing the specified template.

Notes and tips

- The DOCUMENT commands allow you to create and manage HTML pages that can then be sent to a web browser through CICS's web support facility. Prior to the introduction of the DOCUMENT commands in CICS TS 1.3, an HTML template manager was needed. Although it can still be used, we recommend you use the DOCUMENT commands instead.

- The DOCUMENT CREATE command is the first step in creating a document. The document created can be empty or based on another document, template, or data string.

- A template contains generalized information that can be used as the basis for many different documents. When you use the TEMPLATE option, you can code the SYMBOLLIST option to change any of the predefined symbols in the template to values you specify. This allows you to customize your document with specific information related to your task. Any template referenced must first be defined to CICS through the RDO facility.

- Remember to adhere to HTML coding standards when formatting or adding symbols to an HTML document.

- Some characters, such as the ampersand (&), have special meaning in HTML. So to avoid confusion when a user enters a character like that, the HTTP client *escapes* the character. That means the character is converted to the format *%nn*, where *nn* is the ASCII value of the character. *Unescaping* means a character in that format is not converted to a single character but is transmitted as is.

- A host code page and a client code page are used to translate data to the format that's used on the server and the client, respectively. In a IBM environment, usually the host uses EBCDIC code while the clients use ASCII. Specifying what the host and client code pages are if they're not standard EBCDIC and ASCII will ensure that the information being transmitted will be translated correctly.

Coding example

The following code shows how the DOCUMENT CREATE command is used to create an HTML document that displays an order and confirmation number. The template used to create the document is called ORDERCONFIRM, and the SYMBOLLIST option passes information that's specific to the order. The WEB SEND command then passes the HTML page back out to the web server for delivery to the client browser.

```
WORKING-STORAGE SECTION.
.
.
01  CURRORDER       PIC X(16) VALUE SPACES.
01  STATUS-MESSAGE  PIC X(10) VALUE 'OK'.

01  CONFIRM-STRING.
    05  FILLER      PIC X(08) VALUE 'order_no'.
    05  FILLER      PIC X(01) VALUE '='.
    05  CONF-ODR-NO PIC 9(06) VALUE ZERO.
    05  FILLER      PIC X(01) VALUE '&'.
    05  FILLER      PIC X(10) VALUE 'confirm_no'.
    05  FILLER      PIC X(01) VALUE '='.
    05  CONF-NO     PIC X(09) VALUE SPACE.

01  CODEPAGE-INFO.
    05  CODEPAGE-EBCDIC  PIC X(08) VALUE '037'.
    05  CODEPAGE-ASCII   PIC X(40) VALUE 'iso-8859-1'.
.
.
PROCEDURE DIVISION.
.
.
5000-SEND-CONFIRMATION.
.
.
    EXEC CICS
        DOCUMENT CREATE
                DOCTOKEN(CURRORDER)
                TEMPLATE('ORDERCONFIRM')
                SYMBOLLIST(CONFIRM-STRING)
                LISTLENGTH(LENGTH OF CONFIRM-STRING)
                HOSTCODEPAGE(CODEPAGE-EBCDIC)
    END-EXEC.
.
.
    EXEC CICS
        WEB SEND
            DOCTOKEN(CURRORDER)
            STATUSCODE(200)
            STATUS(STATUS-MESSAGE)
            CLNTCODEPAGE(CODEPAGE-ASCII)
    END-EXEC.
```

The DOCUMENT INSERT command

Function

Document services. (TS 1.3 and later) The DOCUMENT INSERT command lets you insert document objects at specified points within a document. For example, you can use this command to add additional text to an HTML document.

Syntax

```
EXEC CICS
    DOCUMENT INSERT    DOCTOKEN(data-area)

                       { FROM(data-area) LENGTH(data-value) }
                       { TEXT(data-area) LENGTH(data-value) }
                       { BINARY(data-area) LENGTH(data-value) }
                       { FROMDOC(data-area) }
                       { TEMPLATE(name) }
                       { SYMBOL(name) }
                       { BOOKMARK(name) }

                       [ DOCSIZE(data-area) ]
                       [ HOSTCODEPAGE(name) ]
                       [ AT(name)
                            [ TO(name) ] ]
    END-EXEC.
```

Options

DOCTOKEN	Specifies the 16-character symbolic name of the document into which the data is inserted.
FROM	Specifies the data area that's to be inserted into the document. This data area can be a template or an existing document that's been retrieved.
TEXT	Specifies a character string data area that's to be inserted into the document. No attempt is made to parse the data for symbol substitution.
BINARY	Specifies a binary data area that's to be inserted into the document. This option lets you insert a block of data that won't be converted to the client's code page when the data is sent, allowing embedded code to be passed to the document.
LENGTH	Specifies a binary fullword (PIC S9(8) COMP) that contains the length of the data area used by the FROM, TEXT, or BINARY option to insert data into the document.
FROMDOC	Specifies the DOCTOKEN name of another document whose contents is to be inserted into the target document.
TEMPLATE	Specifies the 48-character name of a template whose contents is to be inserted into the document. The template must be defined to CICS through the RDO facility.
SYMBOL	Specifies the 32-character name of a symbol whose associated value is to be inserted into the document.

BOOKMARK	Specifies the 16-character symbolic name of a bookmark to be inserted into the document. Once inserted, subsequent DOCU-MENT INSERT commands can then insert data at the point marked by the bookmark.
DOCSIZE	Specifies a binary fullword (PIC S9(8) COMP) that's updated with the current size of the document in bytes.
HOSTCODEPAGE	Specifies the 8-character name of the host code page to be used for the data being added to the document. HOSTCODEPAGE can only be used with the TEXT, SYMBOL, and TEMPLATE options.
AT	Specifies the 16-character name of a bookmark insertion point in the document. Data is then inserted after the bookmark. If AT is not specified, data is inserted at the end of the document. A predefined bookmark named TOP is available that allows you to insert data at the beginning of the document.
TO	Specifies the 16-character name of a bookmark that identifies the end position of an insertion point. The data between the bookmarks specified by the AT and TO options is deleted, and the new data is inserted in its place.

Exceptional conditions

Note: The default action for these conditions is to terminate the task.

DUPREC	The specified bookmark already exists.
INVREQ	The document specified in the FROM option is not in a valid format, the bookmark specified by the TO option appears before the bookmark specified for the AT option, or the bookmark name is invalid.
NOTFND	The document or template specified in the FROMDOC, TEM-PLATE, or SYMBOL option can't be found or is named incorrectly.
TEMPLATERR	An invalid #set, #include, or #echo command was encountered while processing the specified template.

Notes and tips

- The DOCUMENT commands allow you to create and manage HTML pages that can then be sent to a web browser through CICS's web support facility. Prior to the introduction of the DOCUMENT commands in CICS TS 1.3, an HTML template manager was needed. Although it can still be used, we recommend you use the DOCUMENT commands instead.

- Bookmarks allow an application to insert blocks of information into a document in any order yet still control the sequence of that information within the document. In other words, a bookmark serves as an insertion point or placeholder in a document.

- All bookmarks must be defined before they are referenced. Data is then inserted after the position identified by the bookmark.

- If a bookmark name is less than 16 characters long, pad the name with spaces.

- A host code page and a client code page are used to translate data to the format that's used on the server and the client, respectively. In a IBM environment, usually the host uses EBCDIC code while the clients use ASCII. Specifying what the host and client code pages are if they're not standard EBCDIC and ASCII will ensure that the information being transmitted will be translated correctly.

Coding example

The following code shows how the DOCUMENT INSERT command can be used to define two bookmarks in a document and then insert a block of data between them. To start, a DOCUMENT CREATE command is issued to create the document. Then, a DOCUMENT INSERT command is issued to place the first bookmark in the document. After that, a generic name is inserted to hold a place for a customer name. A second bookmark is inserted to identify the end of the customer name block. Finally, a real customer name is inserted into the document.

```
1000-FORMAT-DOCUMENT.
    .
    .

    EXEC CICS
        DOCUMENT CREATE
                DOCTOKEN(CUSTPAGE)
        END-EXEC.
    .
    .

    EXEC CICS
        DOCUMENT INSERT
                DOCTOKEN(CUSTPAGE)
                BOOKMARK('CustBeg          ')
    END-EXEC.

    EXEC CICS
        DOCUMENT INSERT
                DOCTOKEN(CUSTPAGE)
                TEXT('customer name')
                LENGTH(13)
    END-EXEC.

    EXEC CICS
        DOCUMENT INSERT
                DOCTOKEN(CUSTPAGE)
                BOOKMARK('CustEnd          ')
    END-EXEC.
    .
    .
5000-INSERT-CUSTOMER-NAME.
    .
    .

    EXEC CICS
        DOCUMENT INSERT
                DOCTOKEN(CUSTPAGE)
                TEXT(CM-CUST-NAME)
                LENGTH(LENGTH OF CM-CUST-NAME)
                AT ('CustBeg          ')
                TO ('CustEnd          ')
    END-EXEC.
```

The DOCUMENT RETRIEVE command

Function

Document services. (TS 1.3 and later) The DOCUMENT RETRIEVE command lets you retrieve a copy of a specified document and save it in a field defined in your application program. The retrieved document can then be used to create a new document.

Syntax

```
EXEC CICS
    DOCUMENT RETRIEVE     DOCTOKEN(data-area)
                          INTO(data-area)
                          LENGTH(data-value)
                          MAXLENGTH(data-value)
                        [ CLNTCODEPAGE(name) ]
                        [ DATAONLY ]
    END-EXEC.
```

Options

DOCTOKEN	Specifies the 16-character symbolic name of the document to be retrieved.
INTO	Specifies the data area that receives a copy of the document's contents.
LENGTH	Specifies a binary fullword (PIC S9(8) COMP) that contains the length of the data returned.
MAXLENGTH	A binary fullword (PIC S9(8) COMP) that specifies the maximum amount of data that the INTO area can hold. Optional for TS 2.2 and later versions.
CLNTCODEPAGE	Specifies the 40-character name of the client code page to which the data should be converted.
DATAONLY	Specifies that the document's content should be retrieved without any embedded tags.

Exceptional conditions

Note: The default action for these conditions is to terminate the task.

LENGERR	The length of the INTO option isn't long enough to receive the entire contents of the document.
NOTFND	The document specified can't be found or is named incorrectly.

Notes and tips

- The DOCUMENT commands allow you to create and manage HTML pages that can then be sent to a web browser through CICS's web support facility. Prior to the introduction of the DOCUMENT commands in CICS TS 1.3, an HTML template manager was needed. Although it can still be used, we recommend you use the DOCUMENT commands instead.

- Any document you create will exist only as long as the task in which it was created. To save a document so that it can be used by another task, use the DOCUMENT RETRIEVE command to obtain a copy of the document. You can then use a transient data queue or communication area to save the document information so that it can be retrieved at a later time.

- A host code page and a client code page are used to translate data to the format that's used on the server and the client, respectively. In a IBM environment, usually the host uses EBCDIC code while the clients use ASCII. Specifying what the host and client code pages are if they're not standard EBCDIC and ASCII will ensure that the information being transmitted will be translated correctly.

Coding examples

The two coding examples that follow show how to store a document that can later be retrieved by another CICS task.

In this first example, a document is copied into a working-storage area via a DOCUMENT RETREIVE command and then written to a temporary storage queue. Note that the binary fullword LENGTH field used in the DOCUMENT RETRIEVE command must be moved to a binary halfword LENGTH field in the WRITEQ TS command.

```
EXEC CICS
    DOCUMENT RETRIEVE
            DOCTOKEN(CUSTINFO)
            INTO(CUSTOMER-INFO-FORM)
            LENGTH(CUST-FORM-FLENGTH)
            MAXLENGTH(500)
END-EXEC.

MOVE CUST-FORM-FLENGTH TO CUST-FORM-HLENGTH.

EXEC CICS
    WRITEQ TS QUEUE('CUSTDATA')
            FROM(CUSTOMER-INFO-FORM)
            LENGTH(CUST-FORM-HLENGTH)
END-EXEC.
```

In this second example, the document is retrieved from the TS queue and the document is recreated with the DOCUMENT CREATE command.

```
EXEC CICS
    READQ TS QUEUE('CUSTDATA')
                INTO(CUSTOMER-INFO-FORM)
                LENGTH(CUST-FORM-HLENGTH)
END-EXEC.

MOVE CUST-FORM-HLENGTH TO CUST-FORM-FLENGTH.

EXEC CICS
    DOCUMENT CREATE
                DOCTOKEN(CUSTINFO)
                FROM(CUSTOMER-INFO-FORM)
                LENGTH(CUST-FORM-FLENGTH)
END-EXEC.
```

The DOCUMENT SET command

Function

Document services. (TS 1.3 and later) The DOCUMENT SET command lets you add symbols and values to the symbol table that's related to a document.

Syntax

```
EXEC CICS
    DOCUMENT SET      DOCTOKEN(data-area)
                      { SYMBOL(name) VALUE(data-area) }
                      { SYMBOLLIST(data-area)
                          [ DELIMITER(data-value) ]   }
                      LENGTH(data-value)
                          [ UNESCAPED ]
    END-EXEC.
```

Options

DOCTOKEN	Specifies the 16-character symbolic name of the document that owns the symbol table to which symbols and values will be added.
SYMBOL	Specifies a 1- to 32-character field that contains the name of the symbol to be added to the table.
VALUE	Specifies the field that contains the value associated with the SYMBOL option.
SYMBOLLIST	Specifies a field that contains a symbol list to be added to the symbol table. A symbol list is a character string that consists of one or more symbol definitions separated by ampersands. Each symbol definition consists of a name, an equals sign, and a value. Example: tranid=INV1&user=MM01&orderno=123456.
DELIMITER	(TS 2.1 and later) Specifies a 1-character field or literal value used to delimit symbol definitions in the SYMBOLLIST. If not specified, the value defaults to an ampersand.
LENGTH	Specifies a binary fullword (PIC S9(8) COMP) that contains the length of the symbol or symbol list.
UNESCAPED	(TS 2.1 and later) Prevents CICS from escaping symbol values contained in the SYMBOLLIST. If used, plus signs are not converted to spaces, and sequences in the format %*nn* are not converted to single character values (where *nn* is the ASCII value of the character).

Exceptional conditions

Note: The default action for these conditions is to terminate the task.

NOTFND   The document specified can't be found or is named incorrectly.

SYMBOLERR   A symbol specified in the symbol list doesn't conform to the naming rules for symbols.

Notes and tips

- The DOCUMENT commands allow you to create and manage HTML pages that can be sent to a web browser through CICS's web support facility. Prior to the introduction of the DOCUMENT commands in CICS TS 1.3, an HTML template manager was needed. Although it can still be used, we recommend you use the DOCUMENT commands instead.

- The DOCUMENT SET command allows you to add symbols and their associated values to the symbol table for an already existing document. If a symbol already exists, it will be replaced by the new definition.

- If several of the values for a document change, you can use the SYMBOLLIST option instead of the SYMBOL and VALUE options. This allows you to insert multiple symbols and their associated values with only one command.

- Some characters, such as the ampersand (&), have special meaning in HTML. So to avoid confusion when a user enters a character like that, the HTTP client *escapes* the character. That means the character is converted to the format *%nn*, where *nn* is the ASCII value of the character. *Unescaping* means a character in that format is not converted to a single character but is transmitted as is.

Coding example

The following example shows how a DOCUMENT SET command can be used to update the customer name for a document.

```
EXEC CICS
    DOCUMENT SET DOCTOKEN(CUSTINFO)
                 SYMBOL(cust_name)
                 VALUE(CM-CUST-NAME)
                 LENGTH(LENGTH OF CM-CUST-NAME)
END-EXEC.
```

The DUMP TRANSACTION command

Function

Diagnostic services. The DUMP TRANSACTION command forces a storage dump of one or more of the main storage areas related to a task. It can also produce a dump of all of the CICS tables.

Syntax

```
EXEC CICS
    DUMP TRANSACTION  DUMPCODE(name)
                    [ FROM(data-area)
                        [ LENGTH(data-value) | FLENGTH(data-value) ] ]
                    [ SEGMENTLIST(data-area)
                          LENGTHLIST(data-area)
                              NUMSEGMENTS(data-area) ]
                    [ COMPLETE ]
                    [ TRT ]
                    [ TASK ]
                    [ STORAGE ]
                    [ PROGRAM ]
                    [ TERMINAL ]
                    [ TABLES ]
                    [ DCT ]
                    [ FCT ]
                    [ PCT ]
                    [ PPT ]
                    [ SIT ]
                    [ TCT ]
    END-EXEC.
```

Options

Note: If you don't code any options on the DUMP TRANSACTION command, the output produced is similar to that produced if you code the TASK option, except that DL/I control blocks aren't included.

DUMPCODE   Specifies a 1- to 4-character name that identifies the dump. If the name contains any leading or embedded blanks, a dump will still be produced but the INVREQ condition will be raised and no entry will be added to the system dump table.

FROM   Specifies the data area to be dumped. The storage dump begins at the specified data area and continues for the length specified in the LENGTH or FLENGTH option.

LENGTH   Specifies a binary halfword (PIC S9(4) COMP) or literal value that indicates the length of the FROM area to be dumped.

FLENGTH   Specifies a binary fullword (PIC S9(8) COMP) or literal value that indicates the length of the FROM area to be dumped.

SEGMENTLIST	Specifies a data area that contains a list of fullword addresses. Each address represents the starting address of an area of main storage to be included in the dump. If you specify SEGMENTLIST, you must also specify LENGTHLIST and NUMSEGMENTS.
LENGTHLIST	Specifies a data area that contains a list of fullwords. Each fullword supplies the length of the corresponding segment address provided in the SEGMENTLIST data area.
NUMSEGMENTS	Specifies a binary fullword (PIC S9(8) COMP) whose value represents the number of segments in the SEGMENTLIST and LENGTHLIST fields.
COMPLETE	Specifies that all available task information should be dumped, including all CICS tables and DL/I control blocks.
TRT	Specifies that the task's entries in the internal trace table should be included in the dump.
TASK	Specifies that task information should be dumped, including programs and certain control blocks (including DL/I control blocks).
STORAGE	Specifies that task storage areas and certain control blocks should be dumped.
PROGRAM	Specifies that task program areas and certain control blocks should be dumped.
TERMINAL	Specifies that terminal storage areas and certain control blocks should be dumped.
TABLES	Specifies that CICS tables should be dumped.
DCT	Specifies that the Destination Control Table should be dumped.
FCT	Specifies that the File Control Table should be dumped.
PCT	Specifies that the Program Control Table should be dumped.
PPT	Specifies that the Processing Program Table should be dumped.
SIT	Specifies that the System Initialization Table should be dumped.
TCT	Specifies that the Terminal Control Table should be dumped.

Exceptional conditions

Note: The default action for these conditions is to terminate the task.

INVREQ	The DUMPCODE is invalid.
IOERR	An I/O error has occurred during the creation of the specified dumps.
NOSPACE	The dump data set has run out of space.
NOSTG	CICS has run out of storage.
NOTOPEN	The dump data set is not open.
OPENERR	An error occurred opening the dump data set.
SUPPRESSED	The dump was suppressed because of the transaction's resource definition.

Notes and tips

- Storage dumps are written to the CICS dump data sets. You'll have to determine your installation's procedures for printing dumps.

- Usually, a transaction dump is produced automatically when a task abends. So you need to code a DUMP TRANSACTION command only in unusual situations.

- Some of the DUMP TRANSACTION options produce excessive amounts of information that are useful only for debugging CICS system problems. For application program debugging, specify TASK, PROGRAM, or STORAGE, or code the command with just the DUMPCODE option.

Coding example

This example shows how to force a storage dump and assign it an identifier of R100.

```
EXEC CICS
    DUMP TRANSACTION DUMPCODE('R100')
END-EXEC.
```

The ENDBR command

Function

File control. The ENDBR command terminates a browse operation. If you want to perform an update operation on the file you're browsing via a READ UPDATE command, you must end the browse with an ENDBR command. Otherwise, the browse will terminate automatically when the task ends.

Syntax

```
EXEC CICS
    ENDBR    FILE(filename) }
           [ REQID(data-value) ]
           [ SYSID(systemname) ]
END-EXEC.
```

Options

FILE   Specifies the 1- to 8-character name of the data set for which the browse operation is to be ended.

REQID   Specifies a binary halfword (PIC S9(4) COMP) or literal value that identifies the browse operation; used only when your program controls two or more browse operations at the same time. For each I/O command that's part of the same browse operation, specify the same REQID value. If not specified, the default value of zero is assumed.

SYSID   Specifies the 1- to 4-character name of a remote system that contains the file.

Exceptional conditions

Note: The default action for these conditions is to terminate the task.

FILENOTFOUND	The data set name specified in the FILE option isn't defined in the File Control Table.
ILLOGIC	A serious VSAM error occurred.
INVREQ	A browse operation has not been properly started by a STARTBR command.
IOERR	The REQID doesn't match that of any successful STARTBR command.
ISCINVREQ	An undeterminable error occurred on the remote system specified in the SYSID option.
NOTAUTH	A resource security check has failed on the specified file because the user is not authorized to access it.
SYSIDERR	The system identified by SYSID could not be located or accessed.

Notes and tips

- In releases of CICS prior to TS 1.1, you can't update a record within a browse. Instead, you need to issue an ENDBR command to end the browse before issuing any READ UPDATE, WRITE, REWRITE, or DELETE commands. This lets you avoid potential deadlocks.

- Starting in CICS TS 1.1, you can update a record within a browse after issuing a READNEXT or READPREV command with the UPDATE option. However, you should still use the ENDBR command to end a browse before any syncpoints in your program to avoid potential deadlocks.

Coding example

This example terminates a browse operation for a file named ACCOUNT.

```
9100-END-ACCOUNT-BROWSE.
*
    EXEC CICS
        ENDBR FILE('ACCOUNT')
    END-EXEC.
```

The ENQ command

Function

Task control. The ENQ command reserves a user-defined resource for exclusive use by your task. Any other task that issues an ENQ command for the same resource will be suspended until your task ends or issues a DEQ command for the resource.

Syntax

```
EXEC CICS
    ENQ   RESOURCE(data-area)
        [ LENGTH(data-value) ]
        [ UOW | TASK | MAXLIFETIME(data-area) ]
        [ NOSUSPEND ]
END-EXEC.
```

Options

RESOURCE	Identifies the resource to be reserved. If LENGTH is also specified, the character string (up to 255 bytes) contained in the data area is used to identify the resource; if LENGTH is omitted, the address of the data area identifies the resource.
LENGTH	Specifies a binary halfword (PIC S9(4) COMP) or literal value that indicates the length (up to 255 bytes) of the character string specified in the RESOURCE option.
UOW	Specifies that the enqueue should be held until the end of the current unit of work (the default). For compatibility with previous releases of CICS/ESA, LUW can also be used.
TASK	Specifies that the enqueue should be held until the end of the current task.
MAXLIFETIME	Specifies a binary fullword (PIC S9(8) COMP) that indicates the duration of the enqueued resource. The field's value can be set to either DFHVALUE(UOW) or DFHVALUE(TASK).
NOSUSPEND	Indicates that if the resource is already reserved, control is returned immediately to your program at the point following the ENQ command.

Exceptional conditions

Note: The default action for all of these conditions except ENQBUSY is to terminate the task. The default action for the ENQBUSY condition is to suspend the task.

ENQBUSY	Indicates that another task has already issued an ENQ command naming the resource you specified.
INVREQ	The MAXLIFETIME value is incorrect.
LENGERR	The length value is not in the range of 1 to 255.

Notes and tips

- The ENQ/DEQ facility is useful for single threading access to resources that you don't want to be shared: printers, destinations, temporary storage queues, etc.

- The ENQ/DEQ facility will work properly only if all tasks that use a particular resource issue ENQ commands and identify the resource in the same way. The ENQ/DEQ facility does nothing to prevent programs that don't issue an ENQ command from accessing the resource.

- Most installations have a standard that specifies how resources are named. Find out what that standard is and be sure to follow it.

- If the LENGTH option is specified in the ENQ command, it must also be specified in the DEQ command for the same resource and the value must match.

- ENQBUSY is one of the few exceptional conditions that doesn't cause your task to be terminated. Instead, its action depends on whether you handle the condition (using the RESP option or a HANDLE CONDITION command) and whether you specify NOSUSPEND on the ENQ command. If you do neither, ENQBUSY simply causes your task to be suspended until the resource becomes available; then, control returns to your program at the first statement following the ENQ command. If your program handles the ENQBUSY condition, the specified error processing is done, and the program must issue the ENQ command again to reserve the resource. If you specify NOSUSPEND, control is returned to the statement following the ENQ command if the resource is unavailable; again, you'll have to issue another ENQ command to reserve the resource later.

Coding example

This example shows how to issue an ENQ command to reserve a printer so the program can send output to it. The character string in the RESOURCE option is the printer-id. Thus, any other task that issues an ENQ command using the same printer-id will be suspended until this program issues the DEQ command. Without this command, other programs could access the printer at the same time, so the output might be interspersed with data from other applications.

```
          .
          .
 *
  01   PRINTER-ID                    PIC X(04)        VALUE 'L86P'.
 *
          .
          .
 *
  PROCEDURE DIVISION.
 *
  0000-PRODUCE-INVENTORY-LISTING.
 *
          .
          .
      EXEC CICS
          ENQ RESOURCE(PRINTER-ID)
              LENGTH(4)
      END-EXEC.

      PERFORM 2000-PRINT-INVENTORY-LINE
          UNTIL END-OF-REPORT.

      PERFORM 3000-PRINT-TOTAL-LINE.

      EXEC CICS
          DEQ RESOURCE(PRINTER-ID)
              LENGTH(4)
      END-EXEC.
          .
          .
```

The ENTER TRACENUM command

Function

Diagnostic services. The ENTER TRACENUM command writes a user trace entry in the CICS trace table, which is printed when a transaction dump is produced.

Syntax

```
EXEC CICS
    ENTER    TRACENUM(data-value)
           [ FROM(data-area)
               [ FROMLENGTH(data-area) ] ]
           [ RESOURCE(data-area) ]
           [ EXCEPTION ]
    END-EXEC.
```

Options

TRACENUM	Specifies a binary halfword (PIC S9(4) COMP) or literal value that contains the trace identifier that will be associated with the user trace entry. The value must be in the range of 0 to 199.
FROM	Specifies an 8-byte alphanumeric field; the contents of this field are placed in the data field of the user trace entry. If omitted, binary zeroes are passed.
FROMLENGTH	Specifies a binary halfword (PIC S9(4) COMP) that contains the length of the trace entry to be written. The value must be in the range of 0 to 4000. If omitted, a length of 8 bytes is assumed.
RESOURCE	Specifies an 8-byte alphanumeric field; the contents of this field are placed in the resource field of the user trace entry.
EXCEPTION	Specifies that the user trace entry should be written even if user tracing is disabled. Exception trace entries are identified by "*EXCU" when the entries are formatted by the trace utility program.

Exceptional conditions

Note: The default action for these conditions is to terminate the task.

INVREQ	The TRACENUM value is greater than 199, there is no trace table available, or user tracing is disabled and EXCEPTION isn't specified.
LENGERR	The FROMLENGTH value is not in the range 0 to 4000.

Notes and tips

- In general, CICS writes the trace entry only if the master and user trace flags are on (this is usually handled by a systems programmer). However, if you specify the EXCEPTION option, a user trace entry will always be written, even if the trace flags are off.

- You probably won't use the ENTER TRACENUM command often. Although its main function is for program debugging, there are better debugging facilities available. There are few cases where a user trace entry can help.

Coding example

This example shows how to create a user trace entry using 100 as the trace identifier.

```
EXEC CICS
    ENTER TRACENUM(100)
        FROM(WS-TRACE-AREA)
END-EXEC.
```

The EXTRACT ATTACH command

Function

Terminal control. The EXTRACT ATTACH command is used in a back-end transaction to retrieve values from an ATTACH Function Management Header (FMH) that was created by the front-end transaction in an LU6.1 or MRO session. It is not used for LU6.2/APPC sessions.

Syntax

```
EXEC CICS
    EXTRACT ATTACH [ ATTACHID(name) | CONVID(name) | SESSION(name) ]
                   [ PROCESS(data-area) ]
                   [ RESOURCE(data-area) ]
                   [ RPROCESS(data-area) ]
                   [ RRESOURCE(data-area) ]
                   [ QUEUE(data-area) ]
                   [ IUTYPE(data-area) ]
                   [ DATASTR(data-area) ]
                   [ RECFM(data-area) ]
END-EXEC.
```

Options

Note: If ATTACHID, CONVID, and SESSION are all omitted, the ATTACH FMH associated with the principal facility is used.

ATTACHID	Specifies the 1- to 8-character name of the ATTACH FMH to be accessed.
CONVID	Specifies that the ATTACH FMH associated with the named conversation is to be accessed. This 4-character name can identify either the token returned by a previously executed ALLOCATE command in the EIBSRCE field of the EIB, or the token representing the principal session returned by an ASSIGN command.
SESSION	Specifies that the ATTACH FMH associated with the named session is to be accessed.
PROCESS	Returns the name of the process to be started on the remote system. If the remote system is a CICS system, this option names the trans-id of the transaction to be started.
RESOURCE	Returns the value of the resource name field in the ATTACH FMH. Not used if the remote system is a CICS system.
RPROCESS	Returns the value of the return process name field in the ATTACH FMH. Not used if the remote system is a CICS system.
RRESOURCE	Returns the value of the resource field in the ATTACH FMH. Not used if the remote system is a CICS system.
QUEUE	Returns the value of the queue name field in the ATTACH FMH. Not used if the remote system is a CICS system.

IUTYPE	Returns the value of the interchange unit field in the ATTACH FMH. Not used if the remote system is a CICS system.
DATASTR	Returns the value of the data stream profile field in the ATTACH FMH. Not used if the remote system is a CICS system.
RECFM	Returns the value of the deblocking algorithm field in the ATTACH FMH. Not used if the remote system is a CICS system.

Exceptional conditions

Note: The default action for these conditions is to terminate the task.

CBIDERR	The requested ATTACH FMH doesn't exist.
INVREQ	The ATTACH FMH contains invalid data.
NOTALLOC	The session or conversation has not been allocated.

Notes and tips

* You use the EXTRACT ATTACH command in a back-end transaction to extract data that was placed in the ATTACH FMH by the front-end transaction. In most cases, the only data placed in the ATTACH FMH is the name of the back-end transaction.

Coding example

The following example shows how to extract the PROCESS field from an ATTACH FMH.

```
EXEC CICS
    EXTRACT ATTACH PROCESS(FMH-PROCESS)
END-EXEC.
```

The EXTRACT ATTRIBUTES command

Function

APPC mapped conversation/Terminal control. Determines the current state of an MRO or APPC conversation.

Syntax

```
EXEC CICS
    EXTRACT ATTRIBUTES [ CONVID(name) | SESSION(name) ]
                       [ STATE(cvda) ]
END-EXEC.
```

Options

Note: If both CONVID and SESSION are omitted, the conversation with the front-end program (that is, the principal facility) is used.

CONVID   Specifies the name of the conversation obtained from the EIBRSRCE field of the EIB following a successful ALLOCATE command.

SESSION   (MRO only) Specifies the name of the session obtained from the Terminal Control Table. Under APPC, SESSION is accepted as a synonym for CONVID.

STATE   Specifies a binary fullword (PIC S9(8) COMP) where CICS places the state information. The current state can be determined by testing it using the DFHVALUE keyword. Valid states are:

ALLOCATED	RECEIVE
CONFFREE*	ROLLBACK
CONFRECEIVE*	SEND
CONFSEND*	SYNCFREE
FREE	SYNCRECEIVE
PENDFREE	SYNCSEND
PENDRECEIVE*	

*APPC only

Exceptional conditions

Note: The default action for these conditions is to terminate the task.

INVREQ   The command is invalid for the specified conversation.

NOTALLOC   The specified conversation has not been allocated.

Notes and tips

- In most cases, your program should be aware of the state of the conversation following each distributed processing command. So you'll probably use this command only in unusual situations.

Coding example

The following example shows how to determine the state of a conversation.

```
EXEC CICS
    EXTRACT ATTRIBUTES STATE(CONV-STATE)
END-EXEC.

IF CONV-STATE = DFHVALUE(SEND)
    .
    .
```

The EXTRACT CERTIFICATE command

Function

TCP/IP services. (TS 1.3 and later) The EXTRACT CERTIFICATE command lets you extract information from the X.509 certificate sent from a client during a Secure Sockets Layer (SSL) handshake. Besides information that identifies the certificate itself, you can retrieve information on the owner of the certificate or on the Certificate Authority that issued the certificate.

Syntax

```
EXEC CICS
    EXTRACT    CERTIFICATE(pointer-ref)
               [ LENGTH(data-area) ]
               [ SERIALNUM(pointer-ref) ]
               [ SERIALNUMLEN(data-area) ]
               [ USERID(pointer-ref) ]
               [ OWNER | ISSUER ]
               [ COMMONNAME(pointer-ref) ]
               [ COMMONNAMELEN(data-area) ]
               [ COUNTRY(pointer-ref) ]
               [ COUNTRYLEN(data-area) ]
               [ STATE(pointer-ref) ]
               [ STATELEN(data-area) ]
               [ LOCALITY(pointer-ref) ]
               [ LOCALITYLEN(data-area) ]
               [ ORGANIZATION(pointer-ref) ]
               [ ORGANIZATLEN(data-area) ]
               [ ORGUNIT(pointer-ref) ]
               [ ORGUNITLEN(data-area) ]
    END-EXEC.
```

Options

CERTIFICATE	Specifies a pointer field that's set to the address of the full binary certificate received from the client.
LENGTH	A binary fullword (PIC S9(8) COMP) that's set to the length of the body of the certificate.
SERIALNUM	Specifies a pointer field that's set to the address of the serial number of the certificate.
SERIALNUMLEN	A binary fullword (PIC S9(8) COMP) that's set to the length of the serial number of the certificate.
USERID	Specifies a pointer field that's set to the address of the user-id connected with the certificate.
OWNER	Specifies that the values returned refer to the owner of the certificate. This is the default.
ISSUER	Specifies that the values returned refer to the Certificate Authority that issued the certificate.

COMMONNAME	Specifies a pointer field that's set to the address of the actual name of the owner or issuer.
COMMONNAMLEN	A binary fullword (PIC S9(8) COMP) that's set to the length of the common name.
COUNTRY	Specifies a pointer field that's set to the address of the country of the owner or issuer.
COUNTRYLEN	A binary fullword (PIC S9(8) COMP) that's set to the length of the country.
STATE	Specifies a pointer field that's set to the address of the state or province of the owner or issuer.
STATELEN	A binary fullword (PIC S9(8) COMP) that's set to the length of the state or province.
LOCALITY	Specifies a pointer field that's set to the address of the locality of the owner or issuer.
LOCALITYLEN	A binary fullword (PIC S9(8) COMP) that's set to the length of the locality.
ORGANIZATION	Specifies a pointer field that's set to the address of the organization or company that the owner or issuer is related to.
ORGANIZATLEN	A binary fullword (PIC S9(8) COMP) that's set to the length of the organization or company.
ORGUNIT	Specifies a pointer field that's set to the address of the unit or department of the owner or issuer.
ORGUNITLEN	A binary fullword (PIC S9(8) COMP) that's set to the length of the organizational unit.

Exceptional conditions

Note: The default action for these conditions is to terminate the task.

INVREQ	An error occurred retrieving the certificate from CICS intermediate storage or the command was issued in a non-CICS Web Interface application.
LENGERR	A length error occurred on one of the options.

Notes and tips

- Since the certificate contains information for both the certificate owner and issuer, you can select the fields you need by specifying the OWNER or ISSUER option. You can't, however select both OWNER and ISSUER in a single command.
- Any pointer references that are specified are valid only until the next CICS command is issued or until the task ends.

Coding example

The following example shows how to extract the client certificate, user-id, and name for the owner of the certificate.

```
EXEC CICS
    EXTRACT CERTIFICATE(CERT-PTR)
            LENGTH(CERT-LEN)
            USERID(CERT-USERID)
            COMMONNAME(CERT-NAME)
            OWNER
END-EXEC.
```

The EXTRACT PROCESS command

Function

APPC mapped conversation. The EXTRACT PROCESS command is used in a back-end program to obtain information specified in the front-end program's CONNECT PROCESS command.

Syntax

```
EXEC CICS
    EXTRACT PROCESS [ CONVID(name) ]
                    [ PROCNAME(data-area)
                          PROCLENGTH(data-area)
                            [ MAXPROCLEN(data-value) ] ]
                    [ SYNCLEVEL(data-area) ]
                    [ PIPLIST(pointer-ref)
                          PIPLENGTH(data-value) ]
    END-EXEC.
```

Options

CONVID	Specifies the 4-character conversation-id obtained from the Execute Interface Block field EIBRSRCE following a successful ALLOCATE command. If omitted, the conversation with the front-end program (that is, the principal facility) is used.
PROCNAME	Specifies a field where CICS places the PROCNAME value specified on the corresponding CONNECT PROCESS command. This data area can be from 1 to 64 bytes long and should never be shorter than the value specified in the MAXPROCLEN option.
PROCLENGTH	Specifies a binary halfword (PIC S9(4) COMP) where CICS places the length of the PROCNAME field.
MAXPROCLEN	Specifies a binary halfword (PIC S9(4) COMP) or literal value that indicates the size of the field specified in the PROCNAME option. If omitted, 32 is assumed.
SYNCLEVEL	Specifies a binary halfword (PIC S9(4) COMP) where CICS places the number 0, 1, or 2 to indicate the degree of synchronization required between the programs. SYNCLEVEL(0) indicates that no synchronization is required. SYNCLEVEL(1) provides the low-level support required for applications to perform their own synchronization. SYNCLEVEL(2) automatically coordinates SYNCPOINT and SYNCPOINT ROLLBACK commands.
PIPLIST	Specifies a pointer field where CICS places the address of the PIPLIST field specified in the corresponding CONNECT PROCESS command.
PIPLENGTH	Specifies a binary halfword (PIC S9(4) COMP) or literal value where CICS places the length of the PIPLIST area.

Exceptional conditions

Note: The default action for these conditions is to terminate the task.

INVREQ   The command is invalid for the specified conversation.

LENGERR   The PROCNAME data is larger than the MAXPROCLEN specification.

NOTALLOC   The specified conversation has not been allocated.

Notes and tips

- The EXTRACT PROCESS command is usually issued in a back-end program to determine the settings specified on the front-end program's CONNECT PROCESS command. In that case, you should omit the CONVID option.

- The PIPLIST option lets you access data that was passed by the corresponding CONNECT PROCESS command. The PIPLIST consists of one or more Process Initialization Parameters (PIPs). Each PIP consists of a binary halfword length field, a binary halfword field set to zero, and a variable-length data area. The length field is set to the length of the data area plus 4. For example, here's a PIPLIST with two PIPs:

```
 01  PIP-LIST.
 *
     05  PIP-1.
         10  PIP1-LENGTH  PIC S9(04)  COMP.
         10  FILLER       PIC S9(04)  COMP.
         10  PIP1-DATA    PIC X(50).
     05  PIP-2.
         10  PIP2-LENGTH  PIC S9(04)  COMP.
         10  FILLER       PIC S9(04)  COMP.
         10  PIP2-DATA    PIC X(16).
```

The PIPLENGTH option returns the complete length of the PIPLIST field (74 in this case).

Coding example

The following example shows how to use the EXTRACT PROCESS command to retrieve PIPLIST information passed by the front-end program.

```
 1000-EXTRACT-PIPLIST.
 *
     EXEC CICS
         EXTRACT PROCESS PIPLIST(ADDRESS OF PIPLIST)
                         PIPLENGTH(PIPLIST-LENGTH)
     END-EXEC.
```

The EXTRACT TCPIP command

Function

TCP/IP services. (TS 1.3 and later) The EXTRACT TCPIP command lets you obtain information about the TCP/IP characteristics for the current transaction.

Syntax

```
EXEC CICS
    EXTRACT TCPIP   [ CLIENTNAME(data-area) CNAMELENGTH(data-area)
                        [ AUTHENTICATE(cvda) ] ]
                    [ SERVERNAME(data-area) SNAMELENGTH(data-area) ]
                    { CLIENTADDR(data-area)
                          CADDRLENGTH(data-area) }
                    { CLIENTADDRNU(data-area)       }
                    { SERVERADDR(data-area)
                          SADDRLENGTH(data-area) }
                    { SERVERADDRNU(data-area)       }
                    [ SSLTYPE(cvda)             ]
                    [ TCPIPSERVICE(data-area)   ]
                    [ PORTNUMBER(data-area)     ]
                    [ PORTNUMNU(data-area)      ]
    END-EXEC.
```

Options

CLIENTNAME	Specifies a data area that receives the client's name as known by the Domain Name Server (DNS).
CNAMELENGTH	A binary fullword (PIC S9(8) COMP) that's set to the actual length of the data area specified in the CLIENTNAME option.
AUTHENTICATE	(TS 2.1 and later) Specifies a binary fullword (PIC S9(8) COMP) where CICS returns the authentication requested for the client using this transaction. The value can be determined by testing it using the DFHVALUE keyword. Valid values are:

> AUTOAUTH   CERTIFICAUTH
> AUTOREGISTER NOAUTHENTIC
> BASICAUTH

SERVERNAME	Specifies a data area that receives the server's name as known by the Domain Name Server.
SNAMELENGTH	A binary fullword (PIC S9(8) COMP) that's set to the actual length of the data area specified in the SERVERNAME option.
CLIENTADDR	Specifies a data area that receives the client's TCP/IP address.
CADDRLENGTH	A binary fullword (PIC S9(8) COMP) that's set to the actual length of the data area specified in the CLIENTADDR option.

CLIENTADDRNU	A binary fullword (PIC S9(8) COMP) that receives the client's TCP/IP address in binary format.
SERVERADDR	Specifies a data area that receives the server's TCP/IP address.
SADDRLENGTH	A binary fullword (PIC S9(8) COMP) that's set to the actual length of the data area specified in the SERVERADDR option.
SERVERADDRNU	A binary fullword (PIC S9(8) COMP) that receives the server's TCP/IP address in binary format.
SSLTYPE	Specifies a binary fullword (PIC S9(8) COMP) where CICS returns the Secure Socket Layer that's used to secure communications for the transaction. The type can be determined by testing it using the DFHVALUE keyword. Valid types are: SSL NOSSL CLIENTAUTH
TCPIPSERVICE	An 8-character field that receives the name of the TCPIPSERVICE associated with the transaction.
PORTNUMBER	A 5-character field that receives the port number associated with the transaction.
PORTNUMNU	A binary fullword (PIC S9(8) COMP) that receives the port number associated with this transaction.

Exceptional conditions

Note: The default action for these conditions is to terminate the task.

| INVREQ | The command was issued from a non-TCP/IP application. |
| LENGERR | A length error occurred on one of the options. |

Notes and tips

- The EXTRACT TCPIP command was added to support the TCP/IP listener. You can use this command to obtain information about the client's address or the server that sent the transmission. Although you may not need to use it often, you may find it useful in web applications.

Coding example

This command gets the address and name of the server that sent the transmission along with the port number that's associated with the transaction.

```
EXEC CICS
    EXTRACT TCPIP SERVERADDR(TCP-SERVER-ADDR)
                  SADDRLENGTH(LENGTH OF TCP-SERVER-ADDR)
                  SERVERNAME(TCP-SERVER-NAME)
                  PORTNUMBER(TCP-PORT-NUMBER)
    END-EXEC.
```

The FORMATTIME command

Function

Interval control. The FORMATTIME command accepts a time value in the absolute time format and returns a time value in any of several formats.

Syntax

```
EXEC CICS
     FORMATTIME    ABSTIME(data-value)
                 [ DATE(data-area) ]
                 [ FULLDATE(data-area) ]
                 [ DATEFORM(data-area) ]
                 [ DATESEP [(data-value)] ]
                 [ DAYCOUNT(data-area) ]
                 [ DAYOFMONTH(data-area) ]
                 [ DAYOFWEEK(data-area) ]
                 [ DDMMYY(data-area) ]
                 [ DDMMYYYY(data-area) ]
                 [ MONTHOFYEAR(data-area) ]
                 [ MMDDYY(data-area) ]
                 [ MMDDYYYY(data-area) ]
                 [ YEAR(data-area) ]
                 [ YYDDD(data-area) ]
                 [ YYDDMM(data-area) ]
                 [ YYMMDD(data-area) ]
                 [ YYYYDDD (data-area) ]
                 [ YYYYDDMM(data-area) ]
                 [ YYYYMMDD(data-area) ]
                 [ TIME(data-area)
                      [ TIMESEP [(data-value)] ] ] ]
     END-EXEC.
```

Options

Note: In the descriptions that follow, yy *represents a two-digit year (like 90 for 1990);* yyyy *represents a four-digit year (like 2002);* mm *represents a two-digit month (like 04 for April);* dd *represents a two-digit day within the current month;* ddd *represents a three-digit day within the current year; and / or : represent optional separator characters.*

ABSTIME   Specifies a 15-digit packed-decimal field (PIC S9(15) COMP-3) or literal value that represents the number of milliseconds that have elapsed since midnight, January 1, 1900. Usually, the value is obtained with an ASKTIME command.

DATE   Specifies an 8-byte field (example: 03/01/02) where CICS returns the date in the format specified in the DATFORM parameter at the time of system initialization. Separators will be present if specified with the DATESEP option; if not, the value is returned left-justified.

FULLDATE	Specifies a 10-byte field (example: 03/01/2002) where CICS returns the date in the format specified in the DATFORM parameter at the time of system initialization. Separators will be present if specified with the DATESEP option; if not, the value is returned left-justified.
DATEFORM	Specifies a 6-byte field where CICS returns YYMMDD, DDMMYY, or MMDDYY to indicate the installation's standard date format.
DATESEP	Specifies a single character value to be used as a separator between the month, day, and year components of a date value. If you omit DATESEP, no separator is used; if you specify DATESEP but don't provide a value, a slash (/) is used.
DAYCOUNT	Specifies a binary fullword (PIC S9(8) COMP) where CICS returns the number of days that have passed since January 1, 1900 (day 1).
DAYOFMONTH	Specifies a binary fullword (PIC S9(8) COMP) where CICS returns the day within the current month.
DAYOFWEEK	Specifies a binary fullword (PIC S9(8) COMP) where CICS returns a number that corresponds to the current day of the week: Sunday is 0, Monday is 1, and so on.
DDMMYY	Specifies an 8-byte field where CICS returns the day, month, and year in the form *dd/mm/yy* if the DATESEP option is specified. If DATESEP is not present, the value is returned left-justified.
DDMMYYYY	Specifies a 10-byte field where CICS returns the day, month, and year in the form *dd/mm/yyyy* if the DATESEP option is specified. If DATESEP is not present, the value is returned left-justified.
MONTHOFYEAR	Specifies a binary fullword (PIC S9(8) COMP) where CICS returns a number that corresponds to the current month: January is 1, February is 2, and so on.
MMDDYY	Specifies an 8-byte field where CICS returns the month, day, and year in the form *mm/dd/yy* if the DATESEP option is specified. If DATESEP is not present, the value is returned left-justified.
MMDDYYYY	Specifies a 10-byte field where CICS returns the month, day, and year in the form *mm/dd/yyyy* if the DATESEP option is specified. If DATESEP is not present, the value is returned left-justified.
YEAR	Specifies a binary fullword (PIC S9(8) COMP) where CICS returns the 4-digit year (such as 2002).
YYDDD	Specifies a 6-byte field where CICS returns the year and day within the year in the form *yy/ddd* if the DATESEP option is specified. If DATESEP is not present, the value is returned left-justified.
YYDDMM	Specifies an 8-byte field where CICS returns the year, day, and month in the form *yy/dd/mm* if the DATESEP option is specified. If DATESEP is not present, the value is returned left-justified.
YYMMDD	Specifies an 8-byte field where CICS returns the year, month, and day in the form *yy/mm/dd* if the DATESEP option is specified. If DATESEP is not present, the value is returned left-justified.

YYYYDDD	Specifies an 8-byte field where CICS returns the year and day within the year in the form *yyyy/ddd* if the DATESEP option is specified. If DATESEP is not present, the value is returned left-justified.
YYYYDDMM	Specifies a 10-byte field where CICS returns the year, day, and month in the form *yyyy/dd/mm* if the DATESEP option is specified. If DATESEP is not present, the value is returned left-justified.
YYYYMMDD	Specifies a 10-byte field where CICS returns the year, month, and day in the form *yyyy/mm/dd* if the DATESEP option is specified. If DATESEP is not present, the value is returned left-justified.
TIME	Specifies an 8-byte field where CICS returns the current 24-hour clock time in the form *hh:mm:ss*.
TIMESEP	Specifies a single character value to be used as a separator between the hours, minutes, and seconds components of a time value. If you omit TIMESEP, no separator is used; if you specify TIMESEP but don't provide a value, a colon (:) is used.

Exceptional condition

INVREQ	The command is invalid, or the ABSTIME option is specified incorrectly. The default action for this condition is to terminate the task.

Notes and tips

- The FORMATTIME command is usually used in combination with the ASKTIME command to simplify the process of formatting time and date values for output.

- To ensure that dates are displayed in a consistent manner, use the DATE or FULLDATE option, which obtains the format and separator character from the System Initialization Table.

- In applications that require date calculations or comparisons, other options are more useful than DATE and FULLDATE. For example, an accounts receivable application might use the DAYCOUNT option to determine how old (in days) a customer's account is. And the DAYOFMONTH and DAYOFWEEK options might be used in payroll applications. Likewise, an option like MMDDYYYY might be used to compare the month and year to other values.

Coding example

This example shows how to get both the current day-of-week (a number that ranges from 0 to 6) and the CICS system date. The absolute time is first obtained using an ASKTIME command. ABSOLUTE-TIME is a 15-digit packed-decimal field (PIC S9(15) COMP-3), DAY-OF-WEEK is a binary fullword (PIC S9(8) COMP), and CURRENT-DATE is a 10-character field (PIC X(10)).

```
 0500-GET-DAY-OF-WEEK.
*
     EXEC CICS
         ASKTIME ABSTIME(ABSOLUTE-TIME)
     END-EXEC.

     EXEC CICS
         FORMATTIME ABSTIME(ABSOLUTE-TIME)
                    DAYOFWEEK(DAY-OF-WEEK)  DATESEP('/')
                    FULLDATE(CURRENT-DATE)
     END-EXEC.
```

The FREE command

Function

APPC mapped conversation/Terminal control. The FREE command releases a distributed processing session so it can be used by another distributed processing transaction.

Syntax

```
EXEC CICS
    FREE [ CONVID(name) | SESSION(name) ]
         [ STATE(cvda) ]
END-EXEC.
```

Options

Note: If you omit both CONVID and SESSION, the principal facility is freed.

CONVID   Specifies the 4-character conversation-id obtained from the Execute Interface Block field EIBRSRCE following a successful ALLOCATE command.

SESSION   (LUTYPE6.1 and MRO only) Specifies the 4-character symbolic TCTTE identifier of the session to be freed.

STATE   (APPC and MRO only) Specifies a binary fullword (PIC S9(8) COMP) where CICS places the state information. The current state can be determined by testing it using the DFHVALUE keyword. Valid states are:

ALLOCATED	RECEIVE
CONFFREE*	ROLLBACK
CONFRECEIVE*	SEND
CONFSEND*	SYNCFREE
FREE	SYNCRECEIVE
PENDFREE	SYNCSEND
PENDRECEIVE*	

*APPC only

Exceptional conditions

Note: The default action for these conditions is to terminate the task.

INVREQ   The request is not allowed.

NOTALLOC   The conversation has not been properly allocated.

Notes and tips

- If you don't explicitly free a session by issuing a FREE command, CICS automatically frees it when the task terminates. As a result, you should use the FREE command only if your program does substantial processing after the conversation has completed.

Coding example

The following example shows a FREE command that releases a session whose conversation-id is stored in the field CONVERSATION-ID.

```
EXEC CICS
    FREE CONVID(CONVERSATION-ID)
END-EXEC.
```

The FREEMAIN command

Function

Storage control. The FREEMAIN command releases virtual storage that was previously acquired with a GETMAIN command so that CICS can use it for other purposes.

Syntax

```
EXEC CICS
    FREEMAIN { DATA(data-area) | DATAPOINTER(pointer-ref) }
END-EXEC.
```

Options

DATA	Specifies the name of the Linkage Section field that defines the storage area you want freed.
DATAPOINTER	Specifies a pointer variable that contains the address of the storage to be freed. Can also specify ADDRESS OF a Linkage Section field.

Exceptional condition

INVREQ	The storage specified wasn't acquired by a GETMAIN command, or the storage is in CICS key and the program is in user key. The default action for this condition is to terminate the task.

Notes and tips

- Note that if you use the DATA option, you specify the Linkage Section field that defines the storage area you want freed, not the address of the field. In other words, specify the Linkage Section description of the field itself, not the ADDRESS OF special register. If you want to specify an address, use the DATAPOINTER option instead.

- You don't need to specify the length of the storage area to be freed. CICS uses control information that immediately precedes the storage to determine how much to release.

Coding example

This example shows how to release virtual storage that was previously acquired by a GETMAIN command. The storage is addressed by a Linkage Section field named INVENTORY-RECORD. See the coding examples for the GETMAIN command to see how the storage was originally acquired.

```
EXEC CICS
    FREEMAIN DATA(INVENTORY-RECORD)
END-EXEC.
```

The GDS commands

Function

APPC basic conversation. The 14 CICS commands that begin with GDS can be used to implement APPC distributed processing functions in assembler language or C. Because these commands cannot be used in COBOL programs, they aren't covered in detail in this book. Here is a list of them, though:

    GDS ALLOCATE
    GDS ASSIGN
    GDS CONNECT PROCESS
    GDS EXTRACT ATTRIBUTES
    GDS EXTRACT PROCESS
    GDS FREE
    GDS ISSUE ABEND
    GDS ISSUE CONFIRMATION
    GDS ISSUE ERROR
    GDS ISSUE PREPARE
    GDS ISSUE SIGNAL
    GDS RECEIVE
    GDS SEND
    GDS WAIT

The GET COUNTER command

Function

Named counter server. The GET COUNTER command retrieves the current number from the specified named counter and then increments the counter by 1 or a specified increment.

Syntax

```
EXEC CICS
    GET   { COUNTER(name) | DCOUNTER(name) }
          [ POOL(name) ]
            VALUE(data-area)
          [ INCREMENT(data-value)
                REDUCE                ]
          [ WRAP ]
          [ COMPAREMIN(data-area) ]
          [ COMPAREMAX(data-area) ]
END-EXEC.
```

Options

COUNTER	Specifies the 16-character name of the named counter from which the current number is to be retrieved. The COUNTER option requires that signed binary fullwords (PIC S9(8) COMP) be used for the other options.
DCOUNTER	Specifies the 16-character name of the named counter from which the current number is to be retrieved. The DCOUNTER option requires that unsigned binary doublewords (PIC 9(18) COMP) be used for the other options.
POOL	Specifies the 8-character name of the pool in which the named counter resides. If there's no matching entry in the DFHNCOPT options table, the default named counter pool on the NCPLDFT system initialization parameter is used.
VALUE	Specifies a signed binary fullword (PIC S9(8) COMP) or unsigned binary doubleword (PIC 9(18) COMP) that receives the current number from the named counter.
INCREMENT	Specifies a signed binary fullword (PIC S9(8) COMP) or unsigned binary doubleword (PIC 9(18) COMP) increment value that's added to the current number in the counter after the current number is received.
REDUCE	Specifies that the value in the INCREMENT option be reduced if the increment amount causes the counter to exceed its maximum limit (the maximum is given in the counter's DEFINE COUNTER command).
WRAP	Specifies that the named counter server should automatically rewind the named counter if its maximum limit is reached. This sets the counter back to its defined minimum value (the maximum and minimum are given in the counter's DEFINE COUNTER command).

COMPAREMIN   Specifies a signed binary fullword (PIC S9(8) COMP) or unsigned binary doubleword (PIC 9(18) COMP) that's compared against the named counter's current value. If the current value is equal to or greater than the COMPAREMIN value, the current number is returned. Otherwise, an exceptional condition is returned.

COMPAREMAX   Specifies a signed binary fullword (PIC S9(8) COMP) or unsigned binary doubleword (PIC 9(18) COMP) that's compared against the named counter's current value. If the current value is less than or equal to the COMPAREMAX value, the current number is returned. Otherwise, an exceptional condition is returned.

Exceptional conditions

Note: The default action for these conditions is to terminate the task.

INVREQ   The statement was coded improperly, there was a problem accessing the named counter in the coupling facility, or the increment value was invalid.

LENGERR   A DCOUNTER (binary doubleword) value was accessed as a COUNTER (binary fullword) value.

SUPPRESSED   The current value in the named counter is not within the range specified by the COMPAREMIN or COMPAREMAX option; or the maximum value for the named counter was reached and no more counter numbers can be assigned until a REWIND COUNTER command is issued or the WRAP option is specified on the GET COUNTER command.

Notes and tips

- The GET COUNTER command lets you retrieve unique sequence numbers from a named counter for functions such as assigning control numbers (like customer, account, or invoice numbers).

- The named counter facility is designed to run in a Parallel Sysplex environment. That means that the facility is controlled by a named counter server, allowing multiple regions to draw from the same counter.

- Specifying the INCREMENT number allows you to increase the counter by a value other than 1. For example, suppose you issue the GET COUNTER command with an increment of 3, and the value returned is 101. The next time you issue the command, the value returned will be 104. This saves you the time and the system overhead required in having to issue the GET COUNTER command two more times. Plus, it ensures that the numbers you use are consecutive.

- If you use a field, not a literal value, to assign a COUNTER or DCOUNTER name, make sure that the field is padded with trailing spaces if the name is less than 16 characters long.

Coding example

The following example shows a GET COUNTER command that retrieves the current value from the named counter called ORDERINV and places it in a field called ORDERNO. The WRAP option forces an automatic rewind of the counter if its maximum value is reached.

```
EXEC CICS
    GET COUNTER('ORDERINV')
        POOL('MMA')
        VALUE(ORDERNO)
        WRAP
END-EXEC.
```

The GETMAIN command

Function

Storage control. The GETMAIN command acquires a specified amount of virtual storage. That storage is held until a FREEMAIN command is issued or the task ends.

Syntax

```
EXEC CICS
    GETMAIN   SET(pointer-ref)
              { LENGTH(data-value) | FLENGTH(data-value) [BELOW] }
              [ INITIMG(data-value) ]
              [ SHARED ]
              [ NOSUSPEND ]
              [ USERDATAKEY | CICSDATAKEY ]
    END-EXEC.
```

Options

SET	Establishes addressability to the storage to be acquired. For programs compiled under the older OS/VS COBOL compiler, this should be a BLL cell that's associated with the Linkage Section description of the storage; for VS COBOL II and later compilers, use the ADDRESS OF special register for the Linkage Section storage description.
LENGTH	Specifies a binary halfword (PIC S9(4) COMP) or literal value that indicates the length of the storage to be acquired. This option is only supported for compatibility purposes, so use the FLENGTH option instead whenever possible.
FLENGTH	Specifies a binary fullword (PIC S9(8) COMP) or literal value that indicates the length of the storage to be acquired.
BELOW	Specifies that the data is to be acquired from below the 16M line.
INITIMG	Specifies a 1-byte field or literal value used to initialize the storage acquired. If omitted, the storage is not initialized.
SHARED	Specifies that the storage will not be automatically freed when the task ends. Instead, it must be explicitly freed by a FREEMAIN command.
NOSUSPEND	Indicates that if storage is not available, control is returned immediately to your program at the point following the GETMAIN command.
USERDATAKEY	Specifies that the storage is to be allocated from one of the user key storage areas.
CICSDATAKEY	Specifies that the storage is to be allocated from one of the CICS key storage areas.

Note: If you omit both USERDATAKEY and CICSDATAKEY, CICS uses the storage key specified in the transaction's resource definition.

Exceptional conditions

LENGERR   You requested too much storage with the FLENGTH option, or the LENGTH value is zero. The default action for this condition is to terminate the task.

NOSTG   The amount of storage you requested is not immediately available. The default action for this condition is to suspend the task.

Notes and tips

- Although the GETMAIN and FREEMAIN commands allow you to make efficient use of storage, you probably won't need them very often. They're most useful when you use locate-mode I/O rather than move-mode I/O. With locate-mode I/O, you use the SET option on I/O commands to specify the address of an I/O area. For input operations, CICS obtains the required storage and returns its address to you; for output operations, you must first obtain the storage (usually with a GETMAIN command) and provide its address to CICS. With move-mode I/O, you use data areas in your program's Working-Storage Section for I/O areas, and you identify those areas with the INTO and FROM options on I/O commands. Locate-mode I/O is dangerous because it's too easy to access and accidentally damage important system information. And that can terminate not only your task, but the entire CICS system as well. So use move-mode I/O and avoid the GETMAIN and FREEMAIN commands.

- The USERDATAKEY and CICSDATAKEY options were introduced along with the storage protection feature of CICS/ESA 3.3. The storage protection feature is designed to prevent application programs from inadvertently over-writing storage areas owned by CICS. Because few application programs will need to acquire CICS key storage, you'll probably never use these options.

- NOSTG is one of the few exceptional conditions that does not cause your task to be terminated. Instead, its action depends on whether you handle the condition (using the RESP option or the HANDLE CONDITION command) and whether you specify NOSUSPEND on the GETMAIN command. If you do neither, NOSTG simply causes your task to be suspended until the storage becomes available; then, control returns to your program at the first statement following the GETMAIN command. If your program handles the NOSTG condition, the specified error processing is done, and the program must issue the GETMAIN command again to acquire the storage. If you specify NOSUSPEND, control is returned to the statement following the GETMAIN command if the storage is unavailable; again, you'll have to issue another GETMAIN command to acquire the storage later.

Coding example (COBOL for OS/390 and z/OS)

This example shows how to acquire 2048 bytes of virtual storage using the COBOL for OS/390 and z/OS compiler. The storage is initialized to HEX-00 (a working-storage field defined with a value of LOW-VALUE) and addressed via the ADDRESS OF special register. After the GETMAIN command executes, INVENTORY-RECORD (and any data names subordinate to it) can be used.

```
LINKAGE SECTION.
.
.
01  INVENTORY-RECORD.
.
.
PROCEDURE DIVISION.
.
.
    EXEC CICS
        GETMAIN SET(ADDRESS OF INVENTORY-RECORD)
                FLENGTH(2048)
                INITIMG(HEX-00)
    END-EXEC.
.
.
```

Coding example (OS/VS COBOL)

This example shows how to acquire 2048 bytes of virtual storage. The storage is initialized to HEX-00 (a working-storage field defined with a value of LOW-VALUE) and addressed via a BLL cell named BLL-INVENTORY-RECORD. After the GETMAIN command executes, INVENTORY-RECORD (and any data names defined subordinate to it) can be used.

```
LINKAGE SECTION.
*
01  COMMUNICATION-AREA.
.
.
01  BLL-CELLS.
*
    05  FILLER                  PIC S9(8)  COMP.
    05  BLL-INVENTORY-RECORD    PIC S9(8)  COMP.
*
01  INVENTORY-RECORD.
.
.
PROCEDURE DIVISION.
.
.
    EXEC CICS
        GETMAIN SET(BLL-INVENTORY-RECORD)
                LENGTH(2048)
                INITIMG(HEX-00)
    END-EXEC.
.
.
```

The HANDLE ABEND command

Function

Abend support. The HANDLE ABEND command lets you establish an abend exit that receives control whenever an abend occurs.

Syntax

```
EXEC CICS
    HANDLE ABEND { CANCEL         }
                 { PROGRAM(name)  }
                 { LABEL(label)   }
                 { RESET          }
END-EXEC.
```

Options

CANCEL	Specifies that the effect of a previous HANDLE ABEND command at the same program level is to be cancelled. This is the default.
PROGRAM	Specifies the 1- to 8-character name of a program that should be invoked (via a LINK command) if the current program abends.
LABEL	Specifies the COBOL paragraph or section name of a routine within the current program that should be invoked (via a GO TO statement) if the program abends.
RESET	Specifies that a previously cancelled abend exit should be reestablished.

Exceptional conditions

Note: These conditions occur only when you specify the PROGRAM option. The default action is to terminate the task.

NOTAUTH	The transaction's PCT entry specified that resource checking should be done, and the operator is not authorized to access the program.
PGMIDERR	The program you specified isn't defined in the Processing Program Table (PPT).

Notes and tips

- The HANDLE ABEND command is usually used to extend the normal CICS abend facilities. For example, you might want to display a terminal message that's more useful than the standard CICS abend message. Or you might want to record detailed abend information in a log. You might also want to try to recover from certain types of errors, but that's not usually an easy matter. The usual way to provide a standardized abend processing routine is to use the PROGRAM option. Then, all programs simply issue a HANDLE ABEND command to establish the specified program as the abend exit.

- A task can establish more than one abend exit at various program levels (that is, for programs invoked via LINK commands). Whenever an abend occurs, CICS invokes the abend exit that was established by the last HANDLE ABEND command your task issued at the current program level or at a higher level.

Coding example

This example shows how to establish a program named ABEND1 as an abend exit.

```
EXEC CICS
    HANDLE ABEND PROGRAM('ABEND1')
END-EXEC.
```

The HANDLE AID command

Function

Terminal control. The HANDLE AID command lets you establish routines that are invoked when an AID event (such as using the Enter key or a PF or PA key) is detected by a RECEIVE MAP command.

Syntax

```
EXEC CICS
    HANDLE AID option [(label)] ...
END-EXEC.
```

Option

option   Specifies the name of the AID key to be handled. You can code up to 16
              options in a single HANDLE AID command. If you need to handle more than
              16 AID keys at once, just issue more than one HANDLE AID command. If
              you specify a label, control is transferred to that label when the specified key
              is detected; if you omit the label, no action is taken when the specified key is
              pressed. You can specify the following options:

ENTER	Enter key
CLEAR	Clear key
PA1-PA3	Program attention keys
PF1-PF24	Program function keys
ANYKEY	Any PA key, PF key, or the Clear key
CLRPARTN	Clear Partition key
LIGHTPEN	Light pen
OPERID	Magnetic slot reader
TRIGGER	Trigger field

Exceptional condition

INVREQ   You issued the HANDLE AID command in a program invoked via the
            Distributed Program Link (DPL). The default action for this condition is to
            terminate the task.

Notes and tips

*   The HANDLE AID command was commonly used in older programs to tell the
    program what to do when the user pressed an attention key. However, this
    command doesn't detect the use of an AID key itself; the RECEIVE MAP
    command does. So a program with HANDLE AID must issue a RECEIVE
    MAP command, even if it doesn't need to receive any input data from the
    terminal. In addition, the HANDLE AID command forces you to use Go To
    statements and sections to manage the flow of control within your program, as

shown in the example that follows. As a result, when you're developing new programs, check for the use of attention keys by testing the Execute Interface Block field EIBAID instead of using HANDLE AID.

- When the HANDLE AID command is used, the Clear and PA keys should be provided for either explicitly or by specifying ANYKEY. Otherwise, the MAPFAIL condition will be raised for the RECEIVE MAP command because data isn't actually transmitted from the terminal, so there's no data to map.

Coding example

This example shows how to use the HANDLE AID command in a module that receives mapped input from a terminal. Here, the Clear key causes control to branch to 2100-CLEAR-KEY, where CANCEL-ENTRY-SW is set to Y; PF1 causes control to branch to 2100-PF1-KEY, where Y is moved to PF-KEY-1-SW; and any other key (other than the Enter key) causes control to branch to 2100-ANYKEY, where VALID-DATA-SW is set to N. These switches are tested elsewhere in the program.

```
 2100-RECEIVE-KEY-SCREEN SECTION.
 *
     EXEC CICS
         HANDLE AID CLEAR(2100-CLEAR-KEY)
                    PF1(2100-PF1-KEY)
                    ANYKEY(2100-ANYKEY)
     END-EXEC.

     EXEC CICS
         RECEIVE MAP('MNTMAP2')
                 MAPSET('MNTSET1')
                 INTO(CUSTOMER-DATA-MAP)
     END-EXEC.

     GO TO 2100-EXIT.
 *
 2100-CLEAR-KEY.
 *
     MOVE 'Y' TO CANCEL-ENTRY-SW.
     GO TO 2100-EXIT.
 *
 2100-PF1-KEY.
 *
     MOVE 'Y' TO PF-KEY-1-SW.
     GO TO 2100-EXIT.
 *
 2100-ANYKEY.
 *
     MOVE 'N' TO VALID-DATA-SW.
     MOVE 'INVALID KEY PRESSED' TO CDM-D-ERROR-MESSAGE.
 *
 2100-EXIT.
 *
     EXIT.
```

The HANDLE CONDITION command

Function

Exception support. The HANDLE CONDITION command specifies how certain exceptional conditions should be processed.

Syntax

```
EXEC CICS
    HANDLE CONDITION condition-name [(label)] ...
END-EXEC.
```

Option

condition-name   The exceptional condition whose processing is specified. If a label is included, control is transferred to the label when the condition is raised. If a label is not included, the default action for the condition is restored; usually, the default action is to terminate the task. Up to 16 conditions can be specified in a single HANDLE CONDITION command. If you need to handle more than 16 conditions, just issue more than one HANDLE CONDITION command.

Exceptional conditions

No exceptional conditions are raised as a result of the HANDLE CONDITION command.

Notes and tips

- The HANDLE CONDITION command was commonly used in older programs to tell the program what to do when an exceptional condition occurred. However, it establishes exceptional condition handling not just for one CICS command, but for all CICS commands in the program that might raise that condition. As a result, it forces you to take careful control over the execution flow of your program as shown in the coding example that follows, since control can be transferred to the exit from any CICS command in your program. In contrast, the RESP option makes it easy to isolate the error handling code for a command, it's simpler to code and manage because it doesn't require the use of sections and Go Tos, and it's more efficient at run-time. So it's the recommended method for handling exceptional conditions.

- An exceptional condition handling routine established by a HANDLE CONDITION command can be disabled permanently or temporarily in one of several ways. If you issue a HANDLE CONDITION command specifying the condition name but no label, the default processing action is restored for the command. If you issue an IGNORE CONDITION command for the condition, the condition is simply ignored; in that case, you can test the Execute Interface

Block to see if the command executed correctly. If you issue a PUSH HANDLE command, all HANDLE CONDITION exits you've established are ignored until you issue a subsequent POP HANDLE command. Finally, you can code RESP or NOHANDLE on any CICS command to temporarily disable any exceptional condition processing (I recommend RESP, so the NOHANDLE condition isn't covered in any more detail in this book).

- You can use the catchall condition name ERROR to provide a common error handling exit for errors that aren't specified in a HANDLE CONDITION command.

Coding example

This example shows how to establish a routine to process the NOTFND condition in a module that reads a record from a data set. When the module has completed, CUSTOMER-FOUND-SW will contain Y if the record was found or N if the record wasn't found. The HANDLE CONDITION command in 2100-RESET deactivates the processing established by the first HANDLE CONDITION command so it won't affect the handling of conditions raised by CICS commands elsewhere in the program.

```
2100-READ-CUSTOMER-RECORD SECTION.
*
    EXEC CICS
        HANDLE CONDITION NOTFND(2100-NOTFND)
                         ERROR(2100-ERROR)
    END-EXEC.

    EXEC CICS
        READ DATASET('CUSTMAS')
            INTO(CUSTOMER-MASTER-RECORD)
            RIDFLD(CM-CUSTOMER-NUMBER)
    END-EXEC.
    MOVE 'Y' TO CUSTOMER-FOUND-SW.
    GO TO 2100-EXIT.
*
 2100-NOTFND.
*
    MOVE 'N' TO CUSTOMER-FOUND-SW.
    GO TO 2100-RESET.
*
 2100-ERROR.
*
    MOVE 'N' TO CUSTOMER-FOUND-SW.
    MOVE 'Y' TO UNRECOVERABLE-ERROR-SW.
*
 2100-RESET.
*
    EXEC CICS
        HANDLE CONDITION NOTFND
                         ERROR
    END-EXEC.
*
 2100-EXIT.
*
    EXIT.
```

The IGNORE CONDITION command

Function

Exception support. The IGNORE CONDITION command lets you specify that one or more exceptional conditions should be ignored. If the specified conditions are raised, processing continues with the next statement in the program.

Syntax

```
EXEC CICS
    IGNORE CONDITION condition-name ...
END-EXEC.
```

Option

condition-name   The exceptional condition that is to be ignored. Up to 16 conditions can be specified in a single IGNORE CONDITION command. If you need to ignore more than 16 conditions, just issue more than one IGNORE CONDITION command.

Exceptional conditions

No exceptional conditions are raised as a result of the IGNORE CONDITION command.

Notes and tips

- With the IGNORE CONDITION command, you can selectively disable exceptional conditions. Then, you test for those conditions after each command by examining fields in the Execute Interface Block. If you use this technique, however, realize that most of the conditions can be raised by more than one command. For example, the LENGERR condition can be raised by any of 44 different commands, including READ, RECEIVE, WRITEQ TD, and GETMAIN. The point is this: If you issue an IGNORE CONDITION command for a particular condition, you'll have to test the EIB for that condition after every command that can possibly raise that condition. Otherwise, the results could be disastrous.

- The NOHANDLE and RESP options are alternatives to the IGNORE CONDITION command. These options, which can be coded on any CICS command, suspend exceptional condition handling for a single command. Following the command, you must properly test for exceptional conditions.

Coding example

This example shows how to suspend condition handling for three conditions:
NOTFND, DUPREC, and DUPKEY.

```
EXEC CICS
     IGNORE CONDITION NOTFND
                      DUPREC
                      DUPKEY
END-EXEC.
```

The ISSUE commands (APPC)

Function

APPC mapped conversation. These ISSUE commands provide for a variety of
distributed processing functions for APPC conversations.

Syntax

```
EXEC CICS
    ISSUE ABEND [ CONVID(name) ]
                [ STATE(cvda) ]
END-EXEC.

EXEC CICS
    ISSUE CONFIRMATION [ CONVID(name) ]
                       [ STATE(cvda) ]
END-EXEC.

EXEC CICS
    ISSUE ERROR [ CONVID(name) ]
                [ STATE(cvda) ]
END-EXEC.

EXEC CICS
    ISSUE PREPARE [ CONVID(name) ]
                  [ STATE(cvda) ]
END-EXEC.

EXEC CICS
    ISSUE SIGNAL [ CONVID(name) ]
                 [ STATE(cvda) ]
END-EXEC.
```

Options

ABEND	Abends an APPC conversation.
CONFIRMATION	Issues the confirmation required when the partner program specifies the CONFIRM option on a SEND command.
ERROR	Informs the partner program that an error has occurred. Often used when the partner program specifies the CONFIRM option on a SEND command.
PREPARE	Informs the partner program that the sending program is about to issue a SYNCPOINT command.
SIGNAL	Used by a program in receive mode to request a change to send mode so that it may send data to the partner program.
CONVID	Specifies the 4-character conversation-id obtained from the Execute Interface Block field EIBRSRCE following a successful ALLO-CATE command.

STATE   Specifies a binary fullword (PIC S9(8) COMP) where CICS places the state information. The current state can be determined by testing it using the DFHVALUE keyword. Valid states are:

ALLOCATED	RECEIVE
CONFFREE	ROLLBACK
CONFRECEIVE	SEND
CONFSEND	SYNCFREE
FREE	SYNCRECEIVE
PENDFREE	SYNCSEND
PENDRECEIVE	

Exceptional conditions

Note: The default action for all of these conditions except SIGNAL is to terminate the task. The default action for the SIGNAL condition is to ignore it.

INVREQ   The request is not allowed.

NOTALLOC   The conversation has not been properly allocated.

SIGNAL   ISSUE CONFIRMATION and ISSUE ERROR only; the partner program has issued an ISSUE SIGNAL command.

TERMERR   Does not occur for ISSUE SIGNAL. A session error has occurred.

Notes and tips

• These commands are used only in programs that manage complex APPC conversations.

The ISSUE commands (terminal control)

Function

Terminal control. The ISSUE commands initiate various control operations for terminal devices.

Syntax

```
EXEC CICS
    ISSUE  COPY    TERMID(name)
                   [ CTLCHAR(data-value) ]
                   [ WAIT ]
END-EXEC.

EXEC CICS
    ISSUE DISCONNECT
END-EXEC.

EXEC CICS
    ISSUE ERASEAUP [ WAIT ]
END-EXEC.

EXEC CICS
    ISSUE PRINT
END-EXEC.
```

Options

COPY	Specifies that the contents of a specified terminal's screen buffer are to be copied into the current terminal's screen buffer. The terminals must be attached to the same control unit.
TERMID	Specifies the 1- to 4-character name of the terminal whose buffer contents are to be copied. This name must appear in the Terminal Control Table (TCT).
CTLCHAR	Specifies a 1-byte copy control character (CCC); usually omitted.
WAIT	Specifies that CICS is to wait until the operation has completed before returning control to the application program.
DISCONNECT	Breaks the connection between the terminal and the processor.
ERASEAUP	Erases all unprotected fields on the terminal screen.
PRINT	Specifies that the contents of the current terminal's screen buffer are to be copied to a printer; how the printer is selected depends on the terminal type and the how the network is defined. For 3270 terminals attached to the same control unit, the print key gives you the same function without the use of CICS resources.

Exceptional conditions

Note: The default action for these conditions is to terminate the task.

TERMIDERR   ISSUE COPY only; the terminal you specified in the TERMID option hasn't been defined to CICS.

TERMERR   ISSUE ERASEAUP and ISSUE PRINT only; a terminal-related error occurred.

Notes and tips

- These are seldom used commands, for good reason: In a modern telecommunications network, terminal device control operations should not be managed by application programs. Instead, the network itself provides that control. So avoid these commands whenever possible.

The JOURNAL command

Function

Journaling. The JOURNAL command writes a record to a journal file.

Note: The JOURNAL command is supported for compatibility purposes with earlier releases of CICS. It has been replaced by the WRITE JOURNALNAME command.

The LINK command

Function

Program control. The LINK command invokes a program, which causes the program to be loaded into storage if necessary, and passes data to the invoked program if needed. When the invoked program ends, control is returned to the statement following the LINK command in the invoking program. In some cases, the invoked program may reside on another system.

Syntax

```
EXEC CICS
    LINK    PROGRAM(name)
         [ COMMAREA(data-area)
             [ LENGTH(data-value) ]
             [ DATALENGTH(data-value) ] ]
         [ INPUTMSG(data-area)
             [ INPUTMSGLEN(data-value) ] ]
         [ SYSID(systemname) ]
         [ SYNCONRETURN ]
         [ TRANSID(name) ]
    END-EXEC.
```

Options

PROGRAM	Specifies the 1- to 8-character name of the program to be invoked. If this name is not defined in CICS and AUTOINSTALL is active, CICS will supply a definition for the program.
COMMAREA	Specifies a data area that's passed to the invoked program as a communication area. The invoked program accesses the communication area via its DFHCOMMAREA field, which is addressed to the data area specified in the invoking program. In other words, the invoked program accesses the communication area in the same storage locations as the invoking program; the communication area is not copied to another area of storage. (This works differently than it does for an XCTL or RETURN command; see the descriptions of those commands for details.)
LENGTH	Specifies a binary halfword (PIC S9(4) COMP) or literal value that indicates the length of the data area specified in the COMMAREA option. This value can't exceed 32500 bytes if the COMMAREA is to be passed between two CICS systems.
DATALENGTH	Specifies a binary halfword (PIC S9(4) COMP) or literal value that indicates the length of the data to be sent from the area specified in the COMMAREA option. The value may be less than the total length of this area.
INPUTMSG	Specifies a data area that will be used to provide input for a RECEIVE command issued by the invoked program. This option can't be used at the same time as DATALENGTH.

INPUTMSGLEN	Specifies a binary halfword (PIC S9(4) COMP) or literal value that indicates the length of the INPUTMSG field.
SYSID	Specifies the name of the remote system where the specified program resides. If omitted, the program's resource definition is used to determine the location of the program.
SYNCONRETURN	Indicates that the server program should perform a syncpoint when it returns control to the client program. If omitted, the syncpoint is taken when the client program ends.
TRANSID	Specifies the trans-id that the remote system should use to run the invoked program. If omitted, CSMI, CPMI, or CVMI is used.

Note: If you specify INPUTMSG, you cannot specify SYSID, SYNCONRETURN, or TRANSID.

Exceptional conditions

Note: The default action for these conditions is to terminate the task.

INVREQ	INPUTMSG, SYNCONRETURN, or TRANSID is used improperly.
LENGERR	A length error occurred.
NOTAUTH	A resource security check has failed on the program named in the PROGRAM option.
PGMIDERR	The program is not defined in the Processing Program Table (PPT).
ROLLEDBACK	SYNCONRETURN was specified, and the linked-to program could not successfully take a syncpoint. The linked-to program issued a rollback.
SYSIDERR	The remote system could not be found.
TERMERR	A conversation error occurred.

Notes and tips

- The LINK command invokes a CICS program as if it were a subprogram. You can achieve a similar result by using a COBOL Call statement. Although the Call statement is faster and more efficient (because CICS isn't involved), the LINK command has some distinct advantages: It automatically provides addressability to the EIB, and you can invoke a program on either a local or remote system. A COBOL Call statement can only invoke a program on a local system.

- When you invoke a program using LINK, CICS keeps the invoking program in virtual storage while the linked program executes. In contrast, the XCTL command, which also transfers control to another program, doesn't use a return mechanism, so CICS is free to release resources used by the invoking program. Despite that, both XCTL and LINK consume CICS resources. So the choice of one over another should be based on transaction design and not on perceived performance differences.

- If application processing can continue without the linked program, you should handle the PGMIDERR and NOTAUTH conditions. If the program is critical to the application, though, there's little point in handling those conditions.

- The INPUTMSG option is provided to pass data to programs that were originally designed to receive data from the terminal. Data placed in the INPUTMSG area is received by the linked-to program's first RECEIVE command.

- The SYSID, SYNCONRETURN, and TRANSID options were introduced with CICS/ESA 3.3 to support Distributed Program Link (DPL). In most cases, all three can be omitted. Then, the SYSID is specified by the program's resource definition. If the linked-to program updates recoverable resources and the linking program does no updates after issuing the LINK, you can save some communication time by using the SYNCONRETURN option. If you do, however, be sure to test for the ROLLEDBACK condition.

Coding example

This example invokes a program named MMIN2010, passing it a communication area named NEXT-INVOICE-NUMBER.

```
5000-GET-NEXT-INVOICE-NUMBER.
*
    EXEC CICS
        LINK PROGRAM('MMIN2010')
            COMMAREA(NEXT-INVOICE-NUMBER)
    END-EXEC.
```

The LOAD command

Function

Program control. The LOAD command retrieves an object module, loads it into virtual storage, and returns its length and address to the program that issued the LOAD command.

Syntax

```
EXEC CICS
    LOAD   PROGRAM(name)
         [ SET(pointer-ref) ]
         [ LENGTH(data-area) | FLENGTH(data-area) ]
         [ ENTRY(pointer-ref) ]
         [ HOLD ]
    END-EXEC.
```

Options

PROGRAM	Specifies the 1- to 8-character name of the object module to be loaded. If this name is not defined in CICS and AUTOINSTALL is active, CICS will supply a definition for the program.
SET	Specifies a binary fullword (PIC S9(8) COMP) where CICS returns the address of the object module that was loaded. You can use the ADDRESS OF special register in the SET option.
LENGTH	Specifies a binary halfword (PIC S9(4) COMP) that's set to the length of the object module retrieved. To avoid the LENGERR condition, use the FLENGTH option instead.
FLENGTH	Specifies a binary fullword (PIC S9(8) COMP) that's set to the length of the object module retrieved.
ENTRY	Specifies a binary fullword (PIC S9(8) COMP) that's set to the virtual storage address of the entry point of the object module that was loaded.
HOLD	Specifies that the object module should remain in storage after the current task finishes. If specified, the object module can be removed later by a RELEASE command; if omitted, the object module is automatically removed when the task ends. However, if the object module is defined with RELOAD=YES, a FREEMAIN command must be issued to remove the object module.

Exceptional conditions

Note: The default action for these conditions is to terminate the task.

INVREQ   The program manager domain has not yet been initialized.

LENGERR   The LENGTH option was specified, and the length of the specified object
                module is not less than 32KB.

NOTAUTH   A resource security check has failed on the object module named in the
                PROGRAM option.

PGMIDERR   The object module is not defined in the Processing Program Table (PPT).

Notes and tips

- The LOAD command actually loads a program into storage if the program isn't
  already loaded. If the program is already in virtual storage, the LOAD command simply returns the address of the program.

- Although the load module can be an executable program that you can invoke
  via a LINK or XCTL command, it's often a table that is addressed via the
  Linkage Section. Any table whose entries rarely change, such as states or zip
  codes, is a good candidate for this technique.

- Depending on the application, you may or may not need to provide for the
  LENGERR, NOTAUTH, and PGMIDERR conditions.

Coding example

This example shows the Linkage Section and the Procedure Division code required
to load and address a table stored as an object module. The table is held after the
task ends, so it can be released only by a RELEASE command.

```
      LINKAGE SECTION.
      .
      .
      01  STATE-TABLE.
      *
          05  STATE-CODE            OCCURS 52  PIC XX.
      *
      PROCEDURE DIVISION.
      *
      0000-ACCEPT-CUSTOMER-ORDERS.
      *
          EXEC CICS
              LOAD PROGRAM('STATABL')
                  SET(ADDRESS OF STATE-TABLE)
                  HOLD
          END-EXEC.
          .
          .
```

Coding example: The assembler language source code for a constant table

This example shows the assembler language coding required to create a constant table that can be loaded and addressed as shown in the previous example. After the initial comments, the program consists simply of DC statements that define literal values. There are no executable statements.

```
STATABL   START 0
**********************************************************
*                                                        *
*     THIS CONSTANT TABLE CONTAINS 52 TWO-BYTE ENTRIES   *
*     CORRESPONDING TO THE FIFTY STATES PLUS PUERTO RICO *
*     AND THE DISTRICT OF COLUMBIA                       *
*                                                        *
**********************************************************
          DC    CL10'AKALARAZCA'
          DC    CL10'COCTDCDEFL'
          DC    CL10'GAHIIAIDIL'
          DC    CL10'INKSKYLAMA'
          DC    CL10'MDMEMIMNMO'
          DC    CL10'MSMTNCNDNE'
          DC    CL10'NHNJNMNVNY'
          DC    CL10'OHOKORPAPR'
          DC    CL10'RISCSDTNTX'
          DC    CL10'UTVAVTWAWV'
          DC    CL4'WIWY'
          END
```

The POP HANDLE command

Function

Exception support. The POP HANDLE command restores HANDLE ABEND, HANDLE AID, HANDLE CONDITION, and IGNORE CONDITION commands that were temporarily suspended by a PUSH HANDLE command.

Syntax

```
EXEC CICS
    POP HANDLE
END-EXEC.
```

Options

The POP HANDLE command has no options.

Exceptional condition

INVREQ   No PUSH HANDLE command was issued at the current program level. The default action for this condition is to terminate the task.

Notes and tips

- You can think of the PUSH and POP HANDLE commands as implementing a push-down stack for the settings established by HANDLE ABEND, HANDLE AID, HANDLE CONDITION, and IGNORE CONDITION commands. Each time you issue a PUSH HANDLE command, the current HANDLE settings are pushed on top of the stack and all current settings are restored to system defaults. Then, when you issue a POP HANDLE command, the HANDLE settings on top of the stack are removed from the stack and made current.

- PUSH and POP HANDLE are most useful when you invoke subprograms via the COBOL Call statement. A called subprogram can begin by issuing a PUSH HANDLE command. That saves the current HANDLE settings, and the called subprogram can issue whatever HANDLE commands it needs. Then, before it returns to the calling program, the called program can issue a POP HANDLE command to restore the HANDLE settings to their original status.

- When a program is invoked with a LINK command, CICS automatically deactivates the HANDLE AID and HANDLE CONDITION settings of the caller, so the PUSH and POP HANDLE commands aren't needed for that purpose. (Any abend exits established by HANDLE ABEND commands, however, remain active.)

- If you use RESP and EIBAID instead of the HANDLE CONDITION and HANDLE AID commands, you'll probably never need to use the POP HANDLE command.

Coding example

This example shows how you might use PUSH and POP HANDLE commands in a
called subprogram. When used this way, the called subprogram can establish its
own HANDLE settings without altering the settings of the calling program.

```
      PROCEDURE DIVISION USING CUSTOMER-KEY
                               CUSTOMER-RECORD.
*
       0000-GET-CUSTOMER-RECORD SECTION.
*
          EXEC CICS
              PUSH HANDLE
          END-EXEC.

          EXEC CICS
              HANDLE CONDITION NOTFND(1100-NOTFND)
          END-EXEC.
              .
              .
          EXEC CICS
              POP HANDLE
          END-EXEC.
*
       0000-EXIT-PROGRAM.
*
          GOBACK.
```

The POST command

Function

Interval control. The POST command creates a Timer Event Control Area that expires when a specified time interval has elapsed. You can then use a WAIT EVENT command to suspend your task until the posted event expires.

Syntax

```
EXEC CICS
    POST [ { INTERVAL(hhmmss) }
           { TIME(hhmmss)     }
           { AFTER [HOURS(hh)] [MINUTES(mins)] [SECONDS(secs)] }
           { AT [HOURS(hh)] [MINUTES(mins)] [SECONDS(secs)] }    ]
           SET(pointer-ref)
         [ REQID(name) ]
END-EXEC.
```

Options

Note: If INTERVAL, TIME, AFTER, and AT are all omitted, INTERVAL(0) is assumed.

INTERVAL   Specifies a time interval after which the event expires. You can code a literal in the form *hhmmss*; leading zeros can be omitted. Or, you can code a data name for a 7-digit packed-decimal field (PIC S9(7) COMP-3); its value must be in the form *0hhmmss*.

TIME   Specifies a time of day when the event expires. You can code a literal in the form *hhmmss*; leading zeros can be omitted. Or, you can code a data name for a 7-digit packed-decimal field (PIC S9(7) COMP-3); its value must be in the form *0hhmmss*.

AFTER   Specifies that the HOURS, MINUTES, and SECONDS options indicate a duration after which the event expires.

AT   Specifies that the HOURS, MINUTES, and SECONDS options indicate a time of day when the event expires.

HOURS   Specifies a binary fullword (PIC S9(8) COMP) in the range of 0 to 99.

MINUTES   Specifies a binary fullword (PIC S9(8) COMP) in the range of 0 to 59 or 0 to 5999.

SECONDS   Specifies a binary fullword (PIC S9(8) COMP) in the range of 0 to 59 or 0 to 359999.

SET   Specifies a binary fullword (PIC S9(8) COMP) where CICS places the address of the Timer Event Control Area. If you need to access the Timer Event Control Area directly, you should provide the proper linkage using the ADDRESS OF special register. Otherwise, this can be a simple Working-Storage Section field.

REQID   Specifies a 1- to 8-character request identifier that's associated with the Timer Event Control Area. If you issue a CANCEL command specifying the same request identifier, the Timer Event Control Area is cancelled. If you omit REQID, CICS generates a unique request identifier and places it in the EIBREQID field in the Execute Interface Block.

Exceptional conditions

Note: The default action for these conditions is to terminate the task.

EXPIRED   The time you specified in the INTERVAL or TIME option has already arrived.

INVREQ   The command is invalid, or the specified hours, minutes, or seconds are out of range.

Notes and tips

- There are two ways to use the HOURS, MINUTES, and SECONDS options following AFTER. If you use them in combination, the ranges are 0 to 99 for HOURS, 0 to 59 for MINUTES, and 0 to 59 for SECONDS. However, if you specify only one option, you can use the larger ranges: 0 to 99 for HOURS, 0 to 5999 for MINUTES, and 0 to 359999 for SECONDS. For example, you could specify AFTER MINUTES(1) SECONDS(30), or you could specify AFTER SECONDS(90). Both have the same effect.

- One possible, though unlikely, use for the POST and WAIT EVENT commands is to force a minimum response time for terminal transactions. To do that, issue a POST command at the start of the task, specifying the minimum response time (perhaps 3 seconds) in the INTERVAL option. Then, before you issue the final SEND MAP command, issue a WAIT EVENT command. That way, the terminal won't receive output faster than the minimum response time will allow. Of course, this doesn't account for data transmission time, which is often the largest component of total response time.

Coding example

This example shows how to issue POST and WAIT EVENT commands to ensure a minimum response time of 3 seconds. Because this type of function affects the high-level coding of the program, I've included most of the program's top-level module and parts of several subordinate modules. WS-ECA-POINTER is a working storage field defined as PIC S9(8) COMP.

```
     0000-PROCESS-CUSTOMER-INQUIRY.
 *
         IF EIBCALEN > ZERO
             EXEC CICS
                 POST EVENT INTERVAL(3)
                           SET(WS-ECA-POINTER)
             END-EXEC
         END-IF.

         EVALUATE TRUE
             WHEN EIBAID = DFHPF3 OR DFHPF12
                 EXEC CICS
                     XCTL PROGRAM('MENU1')
                 END-EXEC
             WHEN EIBAID = DFHENTER
                 PERFORM 1000-PROCESS-CUSTOMER-MAP
                 .
                 .
                 .
         END-EVALUATE.

         EXEC CICS
             RETURN TRANSID('INQ1')
                     COMMAREA(COMMUNICATION-AREA)
         END-EXEC.
 *
      1000-PROCESS-CUSTOMER-MAP.
 *
         PERFORM 1100-RECEIVE-CUSTOMER-MAP.
         .
         .
         IF VALID-DATA
             PERFORM 1400-SEND-CUSTOMER-MAP
         END-IF.
         .
         .
      1400-SEND-CUSTOMER-MAP.
 *
         EXEC CICS
             WAIT EVENT ECADDR(WS-ECA-POINTER)
         END-EXEC.

         EXEC CICS
             SEND MAP ...
         END-EXEC.
```

The PURGE MESSAGE command

Function

Basic Mapping Support. The PURGE MESSAGE command lets you delete a logical message before your task terminates.

Syntax

```
EXEC CICS
    PURGE MESSAGE
END-EXEC.
```

Options

The PURGE MESSAGE command has no options.

Exceptional condition

Note: The default action for these conditions is to terminate the task.

INVREQ   The command was called in a Distributed Program Link (DPL) program.

TSIOERR   An I/O error has occurred on the temporary storage data set. The default action for this condition is to terminate the task.

Notes and tips

*   A logical message is a single unit of terminal output that's built by one or more SEND TEXT or SEND MAP commands.
*   The PURGE MESSAGE command is useful if, while your program is building a message, it encounters an error that won't let it complete the message. In that case, the program should issue a PURGE MESSAGE command so that all of the CICS resources—especially the temporary storage space occupied by the message—are released.

Coding example

This example shows how to issue a PURGE MESSAGE command. Here, module 1000 is invoked repeatedly to build a message until MESSAGE-COMPLETE-SW is turned on. If a situation arises that prevents the message from being created, MESSAGE-CANCELED-SW is turned on. After module 1000 completes, that switch is tested. If it's on, a PURGE MESSAGE command is issued to delete the portion of the message that was created before the error condition occurred.

```
    .
    .
PERFORM 1000-BUILD-INQUIRY-MESSAGE
    UNTIL MESSAGE-COMPLETE.

IF MESSAGE-CANCELED
    EXEC CICS
        PURGE MESSAGE
    END-EXEC
END-IF.
    .
    .
```

The PUSH HANDLE command

Function

Exception support. The PUSH HANDLE command suspends HANDLE ABEND, HANDLE AID, HANDLE CONDITION, and IGNORE CONDITION commands. A POP HANDLE command can be used to restore the saved settings.

Syntax

```
EXEC CICS
    PUSH HANDLE
END-EXEC.
```

Options

The PUSH HANDLE command has no options.

Exceptional conditions

No exceptional conditions are raised as a result of the PUSH HANDLE command.

Notes and tips

*   You can think of the PUSH and POP HANDLE commands as implementing a push-down stack for the settings established by HANDLE ABEND, HANDLE AID, HANDLE CONDITION, and IGNORE CONDITION commands. Each time you issue a PUSH HANDLE command, the current HANDLE or IG-NORE settings are pushed on top of the stack and all current settings are restored to system defaults. Then, when you issue a POP HANDLE command, the HANDLE or IGNORE settings on top of the stack are removed from the stack and made current.

*   PUSH and POP HANDLE are most useful when you invoke subprograms via the COBOL Call statement. A called subprogram can begin by issuing a PUSH HANDLE command. That saves the current HANDLE settings, and the called subprogram can issue whatever HANDLE commands it needs. Then, before it returns to the calling program, the called program can issue a POP HANDLE command to restore the HANDLE settings to their original status.

*   When a program is invoked with a LINK command, CICS automatically deactivates the HANDLE AID and HANDLE CONDITION settings of the caller, so the PUSH and POP HANDLE commands aren't needed for that purpose. (Any abend exits established by HANDLE ABEND commands, however, remain active.)

*   If you use RESP and EIBAID instead of the HANDLE CONDITION and HANDLE AID commands, you'll probably never need to use the PUSH HANDLE command.

Coding example

This example shows how you might use PUSH and POP HANDLE commands in a
called subprogram. When used this way, the called subprogram can establish its
own HANDLE settings without altering the settings of the calling program.

```
       PROCEDURE DIVISION USING CUSTOMER-KEY
                              CUSTOMER-RECORD.
 *
  0000-GET-CUSTOMER-RECORD SECTION.
 *
       EXEC CICS
           PUSH HANDLE
       END-EXEC.

       EXEC CICS
           HANDLE CONDITION NOTFND(1100-NOTFND)
       END-EXEC.
         .
         .
       EXEC CICS
           POP HANDLE
       END-EXEC.
 *
  0000-EXIT-PROGRAM.
 *
       GOBACK.
```

The QUERY COUNTER command

Function

Named counter server. The QUERY COUNTER command lets you retrieve the current, minimum, and maximum values for the named counter.

Syntax

```
EXEC CICS
    QUERY   { COUNTER(name) | DCOUNTER(name) }
            [ POOL(name) ]
            [ VALUE(data-area) ]
            [ MINIMUM(data-area) ]
            [ MAXIMUM(data-area) ]
END-EXEC.
```

Options

COUNTER	Specifies the 16-character name of the counter to be queried. The COUNTER option requires that signed binary fullword (PIC S9(8) COMP) values be used for the VALUE, MINIMUM, and MAXIMUM options.
DCOUNTER	Specifies the 16-character name of the counter to be queried. The DCOUNTER option requires that unsigned binary doubleword (PIC 9(18) COMP) values be used for the VALUE, MINIMUM, and MAXIMUM options.
POOL	Specifies the 8-character name of the pool in which the named counter resides. If there's no matching entry in the DFHNCOPT options table, the default named counter pool on the NCPLDFT system initialization parameter is used.
VALUE	Specifies a signed binary fullword (PIC S9(8) COMP) or unsigned binary doubleword (PIC 9(18) COMP) that returns the current number from the named counter.
MINIMUM	Specifies a signed binary fullword (PIC S9(8) COMP) or unsigned binary doubleword (PIC 9(18) COMP) that returns the minimum number defined for the named counter.
MAXIMUM	Specifies a signed binary fullword (PIC S9(8) COMP) or unsigned binary doubleword (PIC 9(18) COMP) that returns the maximum number defined for the named counter.

Exceptional conditions

Note: The default action for these conditions is to terminate the task.

INVREQ The statement was coded improperly or there was a problem accessing the named counter in the coupling facility.

LENGERR A DCOUNTER (binary doubleword) value was accessed as a COUNTER (binary fullword) value.

Notes and tips

- A named counter generates sequence numbers that can be used for functions such as assigning control numbers (like customer, account, or invoice numbers).

- The named counter facility is designed to run in a Parallel Sysplex environment. That means that the facility is controlled by a named counter server, allowing multiple regions to draw from the same counter.

- The QUERY COUNTER command lets you find out what the current, minimum, and maximum values are for a specified counter. However, as soon as the command is executed, another task somewhere in the sysplex may change the counter value by issuing a GET COUNTER command. So keep that in mind as you use the counter value you've retrieved.

- If you use a field, not a literal value, to assign a COUNTER or DCOUNTER name, make sure that the field is padded with trailing spaces if the name is less than 16 characters long.

Coding example

The following example shows a QUERY COUNTER command that retrieves the current number stored in a counter named ORDERINV.

```
EXEC CICS
    QUERY COUNTER('ORDERINV')
    POOL('MMA')
    VALUE(ORDERNO)
END-EXEC.
```

The QUERY SECURITY command

Function

Security. The QUERY SECURITY command lets you check the user's authorization to access specific resources defined in the external security manager before an actual attempt is made to access them.

Syntax

```
EXEC CICS
    QUERY SECURITY    RESID(data-value)
                      { RESTYPE(data-value) }
                      { RESCLASS(data-value)
                            RESIDLENGTH(data-value) }
                      [ LOGMESSAGE(cvda) ]
                      [ READ(cvda) ]
                      [ UPDATE(cvda) ]
                      [ CONTROL(cvda) ]
                      [ ALTER(cvda) ]
    END-EXEC.
```

Options

RESID	A 1- to 12-character field or literal value that specifies the name of the CICS or user-defined resource involved in the security check.
RESTYPE	A 1- to 12-character field or literal value that specifies the type of resource involved in the security check.
RESCLASS	An 8-character field or literal value that specifies the name of a valid resource class in the external security manager. If the ESM is RACF, the class can be CICS-supplied or user-defined. The RESCLASS allows you to query at the record or field level for authorization.
RESIDLENGTH	Specifies a binary fullword (PIC S9(8) COMP) or literal value that indicates the length of the resource identifier in the RESID option. You only need to include this option when you specify the RESCLASS option.
LOGMESSAGE	Specifies a binary fullword (PIC S9(8) COMP) that enables you to control security violation messages. You can use the DFHVALUE keyword to set the value to LOG, which enables the security messages, or NOLOG, which inhibits the messages. The default is LOG.
READ	A binary fullword (PIC S9(8) COMP) that specifies whether or not a user has READ authority for the named resource. You can test this value using the DFHVALUE keyword. Valid values are: READABLE and NOTREADABLE.
UPDATE	A binary fullword (PIC S9(8) COMP) that specifies whether or not a user has UPDATE authority for the named resource. You can test this value using the DFHVALUE keyword. Valid values are: UPDATABLE and NOTUPDATABLE.

CONTROL   A binary fullword (PIC S9(8) COMP) that specifies whether or not a user
              has CONTROL authority for the named resource. You can test this value
              using the DFHVALUE keyword. Valid values are: CTRLABLE and
              NOTCTRLABLE.

ALTER   A binary fullword (PIC S9(8) COMP) that specifies whether or not a user
              has ALTER authority for the named resource. You can test this value using
              the DFHVALUE keyword. Valid values are: ALTERABLE and
              NOTALTERABLE.

Exceptional conditions

Note: The default action for these conditions is to terminate the task.

INVREQ   The CICS-value data area provided for the LOGMESSAGE option is
              invalid or the RESID option is invalid or the external security manager is
              inactive.

LENGERR   The length specified in the RESIDLENGTH option is invalid.

NOTFND   One of the following values is not valid: RESID, RESTYPE, RESCLASS.

QIDERR   An indirect queue name associated with the value in the RESID option is
              not found.

Notes and tips

- The resource type you specify in the RESTYPE option must be one of the
  following:

DB2ENTRY	PROGRAM	TRANSACTION
FILE	PSB	TRANSATTACH
JOURNALNAME	SPCOMMAND	TSQUEUE
JOURNALNUM	TDQUEUE	

Coding example

This example prevents CICS from logging security violation messages for the
resource named in WS-RESID.

```
    .
    .
    MOVE DFHVALUE(NOLOG) TO WS-LOG-IND.
    .
    .
    EXEC CICS
        QUERY SECURITY RESID(WS-RESID)
                       LOGMESSAGE(WS-LOG-IND)
    END-EXEC.
```

The READ command

Function

File control. The READ command retrieves one record from a file. The file can be a VSAM KSDS, ESDS, RRDS, or path. (CICS also supports BDAM files, but the BDAM options aren't covered in this book.)

Syntax

```
EXEC CICS
    READ    FILE(filename)
          { INTO(data-area) | SET(pointer-ref) }
            RIDFLD(data-area)
          [ LENGTH(data-area) | SYSID(systemname) LENGTH(data-area) ]
          [ KEYLENGTH(data-value)
              [ GENERIC ] ]
          [ RBA | RRN ]
          [ GTEQ | EQUAL ]
          [ { UPDATE
                [ TOKEN(data-area) ] }
            { CONSISTENT   }
            { REPEATABLE   }
            { UNCOMMITTED } ]
          [ NOSUSPEND ]
    END-EXEC.
```

Options

FILE	Specifies the 1- to 8-character name of the data set that contains the record to be read.
INTO	Specifies the data area that will contain the record being read.
SET	Specifies the data area that will contain the address of the retrieved record.
RIDFLD	Specifies a data area that identifies the record to be retrieved. The content of the RIDFLD field depends on whether RBA or RRN is specified; if neither is specified, the RIDFLD field contains a key for VSAM KSDS or path retrieval. For a generic read (see the KEYLENGTH and GENERIC options below), the RIDFLD must still be as long as the file's defined key length.
LENGTH	Specifies a binary halfword (PIC S9(4) COMP) that contains the length of the record. On entry, the data area indicates the size of the INTO data area, if INTO is specified. On exit, the data area contains the size of the record retrieved. Required if INTO is specified and the file has variable-length records; optional for SET. Also required when SYSID is specified.
SYSID	Specifies the 1- to 4-character name of a remote system that contains the file.

KEYLENGTH	Specifies a binary halfword (PIC S9(4) COMP) or literal value that indicates the length of the key, which must be less than the file's defined key length. Used only for a generic read along with the GENERIC option or when the SYSID option is specified. Not valid if RBA or RRN is specified.
GENERIC	Specifies that only a part of the key in the RIDFLD field should be used, as indicated by the KEYLENGTH option. The first record with a key whose leftmost character positions (as specified by KEYLENGTH) match the RIDFLD field is retrieved.
RBA	Specifies that the RIDFLD field is a relative byte address (RBA) for a VSAM KSDS or ESDS. However, you can't use the RBA option for user-maintained data tables, coupling facility data tables, KSDS files larger than 4GB, or KSDS files opened in RLS mode. An RBA is a binary fullword (PIC S9(8) COMP).
RRN	Specifies that the RIDFLD is a relative record number (RRN) for a VSAM RRDS. An RRN is a binary fullword (PIC S9(8) COMP). The RRN of the first record in an RRDS is 1.
GTEQ	Specifies that the first record whose key value is greater than or equal to the key specified in the RIDFLD field is to be retrieved. This will always retrieve a record from the file unless the specified key is greater than the largest key in the file.
EQUAL	Specifies that only a record whose key matches the RIDFLD field will be retrieved. This is the default.
UPDATE	Specifies that you intend to update the record by rewriting or deleting it. In this case, the entire control interval containing the record is held under exclusive control by your task. No other task can access any record in the control interval until: (1) you issue a REWRITE, DELETE, or UNLOCK command to release the record or (2) your task ends. If the file is recoverable, the control interval is held until the task ends or you issue a SYNCPOINT command, even if you issue a REWRITE, DELETE, or UNLOCK command.
TOKEN	Specifies a binary fullword (PIC S9(8) COMP) that returns a unique identifier for a READ UPDATE request. This identifier can then be used to associate the record retrieved with a subsequent REWRITE, DELETE or UNLOCK command. Using this option makes it possible to perform concurrent updates on two or more records in the same file within the same task.
CONSISTENT	(RLS only) Specifies that the record is to be read with a level of read integrity provided by a VSAM shared lock that lasts until the record is read (that is, until it's returned to your program). If the record is locked by another task, the READ request waits until the lock is released.
REPEATABLE	(RLS only) Specifies that the record is to be read with a level of read integrity provided by a VSAM shared lock that lasts until the unit of work that contains the READ request is ended. If the record is locked by another task, the READ request waits until the lock is released.
UNCOMMITTED	(RLS only) Specifies that the record is to be read with no read integrity.
NOSUSPEND	(RLS only) Specifies that the READ request will not wait if the record is held under exclusive control (locked) by another task.

Exceptional conditions

Note: The default action for these conditions is to terminate the task.

DISABLED	The data set is disabled, probably as a result of the master terminal operator explicitly disabling the file using CEMT SET DISABLE.
DUPKEY	Occurs only when retrieving records via an alternate index (path) that allows duplicate keys; indicates that more than one record with the specified key exists. The READ command retrieves only the first record with the specified key.
FILENOTFOUND	The data set name specified in the FILE option isn't defined in the File Control Table (FCT).
ILLOGIC	A serious VSAM error occurred.
INVREQ	The READ request is prohibited by the file's FCT entry. Can also occur if the KEYLENGTH value is incorrect.
IOERR	An I/O error occurred.
ISCINVREQ	An undeterminable error occurred on the remote system specified in the SYSID option.
LENGERR	The length of the record retrieved exceeds the length specified in the LENGTH option.
LOADING	(TS 1.1 and later) The READ request was issued against a data table that is still being loaded into the CICS system.
LOCKED	A READ UPDATE was issued against a record that is currently locked.
NOTAUTH	The transaction's PCT entry specified that resource security checking should be done, and the operator is not authorized to access the data set.
NOTFND	The specified record could not be located.
NOTOPEN	The file is not open.
RECORDBUSY	(TS 1.1 and later) The NOSUSPEND option was specified on a record held under exclusive control by another task.
SYSIDERR	The system identified by SYSID could not be located or accessed.

Notes and tips

- To read a record via an alternate index, simply specify a path name in the FILE option. If the alternate index allows duplicate keys, only the first record for each alternate key value can be retrieved by the READ command. To retrieve more than one record with the same alternate key value, use the READNEXT command.

- The only exceptional condition you should worry about for the READ command is NOTFND. If you're retrieving records via a path that allows duplicate keys, you should also check for DUPKEY.

- Record-level sharing (RLS) is a VSAM feature available through the SMS facility. It allows files to be shared with update capability between applications and across CICS regions. When you open a file in RLS mode, locking takes place at the record level instead of the control-interval level. This reduces the possibility of deadlocks.

Coding example (fixed-length VSAM KSDS records)

This example retrieves a fixed-length record from a VSAM KSDS. The record, identified by the key value in ACCOUNT-NUMBER, is placed in the field named ACCOUNT-RECORD. The NOTFND condition is handled to provide for invalid key values.

```
2100-READ-ACCOUNT-RECORD.
*
    EXEC CICS
        READ FILE('ACCOUNT')
            INTO(ACCOUNT-RECORD)
            RIDFLD(ACCOUNT-NUMBER)
            RESP(RESPONSE-CODE)
    END-EXEC.

    IF RESPONSE-CODE = DFHRESP(NORMAL)
        MOVE 'Y' TO RECORD-FOUND-SW
    ELSE
        IF RESPONSE-CODE = DFHRESP(NOTFND)
            MOVE 'N' TO RECORD-FOUND-SW
        ELSE
            PERFORM 9999-TERMINATE-PROGRAM
        END-IF
    END-IF.
```

Coding example (variable-length VSAM ESDS records)

This example retrieves a record from a variable-length VSAM ESDS. The record is identified by the RBA value in ACCOUNT-MASTER-RBA. The LENGTH field initially contains the maximum record length the program will accept; after the READ command, it contains the length of the record that was read. NOTFND provides for records that can't be located.

```
    2100-READ-ACCOUNT-RECORD.
*
        EXEC CICS
            READ FILE('ACCOUNT')
                 INTO(ACCOUNT-RECORD)
                 LENGTH(ACCOUNT-RECORD-LENGTH)
                 RIDFLD(ACCOUNT-MASTER-RBA)
                 RBA
                 RESP(RESPONSE-CODE)
        END-EXEC.

        IF RESPONSE-CODE = DFHRESP(NORMAL)
            MOVE 'Y' TO RECORD-FOUND-SW
        ELSE
            IF RESPONSE-CODE = DFHRESP(NOTFND)
                MOVE 'N' TO RECORD-FOUND-SW
            ELSE
                PERFORM 9999-TERMINATE-PROGRAM
            END-IF
        END-IF.
```

The READNEXT command

Function

File control. The READNEXT command retrieves the next sequential record from a file during a browse operation. The file can be a VSAM KSDS, ESDS, RRDS, or path.

Syntax

```
EXEC CICS
    READNEXT   FILE(filename)
               { INTO(data-area) | SET(pointer-ref) }
               RIDFLD(data-area)
               [ { LENGTH(data-area) }
                 { SYSID(systemname) LENGTH(data-area) } ]
               [ KEYLENGTH(data-value) ]
               [ RBA | RRN ]
               [ REQID(data-value) ]
               [ { UPDATE
                     [ TOKEN(data-area) ] }
                 { CONSISTENT  }
                 { REPEATABLE  }
                 { UNCOMMITTED } ]
               [ NOSUSPEND ]
    END-EXEC.
```

Options

FILE	Specifies the 1- to 8-character name of the data set that contains the record to be read.
INTO	Specifies the data area that will contain the record being read.
SET	Specifies the data area that will contain the address of the retrieved record.
RIDFLD	Specifies a data area that identifies the record to be retrieved. The content of the RIDFLD field depends on whether RBA or RRN is specified; if neither is specified, the RIDFLD field contains a key for VSAM KSDS or path retrieval. For a generic browse, the RIDFLD field must still be as long as the file's defined key length. Then, when the READNEXT command finishes, CICS puts the complete key value in the RIDFLD field. Normally, you should leave the contents of the RIDFLD field unchanged during a browse operation. If you change the field before you issue a READNEXT command, the browse is restarted from the new location.
LENGTH	Specifies a binary halfword (PIC S9(4) COMP) that contains the length of the record. On entry, the data area indicates the size of the INTO data area if INTO is specified. On exit, the data area contains the size of the record retrieved. Required if INTO is specified and the file has variable-length records; optional for SET. Also required when SYSID is specified.

SYSID	Specifies the 1- to 4-character name of a remote system that contains the file.
KEYLENGTH	Specifies a binary halfword (PIC S9(4) COMP) or literal value that indicates the length of the key. If you specified GENERIC on the STARTBR or RESETBR command, you can use the KEYLENGTH option to change the length of the generic key. In that case, CICS repositions the browse using the new generic key. Also used when the SYSID option is specified. Not valid if RBA or RRN is specified.
RBA	Specifies that the RIDFLD field is a relative byte address (RBA) for a VSAM KSDS or ESDS. An RBA is a binary fullword (PIC S9(8) COMP).
RRN	Specifies that the RIDFLD is a relative record number (RRN) for a VSAM RRDS. An RRN is a binary fullword (PIC S9(8) COMP). The RRN of the first record in an RRDS is 1.
REQID	Specifies a binary halfword (PIC S9(4) COMP) or literal value that identifies the browse operation; used only when your program controls two or more browse operations at the same time. For each I/O command that's part of the same browse operation, specify the same REQID value.
UPDATE	(TS 1.1 and later) (RLS only) Specifies that you intend to update the record by rewriting or deleting it. The record is held under exclusive control by your task, and no other task can access it until: (1) you issue a REWRITE, DELETE, or UNLOCK command to release the record or (2) your task ends. If the file is recoverable, the record is held until the task ends or you issue a SYNCPOINT command, even if you issue a REWRITE, DELETE, or UNLOCK command. If you specify the UPDATE option, you must also specify the TOKEN option.
TOKEN	(TS 1.1 and later) (RLS only) Specifies a binary fullword (PIC S9(8) COMP) that returns a unique identifier for a READNEXT UPDATE request. This identifier can then be used to associate the record retrieved with a subsequent REWRITE, DELETE, or UNLOCK command. The UPDATE option is assumed if TOKEN is specified.
CONSISTENT	(RLS only) Specifies that the record is to be read with a level of read integrity provided by a VSAM shared lock that lasts until the record is read (that is, until it's returned to your program). If the record is locked by another task, the READ request waits until the lock is released.
REPEATABLE	(RLS only) Specifies that the record is to be read with a level of read integrity provided by a VSAM shared lock that lasts until the unit of work that contains the READ request is ended. If the record is locked by another task, the READ request waits until the lock is released.
UNCOMMITTED	(RLS only) Specifies that the record is to be read with no read integrity.
NOSUSPEND	(RLS only) Specifies that the READNEXT request will not wait if the record is held under exclusive control (locked) by another task.

Exceptional conditions

Note: The default action for these conditions is to terminate the task.

DUPKEY	Occurs only when retrieving records via an alternate index (path) that allows duplicate keys; indicates that at least one more record with the specified key exists. To retrieve all of the records with the same key value, issue successive READNEXT commands; DUPKEY will be raised for each record except the last.
ENDFILE	Occurs when there are no more records to be retrieved.
FILENOTFOUND	The data set name specified in the FILE option isn't defined in the File Control Table (FCT).
ILLOGIC	A serious VSAM error occurred.
INVREQ	A browse operation has not been properly started by a STARTBR command, the meaning of the RIDFLD option (key, RBA, or RRN) was changed during the browse, or the KEYLENGTH value is incorrect.
IOERR	An I/O error occurred.
ISCINVREQ	An undeterminable error occurred on the remote system specified in the SYSID option.
LENGERR	The length of the record retrieved exceeds the length specified in the LENGTH option.
LOADING	(TS 1.1 and later) The READNEXT request was issued against a data table that is still being loaded into the CICS system.
LOCKED	A READNEXT UPDATE was issued against a record that is currently locked.
NOTAUTH	The transaction's PCT entry specified that resource security checking should be done, and the operator is not authorized to access the data set.
NOTFND	The specified record could not be located.
NOTOPEN	The file is not open.
RECORDBUSY	(TS 1.1 and later) The NOSUSPEND option was specified on a record held under exclusive control by another task.
SYSIDERR	The system identified by SYSID could not be located or accessed.

Notes and tips

- Before you can issue a READNEXT command, you must begin a browse operation by issuing a STARTBR command. Browsing is relatively inefficient because a VSAM string is held for the duration of the browse. (A string is required for each concurrent access to a VSAM file, so if 10 strings are specified for a file, 10 simultaneous accesses are permitted.) Because of this inefficiency, you may want to minimize the duration of a browse so you don't tie up a string any longer than is needed.

- Record-level sharing (RLS) is a VSAM feature available through the SMS facility. It allows files to be shared with update capability between applications and across CICS regions. When you open a file in RLS mode, locking takes place at the record level instead of the control-interval level. This reduces the possibility of deadlocks.

- If you have RLS active on your system and you're working in CICS TS 1.1 or higher, you can invoke the READNEXT command with the UPDATE option. This feature allows you to update or delete the record retrieved. Without it, you must first end the browse with an ENDBR command and then issue a READ UPDATE command for the record you want to update or delete.

- To browse a file via an alternate path, specify the path name in the FILE option. Be aware that if the alternate index allows duplicate keys, the DUPKEY condition will be raised if there's more than one record with the same alternate key value. So be sure to check for the DUPKEY condition.

- When you retrieve records with duplicate keys, the records are presented in the sequence they were created. If the alternate indexes were recently rebuilt, that will be in prime key sequence. But don't count on it. (Actually, if the alternate index isn't upgradable, any duplicates will always be in prime key sequence since the alternate index entries can be created only by rebuilding the index.)

- The only exceptional condition you normally need to worry about for the READNEXT command is ENDFILE. If you're browsing via a path that allows duplicate keys, you should also check for DUPKEY.

Coding example (base cluster)

This example shows how to retrieve records during a browse operation. The records are retrieved directly from the base cluster of a VSAM KSDS via the primary key. Several program modules are shown to indicate the program logic necessary to invoke the browse module repeatedly. (The code for module 1100-START-ACCOUNT-BROWSE is shown in the coding example for the STARTBR command later in this unit.)

```
        .
        .
        MOVE LOW-VALUE TO AR-ACCOUNT-NUMBER.
        PERFORM 1100-START-ACCOUNT-BROWSE.
        PERFORM 2000-PROCESS-ACCOUNT-RECORD
            UNTIL END-OF-BROWSE.
        .
        .
*
 2000-PROCESS-ACCOUNT-RECORD.
*
        PERFORM 2100-READ-NEXT-ACCOUNT-RECORD.
        IF NOT END-OF-BROWSE
            .
            .
*
 2100-READ-NEXT-ACCOUNT-RECORD.
*
        EXEC CICS
            READNEXT FILE('ACCOUNT')
                     INTO(ACCOUNT-RECORD)
                     RIDFLD(AR-ACCOUNT-NUMBER)
                     RESP(RESPONSE-CODE)
        END-EXEC.

        IF RESPONSE-CODE = DFHRESP(ENDFILE)
            MOVE 'Y' TO END-OF-BROWSE-SW
        ELSE
            IF RESPONSE-CODE NOT = DFHRESP(NORMAL)
                PERFORM 9999-TERMINATE-PROGRAM
            END-IF
        END-IF.
```

Coding example (alternate index)

This example shows how to retrieve duplicate key records via an alternate index. Here, module 1800 retrieves up to 10 invoice records by customer number, which is an alternate key for the file. The DUPKEY condition indicates whether more invoices are available for the customer. As soon as DUPKEY is not detected, N is moved to MORE-INVOICES-SW.

```
 1800-GET-INVOICE-RECORDS.
*
      PERFORM 1810-START-INVOICE-BROWSE.
      PERFORM 1820-FORMAT-INVOICE-LINE
          VARYING INVOICE-SUB FROM 1 BY 1
          UNTIL INVOICE-SUB > 10.
     .
     .
*
 1820-FORMAT-INVOICE-LINE.
*
      IF MORE-INVOICES
          PERFORM 1830-READ-INVOICE-RECORD
          MOVE INV-INVOICE-NUMBER
              TO IM-D-INVOICE-NUMBER(INVOICE-SUB)
          MOVE INV-PO-NUMBER
              TO IM-D-PO-NUMBER(INVOICE-SUB)
          MOVE INV-INVOICE-DATE
              TO IM-D-INVOICE-DATE(INVOICE-SUB)
          MOVE INV-INVOICE-TOTAL
              TO IM-D-INVOICE-TOTAL(INVOICE-SUB)
      ELSE
          MOVE SPACE TO IM-D-INVOICE-LINE(INVOICE-SUB)
      END-IF.
*
 1830-READ-INVOICE-RECORD.
*
      EXEC CICS
          READNEXT FILE('INVPATH')
                   INTO(INVOICE-RECORD)
                   RIDFLD(CM-CUSTOMER-NUMBER)
                   RESP(RESPONSE-CODE)
      END-EXEC.

      IF RESPONSE-CODE = DFHRESP(NORMAL)
          MOVE 'N' TO MORE-INVOICES-SW
      ELSE
          IF RESPONSE-CODE NOT = DFHRESP(DUPKEY)
              PERFORM 9999-TERMINATE-PROGRAM
          END-IF
      END-IF.
```

The READPREV command

Function

File control. The READPREV command retrieves the previous sequential record from a file during a browse operation. In other words, READPREV reads records backwards. The file can be a VSAM KSDS, ESDS, RRDS, or path.

Syntax

```
EXEC CICS
    READPREV    FILE(filename)
                { INTO(data-area) | SET(pointer-ref) }
                RIDFLD(data-area)

                [ { LENGTH(data-area) }
                  { SYSID(systemname) LENGTH(data-area) } ]

                [ KEYLENGTH(data-value) ]
                [ RBA | RRN ]
                [ REQID(data-value) ]

                [ { UPDATE
                       [ TOKEN(data-area) ] }
                  { CONSISTENT   }
                  { REPEATABLE   }
                  { UNCOMMITTED } ]

                [ NOSUSPEND ]
    END-EXEC.
```

Options

FILE	Specifies the 1- to 8-character name of the data set that contains the record to be read.
INTO	Specifies the data area that will contain the record being read.
SET	Specifies the data area that will contain the address of the retrieved record.
RIDFLD	Specifies a data area that identifies the record to be retrieved. The content of the RIDFLD field depends on whether RBA or RRN is specified; if neither is specified, the RIDFLD field contains a key for VSAM KSDS or path retrieval. For a generic browse, the RIDFLD field must still be as long as the file's defined key length. Then, when the READPREV command finishes, CICS puts the complete key value in the RIDFLD field.
	Normally, you should leave the contents of the RIDFLD field unchanged during a browse operation. If you change the field before you issue a READPREV command, the browse is restarted from the new location.
LENGTH	Specifies a binary halfword (PIC S9(4) COMP) that contains the length of the record. On entry, the data area indicates the size of the INTO data area if INTO is specified. On exit, the data area contains the size of the record retrieved. Required if INTO is specified and the file has variable-length records; optional for SET. Also required when SYSID is specified.

SYSID	Specifies the 1- to 4-character name of a remote system that contains the file.
KEYLENGTH	Specifies a binary halfword (PIC S9(4) COMP) or literal value that indicates the length of the key. Not valid if RBA or RRN is specified.
RBA	Specifies that the RIDFLD field is a relative byte address (RBA) for a VSAM KSDS or ESDS. An RBA is a binary fullword (PIC S9(8) COMP).
RRN	Specifies that the RIDFLD is a relative record number (RRN) for a VSAM RRDS. An RRN is a binary fullword (PIC S9(8) COMP). The RRN of the first record in an RRDS is 1.
REQID	Specifies a binary halfword (PIC S9(4) COMP) or literal value that identifies the browse operation; used only when your program controls two or more browse operations at the same time. For each I/O command that's part of the same browse operation, specify the same REQID value.
UPDATE	(TS 1.1 and later) (RLS only) Specifies that you intend to update the record by rewriting or deleting it. The record is held under exclusive control by your task, and no other task can access it until: (1) you issue a REWRITE, DELETE, or UNLOCK command to release the record or (2) your task ends. If the file is recoverable, the record is held until the task ends or you issue a SYNCPOINT command, even if you issue a REWRITE, DELETE, or UNLOCK command. If you specify the UPDATE option, you must also specify the TOKEN option.
TOKEN	(TS 1.1 and later) (RLS only) Specifies a binary fullword (PIC S9(8) COMP) that returns a unique identifier for a READPREV UPDATE request. This identifier can then be used to associate the record retrieved with a subsequent REWRITE, DELETE, or UNLOCK command. The UPDATE option is assumed if TOKEN is specified.
CONSISTENT	(RLS only) Specifies that the record is to be read with a level of read integrity provided by a VSAM shared lock that lasts until the record is read (that is, until it's returned to your program). If the record is locked by another task, the READ request waits until the lock is released.
REPEATABLE	(RLS only) Specifies that the record is to be read with a level of read integrity provided by a VSAM shared lock that lasts until the unit of work that contains the READ request is ended. If the record is locked by another task, the READ request waits until the lock is released.
UNCOMMITTED	(RLS only) Specifies that the record is to be read with no read integrity.
NOSUSPEND	(RLS only) Specifies that the READPREV request will not wait if the record is held under exclusive control (locked) by another task.

Exceptional conditions

Note: The default action for these conditions is to terminate the task.

DUPKEY	Occurs only when retrieving via an alternate index (path) that allows duplicate keys; indicates that at least one more record with the specified key exists. To retrieve all of the records with the same key value, issue successive READPREV commands; DUPKEY will be raised for each record except the last.
ENDFILE	Occurs when there are no more records to be retrieved (the beginning of the file has been reached).
FILENOTFOUND	The data set name specified in the FILE option isn't defined in the File Control Table (FCT).
ILLOGIC	A serious VSAM error occurred.
INVREQ	A browse operation has not been properly started by a STARTBR command, the meaning of the RIDFLD option (key, RBA, or RRN) was changed during the browse, or the KEYLENGTH value is incorrect.
IOERR	An I/O error occurred.
ISCINVREQ	An undeterminable error occurred on the remote system specified in the SYSID option.
LENGERR	The length of the record retrieved exceeds the length specified in the LENGTH option.
LOADING	(TS 1.1 and later) The READPREV request was issued against a data table that is still being loaded into the CICS system.
LOCKED	A READPREV UPDATE was issued against a record that is currently locked.
NOTAUTH	The transaction's PCT entry specified that resource security checking should be done, and the operator is not authorized to access the data set.
NOTFND	The specified record could not be located.
NOTOPEN	The file is not open.
RECORDBUSY	(TS 1.1 and later) The NOSUSPEND option was specified on a record held under exclusive control by another task.
SYSIDERR	The system identified by SYSID could not be located or accessed.

Notes and tips

- Before you can issue a READPREV command, you must begin a browse operation by issuing a STARTBR command that doesn't include the GENERIC option. Browsing is relatively inefficient because a VSAM string is held for the duration of the browse. (A string is required for each concurrent access to a VSAM file, so if 10 strings are specified for a file, 10 simultaneous accesses are permitted.) Because of this inefficiency, you may want to minimize the duration of a browse so you don't tie up a string any longer than is needed.

- Record-level sharing (RLS) is a VSAM feature available through the SMS facility. It allows files to be shared with update capability between applications and across CICS regions. When you open a file in RLS mode, locking takes place at the record level instead of the control-interval level. This reduces the possibility of deadlocks.

- If you have RLS active on your system and you're working in CICS TS 1.1 or higher, you can invoke the READPREV command with the UPDATE option. This feature allows you to update or delete the record retrieved. Without it, you must first end the browse with an ENDBR command and then issue a READ UPDATE command for the record you want to update or delete.

- To browse a file via an alternate path, specify the path name in the FILE option. Be aware that if the alternate index allows duplicate keys, the DUPKEY condition will be raised if there's more than one record with the same alternate key value. So be sure to check for the DUPKEY condition.

- If you issue a READPREV command immediately following a READNEXT command, the same record is retrieved again. And, because of a peculiarity in the way READPREV works, you should not issue it immediately after a STARTBR command unless the STARTBR command established positioning at the end of the file by specifying hex FF (HIGH-VALUE) in the RIDFLD field; instead, issue READNEXT followed by two READPREV commands.

- The only exceptional condition you normally need to worry about for the READPREV command is ENDFILE. If you're browsing via a path that allows duplicate keys, you should also check for DUPKEY.

Coding example (browse backwards)

This example shows how to retrieve records backwards during a browse operation. Several program modules are shown to indicate the program logic necessary to invoke the browse module repeatedly. (The code for module 1100-START-ACCOUNT-BROWSE is shown in the coding example for the STARTBR command later in this unit.)

```
         .
         .
        MOVE HIGH-VALUE TO AR-ACCOUNT-NUMBER.
        PERFORM 1100-START-ACCOUNT-BROWSE.
        PERFORM 2000-PROCESS-ACCOUNT-RECORD
            UNTIL END-OF-BROWSE.
         .
         .
*
 2000-PROCESS-ACCOUNT-RECORD.
*
        PERFORM 2100-READ-PREV-ACCOUNT-RECORD.
        IF NOT END-OF-BROWSE
            .
            .
*
 2100-READ-PREV-ACCOUNT-RECORD.
*
        EXEC CICS
            READPREV FILE('ACCOUNT')
                     INTO(ACCOUNT-RECORD)
                     RIDFLD(AR-ACCOUNT-NUMBER)
                     RESP(RESPONSE-CODE)
        END-EXEC.

        IF RESPONSE-CODE = DFHRESP(ENDFILE)
            MOVE 'Y' TO END-OF-BROWSE-SW
        ELSE
            IF RESPONSE-CODE NOT = DFHRESP(NORMAL)
                PERFORM 9999-TERMINATE-PROGRAM
            END-IF
        END-IF.
```

Coding example (retrieve previous record after STARTBR)

This example shows how to retrieve the record immediately preceding the record where positioning is established by a STARTBR command. Four browse commands are issued: STARTBR, READNEXT, READPREV, and READPREV. (Module 1100-START-ACCOUNT-BROWSE is shown in the description of the STARTBR command.) This elaborate coding is not required if the STARTBR command establishes positioning at the end of the file by specifying HIGH-VALUE in the RIDFLD field.

```
3000-GET-PREV-ACCOUNT-RECORD.
*
        MOVE WS-ACCOUNT-NUMBER TO AR-ACCOUNT-NUMBER.
        PERFORM 1100-START-ACCOUNT-BROWSE.
        IF NOT END-OF-BROWSE
            PERFORM 3100-READ-NEXT-ACCOUNT-RECORD
            PERFORM 3200-READ-PREV-ACCOUNT-RECORD
            PERFORM 3200-READ-PREV-ACCOUNT-RECORD.
*
 3100-READ-NEXT-ACCOUNT-RECORD.
*
        EXEC CICS
            READNEXT FILE('ACCOUNT')
                     INTO(ACCOUNT-RECORD)
                     RIDFLD(AR-ACCOUNT-NUMBER)
                     RESP(RESPONSE-CODE)
        END-EXEC.

        IF RESPONSE-CODE = DFHRESP(ENDFILE)
            MOVE 'Y' TO END-OF-BROWSE-SW
        ELSE
            IF RESPONSE-CODE NOT = DFHRESP(NORMAL)
                PERFORM 9999-TERMINATE-PROGRAM
            END-IF
        END-IF.
*
 3200-READ-PREV-ACCOUNT-RECORD.
*
        EXEC CICS
            READPREV FILE('ACCOUNT')
                     INTO(ACCOUNT-RECORD)
                     RIDFLD(AR-ACCOUNT-NUMBER)
                     RESP(RESPONSE-CODE)
        END-EXEC.

        IF RESPONSE-CODE = DFHRESP(ENDFILE)
            MOVE 'Y' TO END-OF-BROWSE-SW
        ELSE
            IF RESPONSE-CODE NOT = DFHRESP(NORMAL)
                PERFORM 9999-TERMINATE-PROGRAM
            END-IF
        END-IF.
```

The READQ TD command

Function

Transient data control. The READQ TD command reads a record from a specified transient data queue.

Syntax

```
EXEC CICS
    READQ TD    QUEUE(name)
                { INTO(data-area) | SET(pointer-ref) }
                [ LENGTH(data-area) ]
                [ SYSID(systemname) ]
                [ NOSUSPEND ]
END-EXEC.
```

Options

QUEUE	Specifies the 1- to 4-character name of the transient data queue that contains the data to be retrieved.
INTO	Specifies the data area that will contain the record being read.
SET	Specifies the data area that will contain the address of the retrieved record.
LENGTH	Specifies a binary halfword (PIC S9(4) COMP) that contains the length of the record. On entry, the data area indicates the size of the INTO data area if INTO is specified. On exit, the data area contains the size of the record retrieved. Required if INTO is specified, unless the destination is extrapartition and has fixed-length records; optional for SET.
SYSID	Specifies the 1- to 4-character name of a remote system that contains the destination.
NOSUSPEND	Specifies that if the queue is busy, control is to return immediately to the program at the point following the READQ TD command.

Exceptional conditions

Note: The default action for all of these conditions except QBUSY is to terminate the task. The default action for the QBUSY condition is to suspend the task.

DISABLED	The queue is disabled.
INVREQ	The extrapartition queue is currently opened for output.
IOERR	An I/O error occurred.
ISCINVREQ	An undeterminable error occurred on the remote system.
LENGERR	The length of the record retrieved exceeds the length specified in the LENGTH option.

LOCKED	The use of the queue has been restricted.
NOTAUTH	The transaction's PCT entry specified that resource security checking should be done, and the operator is not authorized to access the queue.
NOTOPEN	The queue is not open.
QBUSY	Another task is writing or deleting a record in the queue.
QIDERR	The specified destination doesn't exist.
QZERO	There are no records in the destination.
SYSIDERR	The system identified by SYSID could not be located or accessed.

Notes and tips

- There are two types of transient data queues: intrapartition and extrapartition. All intrapartition destinations are stored in a VSAM file called DFHNTRA, and access to them is efficient. Extrapartition destinations, however, are QSAM files (on disk or another sequential device like a tape drive or a printer) managed not by CICS, but by the operating system. Because of the way CICS interacts with QSAM, extrapartition destinations are relatively inefficient, so use them only when appropriate. (The syntax of the READQ TD command is the same for both types of destinations.)

- An intrapartition destination can be used with automatic transaction initiation (ATI) so that a transaction is started as soon as the number of records in the destination reaches a specified trigger level. Because of this feature, intrapartition destinations are often used for applications where data from one program needs to be gathered temporarily so it can be processed by another program.

- One common use of ATI is for printer applications: An ATI transaction uses a READQ TD command to retrieve records from a destination, and then the transaction formats the data properly and sends it to a printer. This technique removes detailed printer considerations from the application program that creates the data to be printed. All that program has to do is write records to the proper destination.

- Records are always retrieved from a destination in the order they were written. And each record can be read only once. When you read a record, it's effectively deleted from the destination.

- The transient data facility provides no mechanism for holding a destination for exclusive use. If you need to write several uninterrupted records to a destination, use the ENQ and DEQ commands.

- The only exceptional condition you should normally worry about for the READQ TD command is QZERO.

- QBUSY is one of the few exceptional conditions that doesn't cause your task to be terminated. Instead, its action depends on whether you handle the condition (using the RESP option or a HANDLE CONDITION command) and whether you specify NOSUSPEND on the READQ TD command. If you do neither,

QBUSY simply causes your task to be suspended until the queue is available; then, control returns to your program at the first statement following the READQ TD command. If your program handles the QBUSY condition, the specified error processing is done, and the program must issue the READQ TD command again to read the record. If you specify NOSUSPEND, control is returned to the statement following the READQ TD command if the queue is unavailable; again, you'll have to issue another READQ TD command to read the record later.

Coding example

The following example shows how to retrieve a record from a transient data queue. The QZERO condition is handled to terminate the processing loop when no more records are available.

```
            .
            .
        PERFORM 2000-PROCESS-ACCOUNT-RECORD
            UNTIL QUEUE-EMPTY.
            .
            .
    *
     2000-PROCESS-ACCOUNT-RECORD.
    *
        PERFORM 2100-READ-ACCOUNT-RECORD.
        IF NOT QUEUE-EMPTY
            .
            .
    *
     2100-READ-ACCOUNT-RECORD.
    *
        MOVE LENGTH OF ACCOUNT-RECORD
            TO ACCOUNT-RECORD-LENGTH.

        EXEC CICS
            READQ TD QUEUE('ACCT')
                     INTO(ACCOUNT-RECORD)
                     LENGTH(ACCOUNT-RECORD-LENGTH)
                     RESP(RESPONSE-CODE)
        END-EXEC.

        IF RESPONSE-CODE = DFHRESP(QZERO)
            MOVE 'Y' TO QUEUE-EMPTY-SW
        ELSE
            IF RESPONSE-CODE NOT = DFHRESP(NORMAL)
                PERFORM 9999-TERMINATE-PROGRAM
            END-IF
        END-IF.
```

The READQ TS command

Function

Temporary storage control. The READQ TS command reads a record from a specified temporary storage queue.

Syntax

```
EXEC CICS
    READQ TS { QUEUE(name) | QNAME(name) }
             { INTO(data-area) | SET(pointer-ref) }
             [ LENGTH(data-area) ]
             [ NUMITEMS(data-area) ]
             [ ITEM(data-value) | NEXT ]
             [ SYSID(systemname) ]
END-EXEC.
```

Options

QUEUE	Specifies the 1- to 8-character name of the temporary storage queue that contains the data to be retrieved.
QNAME	Specifies the 1-to 16-character name of the temporary storage queue that contains the data to be retrieved. QNAME is an alternative to the QUEUE option.
INTO	Specifies the data area that will contain the record being read.
SET	Specifies the data area that will contain the address of the retrieved record.
LENGTH	Specifies a binary halfword (PIC S9(4) COMP) that contains the length of the record. On entry, the data area indicates the size of the INTO data area if INTO is specified. On exit, the data area contains the size of the record retrieved.
NUMITEMS	Specifies a binary halfword (PIC S9(4) COMP). CICS places the total number of records in the queue in this field.
ITEM	Specifies a binary halfword (PIC S9(4) COMP) or literal value that identifies the number of the record to be retrieved.
NEXT	Specifies that the next queue record in sequence should be read. This is the default.
SYSID	Specifies the 1- to 4-character name of a remote system that contains the destination.

Exceptional conditions

Note: The default action for these conditions is to terminate the task.

INVREQ	The queue was created for internal use by CICS and therefore can't be read by a user program.
IOERR	An I/O error occurred.
ISCINVREQ	An undeterminable error occurred on the remote system specified in the SYSID option.
ITEMERR	No record exists for the item number specified by the ITEM option.
LENGERR	The length of the record retrieved exceeds the length specified in the LENGTH option.
NOTAUTH	The transaction's PCT entry specified that resource security checking should be done, and the operator is not authorized to access the queue.
QIDERR	The specified queue does not exist.
SYSIDERR	The system identified by SYSID could not be located or accessed.

Notes and tips

- All temporary storage queues are held in one of two places: in virtual storage or in a VSAM file called DFHTEMP. As a result, access to data in temporary storage is efficient.

- To create a unique temporary storage queue name, incorporate the terminal-id that's in the Execute Interface Block field EIBTRMID, your user-id, or some other qualifier.

- The QNAME option provides an alternate way of identifying a temporary storage queue by allowing a name of up to 16 bytes. In practice, though, the QUEUE option is large enough to store a unique queue name.

- The READQ TS command provides both direct and sequential access to temporary storage records. For direct access, specify the number of the record you want to retrieve in the ITEM option; for sequential access, specify NEXT. Note, however, that any task that accesses the same temporary storage queue affects the positioning for a READQ TS NEXT command; CICS does not maintain a separate position within the queue for each task. To safely process the records in sequence, use unique queue names or reserve the queue for exclusive access using the ENQ and DEQ commands.

- Because temporary storage queues are created and deleted dynamically, you should always check for the QIDERR condition. If you specify the ITEM option, you should also check for the ITEMERR condition.

Coding example

This example shows how to read the first record from a temporary storage queue. ITEM is specified to be sure the first record is retrieved. If NEXT were used, another task could affect positioning within the queue.

```
 3000-READ-QUEUE-RECORD.
*
     EXEC CICS
         READQ TS QUEUE(TS-QUEUE-NAME)
                  INTO(TS-QUEUE-AREA)
                  LENGTH(TS-QUEUE-LENGTH)
                  ITEM(1)
                  RESP(RESPONSE-CODE)
     END-EXEC.

     EVALUATE RESPONSE-CODE
         WHEN DFHRESP(NORMAL)
             MOVE 'Y' TO TS-RECORD-FOUND-SW
         WHEN DFHRESP(ITEMERR)
             MOVE 'N' TO TS-RECORD-FOUND-SW
         WHEN DFHRESP(QIDERR)
             MOVE 'N' TO TS-RECORD-FOUND-SW
         WHEN OTHER
             PERFORM 9999-TERMINATE-PROGRAM
     END-EVALUATE.
```

The RECEIVE command (APPC)

Function

APPC mapped conversation. The RECEIVE command receives data sent by a remote process.

Syntax

```
EXEC CICS
    RECEIVE [ CONVID(name) | SESSION(name) ]
            { INTO(data-area) | SET(pointer-ref) }
            { LENGTH(data-area) | FLENGTH(data-area) }
            [ MAXLENGTH(data-value) | MAXFLENGTH(data-value) ]
            [ NOTRUNCATE ]
            [ STATE(cvda) ]
END-EXEC.
```

Options

CONVID	Specifies the 4-character conversation-id obtained from the Execute Interface Block field EIBRSRCE following a successful ALLOCATE command.
SESSION	Specifies the 4-character TCTTE id. If omitted, the principal facility of the task is used. The SESSION option is accepted for compatibility with earlier releases, but use CONVID in new programs.
INTO	Specifies the data area that will contain the data received from the remote program.
SET	Specifies the data area that will contain the address of the received data.
LENGTH	Specifies a binary halfword (PIC S9(4) COMP) where CICS places the length of the received data. If you specify INTO, the initial value of this field is used to determine the maximum length of the data that can be received, unless you code MAXLENGTH.
FLENGTH	Specifies a binary fullword (PIC S9(8) COMP) where CICS places the length of the received data. If you specify INTO, the initial value of this field is used to determine the maximum length of the data that can be received, unless you code MAXLENGTH or MAXFLENGTH.
MAXLENGTH	Specifies a binary halfword (PIC S9(4) COMP) or literal value that indicates the maximum length of the data that can be received.
MAXFLENGTH	Specifies a binary fullword (PIC S9(8) COMP) or literal value that indicates the maximum length of the data that can be received.
NOTRUNCATE	Specifies that if the length of the received data is greater than the maximum specified, the excess data should not be discarded. Instead, it should be saved and used to fulfill subsequent RECEIVE commands. If NOTRUNCATE is omitted, excess data is discarded.

STATE	Specifies a binary fullword (PIC S9(8) COMP) where CICS places state information. Valid states are:

ALLOCATED	RECEIVE
CONFFREE	ROLLBACK
CONFRECEIVE	SEND
CONFSEND	SYNCFREE
FREE	SYNCRECEIVE
PENDFREE	SYNCSEND
PENDRECEIVE	

Exceptional conditions

Note: The default action for all these conditions except EOC and SIGNAL is to terminate the task. The default action for the EOC and SIGNAL conditions is to ignore the condition.

EOC	The end of the message chain has been received. This is the normal response code for RECEIVE.
INBFMH	(MRO only) A function management header (FMH) was sent.
INVREQ	A function shipping error occurred, or the command isn't compatible with the conversation.
LENGERR	The data received from the remote process is longer than the maximum specified, or the specification for the maximum length is invalid.
NOTALLOC	The conversation has not been properly allocated.
SIGNAL	The remote program has executed an ISSUE SIGNAL command.
TERMERR	A session error has occurred.

Notes and tips

- The STATE option returns a value that indicates the current state of the conversation. If the RECEIVE is successful, the STATE field should be set to SEND. The value of the STATE field can be tested using the CICS keyword DFHVALUE, in much the same way as you use DFHRESP to test the response code returned in the RESP field:

  ```
  IF CONVERSATION-STATE = DFHVALUE(SEND)
  ```

- If your conversation is designed to allow the partner program to use the ISSUE SIGNAL command, you should test for the SIGNAL condition. When you do, remember that EOC is a normal response for the RECEIVE command.

Coding example

The following example shows a RECEIVE command that receives data from a back-end transaction. Here, the program first issues a SEND command to send a customer number to the back-end program and invites the program to respond. Then, the program issues a RECEIVE command to receive data related to the customer. (In a production environment, additional error checking would be required.)

```
WORKING-STORAGE SECTION.
*
 .
 .
 .
01  SEND-MESSAGE.
*
    05  SM-CUSTOMER-NUMBER      PIC X(06).
*
01  RECEIVE-MESSAGE.
*
    05  RM-CUSTOMER-FOUND-SW    PIC X(01).
        88  RM-CUSTOMER-FOUND       VALUE 'Y'.
    05  RM-CUST-DATA-1          PIC X(520).
    05  RM-CUST-DATA-2          PIC X(300).
    05  RM-CUST-DATA-3          PIC X(255).
*
01  RECEIVE-LENGTH             PIC S9(04) COMP.
 .
 .
 .
PROCEDURE DIVISION.
 .
 .
 .
*
2300-GET-CUSTOMER-DATA.
*
    MOVE CUSTNOI TO SM-CUSTOMER-NUMBER.
    EXEC CICS
        SEND CONVID(CONVERSATION-ID)
             FROM(SEND-MESSAGE)
             INVITE
             WAIT
    END-EXEC.

    MOVE LENGTH OF RECEIVE-MESSAGE TO RECEIVE-LENGTH.

    EXEC CICS
        RECEIVE CONVID(CONVERSATION-ID)
                INTO(RECEIVE-MESSAGE)
                LENGTH(RECEIVE-LENGTH)
    END-EXEC.

    IF RM-CUSTOMER-FOUND
        MOVE RM-CUST-DATA-1 TO CUSTOMER-MASTER-RECORD
        MOVE RM-CUST-DATA-2 TO ACCOUNT-MASTER-RECORD
        MOVE RM-CUST-DATA-3 TO CUSTOMER-HISTORY-RECORD
    END-IF.
```

The RECEIVE command (terminal control)

Function

Terminal control. The RECEIVE command retrieves input data sent from a terminal device. Basic Mapping Support is not used, so the format of the received data depends on the terminal type.

Syntax

```
EXEC CICS
     RECEIVE [ INTO(data-area) | SET(pointer-ref) ]
             { LENGTH(data-area) | FLENGTH(data-area) }
             [ MAXLENGTH(data-value) | MAXFLENGTH(data-value) ]
             [ NOTRUNCATE ]
             [ ASIS ]
             [ BUFFER ]
     END-EXEC.
```

Options

INTO	Specifies the data area that will contain the data being received.
SET	Specifies the data area that will contain the address of the received data.
LENGTH	Specifies a binary halfword (PIC S9(4) COMP) where CICS places the length of the received data. If you specify INTO, the initial value of this field is used to determine the maximum length of the data that can be received, unless you code MAXLENGTH.
FLENGTH	Specifies a binary fullword (PIC S9(8) COMP) where CICS places the length of the received data. If you specify INTO, the initial value of this field is used to determine the maximum length of the data that can be received, unless you code MAXLENGTH or MAXFLENGTH.
MAXLENGTH	Specifies a binary halfword (PIC S9(4) COMP) or literal value that indicates the maximum length of the data that can be received.
MAXFLENGTH	Specifies a binary fullword (PIC S9(8) COMP) or literal value that indicates the maximum length of the data that can be received.
NOTRUNCATE	Specifies that if the length of the data sent from the terminal is greater than the maximum specified, the excess data is to be retained and presented to the program when it issues subsequent RECEIVE commands. If you omit NOTRUNCATE, the excess data is discarded and the LENGERR condition is raised. In either case, the LENGTH field is updated to reflect the actual amount of data received, including any excess.
ASIS	Specifies that lowercase characters are not to be translated to uppercase. In certain cases, ASIS has no effect. For example, ASIS has no effect for the first RECEIVE command issued by a transaction.

BUFFER   Specifies that the entire 3270 terminal buffer should be retrieved, including null characters and other control sequences. If you omit BUFFER, the received data is a standard 3270 data stream.

Exceptional conditions

Note: The default action for these conditions is to terminate the task.

INVREQ   A function shipping error has occurred.

LENGERR   The length of the data received exceeds the length specified in the LENGTH option. CICS discards the excess data.

NOTALLOC   The task is not associated with a terminal.

TERMERR   (VTAM only) A terminal I/O error occurred.

Notes and tips

- Frankly, the programming requirements for processing terminal input using the RECEIVE command are complicated. As a result, it's unreasonable to use basic terminal control commands for full-screen interactive programs; use BMS instead. Use basic terminal control commands only in special situations where the format of terminal input data is simple.

- One common use for the RECEIVE command is to retrieve the command line the operator entered to initiate the transaction. Normally, that data is entered on an unformatted screen (one without fields defined by attribute bytes), so the format of the data is simple, and it's presented to the program exactly as it was entered. Usually, the first four characters of the data will be the trans-id entered by the operator to start the transaction. The trans-id is then followed by any additional data entered by the operator.

- You should usually check the LENGERR condition for the RECEIVE command.

Coding example

This example shows how to use a RECEIVE command to retrieve the command line entered by the operator to start a transaction. In this case, the command line should consist of the trans-id followed by a space and a 1- to 5-character customer number. If the customer number is missing or too much data is entered, an appropriate error message is formatted and N is moved to VALID-DATA-SW.

```
       WORKING-STORAGE SECTION.
   *
     .
     .
     .
   01  COMMAND-LINE.
   *
       05  CL-TRANS-ID          PIC X(04).
       05  FILLER               PIC X(01).
       05  CL-CUSTOMER-NUMBER   PIC X(05).
   *
   01  COMMAND-LENGTH           PIC S9(04) VALUE +10 COMP.
   *
     .
     .
     .
   PROCEDURE DIVISION.
   *
   0000-PROCESS-CUSTOMER-INQUIRY.
   *
       PERFORM 1000-RECEIVE-INQUIRY-DATA.
     .
     .
     .
   *
   1000-RECEIVE-INQUIRY-DATA.
   *
       EXEC CICS
           RECEIVE  INTO(COMMAND-LINE)
                    LENGTH(COMMAND-LENGTH)
                    RESP(RESPONSE-CODE)
       END-EXEC.

       IF RESPONSE-CODE = DFHRESP(NORMAL)
           IF CL-CUSTOMER-NUMBER = SPACE OR LOW-VALUE
               MOVE 'N' TO VALID-DATA-SW
               MOVE 'YOU MUST SUPPLY A CUSTOMER NUMBER'
                   TO ERROR-MESSAGE
           END-IF
       ELSE IF RESPONSE-CODE = DFHRESP(LENGERR)
           MOVE 'N' TO VALID-DATA-SW
           MOVE 'TOO MUCH DATA ENTERED' TO ERROR-MESSAGE
       ELSE
           PERFORM 9999-TERMINATE-PROGRAM
       END-IF.
```

The RECEIVE MAP command

Function

Basic Mapping Support. Receives data from a terminal and formats it using a BMS map definition.

Syntax

```
EXEC CICS
    RECEIVE   MAP(name)
              [ MAPSET(name) ]
              [ INTO(data-area) | SET(pointer-ref) ]
    END-EXEC.
```

Options

MAP	Specifies the 1- to 7-character name of the map to be used to map the input data.
MAPSET	Specifies the 1- to 7-character name of the mapset that contains the specified map. This name must be defined in the Processing Program Table (PPT). If omitted, the name specified in the MAP option is used.
INTO	Specifies the data area that will contain the mapped input data.
SET	Specifies the data area that will contain the address of the mapped input data.

Exceptional conditions

Note: The default action for these conditions is to terminate the task.

INVMPSZ	The line width specified in the map is larger than the line width supported by the terminal.
INVREQ	The task is not associated with a terminal.
MAPFAIL	The data cannot be formatted. This happens if a SEND MAP command was not issued before the operator entered data, or if the operator presses the Enter key without entering any data, or if the operator presses the Clear key or a PA key.

Notes and tips

- If you omit the INTO and SET options, BMS adds the letter I to the end of the map name you specify to determine the name of the input data area. So, if the map is named CUSTMAP, the input data area is CUSTMAPI. BMS uses the same convention when it assembles the symbolic map, so if you copy the BMS-generated symbolic mapset into your program, the names will match up. However, you must code INTO (or SET) if (1) you want to use your own version of the symbolic map or (2) you specify a data name rather than a literal value in the MAP option.

- You can avoid the MAPFAIL condition altogether by doing two things: (1) testing EIBAID for the Clear key or a PA key before issuing the RECEIVE MAP command and (2) including in the mapset a one-byte dummy field with FSET specified, so at least one byte of data is sent to the program whenever the operator presses Enter or a PF key.

Coding example

This example shows a typical module that receives input data from a terminal. The data is mapped into a data area called MENU-MAP, a symbolic map created by the programmer.

```
1100-RECEIVE-MENU-SCREEN.
*
    EXEC CICS
        RECEIVE MAP('MENUMAP')
                MAPSET('MENUSET')
                INTO(MENU-MAP)
    END-EXEC.
```

The RELEASE command

Function

Program control. The RELEASE command frees the virtual storage occupied by an object module previously loaded by a LOAD command. A RELEASE command is required only if the LOAD command specified the HOLD option.

Syntax

```
EXEC CICS
    RELEASE PROGRAM(name)
END-EXEC.
```

Option

PROGRAM   Specifies the 1- to 8-character name of the load module to be released.

Exceptional conditions

Note: The default action for these conditions is to terminate the task.

INVREQ   The program can't be released or is not loaded.

NOTAUTH   The transaction's PCT entry specified that resource security checking should be done, and the operator is not authorized to access the specified object module.

PGMIDERR   The object module is not defined in the Processing Program Table (PPT).

Notes and tips

* If you specify the HOLD option on a LOAD command, you should release the program using a RELEASE command unless you want the program to remain in virtual storage indefinitely. If the program is needed only by a particular application, make sure you release it when that application is no longer active.

* As a general rule, provide for exceptional conditions in the same way as you do for the LOAD command that loads the program you're releasing.

Coding example

This example shows how to release an object module originally retrieved by a LOAD command.

```
0500-RELEASE-STATE-TABLE.
*
    EXEC CICS
        RELEASE PROGRAM('STATABLE')
    END-EXEC.
```

The RESETBR command

Function

File control. The RESETBR command resets the current position of a browse operation. The RESETBR command itself does not retrieve a record; it just establishes position for subsequent retrieval. The browse operation should always end with an ENDBR command.

Syntax

```
EXEC CICS
    RESETBR    FILE(filename)
               RIDFLD(data-area)
              [ KEYLENGTH(data-value)
                  [ GENERIC ] ]
              [ RBA | RRN ]
              [ GTEQ | EQUAL ]
              [ REQID(data-value) ]
              [ SYSID(systemname) ]
    END-EXEC.
```

Options

FILE	Specifies the 1- to 8-character name of the data set that contains the records to be browsed.
RIDFLD	Specifies a data area that identifies the record where the browse operation is to continue. The content of the RIDFLD field depends on whether RBA or RRN is specified; if neither is specified, the RIDFLD field contains a key for VSAM KSDS or path retrieval. For generic positioning (see the KEYLENGTH and GENERIC options below), the RIDFLD field must still be as long as the file's defined key length. To begin a browse operation at the first record in the file, place hex zeros (LOW-VALUE) in the RIDFLD field. To begin a browse operation at the last record in the file, place hex FFs (HIGH-VALUE) in the RIDFLD field.
KEYLENGTH	Specifies a binary halfword (PIC S9(4) COMP) or literal value that indicates the length of the key, which must be less than the file's defined key length. Used only for generic retrieval along with the GENERIC option or when the SYSID option is specified. Not valid if RBA or RRN is specified.
GENERIC	Specifies that only a part of the key in the RIDFLD field should be used, as indicated by the KEYLENGTH option. Positioning is established at the first record with a key whose leftmost character positions (as specified by KEYLENGTH) match the RIDFLD field.
RBA	Specifies that the RIDFLD field is a relative byte address (RBA) for a VSAM KSDS or ESDS. An RBA is a binary fullword (PIC S9(8) COMP).

RRN   Specifies that the RIDFLD is a relative record number (RRN) for a VSAM RRDS. An RRN is a binary fullword (PIC S9(8) COMP). The RRN of the first record in an RRDS is 1.

GTEQ   Specifies that positioning is to be established at the first record whose key value is greater than or equal to the key specified in the RIDFLD field. This will always establish positioning in the file unless the specified key is greater than the largest key in the file. Not valid for ESDS files.

EQUAL   Specifies that positioning will be established at the record whose key matches the RIDFLD field exactly. If no such record exists, the NOTFND condition is raised and the browse operation is not started.

REQID   Specifies a binary halfword (PIC S 9(4) COMP) or literal value that identifies the browse operation; used only when your program controls two or more browse operations at the same time. For each I/O command that's part of the same browse operation, specify the same REQID value.

SYSID   Specifies the 1- to 4-character name of a remote system that contains the file.

Exceptional conditions

Note: The default action for these conditions is to terminate the task.

DISABLED   The data set is disabled, probably as a result of the master terminal operator explicitly disabling the file using CEMT SET DISABLE.

FILENOTFOUND   The data set name specified in the FILE option isn't defined in the File Control Table.

ILLOGIC   A serious VSAM error occurred.

INVREQ   A browse has not been started on the file, or the KEYLENGTH value is incorrect.

IOERR   An I/O error occurred.

ISCINVREQ   An undeterminable error occurred on the remote system specified in the SYSID option.

NOTAUTH   The transaction's PCT entry specified that resource security checking should be done, and the operator is not authorized to access the data set.

NOTFND   The specified record could not be located.

NOTOPEN   The file is not open.

SYSIDERR   The system identified by SYSID could not be located or accessed.

Notes and tips

• Before you can issue a RESETBR command, you must begin a browse operation by issuing a STARTBR command. Browsing is relatively inefficient because a VSAM string is held for the duration of the browse. (A string is required for each concurrent access to a VSAM file, so if 10 strings are specified for a file, 10 simultaneous accesses are permitted.) Because of this inefficiency, you may want to minimize the duration of a browse so you don't tie up a string any longer than is needed.

- To browse a file via an alternate path, specify the path name in the FILE option.

- Another way to change the position during a browse is to simply change the value of the RIDFLD specified in the READNEXT or READPREV command. Then, the new key value you supply becomes the new browse position. This is the most efficient technique if the record you want to skip to is close to the current record. Because you usually won't know if the records are close together, though, I recommend using the RESETBR command instead.

- You can also use the RESETBR command to change the characteristics of the browse from those specified in the STARTBR command without ending the browse. The characteristics that can be changed include those specified in the GENERIC, GTEQ, and RBA options.

- The only exceptional condition you should normally worry about for the RESETBR command is NOTFND.

Coding example

This example resets a browse operation for a file named ACCOUNT. The browse operation will continue at the record indicated by AR-ACCOUNT-NUMBER. If this field contains hex zeros (LOW-VALUE), the browse starts at the beginning of the file; if it contains hex FFs (HIGH-VALUE), the browse starts at the end of the file; otherwise, the browse starts at the first record whose key is equal to or greater than the RIDFLD.

```
4500-RESET-ACCOUNT-BROWSE.
*
    EXEC CICS
        RESETBR FILE('ACCOUNT')
                RIDFLD(AR-ACCOUNT-NUMBER)
                RESP(RESPONSE-CODE)
    END-EXEC.

    IF RESPONSE-CODE = DFHRESP(NORMAL)
        MOVE 'N' TO END-OF-BROWSE-SW
    ELSE
        IF RESPONSE-CODE = DFHRESP(NOTFND)
            MOVE 'Y' TO END-OF-BROWSE-SW
        ELSE
            PERFORM 9999-TERMINATE-PROGRAM
        END-IF
    END-IF.
```

The RETRIEVE command

Function

Interval control. The RETRIEVE command is used in transactions that were invoked via a START command. It retrieves data passed to the program via the START command's FROM option.

Syntax

```
EXEC CICS
    RETRIEVE { INTO(data-area) | SET(pointer-ref) }
             [ LENGTH(data-area) ]
             [ RTRANSID(data-area) ]
             [ RTERMID(data-area) ]
             [ QUEUE(data-area) ]
             [ WAIT ]
    END-EXEC.
```

Options

INTO	Specifies the data area that will contain the data specified in the FROM option of the START command that started the task.
SET	Specifies a binary halfword (PIC S9(4) COMP) that will contain the address of the data specified in the FROM or SET option of the START command that started the task.
LENGTH	Specifies a binary halfword (PIC S9(4) COMP) where CICS places the length of the received data. If you specify INTO, the initial value of the LENGTH field is used to determine the maximum length that can be retrieved.
RTRANSID	Specifies a 4-character field that will contain the data specified in the RTRANSID option of the START command that started the task.
RTERMID	Specifies a 4-character field that will contain the data specified in the RTERMID option of the START command that started the task.
QUEUE	Specifies an 8-character field that will contain the data specified in the QUEUE option of the START command that started the task.
WAIT	Specifies that if no data is currently available, the task is to be suspended until more data is made available; that is, when an unexpired START command expires.

Exceptional conditions

Note: The default action for these conditions is to terminate the task.

ENDDATA	No data is available for the started task.
ENVDEFERR	The RETRIEVE command specified a SET, RTRANSID, RTERMID, or QUEUE option and no corresponding option was specified in the START command.
INVREQ	The command is not valid.
IOERR	An I/O error occurred.
LENGERR	The length specified in the LENGTH option is less than the length of the data retrieved.
NOTFND	The data has been deleted by another task.

Notes and tips

- When more than one START command is issued for the same trans-id specifying the same expiration time and each START command passes data to the task to be started, a single execution of the transaction can process all of the data sent by the START commands. To do that, the program should issue RETRIEVE commands repeatedly until the ENDDATA condition is raised. You don't have to code your programs in this way, though. If you code the program so that just one RETRIEVE command is issued, each START command will result in a separate invocation of the program.

- The RTRANSID, RTERMID, and QUEUE options are designed to let you pass specific types of information to a started task: RTRANSID passes a transaction identifier, RTERMID passes a terminal identifier, and QUEUE passes the name of a transient data queue. If your application requires you to pass this information to a started task, you might consider using these options. However, there's no reason you can't pass that same data using the FROM/INTO options. And, as a matter of fact, you can pass any information you wish in the RTRANSID, RTERMID, or QUEUE fields; CICS doesn't make any assumptions about the contents of those fields other than their lengths.

- The WAIT option can be used for applications that make heavy use of data passed via START commands; it causes the task to remain active even if there isn't currently any data to process. Because the task remains active, however, it consumes CICS resources even when it's idle. So don't specify WAIT unless your application uses data passed via interval control almost constantly.

- You should always check for the ENDDATA condition.

Coding example

This example shows the top-level modules of a program that processes data sent to it from START commands. For efficiency, the program processes as many data items as are available before it terminates.

```
    0000-PROCESS-ORDERS.
*
        PERFORM 1000-PROCESS-ORDER
            UNTIL END-OF-DATA.

        EXEC CICS
            RETURN
        END-EXEC.
*
    1000-PROCESS-ORDER.
*
        PERFORM 1100-RETRIEVE-ORDER-DATA.
        IF NOT END-OF-DATA
            .
            .
*
    1100-RETRIEVE-ORDER-DATA.
*
        MOVE LENGTH OF CUSTOMER-ORDER
            TO CUSTOMER-ORDER-LENGTH.

        EXEC CICS
            RETRIEVE INTO(CUSTOMER-ORDER)
                     LENGTH(CUSTOMER-ORDER-LENGTH)
                     RESP(RESPONSE-CODE)
        END-EXEC.

        IF RESPONSE-CODE = DFHRESP(ENDDATA)
            MOVE 'Y' TO END-OF-DATA-SW
        ELSE
            IF RESPONSE-CODE NOT = DFHRESP(NORMAL)
                PERFORM 9999-TERMINATE-PROGRAM
            END-IF
        END-IF.
```

The RETURN command

Function

Program control. The RETURN command terminates program execution, returning control to the invoking program.

Syntax

```
EXEC CICS
    RETURN [ TRANSID(name)
               [ COMMAREA(data-area)
                   [ LENGTH(data-value) ] ]
               [ IMMEDIATE ] ]
            [ INPUTMSG(data-area)
                [ INPUTMSGLEN(data-value) ] ]
            [ ENDACTIVITY ]
    END-EXEC.
```

Options

TRANSID	Specifies the 1- to 4-character name of the transaction to be invoked when the terminal operator presses an attention key. The trans-id must be defined in the Program Control Table (PCT). TRANSID is valid only for programs that are invoked by terminal users.
COMMAREA	Specifies a data area that's passed to the next execution of a pseudo-conversational program. The next program execution accesses the communication area via its DFHCOMMAREA field, which addresses a copy of the communication area specified in the RETURN command. (This works differently than it does for a LINK command; see the description of that command for details.) COMMAREA is valid only when TRANSID is specified.
LENGTH	Specifies a binary halfword (PIC S9(4) COMP) or literal value that indicates the length of the data area specified in the COMMAREA option.
IMMEDIATE	Causes the transaction specified in the TRANSID option to be started immediately, without waiting for user input.
INPUTMSG	Specifies a data area that supplies input data for the next RECEIVE command. If the TRANSID option is specified, the INPUTMSG data is processed by the first RECEIVE command issued by the specified transaction. If TRANSID is not specified and the current program was invoked by a LINK command, a RECEIVE command in the calling program can process the data.
INPUTMSGLEN	Specifies a binary halfword (PIC S9(4) COMP) or literal value that specifies the length of the INPUTMSG field.
ENDACTIVITY	This option is only valid for programs that implement the CICS Business Transaction Services (BTS). It's ignored if specified for programs outside the BTS environment.

Exceptional conditions

Note: The default action for these conditions is to terminate the task.

INVREQ   You used the TRANSID or COMMAREA options incorrectly.

LENGERR   A length error occurred.

Notes and tips

- You use the RETURN command to implement a pseudo-conversational program by specifying both the TRANSID option and the COMMAREA option. In the TRANSID option, you specify the trans-id that will be used to restart the program when the operator presses an AID key (Enter, Clear, or a PA or PF key). The COMMAREA option passes data forward to the next program execution. Even if you don't need to pass data, you can use the presence of a communication area to determine whether or not a program is being executed for the first time.

- The COMMAREA passed in the RETURN command can be from 0 to 32763 bytes long. If the length is longer, a LENGERR condition will occur.

Coding example

This example shows the complete high-level module of a pseudo-conversational program. EIBCALEN is a CICS-defined field that indicates the length of the communication area, which is used as a switch to trigger first-time processing. On all executions of the program but the first in a terminal session, a one-byte communication area is passed.

```
0000-PROCESS-CUSTOMER-INQUIRY.
*
    EVALUATE TRUE
        WHEN EIBCALEN = ZERO
            MOVE LOW-VALUE TO INQMAP1O
            MOVE '1' TO SEND-FLAG
            PERFORM 1400-SEND-CUSTOMER-MAP
        WHEN EIBAID = DFHCLEAR
            MOVE LOW-VALUE TO INQMAP1O
            MOVE '1' TO SEND-FLAG
            PERFORM 1400-SEND-CUSTOMER-MAP
        WHEN EIBAID = DFHPA1 OR DFHPA2 OR DFHPA3
            CONTINUE
        WHEN EIBAID = DFHPF3 OR DFHPF12
            EXEC CICS
                XCTL PROGRAM('INVMENU')
            END-EXEC
        WHEN EIBAID = DFHENTER
            PERFORM 1000-PROCESS-CUSTOMER-MAP
        WHEN OTHER
            MOVE LOW-VALUE TO INQMAP1O
            MOVE 'Invalid key pressed.' TO MESSAGEO
            MOVE '3' TO SEND-FLAG
            PERFORM 1400-SEND-CUSTOMER-MAP
    END-EVALUATE.

    EXEC CICS
        RETURN TRANSID('INQ1')
                COMMAREA(COMMUNICATION-AREA)
    END-EXEC.
*
```

The REWIND COUNTER command

Function

Named counter server. The REWIND COUNTER command resets the current value of the named counter to its defined minimum.

Syntax

```
EXEC CICS
    REWIND   { COUNTER(name) | DCOUNTER(name) }
             [ POOL(name) ]
             [ INCREMENT(data-value) ]
END-EXEC.
```

Options

COUNTER	Specifies the 16-character name of the counter that is to be reset to its defined minimum value. The COUNTER option requires that a signed binary fullword (PIC S9(8) COMP) value be used for the INCREMENT option.
DCOUNTER	Specifies the 16-character name of the counter that is to be reset to its defined minimum value. The DCOUNTER option requires that an unsigned binary doubleword (PIC 9(18) COMP) value be used for the INCREMENT option.
POOL	Specifies the 8-character name of the pool in which the named counter resides. If there's no matching entry in the DFHNCOPT options table, the default named counter pool on the NCPLDFT system initialization parameter is used.
INCREMENT	Specifies a signed binary fullword (PIC S9(8) COMP) or unsigned binary doubleword (PIC 9(18) COMP) increment value. Use this option if the INCREMENT fails on a GET COUNTER command due to the maximum counter value being reached. The increment value is added to the current counter number after the counter is rewound.

Exceptional conditions

Note: The default action for these conditions is to terminate the task.

INVREQ	The statement was coded improperly, there was a problem accessing the named counter in the coupling facility, or the increment value was invalid.
SUPPRESSED	The named counter hasn't yet reached its maximum limit.

Notes and tips

- The minimum and maximum values for a counter are specified in its DEFINE COUNTER command. The REWIND COUNTER command can only be used if the counter has reached its maximum limit. Otherwise, a SUPPRESSED exceptional condition is raised.

- You can also reset a counter to its minimum value by using the UPDATE COUNTER command or by deleting and redefining it.

- The named counter facility is designed to run in a Parallel Sysplex environment. That means that the facility is controlled by a named counter server, allowing multiple regions to draw from the same counter.

- If you use a field, not a literal value, to assign a COUNTER or DCOUNTER name, make sure that the field is padded with trailing spaces if the name is less than 16 characters long.

Coding example

The following example shows a REWIND COUNTER command that resets the number in the counter named ORDERINV back to its defined minimum value.

```
EXEC CICS
    REWIND COUNTER('ORDERINV')
            POOL('MMA')
END-EXEC.
```

The REWRITE command

Function

File control. The REWRITE command updates a record in a file. The record must have been previously read by a READ, READNEXT, or READPREV command with the UPDATE option. The file can be a VSAM KSDS, ESDS, RRDS, or path. (CICS also supports BDAM files, but the BDAM options aren't covered in this book.)

Syntax

```
EXEC CICS
    REWRITE    FILE(filename)
               FROM(data-area)
          [ { LENGTH(data-area)
            { SYSID(systemname) LENGTH(data-area) } ]
          [ TOKEN(data-area) ]
          [ NOSUSPEND ]
END-EXEC.
```

Options

FILE	Specifies the 1- to 8-character name of the data set that contains the record to be updated.
FROM	Specifies the data area that contains the record to be written.
LENGTH	Specifies a binary halfword (PIC S9(4) COMP) that contains the length of the record to be updated. Required when the file has variable-length records or the SYSID option is specified.
SYSID	Specifies the 1- to 4-character name of a remote system that contains the file.
TOKEN	Specifies a binary fullword (PIC S9(8) COMP) that contains a unique request identifier for the REWRITE command. You can use this identifier to associate the REWRITE with a specific READ, READNEXT, or READPREV command that specified the UPDATE option.
NOSUSPEND	(RLS only) The REWRITE request will not wait if there is an exclusive hold on the record. Since you would have had to issue a READ, READNEXT, or READPREV for UPDATE in order to rewrite the record, you'll probably never use the NOSUSPEND option.

Exceptional conditions

Note: The default action for these conditions is to terminate the task.

CHANGED	The record in a coupling facility data table has been changed since the program read it for update.
DUPREC	The record contains an alternate key value that already exists, the alternate index does not allow duplicate keys, and the alternate index is a part of the file's upgrade set.
FILENOTFOUND	The data set name specified in the FILE option isn't defined in the File Control Table.
ILLOGIC	A serious VSAM error occurred.
INVREQ	The record was not previously retrieved by a READ, READNEXT, or READPREV command with the UPDATE option.
IOERR	An I/O error occurred.
ISCINVREQ	An undeterminable error occurred on the remote system specified in the SYSID option.
LENGERR	The length specified in the LENGTH option exceeds the maximum record length allowed for the file.
NOSPACE	There is not enough space allocated to the data set to contain the record.
NOTAUTH	The transaction's PCT entry specified that resource security checking should be done, and the operator is not authorized to access the data set.
NOTOPEN	The file is not open.
RECORDBUSY	(TS 1.1 and later) The NOSUSPEND option was specified on a record with an alternate index key that has caused the request to wait.
SYSIDERR	The system identified by SYSID could not be located or accessed.

Notes and tips

- To rewrite a record, you must first read the record with the UPDATE option. This places a lock on the control interval that contains the record so that other CICS tasks can't access it, unless RLS (record level sharing) is being used. In that case, only the record is locked and other programs can read it, though they can't update it. In either case, if the file is recoverable, the lock is held until the task ends or a syncpoint is issued. Otherwise, it's released when a REWRITE or UNLOCK command is issued for the file.

- When you rewrite a record, you can change any data within the record except the file's primary key. You can also change the record's length.

Coding example (READ UPDATE and REWRITE)

This example retrieves and updates a VSAM KSDS record. The field named AR-ACCOUNT-NUMBER identifies the record to be read and the field named NEW-ACCOUNT-RECORD contains the data that's to replace the current record. The NOTFND condition is checked in case the READ command can't locate the record.

```
    4100-UPDATE-ACCOUNT-RECORD.
*
        EXEC CICS
            READ FILE('ACCOUNT')
                INTO(ACCOUNT-RECORD)
                RIDFLD(AR-ACCOUNT-NUMBER)
                UPDATE
                RESP(RESPONSE-CODE)
        END-EXEC.

        IF RESPONSE-CODE = DFHRESP(NORMAL)
            EXEC CICS
                REWRITE FILE('ACCOUNT')
                        FROM(NEW-ACCOUNT-RECORD)
            END-EXEC
        ELSE
            IF RESPONSE-CODE = DFHRESP(NOTFND)
                MOVE 'N' TO RECORD-FOUND-SW
            ELSE
                PERFORM 9999-TERMINATE-PROGRAM
            END-IF
        END-IF.
```

The ROUTE command

Function

Basic Mapping Support. The ROUTE command lets you specify one or more terminals as delivery points for a BMS message.

Syntax

```
EXEC CICS
    ROUTE [ LIST(data-area) ]
          [ OPCLASS(data-area) ]
          [ { INTERVAL(hhmmss)  }
            { TIME(hhmmss)       }
            { AFTER [HOURS(hh)][MINUTES(mins)][SECONDS(secs)] }
            { AT [HOURS(hh)][MINUTES(mins)][SECONDS(secs)]    } ]
          [ ERRTERM[(name)] ]
          [ TITLE(data-area) ]
          [ REQID(name) ]
          [ NLEOM ]
END-EXEC.
```

Options

Note: If INTERVAL, TIME, AFTER, and AT are all omitted, INTERVAL(0) is assumed.

LIST
: Specifies a list of terminals where the logical message should be routed. The route list is a data area consisting of one or more 16-byte entries, each identifying one terminal or operator. I'll describe the format of each under "Notes and tips."

OPCLASS
: Specifies a 3-byte field that indicates which classes of operators the message should be delivered to. Each bit in the 3-byte field corresponds to one of the 24 allowable operator classes: the first bit corresponds to operator class 24, and the last bit corresponds to operator class 1. If a bit position is on, the message is delivered to operators of the corresponding class. If a bit position is off, the message is not delivered to operators of that class.

INTERVAL
: Specifies how long BMS should wait before it delivers the logical message. You can code a literal in the form *hhmmss*; leading zeros can be omitted. Or, you can code a data name for a 7-digit packed-decimal field (PIC S9(7) COMP-3); its value must be in the form *0hhmmss*.

TIME
: Specifies the time of day for delivering the logical message. You can code a literal in the form *hhmmss*; leading zeros can be omitted. Or, you can code a data name for a 7-digit packed-decimal field (PIC S9(7) COMP-3); its value must be in the form *0hhmmss*.

AFTER
: Specifies that the HOURS, MINUTES, and SECONDS options indicate a duration after which the message will be delivered.

AT	Specifies that the HOURS, MINUTES, and SECONDS options indicate a time of day when the message is to be delivered.
HOURS	Specifies a binary fullword (PIC S9(8) COMP) in the range of 0 to 99.
MINUTES	Specifies a binary fullword (PIC S9(8) COMP) in the range of 0 to 59 or 0 to 5999.
SECONDS	Specifies a binary fullword (PIC S9(8) COMP) in the range of 0 to 59 or 0 to 359999.
ERRTERM	Specifies the 1- to 4-character terminal-id of a terminal that should be notified if the message can't be delivered. If you specify ERRTERM without a name, the terminal attached to the task that originated the message is assumed.
TITLE	Specifies a data area that includes the title used to identify the message during page retrieval. The title field must begin with a binary halfword (PIC S9(4) COMP) that indicates the length of the entire title field, including the two bytes occupied by the length field.
REQID	Specifies a two-character name that's used for message recovery. If omitted, '**' is assumed.
NLEOM	Specifies that BMS should use new-line (NL) and end-of-message (EM) orders as it builds the logical message. If you specify NLEOM on the ROUTE command, you should also specify it on the SEND MAP/SEND TEXT commands that build the message.

Exceptional conditions

Note: The default action for all of these conditions except RTEFAIL and RTESOME is to terminate the task. The default action for the RTEFAIL and RTESOME conditions is to ignore the condition.

IGREQID	The prefix specified in the REQID option is different from the prefix established in a previous REQID.
INVERRTERM	The terminal identifier specified in the ERRTERM option isn't defined in the Terminal Control Table (TCT) or the type of terminal isn't supported by BMS.
INVREQ	There is a format error in the route list, the specified hours, minutes, or seconds are out of range, or a distributed program link error occurred.
RTEFAIL	The ROUTE command does not specify any terminals other than the one attached to the current task.
RTESOME	BMS is able to route the message to some, but not all, of the specified terminals.

Notes and tips

- To route a logical message, you must issue a ROUTE command before you issue the SEND MAP, SEND TEXT, or SEND CONTROL commands to build the message. To properly build the message, each of these commands should specify the ACCUM and PAGING options. To complete the message so it can be delivered, issue a SEND PAGE command.

- Routed logical messages are held in temporary storage until they can be delivered. A parameter in the System Initialization Table (SIT) lets an installation specify how long undelivered messages are kept. If this time is exceeded, the undelivered message is automatically deleted.

- Each entry in a route list is 16 bytes long and contains the following information:

  Bytes 0-3   The terminal identifier of a terminal where you want the message sent.

  Bytes 4-5   A logical device code name for logical units that support LDC.

  Bytes 6-8   The operator identifier of an operator to whom you want the message sent or blanks.

  Byte 9   A status value that CICS updates to indicate whether or not the message was successfully routed to the terminal or operator specified in this entry. Any value other than hex zeros (LOW-VALUE) indicates that the message wasn't routed to this terminal or operator.

  Bytes 10-15   Must be spaces.

  After the last entry in the list, code a binary halfword (PIC S9(4) COMP) initialized to -1.

- If you're routing a message to a printer terminal, you should code the NLEOM option to control printer line spacing. That reduces the number of bytes that must be sent to the printer.

- There are two ways to use the HOURS, MINUTES, and SECONDS options following AFTER. If you use them in combination, the ranges are 0 to 99 for HOURS, 0 to 59 for MINUTES, and 0 to 59 for SECONDS. However, if you specify only one option, you can use the larger ranges: 0 to 99 for HOURS, 0 to 5999 for MINUTES, and 0 to 359999 for SECONDS. For example, you could specify AFTER MINUTES(1) SECONDS(30), or you could specify AFTER SECONDS(90). Both have the same effect.

- Be sure to test the RTEFAIL and RTESOME conditions to ensure that the route command was successful.

Coding example

This example shows portions of a program that builds a logical message and routes
it to two printer terminals. The terminal-ids for the printers are L1P1 and L2P5.

```
01  ROUTE-LIST.
*
    05   LIST-ENTRY-1.
         10   LE1-TERMINAL-ID  PIC X(04)   VALUE 'L1P1'.
         10   FILLER           PIC X(12)   VALUE SPACE.
    05   LIST-ENTRY-2.
         10   LE2-TERMINAL-ID  PIC X(04)   VALUE 'L2P5'.
         10   FILLER           PIC X(12)   VALUE SPACE.
    05   FILLER               PIC S9(04) VALUE -1      COMP.
*
  .

  .
 PROCEDURE DIVISION.
*
 0000-PRODUCE-INVENTORY-LISTING.
*
     EXEC CICS
         ROUTE LIST(ROUTE-LIST)
               NLEOM
     END-EXEC.
     .
     .
     EXEC CICS
         SEND PAGE
     END-EXEC.
     .
     .
```

The SEND command (APPC)

Function

APPC mapped conversation. The SEND command sends data to a remote process.

Syntax

```
EXEC CICS
    SEND [ CONVID(name) | SESSION(name) ]
         [ ATTACHID(name) ]
         [ FROM(data-area)
             [ LENGTH(data-value) | FLENGTH(data-value) ] ]
         [ INVITE | LAST ]
         [ CONFIRM | WAIT ]
         [ STATE(cvda) ]
END-EXEC.
```

Options

CONVID	Specifies the 4-character conversation-id obtained from the Execute Interface Block field EIBRSRCE following a successful ALLOCATE command.
SESSION	A synonym for CONVID provided for compatibility with earlier releases. CONVID is preferred.
ATTACHID	Specifies the 1- to 8-character name of the ATTACH FMH that was specified on the BUILD ATTACH command.
FROM	Specifies the area that contains the data to be sent.
LENGTH	Specifies a binary halfword (PIC S9(4) COMP) or literal value that indicates the length of the FROM area.
FLENGTH	Specifies a binary fullword (PIC S9(8) COMP) or literal value that indicates the length of the FROM area.
INVITE	Informs the remote process that it may respond by sending data and places the current program in receive state.
LAST	Informs the remote process that this is the last transmission of the conversation.
CONFIRM	Informs the remote process that confirmation is required. The remote process should respond by executing an ISSUE CONFIRMATION or ISSUE ERROR command.
WAIT	Does not return control to the application program until the contents of the transmission buffer are sent to the remote process.
STATE	Specifies a binary fullword (PIC S9(8) COMP) where CICS places state information.

Exceptional conditions

Note: The default action for all these conditions except EOC and SIGNAL is to terminate the task. The default action for the EOC and SIGNAL conditions is to ignore the condition.

CBIDERR	The Attach Header Control Block cannot be found.
EOC	The end of the message chain has been received. This is the normal response code for SEND.
INVREQ	A function shipping error occurred, the command isn't compatible with the conversation, or CONFIRM was specified and the conversation isn't sync level 1 or 2.
LENGERR	The data received from the remote process is longer than the maximum specified, or the specification for the maximum length is invalid.
NOTALLOC	The conversation has not been properly allocated.
SIGNAL	The remote program has executed an ISSUE SIGNAL command.
TERMERR	A session error has occurred.

Notes and tips

- The CONVID value is obtained from the Execute Interface Block field EIBRSRCE following the successful execution of an ALLOCATE command.

- The STATE option returns a value that indicates the current state of the conversation. If the SEND is successful, the STATE value depends on the options you coded, as follows:

Options	Resulting state
None	SEND
INVITE	PENDRECEIVE
INVITE WAIT	RECEIVE
LAST	PENDFREE
LAST WAIT	FREE
CONFIRM	SEND
INVITE CONFIRM	RECEIVE
LAST CONFIRM	FREE

  The value of the STATE field can be tested using the CICS keyword DFHVALUE, in much the same way as you use DFHRESP to test the response code returned in the RESP field:

```
IF CONVERSATION-STATE = DFHVALUE(RECEIVE)
```

- If your conversation is designed to allow the partner program to use the ISSUE SIGNAL command, you should test for the SIGNAL condition. When you do, remember that EOC is a normal response for the SEND command.

Coding example

The following example shows a SEND command that sends data to a back-end transaction. Here, the data sent to the back-end transaction is a customer number. After the SEND command, the program issues a RECEIVE command to receive the customer data retrieved by the back-end transaction. (In a production environment, additional error checking would be required.)

```
      WORKING-STORAGE SECTION.
*
   .
   .
   .
  01   SEND-MESSAGE.
*
      05   SM-CUSTOMER-NUMBER        PIC X(06).
*
  01   RECEIVE-MESSAGE.
*
      05   RM-CUSTOMER-FOUND-SW      PIC X(01).
         88  RM-CUSTOMER-FOUND          VALUE 'Y'.
      05   RM-CUST-DATA-1            PIC X(520).
      05   RM-CUST-DATA-2            PIC X(300).
      05   RM-CUST-DATA-3            PIC X(255).
*
  01   RECEIVE-LENGTH               PIC S9(04) COMP.
   .
   .
   .
  PROCEDURE DIVISION.
   .
   .
   .
*
  2300-GET-CUSTOMER-DATA.
*
      MOVE CUSTNOI TO SM-CUSTOMER-NUMBER.

      EXEC CICS
          SEND CONVID(CONVERSATION-ID)
              FROM(SEND-MESSAGE)
              INVITE
              WAIT
      END-EXEC.

      MOVE LENGTH OF RECEIVE-MESSAGE TO RECEIVE-LENGTH.

      EXEC CICS
          RECEIVE CONVID(CONVERSATION-ID)
                  INTO(RECEIVE-MESSAGE)
                  LENGTH(RECEIVE-LENGTH)
      END-EXEC.

      IF RM-CUSTOMER-FOUND
          MOVE RM-CUST-DATA-1 TO CUSTOMER-MASTER-RECORD
          MOVE RM-CUST-DATA-2 TO ACCOUNT-MASTER-RECORD
          MOVE RM-CUST-DATA-3 TO CUSTOMER-HISTORY-RECORD
      END-IF.
```

The SEND command (terminal control)

Function

Terminal control. The SEND command transmits data to a terminal without using BMS services to format the data.

Syntax

```
EXEC CICS
    SEND   FROM(data-area)
           { LENGTH(data-value) | FLENGTH(data-value) }
           [ DEST(name) ]
           [ WAIT ]
           [ INVITE | LAST ]
           [ DEFRESP ]
           [ STRFIELD ] | [ ERASE ] [ CTLCHAR(data-area) ]
END-EXEC.
```

Options

FROM	Specifies the data area that contains the output data.
LENGTH	Specifies a binary halfword (PIC S9(4) COMP) or literal value that indicates the length of the FROM area.
FLENGTH	Specifies a binary fullword (PIC S9(8) COMP) or literal value that indicates the length of the FROM area.
DEST	(TCAM only) Specifies the 4-character name of the terminal where the output data should be sent.
WAIT	Specifies that the application program should be suspended until the output operation has completed.
INVITE	(VTAM only) Specifies that the next terminal control operation will be a RECEIVE command.
LAST	(VTAM only) Specifies that this is the last terminal output operation for the transaction.
DEFRESP	(VTAM only) Specifies that the terminal must issue a response to the output message whether the operation was successful or not. Normally, a response is required only when an error occurs.
STRFIELD	Specifies that the output data contains structured fields. If you code STRFIELD, you cannot code ERASE or CTLCHAR.
ERASE	Specifies that the terminal's display screen is to be erased before data is sent. If you code ERASE, you cannot code STRFIELD.
CTLCHAR	Specifies a 1-byte field that contains a write control character. If you code CTLCHAR, you cannot code STRFIELD.

Exceptional conditions

Note: The default action for these conditions is to terminate the task.

INVREQ   A function shipping error has occurred.

LENGERR   A length error has occurred.

NOTALLOC   The task is not associated with a terminal.

TERMERR   (VTAM only) A terminal I/O error has occurred.

Notes and tips

• The SEND command is best used to send small amounts of unformatted data to a terminal. If any but the simplest formatting is required, you're better off using BMS to handle the formatting.

• Under VTAM, you can improve performance by coordinating SEND and RECEIVE commands using the INVITE and LAST options. When you issue a SEND command, code INVITE if the next operation will be RECEIVE. For the transaction's last SEND command, code LAST.

Coding example

This program segment shows how data can be sent to a 3270 terminal without using BMS. Here, the output data consists of four display lines, each padded with spaces so it's 80 characters long. As a result, the display will be correct only for standard 80-column displays. Module 3000 begins by moving data from a customer record to the output area and then issues the SEND command. The ERASE option is specified so that the previous contents of the terminal screen are erased.

```
 *
  WORKING-STORAGE SECTION.
 *
   .
   .
   .
 *
  01   CUSTOMER-DATA-LINES.
 *
      05   CUSTOMER-LINE-1.
          10   FILLER                PIC X(10)    VALUE 'Customer: '.
          10   CDL-CUSTOMER-NUMBER PIC X(06).
          10   FILLER                PIC X(04)    VALUE SPACE.
          10   CDL-LAST-NAME         PIC X(30).
          10   FILLER                PIC X(30)    VALUE SPACE.
      05   CUSTOMER-LINE-2.
          10   FILLER                PIC X(20)    VALUE SPACE.
          10   CDL-FIRST-NAME        PIC X(20).
          10   FILLER                PIC X(40)    VALUE SPACE.
      05   CUSTOMER-LINE-3.
          10   FILLER                PIC X(20)    VALUE SPACE.
          10   CDL-ADDRESS           PIC X(30).
          10   FILLER                PIC X(30)    VALUE SPACE.
```

```
        05  CUSTOMER-LINE-4.
            10  FILLER              PIC X(20)    VALUE SPACE.
            10  CDL-CITY            PIC X(20).
            10  FILLER              PIC X(01)    VALUE SPACE.
            10  CDL-STATE           PIC X(02).
            10  FILLER              PIC X(01)    VALUE SPACE.
            10  CDL-ZIP-CODE        PIC X(10).
            10  FILLER              PIC X(26)    VALUE SPACE.
    .
    .
    .
*
   PROCEDURE DIVISION.
*
   0000-PROCESS-CUSTOMER-INQUIRY.
*
       PERFORM 1000-RECEIVE-INQUIRY-DATA.
       IF VALID-DATA
           PERFORM 2000-READ-CUSTOMER-RECORD
           IF CUSTOMER-FOUND
               PERFORM 3000-SEND-CUSTOMER-DATA
           END-IF
       END-IF.

       IF NOT VALID-DATA
           PERFORM 4000-SEND-ERROR-MESSAGE
       END-IF.

       EXEC CICS
           RETURN
       END-EXEC.
*
    .
    .
    .
*
   3000-SEND-CUSTOMER-DATA.
*
       MOVE CM-CUSTOMER-NUMBER TO CDL-CUSTOMER-NUMBER.
       MOVE CM-LAST-NAME        TO CDL-LAST-NAME.
       MOVE CM-FIRST-NAME       TO CDL-FIRST-NAME.
       MOVE CM-ADDRESS          TO CDL-ADDRESS.
       MOVE CM-CITY             TO CDL-CITY.
       MOVE CM-STATE            TO CDL-STATE.
       MOVE CM-ZIP-CODE         TO CDL-ZIP-CODE.

       EXEC CICS
           SEND FROM(CUSTOMER-DATA-LINES)
               ERASE
       END-EXEC.
*
```

The SEND CONTROL command

Function

Basic Mapping Support. The SEND CONTROL command lets you send device control instructions to a terminal. No mapped data is sent.

Syntax

```
EXEC CICS
    SEND CONTROL [ ERASEAUP | ERASE ]
                 [ ALARM ]
                 [ FREEKB ]
                 [ FRSET ]
                 [ CURSOR (data-value) ]
                 [ PRINT ]
                 [ FORMFEED ]
                 [ ACCUM ]
                 [ { PAGING }
                   { SET(pointer-ref) }
                   { TERMINAL [WAIT] [LAST] } ]
                 [ L40 | L64 | L80 | HONEOM ]
                 [ REQID(name) ]
    END-EXEC.
```

Options

ERASEAUP	Erases all of the unprotected fields on the screen.
ERASE	Erases the entire display screen.
ALARM	Sounds the terminal's alarm.
FREEKB	Unlocks the terminal's keyboard.
FRSET	Resets the Modified Data Tag (MDT) bit of each attribute byte to zero.
CURSOR	Specifies a binary halfword (PIC S9(4) COMP) or literal value that indicates the screen position where the cursor is to be placed. The row and column corresponding to a given cursor position value depend on the number of columns in each line. For a standard 80-column display, column 1 of row 1 is cursor position 0, column 1 of row 2 is cursor position 80, and so on. If you omit CURSOR, the cursor is placed in position 0.
PRINT	When used with a printer, specifies that the data is to be printed. If PRINT is omitted, the data is sent to the printer but not printed.
FORMFEED	Causes the printer to advance to the top of the next page.
ACCUM	Specifies that this command is part of a message building operation.
PAGING	Specifies that output should be held in temporary storage until it can be delivered to its final destination.
SET	Specifies a pointer to be set to the address of the output data.

TERMINAL	Specifies that output should be sent directly to the terminal. This is the default.
WAIT	Specifies that the task should be suspended until the output operation has completed.
LAST	For logical units only, specifies the last terminal output operation for the task.
L40	Specifies that the maximum line length for printed output is 40 characters.
L64	Specifies that the maximum line length for printed output is 64 characters.
L80	Specifies that the maximum line length for printed output is 80 characters.
HONEOM	Specifies that CICS should honor the printer's default end-of-margin setting when determining the maximum print line length. This is the default.
REQID	Specifies a two-character name that's used for message recovery. If omitted, '**' is assumed. All BMS commands for the same logical message must specify the same REQID value.

Exceptional conditions

Note: The default action for these conditions is to terminate the task.

IGREQCD	A VTAM error has occurred.
IGREQID	The prefix specified in the REQID option is different from the prefix established in a previous REQID.
INVREQ	A function shipping error has occurred.
TSIOERR	A temporary storage I/O error has occurred.

Notes and tips

- You should use the SEND CONTROL command only when you need to send control information to a terminal without sending data. All of the options you can specify on a SEND CONTROL command can also be specified on a SEND MAP or SEND TEXT command. As a result, coding a SEND CONTROL command is equivalent to moving hex zeros (LOW-VALUE) to a symbolic map and issuing a SEND MAP command with the DATAONLY option. In both cases, control information is sent without any data.

- Several SEND CONTROL options are particularly useful when sending data to a printer. In particular, the FORMFEED option causes the printer to advance to the next page; the L40, L64, L80, and HONEOM options let you specify print line lengths (usually, you'll specify HONEOM or let it default); and the PRINT option instructs the printer to begin printing the data it has received. Like any of the other SEND CONTROL options, however, you can code these options on a SEND MAP or SEND TEXT command as well.

- If you're building a logical message, be sure to include ACCUM and PAGING.

Coding example

This example shows a SEND CONTROL command that initiates a form feed operation and causes the printer to start printing.

```
EXEC CICS
     SEND CONTROL FORMFEED
                  PRINT
END-EXEC.
```

The SEND MAP command

Function

Basic Mapping Support. The SEND MAP command lets you send data to a terminal, mapping it according to the specifications in a BMS map definition.

Syntax

```
EXEC CICS
    SEND    MAP(name)
         [ MAPSET(name) ]
         [ FROM(data-area) ]
         [ LENGTH(data-value) ]
         [ DATAONLY | MAPONLY ]
         [ ERASEAUP | ERASE ]
         [ ALARM ]
         [ FREEKB ]
         [ FRSET ]
         [ CURSOR [(data-value)] ]
         [ PRINT ]
         [ FORMFEED ]
         [ NLEOM ]
         [ ACCUM ]
         [ PAGING | SET(pointer-ref) | TERMINAL [WAIT] [ LAST] ]
         [ L40 | L64 | L80 | HONEOM ]
         [ REQID(name) ]
         [ NOFLUSH ]
    END-EXEC.
```

Options

MAP	Specifies the 1- to 7-character name of the map to be used to map the output data.
MAPSET	Specifies the 1- to 8-character name of the mapset that contains the map. If omitted, the map name is used. This name must be defined in the Processing Program Table (PPT).
FROM	Specifies the data area that contains the data to be mapped.
LENGTH	Specifies a binary halfword (PIC S9(4) COMP) or literal value that indicates the length of the data to be mapped. Required only if less than the entire data area specified in the FROM option is to be used.
DATAONLY	Data from the FROM area is to be mapped, but not constant data included in the BMS map definition.
MAPONLY	Only constant data from the BMS map definition is to be sent; no FROM area is used.
ERASEAUP	Erases all of the unprotected fields on the screen.
ERASE	Erases the entire display screen. When used with the ACCUM option, ERASE causes the display to be erased as each page is displayed, not as each map is written.

ALARM	Sounds the terminal's alarm.
FREEKB	Unlocks the terminal's keyboard.
FRSET	Resets the Modified Data Tag (MDT) bit of each attribute byte to zero.
CURSOR	Specifies a binary halfword (PIC S9(4) COMP) or literal value that indicates the position where the cursor is to be placed. The row and column corresponding to a given cursor position depends on the number of columns in each line. For an 80-column display, column 1 of row 1 is cursor position 0, column 1 of row 2 is cursor position 80, and so on. If you specify CURSOR but omit the data value, the symbolic cursor positioning technique (described in Unit 2) is used.
PRINT	When used with a printer, specifies that the data is to be printed. If PRINT is omitted, the data is sent to the printer but not printed.
FORMFEED	Causes the printer to advance to the top of the next page.
NLEOM	Specifies that BMS is to use new-line (NL) and end-of-message (EM) orders to build the output; should be used for output intended for a printer.
ACCUM	Specifies that this command is part of a message building operation.
PAGING	Specifies that output should be held in temporary storage until it can be delivered to its final destination.
SET	Specifies a pointer to be set to the address of the output data.
TERMINAL	Specifies that output should be sent directly to the terminal. This is the default.
WAIT	Specifies that the task should be suspended until the output operation has completed.
LAST	For logical units only, specifies the last terminal output operation for the task.
L40	Specifies that the maximum line length for printed output is 40 characters.
L64	Specifies that the maximum line length for printed output is 64 characters.
L80	Specifies that the maximum line length for printed output is 80 characters.
HONEOM	Specifies that CICS should honor the printer's default end-of-margin setting when determining the maximum print line length. This is the default.
REQID	Specifies a two-character name that's used for message recovery. If omitted, '**' is assumed. All BMS commands for the same logical message must specify the same REQID value.
NOFLUSH	Specifies that the system not clear pages if an OVERFLOW condition occurs.

Exceptional conditions

*Note: The default action for all of these conditions except OVERFLOW is to
terminate the task. The default action for OVERFLOW is to ignore the condition.*

IGREQCD	A VTAM error has occurred.
IGREQID	The prefix specified in the REQID option is different from the prefix established in a previous REQID.
INVMPSZ	The map is too large for the terminal.
INVREQ	The request is not allowed.
OVERFLOW	There is not enough room on the screen for the map. If you test the RESP or EIBRESP field to detect this condition, you can issue additional SEND MAP commands to complete the current page by sending a trailer map and/or a header map for the next page.
TSIOERR	A temporary storage I/O error has occurred.

Notes and tips

- If you omit the FROM option, BMS adds the letter O to the end of the map name you specify to determine the name of the output data area. So, if the map is named CUSTMAP, the output data area is CUSTMAPO. BMS uses the same convention when it assembles the symbolic map, so if you copy the BMS-generated symbolic mapset into your program, the names will match up. However, you must code FROM if (1) you want to use your own version of the symbolic map or (2) you specify a data name rather than a literal value in the MAP option.

- The DATAONLY and MAPONLY options let you add data to a display. Code DATAONLY when the screen already contains the correct captions, but you want to change the data that's displayed. Code MAPONLY when you want to display just captions with no data. Omit both if you want data from the symbolic map to be combined with captions coded in the BMS map definition. When you code these options, remember that hex zeros (LOW-VALUE) in the symbolic map are never sent to the terminal. So, moving LOW-VALUE to the symbolic map and issuing a SEND MAP command without coding MAPONLY or DATAONLY is equivalent to issuing the same command with MAPONLY. Usually, you'll omit both MAPONLY and DATAONLY and move LOW-VALUE to the symbolic map fields that don't need to be sent to the terminal.

- Although the CURSOR option lets you place the cursor at any screen location, you'll usually want to use the symbolic cursor positioning technique instead. Symbolic cursor positioning is described in Unit 2.

- If you're building a logical message, be sure to include the ACCUM and PAGING options and test for the OVERFLOW condition.

Coding example (general-purpose SEND MAP module)

This example shows a module that issues one of several varieties of SEND MAP commands depending on the setting of a control flag. In each case, the cursor position is specified using symbolic cursor positioning, as described in Unit 2.

```
     1400-SEND-CUSTOMER-MAP.
*
         EVALUATE TRUE
             WHEN SEND-ERASE
                 EXEC CICS
                     SEND MAP('MNTMAP1')
                          MAPSET('MNTSET1')
                          FROM(MNTMAP1O)
                          ERASE
                          CURSOR
                 END-EXEC
             WHEN SEND-ERASE-ALARM
                 EXEC CICS
                     SEND MAP('MNTMAP1')
                          MAPSET('MNTSET1')
                          FROM(MNTMAP1O)
                          ERASE
                          ALARM
                          CURSOR
                 END-EXEC
             WHEN SEND-DATAONLY
                 EXEC CICS
                     SEND MAP('MNTMAP1')
                          MAPSET('MNTSET1')
                          FROM(MNTMAP1O)
                          DATAONLY
                          CURSOR
                 END-EXEC
             WHEN SEND-DATAONLY-ALARM
                 EXEC CICS
                     SEND MAP('MNTMAP1')
                          MAPSET('MNTSET1')
                          FROM(MNTMAP1O)
                          DATAONLY
                          ALARM
                          CURSOR
                 END-EXEC
         END-EVALUATE.
```

Coding example (message building)

This long example shows how to use SEND MAP commands to build message
pages, each consisting of multiple maps. Each page consists of three types of maps:
a header map (LSTMAP1), which is displayed at the top of each page; a detail map
(LSTMAP2), which is displayed several times on each page; and a trailer map
(LSTMAP3), which is displayed at the bottom of each page. The OVERFLOW
condition is tested to determine when header and trailer maps should be sent.

```
0000-PRODUCE-PRODUCT-LISTING.
*
  .
  .
     PERFORM 2230-SEND-HEADER-MAP.
     PERFORM 2000-PRODUCE-PRODUCT-LINE
         UNTIL PRODUCT-EOF.
     EXEC CICS
         SEND PAGE OPERPURGE
     END-EXEC.
     EXEC CICS
         RETURN
     END-EXEC.
*
  .
  .
2000-PRODUCE-PRODUCT-LINE.
*
     PERFORM 2100-READ-PRODUCT-RECORD.
     IF NOT PRODUCT-EOF
         PERFORM 2200-SEND-PRODUCT-LINE.
*
  .
  .
2200-SEND-PRODUCT-LINE.
*
     MOVE PRM-PRODUCT-CODE        TO PCODEO.
     MOVE PRM-PRODUCT-DESCRIPTION TO DESCRO.
     MOVE PRM-UNIT-PRICE          TO UPRICEO.
     MOVE PRM-QUANTITY-ON-HAND    TO ONHANDO.
     PERFORM 2210-SEND-DETAIL-MAP.
     IF PAGE-OVERFLOW
         PERFORM 2220-SEND-TRAILER-MAP
         PERFORM 2230-SEND-HEADER-MAP
         PERFORM 2210-SEND-DETAIL-MAP
         MOVE 'N' TO PAGE-OVERFLOW-SW.
*
2210-SEND-DETAIL-MAP.
*
     EXEC CICS
         SEND MAP('LSTMAP2')
             MAPSET('LSTSET1')
             FROM(LSTMAP2O)
             ACCUM
             PAGING
             ERASE
             RESP(RESPONSE-CODE)
     END-EXEC.
```

```
            IF RESPONSE-CODE = DFHRESP(OVERFLOW)
                MOVE 'Y' TO PAGE-OVERFLOW-SW
            ELSE
                IF RESPONSE-CODE NOT = DFHRESP(NORMAL)
                    PERFORM 9999-TERMINATE-PROGRAM
                END-IF
            END-IF.
*
2220-SEND-TRAILER-MAP.
*
        EXEC CICS
            SEND MAP('LSTMAP3')
                MAPSET('LSTSET1')
                MAPONLY
                ACCUM
                PAGING
                ERASE
        END-EXEC.
*
2230-SEND-HEADER-MAP.
*
        EXEC CICS
            SEND MAP('LSTMAP1')
                MAPSET('LSTSET1')
                FROM(LSTMAP1O)
                ACCUM
                PAGING
                ERASE
        END-EXEC.

        ADD 1 TO PAGE-NO.
```

The SEND PAGE command

Function

Basic Mapping Support. The SEND PAGE command writes the last page of a BMS logical message to temporary storage.

Syntax

```
EXEC CICS
    SEND PAGE { RELEASE [TRANSID(name)] | RETAIN }
              [ SET(pointer-ref) ]
              [ AUTOPAGE | NOAUTOPAGE ]
              [ OPERPURGE ]
              [ TRAILER(data-area) ]
END-EXEC.
```

Options

Note: If both RELEASE and RETAIN are omitted, the terminal paging transaction is started as soon as the current task ends.

RELEASE	Specifies that the terminal paging transaction is to be initiated immediately. After the message is delivered to the terminal, control is to return directly to CICS as if the program had issued a RETURN command.
TRANSID	Specifies a transaction identifier to be associated with the next terminal input. Valid only if RELEASE is also specified.
RETAIN	Specifies that the terminal paging transaction is to be initiated immediately. After the message is delivered to the terminal, control is to return to the statement following the SEND PAGE command.
SET	Specifies a pointer to be set to the address of the output data.
AUTOPAGE NOAUTOPAGE	Overrides the Terminal Control Table's specification for the terminal's paging status. AUTOPAGE specifies that the pages should be sent to the terminal automatically. NOAUTOPAGE specifies that the pages should be sent to the terminal under operator control.
OPERPURGE	Specifies that the operator must enter a message termination command to delete the message. If you omit OPERPURGE, the message is automatically deleted when the operator enters anything that's not a page retrieval command.
TRAILER	Specifies a data area that contains the data to be used as a trailer that's placed at the bottom of the last page. For a description of the format of this trailer data, see the description of the SEND TEXT command.

Exceptional conditions

Note: The default action for these conditions is to terminate the task.

IGREQCD   A VTAM error has occurred.

INVREQ   The request is not allowed.

TSIOERR   A temporary storage I/O error has occurred.

Notes and tips

* You should always include a SEND PAGE command in any program that builds a logical message. Usually, you'll omit AUTOPAGE and NOAUTOPAGE so that the terminal's default setting will apply. For display terminals, however, I recommend you always code OPERPURGE. Otherwise, it's too easy for the operator to accidentally delete the message.

Coding example

This example shows a portion of the high-level module of a program that creates a logical message. As you can see, the program issues a SEND PAGE command immediately before it issues a RETURN command. That way, the last page of the logical message will be handled properly.

```
0000-PRODUCE-PRODUCT-LISTING.
*
        .
        .
    PERFORM 2000-PRODUCE-PRODUCT-LINE
        UNTIL PRODUCT-EOF.
    PERFORM 3000-SEND-TOTAL-MAP.

    EXEC CICS
        SEND PAGE
            OPERPURGE
    END-EXEC.

    EXEC CICS
        RETURN
    END-EXEC.
```

The SEND TEXT command

Function

Basic Mapping Support. The SEND TEXT command lets you send text to a terminal. A map definition is not used to format the data; instead, BMS automatically formats the data, breaking lines between words where possible.

Syntax

```
EXEC CICS
    SEND TEXT    FROM(data-area)
                 [ LENGTH(data-value) ]
                 [ ERASE ]
                 [ ALARM ]
                 [ FREEKB ]
                 [ CURSOR (data-value) ]
                 [ PRINT ]
                 [ FORMFEED ]
                 [ NLEOM ]
                 [ ACCUM ]

                 [ { PAGING }
                   { SET(pointer-ref) }
                   { TERMINAL [WAIT] [ LAST ] } ]

                 [ HEADER(data-area) ]
                 [ TRAILER(data-area) ]
                 [ JUSTIFY(data-value) | JUSFIRST | JUSLAST ]
                 [ L40 | L64 | L80 | HONEOM ]
                 [ REQID(name) ]
    END-EXEC.
```

Options

FROM	Specifies the data area that contains the data to be sent.
LENGTH	Specifies a binary halfword (PIC S9(4) COMP) or literal value that indicates the length of the data to be sent.
ERASE	Erases the entire display screen. When used with the ACCUM option, ERASE causes the display to be erased as each page is displayed, not as each map is written.
ALARM	Sounds the terminal's alarm.
FREEKB	Unlocks the terminal's keyboard.
CURSOR	Specifies a binary halfword (PIC S9(4) COMP) or literal value that indicates the screen position where the cursor is to be placed. The row and column corresponding to a given cursor position value depends on the number of columns in each line. For a standard 80-column display, column 1 of row 1 is cursor position 0, column 1 of row 2 is cursor position 80, and so on.

PRINT	When used with a printer, specifies that the data is to be printed. If PRINT is omitted, the data is sent to the printer but not printed.
FORMFEED	Causes the printer to advance to the top of the next page.
NLEOM	Specifies that BMS is to use new-line (NL) and end-of-message (EM) orders to build the output; should be used for output intended for a printer.
ACCUM	Specifies that this command is part of a message building operation.
PAGING	Specifies that output should be held in temporary storage until it can be delivered to its final destination.
SET	Specifies a pointer to be set to the address of the data.
TERMINAL	Specifies that output should be sent directly to the terminal. This is the default.
WAIT	Specifies that the task should be suspended until the output operation has completed.
LAST	For logical units only, specifies the last terminal output operation for the task.
HEADER	Specifies a data area that contains the data to be used as the header area that's placed at the top of each page. I'll describe the format of the header area data under "Notes and tips."
TRAILER	Specifies a data area that contains the data to be used as the trailer area that's placed at the bottom of each page. I'll describe the format of the trailer area data under "Notes and tips."
JUSTIFY	Specifies a binary halfword (PIC S9(4) COMP) or literal value that indicates the number of the line where the data is to be placed; the first line on the page is line 1. When a data area is specified, the value -1 is the same as specifying JUSFIRST, and -2 is the same as JUSLAST.
JUSFIRST	Specifies that the data is to be placed on the first available line following the header area.
JUSLAST	Specifies that the data is to be placed at the bottom of the page, immediately before the trailer area.
L40	Specifies that the maximum line length for printed output is 40 characters.
L64	Specifies that the maximum line length for printed output is 64 characters.
L80	Specifies that the maximum line length for printed output is 80 characters.
HONEOM	Specifies that CICS should honor the printer's default end-of-margin setting when determining the maximum print line length. This is the default.
REQID	Specifies a two-character name that's used for message recovery. If omitted, '**' is assumed. All BMS commands for the same logical message must specify the same REQID value.

Exceptional conditions

Note: The default action for these conditions is to terminate the task.

IGREQCD	A VTAM error has occurred.
IGREQID	The prefix specified in the REQID option is different from the prefix established in a previous REQID.
INVREQ	The request is not allowed.
LENGERR	The length specified in the LENGTH option is out of range.
TSIOERR	A temporary storage I/O error has occurred.

Notes and tips

- When you use the SEND TEXT command, BMS formats data by breaking it into lines. Lines are split at spaces, so words aren't split across lines. You can force a line break at any time by including a new-line character (hex 15) in the data.

- When you use message building, be sure to code the ACCUM and PAGING options. The HEADER and TRAILER options let you specify data areas that contain header and trailer information. This data is included in the output if the text data overflows the current page. The header and trailer areas must begin with a 4-byte prefix that contains control information. The first two bytes make up a binary halfword (PIC S9(4) COMP) that indicates the length of the area, not including the 4-byte prefix; the next byte indicates whether pages should be automatically numbered (I'll explain that in a moment); and the fourth byte is reserved for use by BMS.

- To use automatic page numbering, code a non-blank value in the third byte of a header or trailer prefix area. When an overflow situation occurs, BMS scans the header or trailer data until it finds one or more occurrences of the character you specified in byte 3 of the prefix. Then, it replaces those characters with the current page number. For example, if you specify an asterisk in byte 3 of the header area's prefix, BMS scans the header data until it finds one or more asterisks; then, it places the current page number in the positions occupied by the asterisks.

- The JUSTIFY, JUSFIRST, and JUSLAST options let you alter the output data's position. JUSTIFY lets you specify the line number of the line where you want the output to begin. JUSFIRST and JUSLAST let you position data at the top or bottom of the page, allowing for any header or trailer areas. If you omit JUSTIFY, JUSFIRST, and JUSLAST, data is positioned starting at the next available line.

Coding example (sending a single block of text)

This example shows how to use a SEND TEXT command to send text to a terminal.
The example is from an online problem reporting system, and the data consists of a
problem number followed by a free-form textual description of the problem. The
fields PROB-N-1 and PROB-N-2 contain new-line characters (hex 15) to force line
breaks.

```
       .
       .
    01    PROBLEM-DESCRIPTION-AREA.
    *
         05    FILLER            PIC X(16)    VALUE 'PROBLEM NUMBER: '.
         05    PROB-NUMBER       PIC X(05).
         05    PROB-N-1          PIC X(01)    VALUE X'15'.
         05    FILLER            PIC X(11)    VALUE 'DESCRIPTION'.
         05    PROB-N-2          PIC X(01)    VALUE X'15'.
         05    PROB-DESCRIPTION  PIC X(1000).
    *
       .
       .
         EXEC CICS
             SEND TEXT FROM(PROBLEM-DESCRIPTION-AREA)
                       ERASE
                       FREEKB
         END-EXEC.
```

Coding example (message building)

This long example shows how to use SEND TEXT commands to create a report
using message building facilities. Each page of the report has a header area at the
top and a trailer area at the bottom. A single SEND TEXT command is used to send
each line of the report. Whenever BMS detects a page overflow condition, it
automatically sends the header and trailer areas. Automatic page numbering is used
to replace the three asterisks in the header area by a three-digit page number.

```
*
 WORKING-STORAGE SECTION.
*
 .
 .
 .
 01  HEADER-AREA.
*
     05  HA-PREFIX.
         10  HA-LENGTH    PIC S9(04)  VALUE 176    COMP.
         10  HA-PAGE-CODE PIC X(01)   VALUE '*'.
         10  FILLER       PIC X(01)   VALUE SPACE.
     05  HEADER-LINE-1.
         10  FILLER       PIC X(20)   VALUE '              Produ'.
         10  FILLER       PIC X(20)   VALUE 'ct Listing         '.
         10  FILLER       PIC X(17)   VALUE '        Page: ***'.
         10  HA1-N        PIC X(02)   VALUE X'1515'.
     05  HEADER-LINE-2.
         10  FILLER       PIC X(20)   VALUE 'Product            '.
         10  FILLER       PIC X(20)   VALUE SPACE.
         10  FILLER       PIC X(17)   VALUE ' Unit    Quantity'.
         10  HA2-N        PIC X(01)   VALUE X'15'.
     05  HEADER-LINE-3.
         10  FILLER       PIC X(20)   VALUE 'Code         Descript'.
         10  FILLER       PIC X(20)   VALUE 'ion                '.
         10  FILLER       PIC X(17)   VALUE ' Price    On Hand'.
         10  HA3-N        PIC X(02)   VALUE X'1515'.
 *
 01  PRODUCT-LINE.
 *
     05  PL-PRODUCT-CODE  PIC X(10).
     05  FILLER           PIC X(02)   VALUE SPACE.
     05  PL-DESCRIPTION   PIC X(20).
     05  FILLER           PIC X(02)   VALUE SPACE.
     05  PL-UNIT-PRICE    PIC Z,ZZZ,ZZZ.99.
     05  FILLER           PIC X(02)   VALUE SPACE.
     05  PL-QUANTITY      PIC Z,ZZZ,ZZ9.
     05  PL-N             PIC X(01)   VALUE X'15'.
 *
 01  TRAILER-AREA.
 *
     05  TA-PREFIX.
         10  TA-LENGTH    PIC S9(04)  VALUE 26   COMP.
         10  FILLER       PIC X(02)   VALUE SPACE.
     05  TRAILER-LINE.
         10  TA-N         PIC X(01)   VALUE X'15'.
         10  FILLER       PIC X(20)   VALUE 'Continued on next pa'.
         10  FILLER       PIC X(05)   VALUE 'ge...'.
 *
```

```
      0000-PRODUCE-PRODUCT-LISTING.
*
  .
  .
      PERFORM 2000-PRODUCE-PRODUCT-LINE
          UNTIL PRODUCT-EOF.

      EXEC CICS
          SEND PAGE
              OPERPURGE
      END-EXEC.

      EXEC CICS
          RETURN
      END-EXEC.
*
  .
  .
  2000-PRODUCE-PRODUCT-LINE.
*
      PERFORM 2100-READ-PRODUCT-RECORD.
      IF NOT PRODUCT-EOF
          PERFORM 2200-SEND-PRODUCT-LINE
      END-IF.
*
  .
  .
  2200-SEND-PRODUCT-LINE.
*
      MOVE PRM-PRODUCT-CODE         TO PL-PRODUCT-CODE.
      MOVE PRM-PRODUCT-DESCRIPTION  TO PL-DESCRIPTION.
      MOVE PRM-UNIT-PRICE           TO PL-UNIT-PRICE.
      MOVE PRM-QUANTITY-ON-HAND     TO PL-QUANTITY.
      EXEC CICS
          SEND TEXT FROM(PRODUCT-LINE)
                    ACCUM
                    PAGING
                    ERASE
                    HEADER(HEADER-AREA)
                    TRAILER(TRAILER-AREA)
      END-EXEC.
*
```

The SEND TEXT NOEDIT command

Function

Basic Mapping Support. The SEND TEXT NOEDIT command lets you send a device-dependent data stream to a terminal. It is similar to the terminal control SEND command, but it lets you direct its output to temporary storage by coding the PAGING option.

Syntax

```
EXEC CICS
    SEND TEXT NOEDIT    FROM(data-area)
                        [ LENGTH(data-value) ]
                        [ ERASE ]
                        [ ALARM ]
                        [ FREEKB ]
                        [ PRINT ]
                        [ PAGING | TERMINAL [WAIT] [LAST] ]
                        [ L40 | L64 | L80 | HONEOM ]
                        [ REQID(name) ]
    END-EXEC.
```

Options

FROM	Specifies the data area that contains the data to be sent.
LENGTH	Specifies a binary halfword (PIC S9(4) COMP) or literal value that indicates the length of the data to be sent.
ERASE	Erases the entire display screen.
ALARM	Sounds the terminal's alarm.
FREEKB	Unlocks the terminal's keyboard.
PRINT	When used with a printer, specifies that the data is to be printed. If PRINT is omitted, the data is sent to the printer but not printed.
PAGING	Specifies that output should be held in temporary storage until it can be delivered to its final destination.
TERMINAL	Specifies that output should be sent directly to the terminal. This is the default.
WAIT	Specifies that the task should be suspended until the output operation has completed.
LAST	For logical units only, specifies the last terminal output operation for the task.
L40	Specifies that the maximum line length for printed output is 40 characters.
L64	Specifies that the maximum line length for printed output is 64 characters.
L80	Specifies that the maximum line length for printed output is 80 characters.

HONEOM   Specifies that CICS should honor the printer's default end-of-margin setting when determining the maximum print line length. This is the default.

REQID   Specifies a two-character name that's used for message recovery. If omitted, '**' is assumed. All BMS commands for the same logical message must specify the same REQID value.

Exceptional conditions

Note: The default action for these conditions is to terminate the task.

IGREQCD   A VTAM error has occurred.

IGREQID   The prefix specified in the REQID option is different from the prefix established in a previous REQID.

INVREQ   The request is not allowed.

TSIOERR   A temporary storage I/O error has occurred.

Notes and tips

- When you use the SEND TEXT NOEDIT command, the data in the FROM area should be in device-dependent format, containing any control characters required by the device to format the data appropriately.

- You can use the PAGING option to direct the output to temporary storage. Then, the user retrieves the data by using the paging transaction. If you don't use the PAGING option, you should probably use the terminal control SEND command instead.

Coding example

This example shows how to use a SEND TEXT NOEDIT command to send text to a temporary storage queue so it can be later retrieved by the paging transaction. The example is from an online problem reporting system, and the data consists of a problem number followed by a free-form textual description of the problem. Note that the output is broken down into 80-character lines, so the display will be correct for standard 80-column displays.

```
      .
      .
 01    PROBLEM-DESCRIPTION-AREA.
*
      05   FILLER            PIC X(16)   VALUE 'PROBLEM NUMBER: '.
      05   PROB-NUMBER       PIC X(05).
      05   FILLER            PIC X(59)   VALUE SPACE.
      05   FILLER            PIC X(11)   VALUE 'DESCRIPTION'
      05   FILLER            PIC X(69)   VALUE SPACE.
      05   PROB-DESCRIPTION.
           10   PROB-LINE    OCCURS 10
                             PIC X(80).
*
      .
      .
      EXEC CICS
          SEND TEXT NOEDIT FROM(PROBLEM-DESCRIPTION-AREA)
                           ERASE
                           FREEKB
                           PAGING
      END-EXEC.
```

The SIGNOFF command

Function

Authentication. The SIGNOFF command signs the user off the CICS system, as if he or she had entered the CESF transaction.

Syntax

```
EXEC CICS
    SIGNOFF
END-EXEC.
```

Options

The SIGNOFF command has no options.

Exceptional condition

INVREQ   The request is not allowed. In most cases, this condition means the user isn't signed on. The default action for this condition is to terminate the task.

Notes and tips

* The SIGNON and SIGNOFF commands are useful when you want to build security into a menu system so the user doesn't have to enter the CESN and CESF transactions directly.

The SIGNON command

Function

Authentication. The SIGNON command signs the user on to the CICS system, as if he or she had entered the CESN transaction.

Syntax

```
EXEC CICS
    SIGNON   USERID(data-value)
             [ PASSWORD(data-value) ]
             [ NEWPASSWORD(data-value) ]
             [ ESMREASON(data-area) ]
             [ ESMRESP(data-area) ]
             [ GROUPID(data-value) ]
             [ OIDCARD(data-value) ]
             [ NATLANG(data-value) | LANGUAGECODE(data-value) ]
             [ NATLANGINUSE(data-area) ]
             [ LANGINUSE(data-area) ]
    END-EXEC.
```

Options

USERID	Specifies the user's 8-character signon-id.
PASSWORD	Specifies the user's 8-character password.
NEWPASSWORD	Specifies a new password. Valid only if PASSWORD is also coded.
ESMREASON	Specifies a binary fullword (PIC S9(8) COMP) where CICS places the reason code returned by an external security manager like RACF.
ESMRESP	Specifies a binary fullword (PIC S9(8) COMP) where CICS places an error code returned by an external security manager if the signon fails.
GROUPID	Specifies the RACF user group that the user is being signed on to.
OIDCARD	Specifies a 65-byte field that contains security data recorded on a magnetic operator-id card.
NATLANG	Specifies a 1-character value that indicates the national language to be used. Some of the values available are:

E	US English	G	German
A	UK English	I	Italian
C	Simplified Chinese	9	Dutch
F	French		

LANGUAGECODE	Specifies a 3-character value that indicates the language to be used. This is an alternative to the NATLANG option. Some of the values available are:

ENU	US English	DEU	German
ENG	UK English	ITA	Italian
CHS	Simplified Chinese	NLD	Dutch
FRA	French		

NATLANGINUSE	Specifies a 1-character field where CICS places a value that indicates the national language currently in use. The values are the same as those for the NATLANG option.
LANGINUSE	Specifies a 3-character field where CICS places a value that indicates the language currently in use. This is an alternative to the NATLANGINUSE option. The values are the same as those for the LANGUAGECODE option.

Exceptional conditions

Note: The default action for these conditions is to terminate the task.

INVREQ   The request is not allowed. The RESP2 field provides additional information:

9	The terminal is already signed on
10	Task is not associated with a terminal
11	Terminal has preset security
12	Invalid response from external security manager
13	External security manager returned invalid code
14	National language not available
15	Transaction routing error
18	External security manager is not initialized
25	Invalid terminal type
26	The limit of MVS ENQ requests was reached
27	External security manager is not active
28	National language is invalid
29	The user is already signed on

NOTAUTH   The user is not authorized. The RESP2 field provides additional information:

1	Password is required
2	Password is incorrect
3	A new password is required
4	The new password is invalid
5	OIDCARD is required
6	OIDCARD is incorrect
16	The user is not authorized for this terminal
17	The user is not authorized for this application
19	The user-id has been revoked
20	The user-id group access has been revoked
21	Signon failure during SECLABEL checking
22	The external security manager is not accepting signons

USERIDERR   The user-id is incorrect. The RESP2 field provides additional information:

8	The user-id is not defined
30	The user-id is all blanks or nulls

Notes and tips

- The SIGNON and SIGNOFF commands are useful when you want to build security into a menu system so the user doesn't have to enter the CESN and CSSF transactions directly.

- Since a user's password is passed as a parameter in this command, it may become visible should the program abend and a dump be produced. For that reason, it's a good idea to move blanks into the password field in your program as soon as you're finished using it.

- There is no signoff implied when the SIGNON command is issued. That means if a user is already signed on to the terminal, you must first issue a SIGNOFF command.

Coding example

The following example shows how to use the SIGNON command. Here, the user-id and password fields have been previously read from the terminal using a RECEIVE MAP command. (In a production program, you would probably want to evaluate the RESP and RESP2 values to provide a more meaningful error message if the signon fails.)

```
 2100-SIGN-ON.
*
`
     EXEC CICS
         SIGNON USERID(USERI)
                PASSWORD(PASSI)
                RESP(RESPONSE-CODE)
     END-EXEC.

     IF RESPONSE-CODE = DFHRESP(NORMAL)
         MOVE 'Signed on.' TO MSGO
         MOVE 'Y' TO SIGNED-ON-SW
     ELSE
         MOVE 'Signon failed.' TO MSGO
         MOVE 'N' TO SIGNED-ON-SW
     END-IF.
```

The START command

Function

Interval control. The START command initiates another task that will begin execution when a specified time period has expired. Optionally, the START command can pass data to the task.

Syntax

```
EXEC CICS
     START    TRANSID(name)
              [ { INTERVAL(hhmmss) }
                { TIME(hhmmss) }
                { AFTER [HOURS(hh)] [MINUTES(mins)] [SECONDS(secs)] }
                { AT [HOURS(hh)] [MINUTES(mins)] [SECONDS(secs)] } ]
              [ TERMID(name) | USERID(data-value) ]
              [ SYSID(systemname) ]
              [ REQID(name) ]
              [ FROM(data-area)
                   [ LENGTH(data-value) ] ]
              [ RTRANSID(name) ]
              [ RTERMID(name) ]
              [ QUEUE(name) ]
              [ NOCHECK ]
              [ PROTECT ]
     END-EXEC.
```

Options

Note: If INTERVAL, TIME, AFTER, and AT are all omitted, INTERVAL(0) is assumed.

TRANSID	Specifies the 1- to 4-character transaction identifier that will be used to start the task.
INTERVAL	Specifies a time interval; the task will be started when this interval has elapsed. You can code a literal in the form *hhmmss*; leading zeros can be omitted. Or, you can code a data name for a 7-digit packed-decimal field (PIC S9(7) COMP-3); its value must be in the form *0hhmmss*.
TIME	Specifies a time of day when the task will be started. You can code a literal in the form *hhmmss*; leading zeros can be omitted. Or, you can code a data name for a 7-digit packed-decimal field (PIC S9(7) COMP-3); its value must be in the form *0hhmmss*.
AFTER	Specifies that the HOURS, MINUTES, and SECONDS options indicate a duration after which the task will be started.
AT	Specifies that the HOURS, MINUTES, and SECONDS options indicate a time of day when the task will be started.
HOURS	Specifies a binary fullword (PIC S9(8) COMP) in the range of 0 to 99.

MINUTES	Specifies a binary fullword (PIC S9(8) COMP) in the range of 0 to 59 or 0 to 5999.
SECONDS	Specifies a binary fullword (PIC S9(8) COMP) in the range of 0 to 59 or 0 to 359999.
TERMID	Specifies a 1- to 4-character terminal identifier that identifies the terminal where the started task will be attached. If specified, it must be defined in the Terminal Control Table (TCT). If omitted, the task is not attached to any terminal and, as a result, can't do any terminal I/O.
USERID	Specifies the user-id under whose authority the started task is to run if the task is not associated with a terminal. If TERMID is used instead, the user-id defaults to userid1.
SYSID	Specifies the 1- to 4-character name of a remote system where the task is to be started.
REQID	Specifies a 1- to 8-character name used to uniquely identify this START command. If specified, a CANCEL command can be issued later to cancel the task before it begins executing. (Once the task has started, however, the CANCEL command has no effect.)
FROM	Specifies a data area that contains data to be passed to the started task. The started task receives this data by issuing a RETRIEVE command with the INTO or SET option.
LENGTH	Specifies a binary halfword (PIC S9(4) COMP) or literal value that indicates the length of the FROM area.
RTRANSID	Specifies a 1- to 4-character name that's passed to the started task. The started task receives the name by issuing a RETRIEVE command with the RTRANSID option.
RTERMID	Specifies a 1- to 4-character name that's passed to the started task. The started task receives the name by issuing a RETRIEVE command with the RTERMID option.
QUEUE	Specifies a 1- to 8-character name that's passed to the started task. The started task receives the name by issuing a RETRIEVE command with the QUEUE option.
NOCHECK	Specifies that when the started task is to be initiated on another system, the task issuing the START command should not wait for confirmation that the START command was successfully processed.
PROTECT	Specifies that the task can not be started until the task issuing the START command issues a syncpoint, either by ending or by issuing a SYNCPOINT command.

Exceptional conditions

Note: The default action for these conditions is to terminate the task.

INVREQ	The START command is invalid, the specified hours, minutes, or seconds are out of range, or the REQID name already exists.
IOERR	An I/O error occurred.
ISCINVREQ	An undeterminable error occurred on the remote system specified in the SYSID option.

LENGERR	A length error occurred.
NOTAUTH	The current transaction's PCT entry specified that resource security checking should be done, and the operator is not authorized to access the transaction to be started.
SYSIDERR	The system identified by SYSID could not be located or accessed.
TERMIDERR	The terminal identified by the TERMID option isn't defined in the Terminal Control Table (TCT).
TRANSIDERR	The transaction identified by the TRANSID option isn't defined in the Program Control Table (PCT).
USERIDERR	The user-id specified in the USERID option is not known to the external security manager.

Notes and tips

- The START command has three common uses:

  The first is when an application function is divided into two or more independent programs that can be executed simultaneously because they don't depend on one another. In this case, use one or more START commands to immediately start one or more tasks.

  The second is when you need to begin a task at some time in the future. For example, you might use a START command to schedule a task for execution at 6:00 a.m., when the system's usage is low. To do that, you can issue a START command with the TIME or AT option. Or you might have a program that needs to restart itself at regular intervals. In that case, the program can issue a START command with the INTERVAL or AFTER option before it ends.

  The third is to implement a menu structure. When you use the XCTL command to execute applications from a menu, the user and the application continue to run under the trans-id of the menu transaction. In contrast, you can use the START command if you want to run under the trans-id of the application program chosen from the menu instead.

- Usually, if two or more START commands specify the same expiration time and the same trans-id, one task will be started for each START command. However, if data is passed to the started task, only one task is started. If this task repeatedly issues RETRIEVE commands to process all of the data sent to it, then no additional tasks are started. But if it does not, the task is started again and again until all of the passed data has been processed.

- There are two ways to use the HOURS, MINUTES, and SECONDS options following AFTER. If you use them in combination, the ranges are 0 to 99 for HOURS, 0 to 59 for MINUTES, and 0 to 59 for SECONDS. However, if you specify only one option, you can use the larger ranges: 0 to 99 for HOURS, 0 to 5999 for MINUTES, and 0 to 359999 for SECONDS. For example, you could specify AFTER MINUTES(1) SECONDS(30), or you could specify AFTER SECONDS(90). Both have the same effect.

Coding example (no data, no terminal)

These examples show how to issue a START command to start the transaction named RFK4 at 6:30 a.m. The first uses the TIME option, the second uses the AT option. No data is passed to the task, and no terminal is associated with the task.

```
EXEC CICS
    START TRANSID('RFK4')
          TIME(063000)
END-EXEC.

EXEC CICS
    START TRANSID('RFK4')
          AT HOURS(6) MINUTES(30)
END-EXEC.
```

Coding example (data, terminal)

These examples show how to start a transaction named DKM3 in 10 minutes, passing it the 100 bytes of data in the field named DKM3-DATA. The first uses the INTERVAL option, the second uses the AFTER option. The task will be attached to the terminal named L580.

```
EXEC CICS
    START TRANSID('DKM3')
          INTERVAL(1000)
          TERMID('L580')
          FROM(DKM3-DATA)
          LENGTH(100)
END-EXEC.

EXEC CICS
    START TRANSID('DKM3')
          AFTER MINUTES(10)
          TERMID('L580')
          FROM(DKM3-DATA)
          LENGTH(100)
END-EXEC.
```

The START ATTACH command

Function

Scheduling. (TS 1.3 and later) The START ATTACH command lets you start a non-terminal task immediately in a local CICS region.

Syntax

```
EXEC CICS
    START ATTACH    TRANSID(name)
                  [ FROM(data-area)
                        LENGTH(data-value) ]
    END-EXEC.
```

Options

TRANSID	Specifies the 1- to 4-character transaction identifier that will be used to start the task.
FROM	Specifies a data area that contains data to be passed to the started task. The started task receives this data by issuing a RETRIEVE command with the INTO or SET option.
LENGTH	Specifies a binary halfword (PIC S9(4) COMP) or literal value that indicates the length of the FROM area.

Exceptional conditions

Note: The default action for these conditions is to terminate the task.

INVREQ	An attempt was made to route a START ATTACH request to another CICS region or the START ATTACH request failed.
LENGERR	A length error occurred.
NOTAUTH	The current transaction's PCT entry specified that resource security checking should be done, and the operator is not authorized to access the transaction to be started.
TRANSIDERR	The transaction identified by the TRANSID option isn't defined in the Program Control Table (PCT).

Notes and tips

* To simplify the use of the START command, IBM has documented it as three distinct variations: START, START ATTACH, and START BREXIT. The START ATTACH command lets you to start a task immediately as long as it's not associated with a terminal, and the START BREXIT command defines a 3270 Bridge exit.

Coding example

This example shows how to use the START ATTACH command to immediately
start a task with a transaction-id of INV1 and pass it a data area named INV-DATA.

```
EXEC CICS
    START ATTACH TRANSID('INV1')
                 FROM(INV-DATA)
                 LENGTH(200)
END-EXEC.
```

The START BREXIT command

Function

Scheduling. (TS 1.3 and later) The START BREXIT command lets you start a task in a 3270 Bridge environment and associate that task with a bridge exit program. The bridge exit handles the terminal I/O in the task so that it can be displayed in a web browser instead of at a 3270-type terminal.

Syntax

```
EXEC CICS
    START { BREXIT | BREXIT(name) }
          TRANSID(name)
        [ BRDATA(data-area)
             BRDATALENGTH(data-value) ]
        [ USERID(data-value) ]
END-EXEC.
```

Options

BREXIT	Specifies the 1- to 8-character name of the bridge exit that's associated with the task. If you don't specify a name here, the value of BREXIT on the TRANSACTION resource definition will be used.
TRANSID	Specifies the 1- to 4-character transaction identifier that will be started by the task. The transaction is started in the 3270 Bridge environment and executes in association with the bridge exit program specified in the BREXIT optión.
BRDATA	Specifies the data area that's passed to the bridge exit program named in the BREXIT option when the task is started.
BRDATALENGTH	Specifies a binary halfword (PIC S9(4) COMP) or literal value that indicates the length of the BRDATA area.
USERID	Specifies the user-id under whose authority the started task is to run.

Exceptional conditions

Note: The default action for these conditions is to terminate the task.

INVREQ	An attempt was made to route a START BREXIT request to another CICS region or the START BREXIT request failed.
LENGERR	A length error occurred.
NOTAUTH	The current transaction's PCT entry specified that resource security checking should be done, and the operator is not authorized to access the transaction to be started.
PGMIDERR	A name was not supplied in the BREXIT option and a BREXIT program isn't defined in the TRANSACTION resource definition.

TRANSIDERR   The transaction identified by the TRANSID option isn't defined in the Program Control Table (PCT).

USERIDERR   The user-id specified in the USERID option is not known to the external security manager.

Notes and tips

- In a 3270 Bridge environment, all the 3270 terminal requests that are issued by the transaction specified in the TRANSID option are intercepted and passed to the bridge exit program specified in the BREXIT option. The bridge exit program then emulates a 3270 display and passes along the display information to a client application executing inside or outside of CICS. In most cases, this means that the display data is passed back to a web server that then displays the data in an HTML page on a client web browser.

- The most powerful feature of the 3270 Bridge environment is that you can convert existing BMS mapsets to HTML pages (Unit 10 describes how to do that). Once your mapsets are converted to HTML, the bridge exit program simply moves the mapset fields directly to the form fields in the HTML document.

- You can specify an IBM-supplied bridge exit program in the BREXIT option or you can write your own. In most cases though, you're better off using the program IBM supplies.

Coding example

The following example shows a START BREXIT command that names an IBM-supplied program called DFH0CBRE as the bridge exit program and specifies that the transaction with trans-id INV1 is to be started.

```
EXEC CICS
    START  BREXIT('DFH0CBRE')
           TRANSID('INV1')
           BRDATA(INV-DATA)
           BRDATALENGTH(200)
END-EXEC.
```

The STARTBR command

Function

File control. The STARTBR command initiates a browse operation so records can be retrieved using READNEXT or READPREV commands. The STARTBR command itself does not retrieve a record; it just establishes positioning for subsequent retrieval. The browse operation should always be ended with an ENDBR command.

Syntax

```
EXEC CICS
    STARTBR    FILE(filename)
               RIDFLD(data-area)
              [ KEYLENGTH(data-value) [ GENERIC ] ]
              [ RBA | RRN ]
              [ GTEQ | EQUAL ]
              [ REQID(data-value) ]
              [ SYSID(systemname) ]
    END-EXEC.
```

Options

FILE	Specifies the 1- to 8-character name of the data set for which a browse operation is to be started.
RIDFLD	Specifies a data area that identifies the record where the browse operation is to begin. The content of the RIDFLD field depends on whether RBA or RRN is specified; if neither is specified, the RIDFLD field contains a key for VSAM KSDS or path retrieval. For generic positioning (see the KEYLENGTH and GENERIC options below), the RIDFLD field must still be as long as the file's defined key length.
	To begin a browse operation at the first record in the file, place hex zeros (LOW-VALUE) in the RIDFLD field. To begin a browse operation at the last record in the file, place hex FFs (HIGH-VALUE) in the RIDFLD field.
KEYLENGTH	Specifies a binary halfword (PIC S9(4) COMP) or literal value that indicates the length of the key, which must be less than the file's defined key length. Used only for a generic read along with the GENERIC option or when the SYSID option is specified. Not valid if RBA or RRN is specified.
GENERIC	Specifies that only a part of the key in the RIDFLD field should be used, as indicated by the KEYLENGTH option. Positioning is established at the first record with a key whose leftmost character positions (as specified by KEYLENGTH) match the RIDFLD field.
RBA	Specifies that the RIDFLD field is a relative byte address (RBA) for a VSAM KSDS or ESDS. An RBA is a binary fullword (PIC S9(8) COMP).

RRN	Specifies that the RIDFLD is a relative record number (RRN) for a VSAM RRDS. An RRN is a binary fullword (PIC S9(8) COMP). The RRN of the first record in an RRDS is 1.
GTEQ	Specifies that positioning is to be established at the first record whose key value is greater than or equal to the key specified in the RIDFLD field. This will always establish positioning in the file unless the specified key is greater than the largest key in the file. This is the default for KSDS and RRDS files; it's not valid for ESDS files.
EQUAL	Specifies that positioning will be established at the record whose key matches the RIDFLD field exactly. If no such record exists, the NOTFND condition is raised, and the browse operation is not started. This is the default for ESDS files.
REQID	Specifies a binary halfword (PIC S9(4) COMP) or literal value that identifies the browse operation; used only when your program controls two or more browse operations at the same time. For each I/O command that's part of the same browse operation, specify the same REQID value.
SYSID	Specifies the 1- to 4-character name of a remote system that contains the file.

Exceptional conditions

Note: The default action for these conditions is to terminate the task.

DISABLED	The data set is disabled, probably as a result of the master terminal operator explicitly disabling the file using CEMT SET DISABLE.
FILENOTFOUND	The data set name specified in the FILE option isn't defined in the File Control Table (FCT).
ILLOGIC	A serious VSAM error occurred.
INVREQ	The STARTBR request is prohibited by the file's FCT entry, the REQID name already exists, the KEYLENGTH value is incorrect, or the file is a user-maintained table.
IOERR	An I/O error occurred.
ISCINVREQ	An undeterminable error occurred on the remote system specified in the SYSID option.
LOADING	(TS 1.1 and later) The STARTBR request was made against a data table that is still being loaded into the CICS system.
NOTAUTH	The transaction's PCT entry specified that resource security checking should be done, and the operator is not authorized to access the data set.
NOTFND	The specified record could not be located.
NOTOPEN	The file is not open.
SYSIDERR	The system identified by SYSID could not be located or accessed.

Notes and tips

- You must issue a STARTBR command before you can issue READNEXT or READPREV commands to sequentially retrieve records during a browse operation. Browsing is relatively inefficient because a VSAM string is held for the duration of the browse. (A string is required for each concurrent access to a VSAM file, so if 10 strings are specified for a file, 10 simultaneous accesses are allowed.) Because of this inefficiency, you may want to minimize the duration of a browse so you don't tie up a string any longer than is needed.

- To browse a file via an alternate index, specify a path name in the FILE option.

- There are two ways to change positioning during a browse. One is to simply change the value of the RIDFLD field before you issue a READNEXT or READPREV command; the key value you specify establishes a new position for the browse. (This is called skip-sequential processing.) The second is to issue a RESETBR command, whose function is basically the same as the STARTBR command.

- The only exceptional condition you should normally check for following a STARTBR command is NOTFND.

Coding example

This example starts a browse operation for a file named ACCOUNT. The browse operation will start at the record indicated by AR-ACCOUNT-NUMBER. If this field contains hex zeros (LOW-VALUE), the browse starts at the beginning of the file. If it contains hex FFs (HIGH-VALUE), the browse starts at the end of the file. Otherwise, the browse starts at the indicated record.

```
 1100-START-ACCOUNT-BROWSE.
*
     EXEC CICS
         STARTBR FILE('ACCOUNT')
                 RIDFLD(AR-ACCOUNT-NUMBER)
                 RESP(RESPONSE-CODE)
     END-EXEC.

     IF RESPONSE-CODE = DFHRESP(NORMAL)
         MOVE 'N' TO END-OF-BROWSE-SW
     ELSE
         IF RESPONSE-CODE = DFHRESP(NOTFND)
             MOVE 'Y' TO END-OF-BROWSE-SW
         ELSE
             PERFORM 9999-TERMINATE-PROGRAM
         END-IF
     END-IF.
```

The SUSPEND command

Function

Task control. The SUSPEND command temporarily returns control to CICS. That allows CICS to dispatch other tasks that may have been waiting while your task executed. Control will eventually return to your task, according to its priority. The SUSPEND command is appropriate only for applications that require an unusually large amount of CPU time without an intervening CICS command.

Syntax

```
EXEC CICS
    SUSPEND
END-EXEC.
```

Options

The SUSPEND command has no options.

Exceptional conditions

No exceptional conditions are raised as a result of the SUSPEND command.

Notes and tips

*   If your program includes a long series of processing that doesn't involve CICS commands, you should issue a SUSPEND command. If you don't, CICS may cancel your task because it thinks it's a runaway task. You don't have to use SUSPEND if the processing issues CICS commands, though. That's because almost all of the CICS commands suspend your task anyway.

Coding example

This example shows how to issue a SUSPEND command once in every 100
invocations of a program routine. In this example, a working-storage field named
WS-SUSPEND-COUNT is used as a counter to determine when the SUSPEND
command should be issued.

```
IF WS-SUSPEND-COUNT = 100
    EXEC CICS
        SUSPEND
    END-EXEC
    MOVE ZERO TO WS-SUSPEND-COUNT
END-IF.

ADD 1 TO WS-SUSPEND-COUNT.
```

The SYNCPOINT command

Function

Syncpoint. The SYNCPOINT command has two distinct functions. When coded without the ROLLBACK option, it makes all of the updates applied to protected resources permanent, so they aren't reversed if an abend occurs. When coded with the ROLLBACK option, the SYNCPOINT command reverses all updates made since the last SYNCPOINT command was issued (or since the task began).

Syntax

```
EXEC CICS
    SYNCPOINT [ ROLLBACK ]
END-EXEC.
```

Option

ROLLBACK   Specifies that all updates made since the last SYNCPOINT command or the beginning of the task should be reversed. If omitted, the SYNCPOINT command permanently commits all of the updates made so far by the task.

Exceptional conditions

Note: The default action for these conditions is to terminate the task.

INVREQ   The program was invoked by a distributed LINK command.

ROLLEDBACK   Indicates that a remote system was not able to complete the syncpoint. As a result, a ROLLBACK operation is forced.

Notes and tips

- When a CICS task abends, any updates made to recoverable resources are normally reversed. Sometimes, however, it's not necessary to reverse all of the updates made by an abending task. In those cases, you can use the SYNCPOINT command to limit the number of updates that are reversed to those that were made since the last SYNCPOINT command was issued. To illustrate, consider a program that reads a file of invoice records and updates corresponding master records in several files. If the program abends (or if CICS itself abends) after 100 records have been processed, the updates for all 100 records are reversed, even though that's probably not necessary; just the updates for the invoice that was being processed when the abend occurred need to be reversed. So, a SYNCPOINT command should be issued after all of the updates for each invoice record have been made.

- When the SYNCPOINT command is executed, it also releases locked records, enabling other tasks that are waiting for them to proceed.

- The SYNCPOINT command with the ROLLBACK option invokes the dynamic transaction backout facility as if the task were abended. You might find it useful in error handling routines when you want to reverse all of the updates made by a task, but you don't want the task to be abended.

Coding example

This example shows how to issue a SYNCPOINT command in a program that updates several files based on records in a transaction file. If the updates for each transaction record are successful, the program issues a SYNCPOINT command. Otherwise, it issues a SYNCPOINT ROLLBACK command.

```
0000-POST-INVOICE-TRANSACTIONS.
*
        .
        .
    PERFORM 1000-POST-INVOICE-TRANSACTION
        UNTIL INVOICE-EOF.
        .
        .
*
 1000-POST-INVOICE-TRANSACTION.
*
    PERFORM 1100-READ-INVOICE-TRANSACTION.
    IF NOT INVOICE-EOF
        PERFORM 1200-UPDATE-MASTER-FILES
        IF UPDATES-SUCCESSFUL
            EXEC CICS
                SYNCPOINT
            END-EXEC
        ELSE
            EXEC CICS
                SYNCPOINT ROLLBACK
            END-EXEC
        END-IF
    END-IF.
*
```

The UNLOCK command

Function

File control. The UNLOCK command releases a record that's being held under exclusive control by the UPDATE option of a READ, READNEXT, or READPREV command. If you don't issue an UNLOCK command, the record is released automatically when you issue a SYNCPOINT command or when your task terminates. The UNLOCK command is also used to terminate a mass insert operation done with the WRITE command.

Syntax

```
EXEC CICS
    UNLOCK   FILE(filename)
           [ TOKEN(data-area) ]
           [ SYSID(systemname) ]
END-EXEC.
```

Options

FILE	Specifies the 1- to 8-character name of the data set containing the record to be released.
TOKEN	Specifies a binary fullword (PIC S9(8) COMP) as a unique identifier for the UNLOCK request. You can use this value to associate the UNLOCK with a previous READ UPDATE, READNEXT UPDATE, or READPREV UPDATE that shares the same TOKEN identifier.
SYSID	Specifies the 1- to 4-character name of a remote system that contains the file.

Exceptional conditions

Note: The default action for these conditions is to terminate the task.

DISABLED	The data set is disabled, probably as a result of the master terminal operator explicitly disabling the file using CEMT SET DISABLE.
FILENOTFOUND	The data set name specified in the FILE option isn't defined in the File Control Table.
ILLOGIC	A serious VSAM error occurred.
IOERR	An I/O error occurred.
ISCINVREQ	An undeterminable error occurred on the remote system specified in the SYSID option.
NOTAUTH	The transaction's PCT entry specified that resource security checking should be done, and the operator is not authorized to access the data set.

NOTOPEN   The file is not open.

SYSIDERR   The system identified by SYSID could not be located or accessed.

Notes and tips

*   Whenever you issue a READ UPDATE, READNEXT UPDATE, or READPREV UPDATE command, CICS prevents other users from accessing any record in the control interval until one of three things happens: your task ends, you issue a SYNCPOINT command, or you issue an UNLOCK command (and you haven't updated or deleted the record). As a result, if your program reads a record with the UPDATE option and then decides not to update the record, it should issue an UNLOCK command (unless the program will end immediately after making the decision not to update the file anyway; don't issue an UNLOCK command if it's the last CICS command issued before the RETURN command).

Coding example

This example shows how to release control of a record in the ACCOUNT file that was previously read with the UPDATE option.

```
4250-UNLOCK-ACCOUNT-FILE.
*
    EXEC CICS
        UNLOCK FILE('ACCOUNT')
    END-EXEC.
```

The UPDATE COUNTER command

Function

Named counter server. The UPDATE COUNTER command lets you set a new current value for the named counter. You can use the COMPAREMIN and COMPAREMAX options to check that the new value is within a certain range before the counter is reset.

Syntax

```
EXEC CICS
    UPDATE   { COUNTER(name) | DCOUNTER(name) }
             [ POOL(name) ]
              VALUE(data-value)
             [ COMPAREMIN(data-value) ]
             [ COMPAREMAX(data-value) ]
    END-EXEC.
```

Options

COUNTER	Specifies the 16-character name of the counter whose current value is to be changed. The COUNTER option requires that signed binary fullword (PIC S9(8) COMP) values be used for the VALUE, COMPAREMIN, and COMPAREMAX options.
DCOUNTER	Specifies the 16-character name of the counter whose current value is to be changed. The DCOUNTER option requires that unsigned binary doubleword (PIC 9(18) COMP) values be used for the VALUE, COMPAREMIN, and COMPAREMAX options.
POOL	Specifies the 8-character name of the pool in which the named counter resides. If there's no matching entry in the DFHNCOPT options table, the default named counter pool on the NCPLDFT system initialization parameter is used.
VALUE	Specifies a signed binary fullword (PIC S9(8) COMP) or unsigned binary doubleword (PIC 9(18) COMP) that contains the new number that the counter's current value is to be set to.
COMPAREMIN	Specifies a signed binary fullword (PIC S9(8) COMP) or unsigned binary doubleword (PIC 9(18) COMP) that's compared against the new current value in the VALUE option. If the new current value is equal to or greater than the COMPAREMIN value, the counter is set to the new value. Otherwise, an exceptional condition is returned.
COMPAREMAX	Specifies a signed binary fullword (PIC S9(8) COMP) or unsigned binary doubleword (PIC 9(18) COMP) that's compared against the new current value in the VALUE option. If the new current value is less than or equal to the COMPAREMAX value, the counter is set to the new value. Otherwise, an exceptional condition is returned.

Exceptional conditions

Note: The default action for these conditions is to terminate the task.

INVREQ   The statement was coded improperly, there was a problem accessing the named counter in the coupling facility, or the new value specified was invalid.

SUPPRESSED   The new value specified for the named counter is not within the range specified by the COMPAREMIN and COMPAREMAX options.

Notes and tips

• The UPDATE COUNTER command can be useful if your application has to skip several numbers in a named counter. However, this command can't update the minimum or maximum values specified for the counter in the DEFINE COUNTER command.

• The named counter facility is designed to run in a Parallel Sysplex environment. That means that the facility is controlled by a named counter server, allowing multiple regions to draw from the same counter.

• If you use a field, not a literal value, to assign a COUNTER or DCOUNTER name for the command, make sure that the field is padded with trailing spaces if the name is less than 16 characters long.

Coding example

The following example shows an UPDATE COUNTER command that changes the current number in counter ORDERINV to 500.

```
EXEC CICS
    UPDATE COUNTER('ORDERINV')
           POOL('MMA')
           VALUE(500)
END-EXEC.
```

The VERIFY PASSWORD command

Function

Authentication. The VERIFY PASWORD command allows you to check that the password specified matches the password recorded in the external security manager for the specified user.

Syntax

```
EXEC CICS
    VERIFY    PASSWORD(data-value)
              USERID(data-value)
            [ CHANGETIME(data-area) ]
            [ DAYSLEFT(data-area) ]
            [ EXPIRYTIME(data-area) ]
            [ LASTUSETIME(data-area) ]
            [ INVALIDCOUNT(data-area) ]
            [ ESMREASON(data-area) ]
            [ ESMRESP(data-area) ]
    END-EXEC.
```

Options

PASSWORD	Specifies an 8-character field or literal value for the password that you want checked against the external security manager for the specified user. If the password is incorrect, the other data areas specified for this command are not returned.
USERID	Specifies an 8-character field or literal value for the user-id whose password is to be checked.
CHANGETIME	Specifies a 15-digit packed-decimal field (PIC S9(15) COMP-3) that returns an ABSTIME value for the date and time the password was last changed. If the external security manager is RACF, the time returned is midnight.
DAYSLEFT	Specifies a binary halfword (PIC S9(4) COMP) that returns the number of days, from the current date, until the password expires. If the password is non-expiring, the value returned is -1.
EXPIRYTIME	Specifies a 15-digit packed-decimal field (PIC S9(15) COMP-3) that returns an ABSTIME value for the date and time the password will expire. If the external security manager is RACF, the time returned is midnight.
LASTUSETIME	Specifies a 15-digit packed-decimal field (PIC S9(15) COMP-3) that returns an ABSTIME value for the date and time the user-id was last accessed.
INVALIDCOUNT	Returns the number of times an invalid password was entered for the user-id specified.

ESMREASON   Specifies a binary fullword (PIC S9(8) COMP) that returns a reason condition from the external security manager.

ESMRESP   Specifies a binary fullword (PIC S9(8) COMP) that returns a response code from the external security manager.

Exceptional conditions

Note: The default action for these conditions is to terminate the task.

INVREQ   Either the external security manager is not responding or there is an unknown return code in ESMRESP.

NOTAUTH   The supplied password is wrong, a new password is required, or the user-id specified in the USERID option is revoked.

USERIDERR   The user-id specified in the USERID option is not known to the external security manager.

Notes and tips

- If the external security manager is RACF, the CHANGETIME and EXPIRYTIME times will always show as midnight.

- Just because a VERIFY PASSWORD request is successful doesn't necessarily mean that a SIGNON request will be. That's because the user-id may be revoked in one or more RACF group connections or the user may not have access to the current CICS region.

- Remember to clear the password field as soon as you can. That's because this field can potentially be revealed in a transaction or system dump if the transaction abends.

Coding example

The following code shows how the VERIFY PASSWORD command can be used to check how many days are left before a password expires.

```
EXEC CICS
    VERIFY PASSWORD(USER-PASSWORD)
           USERID(USER-USERID)
           DAYSLEFT(PASSWORD-DAYS-LEFT)
           ESMRESP(RACF-RESPONSE-CODE)
END-EXEC.
```

The WAIT CONVID command

Function

APPC mapped conversation. The WAIT CONVID command suspends the task until accumulated data has been transmitted during an APPC conversation.

Syntax

```
EXEC CICS
    WAIT    CONVID(name)
          [ STATE(cvda) ]
END-EXEC.
```

Options

CONVID   Specifies the 4-character conversation-id obtained from the Execute Interface Block field EIBRSRCE following a successful ALLOCATE command.

STATE   Specifies a binary fullword (PIC S9(8) COMP) where CICS places state information. Valid states are:

ALLOCATED	RECEIVE
CONFFREE	ROLLBACK
CONFRECEIVE	SEND
CONFSEND	SYNCFREE
FREE	SYNCRECEIVE
PENDFREE	SYNCSEND
PENDRECEIVE	

Exceptional conditions

Note: The default action for these conditions is to terminate the task.

INVREQ   The command is not supported or is not compatible with the conversation.

NOTALLOC   The conversation has not been properly allocated.

Coding example

The following example forces CICS to send any data accumulated in the send buffer before continuing.

```
EXEC CICS
    WAIT CONVID(CONVERSATION-ID)
END-EXEC.
```

The WAIT EVENT command

Function

Interval control. The WAIT EVENT command delays the task until a previously issued POST command has expired.

Syntax

```
EXEC CICS
    WAIT EVENT    ECADDR(pointer-value)
END-EXEC.
```

Option

ECADDR   Specifies a binary fullword (PIC S9(8) COMP) that contains the address of the Timer Event Control Area that must expire before the task can continue. You can obtain this value from the SET option of the POST command that creates the Timer Event Control Area.

Exceptional condition

INVREQ   The Timer Event Control Area address is invalid. The default action for this condition is to terminate the task.

Notes and tips

* One possible, though unlikely, use for the POST and WAIT EVENT commands is to force a minimum response time for terminal transactions. To do that, issue a POST command at the start of the task, specifying the minimum response time (perhaps 3 seconds) in the INTERVAL option. Then, before you issue the final SEND MAP command, issue a WAIT EVENT command. That way, the terminal won't receive output faster than the minimum response time will allow. Of course, this doesn't account for data transmission time, which is often the largest component of total response time.

Coding example

This example shows how to issue POST and WAIT EVENT commands to ensure a minimum response time of three seconds. Because this type of function affects the high-level coding of the program, I've included most of the program's top-level module and parts of several subordinate modules. WS-ECA-POINTER is a working storage field defined as PIC S9(8) COMP.

```
    0000-PROCESS-CUSTOMER-INQUIRY.
*
        IF EIBCALEN > ZERO
            EXEC CICS
                POST EVENT INTERVAL(3)
                            SET(WS-ECA-POINTER)
            END-EXEC
        END-IF.

        EVALUATE TRUE
            .
            .
            WHEN EIBAID = DFHPF3 OR DFHPF12
                EXEC CICS
                    XCTL PROGRAM('MENU1')
                END-EXEC
            WHEN EIBAID = DFHENTER
                PERFORM 1000-PROCESS-CUSTOMER-MAP
            .
            .
        END-EVALUATE.

        EXEC CICS
            RETURN TRANSID('INQ1')
                    COMMAREA(COMMUNICATION-AREA)
        END-EXEC.
*
    1000-PROCESS-CUSTOMER-MAP.
*
        PERFORM 1100-RECEIVE-CUSTOMER-MAP.
        .
        .
        IF VALID-DATA
            PERFORM 1400-SEND-CUSTOMER-MAP
        END-IF.
        .
        .
    1400-SEND-CUSTOMER-MAP.
*
        EXEC CICS
            WAIT EVENT ECADDR(WS-ECA-POINTER)
        END-EXEC.

        EXEC CICS
            SEND MAP ...
        END-EXEC.
```

The WAIT JOURNALNAME command

Function

Journaling. (TS 1.1 and later) The WAIT JOURNALNAME command synchro-nizes the current task with a previously written journal record by suspending the task until the record has been successfully written to the journal file. The WAIT JOURNALNAME command is used only for asynchronous journal output; that is, when the WRITE JOURNALNAME command that writes the journal record does not specify WAIT.

Syntax

```
EXEC CICS
    WAIT    JOURNALNAME(data-value)
         [ REQID(data-value) ]
END-EXEC.
```

Options

JOURNALNAME	Specifies a 1- to 8-character journal name that identifies the journal file with which the task is to be synchronized.
REQID	Specifies a binary fullword (PIC S9(8) COMP) or literal value that identifies the specific journal record for which the task is to wait. You can obtain this value from the REQID option of the WRITE JOURNALNAME command that creates the record. If you omit REQID, the task is suspended until the record created by the most recently issued WRITE JOURNALNAME command is written.

Exceptional conditions

Note: The default action for these conditions is to terminate the task.

INVREQ	A WRITE JOURNALNAME command has not been issued.
IOERR	An I/O error occurred.
JIDERR	The journal identifier you specified in the JOURNALNAME option isn't defined in the Journal Control Table.
NOTOPEN	The journal data set is not open.

Notes and tips

- When you write a journal record asynchronously, control returns to your task as soon as the record has been placed in a buffer. The record will be written to disk later (usually within one second).

- The WAIT JOURNALNAME command can be used to synchronize your task to more than one journal record created asynchronously. Whenever you issue a WAIT JOURNALNAME command, your task is suspended until all journal records created asynchronously have been written to the journal data set. Thus, your program should issue just one WAIT JOURNALNAME command even if it's issued more than one asynchronous WRITE JOURNALNAME command.

- If the journal record has already been written to the journal data set, the WAIT JOURNALNAME command has no effect. Control returns immediately to the application program.

Coding example

This example shows how to delete a data set record after first recording the record in a journal. Asynchronous journal output is used, so the program does not wait for the journal record to be written to disk before it deletes the data set record. However, a WAIT JOURNALNAME command is issued so that the program will not continue beyond the DELETE command before the journal record is written to disk.

```
    3100-DELETE-CUSTOMER-RECORD.
*
    EXEC CICS
        WRITE JOURNALNAME('CUSTOMER')
              JTYPEID('CD')
              FROM(CUSTOMER-MASTER-RECORD)
              FLENGTH(97)
              REQID(WS-REQID)
    END-EXEC.

    EXEC CICS
        DELETE FILE('CUSTMAS')
               RIDFLD(CM-CUSTOMER-NUMBER)
    END-EXEC.

    EXEC CICS
        WAIT JOURNALNAME('CUSTOMER')
             REQID(WS-REQID)
    END-EXEC.
```

The WAIT JOURNALNUM command

Function

Journaling. The WAIT JOURNALNUM command synchronizes the current task with a previously written journal record by suspending the task until the record has been successfully written to the journal file.

Note: The WAIT JOURNALNUM command is supported for compatibility purposes with earlier releases of CICS. It has been replaced by the WAIT JOURNALNAME command.

The WEB ENDBROWSE FORMFIELD command

Function

Web services. (TS 2.1 and later) The WEB ENDBROWSE FORMFIELD command ends the browse of a set of name-value pairs in an HTML form that was started with a WEB STARTBROWSE FORMFIELD command. The HTML form is sent to CICS as part of the body of an HTTP request.

Syntax

```
EXEC CICS
    WEB ENDBROWSE FORMFIELD
END-EXEC.
```

Options

The WEB ENDBROWSE FORMFIELD command has no options.

Exceptional condition

INVREQ   The command was issued before a WEB STARTBROWSE command was issued, or the program isn't a CICS Web interface application. The default action for this condition is to terminate the task.

Notes and tips

- IBM introduced the WEB commands in CICS TS 1.3 as a way of simplifying the communication between CICS and an external web environment. Prior to TS 1.3, the HTML template manager was required to process HTTP header and HTML form information.

- The WEB browse process for HTML forms allows you to retrieve individual name-value pairs from an HTML form sent from a client browser. Your application can then process the information and create an HTML document that can be sent back to the client browser. Executing the WEB ENDBROWSE FORMFIELD command is similar to executing an ENDBR command for a VSAM file. In both cases, the browse is terminated.

The WEB ENDBROWSE HTTPHEADER command

Function

Web services. (TS 1.3 and later) The WEB ENDBROWSE HTTPHEADER command ends an HTTP header browse that was started with the WEB STARTBROWSE HTTPHEADER command.

Syntax

```
EXEC CICS
    WEB ENDBROWSE HTTPHEADER
END-EXEC.
```

Options

The WEB ENDBROWSE HTTPHEADER command has no options.

Exceptional condition

INVREQ   The command was issued before a WEB STARTBROWSE command was issued, or the program isn't a CICS Web interface application. The default action for this condition is to terminate the task.

Notes and tips

* IBM introduced the WEB commands in CICS TS 1.3 as a way of simplifying the communication between CICS and an external web environment. Prior to TS 1.3, the HTML template manager was required to process HTTP header and HTML form information.

* The headers at the beginning of an HTTP request sent by a web browser to the web server include information on the type of browser being used, its versions, and the types of capabilities it has.

* The WEB ENDBROWSE HTTPHEADER command is similar to the ENDBR command. In both cases, these commands terminate a browse function.

The WEB EXTRACT command

Function

Web services. (TS 1.3 and later) The WEB EXTRACT command lets you obtain relevant information from an inbound HTTP request.

Syntax

```
EXEC CICS
    WEB EXTRACT [ HTTPMETHOD(data-area)
                      METHODLENGTH(data-area) ]
                [ HTTPVERSION(data-area)
                      VERSIONLEN(data-area)    ]
                [ PATH(data-area)
                      PATHLENGTH(data-area)    ]
                [ QUERYSTRING(data-area)
                      QUERYSTRLEN(data-area)   ]
                [ REQUESTTYPE(cvda) ]
    END-EXEC.
```

Options

HTTPMETHOD	Specifies a data area that returns the HTTP method string on the request line of the inbound message.
METHODLENGTH	Specifies a data area that receives the length of the HTTP method string.
HTTPVERSION	Specifies a data area that returns the HTTP version string on the request line of the inbound message.
VERSIONLEN	Specifies a data area that receives the length of the HTTP version string.
PATH	Specifies a data area that returns the PATH specified on the request line of the inbound message.
PATHLENGTH	Specifies a data area that receives the length of the PATH.
QUERYSTRING	(TS 2.1 and later) Specifies a data area that returns the value or values encoded after the question mark delimiter at the end of the path on the request line of the inbound message.
QUERYSTRLEN	(TS 2.1 and later) Specifies a data area that receives the length of the QUERYSTRING string.
REQUESTTYPE	Specifies a binary fullword (PIC S9(8) COMP) where the HTTP request type is returned. The HTTP request type can be determined by testing it using the DFHVALUE keyword. Valid request types are: HTTP NONHTTP

Exceptional conditions

Note: The default action for these conditions is to terminate the task.

INVREQ   The program isn't a CICS Web interface application or the command was issued using the HTTPMETHOD, HTTPVERSION, or PATH option for a non-HTTP request.

LENGERR   The length on METHODLENGTH, VERSIONLEN, PATHLENGTH, or QUERYSTRLEN is less than or equal to zero.

Notes and tips

- IBM introduced the WEB commands in CICS TS 1.3 as a way of simplifying the communication between CICS and an external web environment. Prior to TS 1.3, the HTML template manager was required to process HTTP header and HTML form information.

- The WEB EXTRACT command allows you to extract important information from an HTTP inbound request. For example, to process an HTML form, it's important to know what type of HTTP method is being used. With the HTTPMETHOD option, you can determine if the form method is "GET" or "POST."

- The WEB EXTRACT command can also be specified as EXTRACT WEB.

Coding example

The following example shows a WEB EXTRACT command that's used to determine the HTTP method used.

```
EXEC CICS
    WEB EXTRACT
        HTTPMETHOD(HTTP-METHOD-TYPE)
        METHODLENGTH(HTTP-METHOD-LEN)
END-EXEC.
```

The WEB READ FORMFIELD command

Function

Web services. (TS 2.1 and later) The WEB READ command retrieves the value of a specified field from an HTML form. The name of the field to be extracted is given in the FORMFIELD option.

Syntax

```
EXEC CICS
    WEB READ    FORMFIELD(data-area)
                [ NAMELENGTH(data-value) ]
                { VALUE(data-area) | SET(pointer-ref) }
                VALUELENGTH(data-area)
                [ CLNTCODEPAGE(name)
                        HOSTCODEPAGE(name) ]
    END-EXEC.
```

Options

FORMFIELD	Specifies the name of the form field to extract a value from. CICS will find the matching name on the HTML form and return the value associated with the field. The name you specify here is not case-sensitive.
NAMELENGTH	Specifies a binary fullword (PIC S9(8) COMP) or literal value that gives the length of the name in the FORMFIELD option.
VALUE	Specifies a data area that receives the form field value.
SET	Specifies a binary fullword (PIC S9(8) COMP) where the address of the received data is placed.
VALUELENGTH	Specifies a binary fullword (PIC S9(8) COMP) or literal value that gives the length of the form field value.
CLNTCODEPAGE	Specifies the 40-character name of the code page used when data is converted from the client code page. When you use this option, you must also specify the HOSTCODEPAGE option.
HOSTCODEPAGE	Specifies the 8-character name of the host code page that's used when the forms data is converted from the ASCII code page. When you use this option, you must also specify the CLNTCODEPAGE option.

Exceptional conditions

Note: The default action for these conditions is to terminate the task.

INVREQ   The program is a non-CICS Web interface application, no forms were provided in the body of the HTTP request, or the codepage combination for the client and server is invalid.

LENGERR   The length on VALUELENGTH is less than or equal to zero.

NOTFND   A form field with the specified name can't be found.

Notes and tips

* IBM introduced the WEB commands in CICS TS 1.3 as a way of simplifying the communication between CICS and an external web environment. Prior to TS 1.3, the HTML template manager was required to process HTTP header and HTML form information.

* Provided that you know the names of the form fields in the HTML document, the WEB READ command allows you to process each field individually. If you don't know the names of the form fields, or if you need to process all of the fields on the HTML form, use the WEB READNEXT FORMFIELD command in a browse operation instead.

* A host code page and a client code page are used to translate data to the format that's used on the server and the client, respectively. In a IBM environment, usually the host uses EBCDIC code while the clients use ASCII. Specifying what the host and client code pages are if they're not standard EBCDIC and ASCII will ensure that the information being transmitted will be translated correctly.

Coding example

The following example shows how you can read in the value associated with the form field named "BOOKNO" from the HTML form.

```
1000-WEB-READ.
*
     MOVE 'BOOKNO' TO FORM-FIELD-NAME.
     MOVE LENGTH OF FORM-FIELD-NAME  TO FORM-FIELD-NAME-LEN.
     MOVE LENGTH OF FORM-FIELD-VALUE TO FORM-FIELD-VALUE-LEN.

     EXEC CICS
         WEB READ FORMFIELD(FORM-FIELD-NAME)
                  NAMELENGTH(FORM-FIELD-NAME-LEN)
                  VALUE(FORM-FIELD-VALUE)
                  VALUELENGTH(FORM-FIELD-VALUE-LEN)
     END-EXEC.
```

The WEB READ HTTPHEADER command

Function

Web services. (TS 1.3 and later) The WEB READ HTTPHEADER command lets you extract information from a specific HTTP header.

Syntax

```
EXEC CICS
    WEB READ HTTPHEADER(data-area)
             NAMELENGTH(data-value)
             VALUE(data-area)
             VALUELENGTH(data-value)
END-EXEC.
```

Options

HTTPHEADER	Specifies the name of the HTTP header you want to extract information from.
NAMELENGTH	Specifies a binary fullword (PIC S9(8) COMP) or literal value that gives the length of the name in the HTTPHEADER option.
VALUE	Specifies a data area that receives the value returned for the named HTTP header.
VALUELENGTH	Specifies a binary fullword (PIC S9(8) COMP) or literal value that gives the length of the HTTP header value.

Exceptional conditions

Note: The default action for these conditions is to terminate the task.

INVREQ	The program isn't a CICS Web interface application, or the command is being issued for a non-HTTP request.
LENGERR	The length on VALUELENGTH is less than or equal to zero.
NOTFND	An HTTP header with the specified name can't be found.

Notes and tips

- IBM introduced the WEB commands in CICS TS 1.3 as a way of simplifying the communication between CICS and an external web environment. Prior to TS 1.3, the HTML template manager was required to process HTTP header and HTML form information.

- The WEB READ HTTPHEADER command lets you obtain information from a specific header. Although not often used, this command can be helpful when debugging a CICS Web Interface application. For example, if an HTML form isn't displaying properly, you can use the information in the HTTP headers to determine what browser or what version of the browser is being used to help you pinpoint the problem.

The WEB READNEXT FORMFIELD command

Function

Web services. (TS 2.1 and later) The WEB READNEXT FORMFIELD command lets you retrieve the next name-value pair in an HTML form during a form field browse.

Syntax

```
EXEC CICS
    WEB READNEXT FORMFIELD(data-area)
                 NAMELENGTH(data-value)
                 VALUE(data-area)
                 VALUELENGTH(data-area)
    END-EXEC.
```

Options

FORMFIELD	Specifies a data area that receives the name of the next form field being retrieved. The case of the name remains the same as it appears in the HTML form.
NAMELENGTH	Specifies a binary fullword (PIC S9(8) COMP) or literal value that gives the length of the name in the FORMFIELD option.
VALUE	Specifies a data area that receives the form field value.
VALUELENGTH	Specifies a binary fullword (PIC S9(8) COMP) or literal value that gives the length of the form field value.

Exceptional conditions

Note: The default action for these conditions is to terminate the task.

ENDFILE	The end of the list of name-value pairs was reached.
INVREQ	The command was issued before a WEB STARTBROWSE FORMFIELD command was issued, a form field was found that is not in the format NAME:VALUE, or the program isn't a CICS Web interface application.
LENGERR	The length on NAMELENGTH or VALUELENGTH is less than or equal to zero.

Notes and tips

- IBM introduced the WEB commands in CICS TS 1.3 as a way of simplifying the communication between CICS and an external web environment. Prior to TS 1.3, the HTML template manager was required to process HTTP header and HTML form information.
- Before you can issue the WEB READNEXT FORMFIELD command, you must issue a WEB STARTBROWSE FORMFIELD command.
- The WEB READNEXT FORMFIELD command will retrieve a name-value pair every time it is issued until an ENDFILE condition occurs. Once the ENDFILE condition occurs, issue a WEB ENDBROWSE FORMFIELD command to end the browse session.

Coding example

The following example shows how to read and process the name-value pairs in an HTML form using the WEB READNEXT FORMFIELD command.

```
    3000-PROCESS-HTML-FORM.
*
        EXEC CICS
            WEB STARTBROWSE FORMFIELD
        END-EXEC.

        PERFORM 3100-GET-FIELDS
            UNTIL END-OF-FORM.

        EXEC CICS
            WEB ENDBROWSE FORMFIELD
        END-EXEC.
*
    3100-GET-FIELDS.
*
        PERFORM 3200-READNEXT-FORM-FIELD.

        IF NOT END-OF-FORM
            EVALUATE FORM-FIELD-NAME
                WHEN 'BOOKNO'
                    MOVE FORM-FIELD-VALUE(1:FORM-FIELD-VALUE-LEN)
                        TO BOOK-NO
                WHEN 'QTY'
                    MOVE FORM-FIELD-VALUE(1:FORM-FIELD-VALUE-LEN)
                        TO BOOK-QTY
                WHEN 'PRICE'
                    MOVE FORM-FIELD-VALUE(1:FORM-FIELD-VALUE-LEN)
                        TO BOOK-PRICE
            END-EVALUATE
        END-IF.
        .
        .
```

```
 3200-READNEXT-FORM-FIELD.
*
     MOVE LENGTH OF FORM-FIELD-NAME  TO FORM-FIELD-NAME-LEN.
     MOVE LENGTH OF FORM-FIELD-VALUE TO FORM-FIELD-VALUE-LEN.

     EXEC CICS
         WEB READNEXT FORMFIELD(FORM-FIELD-NAME)
                      NAMELENGTH(FORM-FIELD-NAME-LEN)
                      VALUE(FORM-FIELD-VALUE)
                      VALUELENGTH(FORM-FIELD-VALUE-LEN)
                      RESP(RESPONSE-CODE)
     END-EXEC.

     IF RESPONSE-CODE = DFHRESP(ENDFILE)
         SET END-OF-FORM TO TRUE
     ELSE
        IF RESPONSE-CODE NOT = DFHRESP(NORMAL)
            PERFORM 9999-TERMINATE-PROGRAM
        END-IF
     END-IF.
```

The WEB READNEXT HTTPHEADER command

Function

Web services. (TS 1.3 and later) The WEB READNEXT HTTPHEADER command lets you retrieve the next HTTP header in a list of HTTP headers during an HTTP header browse.

Syntax

```
EXEC CICS
    WEB READNEXT  HTTPHEADER(data-area)
                  NAMELENGTH(data-value)
                  VALUE(data-area)
                  VALUELENGTH(data-value)
    END-EXEC.
```

Options

HTTPHEADER	Specifies the data area that receives the name of the next HTTP header being retrieved.
NAMELENGTH	Specifies a binary fullword (PIC S9(8) COMP) or literal value that gives the length of the name in the HTTPHEADER option.
VALUE	Specifies a data area that receives the HTTP header value.
VALUELENGTH	Specifies a binary fullword (PIC S9(8) COMP) or literal value that gives the length of the HTTP header value.

Exceptional conditions

Note: The default action for these conditions is to terminate the task.

ENDFILE	The end of the HTTP headers was reached.
INVREQ	The command was issued before a WEB STARTBROWSE HTTPHEADER command was issued, or the program is a non-CICS Web interface application.
LENGERR	The length on NAMELENGTH or VALUELENGTH is less than or equal to zero.

Notes and tips

- IBM introduced the WEB commands in CICS TS 1.3 as a way of simplifying the communication between CICS and an external web environment. Prior to TS 1.3, the HTML template manager was required to process HTTP header and HTML form information.

- Before you can issue the WEB READNEXT HTTPHEADERcommand, you must issue a WEB STARTBROWSE HTTPHEADER command.

- The WEB READNEXT HTTPHEADER command lets you obtain information from the HTTP headers. Although not often used, this command can be helpful when debugging a CICS Web Interface application. For example, if an HTML form isn't displaying properly, you can use the information in the HTTP headers to determine what browser or what version of the browser is being used to help you pinpoint the problem.

The WEB RECEIVE command

Function

Web services. (TS 1.3 and later) The WEB RECEIVE command receives the body of an HTTP request from the CICS Web interface or Business Logic Interface into a data area supplied by the application program.

Syntax

```
EXEC CICS
    WEB RECEIVE { INTO(data-area) | SET(pointer-ref) }
                   LENGTH(data-area)
                   MAXLENGTH(data-value)
                 [ TYPE(cvda) ]
                 [ NOTRUNCATE ]
                 [ CLNTCODEPAGE(name)
                        HOSTCODEPAGE(name) ]
    END-EXEC.
```

Options

INTO	Specifies the data area that receives the body of the HTTP request.
SET	Specifies the data area that will contain the address of the retrieved HTTP request.
LENGTH	Specifies a binary fullword (PIC S9(8) COMP) or literal value that gives the length of the data received.
MAXLENGTH	Specifies a binary fullword (PIC S9(8) COMP) or literal value that gives the maximum length of the data that CICS can retrieve when the INTO option is specified. Optional in TS 2.2 and later versions.
TYPE	Specifies a binary fullword (PIC S9(8) COMP) that identifies whether the data received is an HTTP or non-HTTP message. The value can be determined by testing it using the DFHVALUE keyword. Valid types are: HTTPYES HTTPNO
NOTRUNCATE	Specifies that if the data in the HTTP request exceeds the maximum length, the remaining data is to be retained for retrieval by subsequent RECEIVE commands.
CLNTCODEPAGE	Specifies the 40-character name of the code page used when data is converted from the client code page. If specified, you must also specify HOSTCODEPAGE. If omitted, the data is passed to the application in the format in which it was transmitted, without any conversion.
HOSTCODEPAGE	Specifies the 8-character name of the host code page that's used when the form's data is converted from the ASCII code page. If specified, you must also specify CLNTCODEPAGE. If omitted, the data is passed to the application in the format in which it was transmitted, without any conversion.

Exceptional conditions

Note: The default action for these conditions is to terminate the task.

INVREQ   The program isn't a CICS Web interface application.

LENGERR   The length of the data exceeds the amount specified in the MAXLENGTH
            option.

NOTFND   The HOSTCODEPAGE or CLNTCODEPAGE specified is invalid.

Notes and tips

- IBM introduced the WEB commands in CICS TS 1.3 as a way of simplifying
  the communication between CICS and an external web environment. Prior to
  TS 1.3, the HTML template manager was required to process HTTP header and
  HTML form information.
- A host code page and a client code page are used to translate data to the format
  that's used on the server and the client, respectively. In a IBM environment,
  usually the host uses EBCDIC code while the clients use ASCII.

Coding example

The following example shows how you can code the WEB RECEIVE command to
pass information from the HTTP request into your application.

```
3000-RECEIVE-HTTP-REQUEST.
*
    MOVE +1500 TO MAX-LEN.

    EXEC CICS
        WEB RECEIVE INTO(HTTP-RECORD)
                    LENGTH(HTTP-LEN)
                    MAXLENGTH(MAX-LEN)
                    TYPE(REQ-TYPE)
                    RESP(RESPONSE-CODE)
    END-EXEC.

    IF REQ-TYPE = DFHVALUE(HTTPYES)
        SET HTTP-REQUEST TO TRUE
    ELSE
        SET NONHTTP-REQUEST TO TRUE
    END-IF.
    .
    .
```

The WEB RETRIEVE command

Function

Web services. (TS 1.3 and later) The WEB RETRIEVE command retrieves the DOCTOKEN of a document which was sent earlier using a WEB SEND command.

Syntax

```
EXEC CICS
    WEB RETRIEVE DOCTOKEN(data-area)
END-EXEC.
```

Options

DOCTOKEN   Specifies the 16-character symbolic name of the document to be retrieved.

Exceptional conditions

INVREQ   A WEB SEND command has not been issued, or the program isn't a CICS Web interface application. The default action for this condition is to terminate the task.

Notes and tips

- IBM introduced the WEB commands in CICS TS 1.3 as a way of simplifying the communication between CICS and an external web environment. Prior to TS 1.3, the HTML template manager was required to process HTTP header and HTML form information.

The WEB SEND command

Function

Web services. (TS 1.3 and later) The WEB SEND command lets you select a
document, typically an HTML document, for delivery by the CICS Web Interface
or the Business Logic Interface.

Syntax

```
EXEC CICS
    WEB SEND   DOCTOKEN(data-area)
               [ CLNTCODEPAGE(name) ]
               [ STATUSCODE(data-value) ]
               [ STATUSTEXT(data-area)
                      LENGTH(data-value) ]
    END-EXEC.
```

Options

DOCTOKEN	Specifies the 16-character symbolic name of the document to be sent.
CLNTCODEPAGE	Specifies the 40-character name of the code page used when data is converted from the application to the browser. If omitted, no data conversion is done.
STATUSCODE	Specifies a binary halfword (PIC S9(4) COMP) or literal value that gives the HTTP status code and is inserted on the status line. It is the programmer's responsibility to ensure that the code specified is valid and conforms to the rules for HTTP status codes.
STATUSTEXT	Specifies a data area that describes the status code.
LENGTH	A binary fullword (PIC S9(8) COMP) or literal value that indicates the length of the data area specified in the STATUSTEXT option.

Exceptional conditions

Note: The default action for these conditions is to terminate the task.

INVREQ	The program isn't a CICS Web interface application.
NOTFND	The DOCTOKEN or CLNTCODEPAGE is incorrectly specified.

Notes and tips

• IBM introduced the WEB commands in CICS TS 1.3 as a way of simplifying
  the communication between CICS and an external web environment. Prior to
  TS 1.3, the HTML template manager was required to process HTTP header and
  HTML form information.

- You'll use the WEB SEND command most often directly after a document has been created or modified by one of the CICS DOCUMENT commands.

- A client code page is used to translate data to the format that's used on the client (usually ASCII).

Coding example

The following code shows how an HTML document is first created and then sent using the WEB SEND command.

```
WORKING-STORAGE SECTION.
.
.
01  CURRORDER        PIC X(16) VALUE SPACE.
*
01  STATUS-MESSAGE  PIC X(10) VALUE 'OK'.
*
01  CONFIRM-STRING.
*
    05  FILLER       PIC X(08) VALUE 'order_no'.
    05  FILLER       PIC X(01) VALUE '='.
    05  CONF-ODR-NO PIC 9(06) VALUE ZERO.
    05  FILLER       PIC X(01) VALUE '&'.
    05  FILLER       PIC X(10) VALUE 'confirm_no'.
    05  FILLER       PIC X(01) VALUE '='.
    05  CONF-NO      PIC X(09) VALUE SPACE.
*
01  CODEPAGE-INFO.
*
    05  CODEPAGE-EBCDIC  PIC X(08) VALUE '037'.
    05  CODEPAGE-ASCII   PIC X(40) VALUE 'iso-8859-1'.
.
.
PROCEDURE DIVISION.
.
.
5000-SEND-CONFIRMATION.
.
.
    EXEC CICS
        DOCUMENT CREATE DOCTOKEN(CURRORDER)
                        TEMPLATE('ORDERCONFIRM')
                        SYMBOLLIST(CONFIRM-STRING)
                        LISTLENGTH(LENGTH OF ORDERINFO)
                        HOSTCODEPAGE(CODEPAGE-EBCDIC)
    END-EXEC.

    EXEC CICS
        WEB SEND DOCTOKEN(CURRORDER)
                 STATUSCODE(200)
                 STATUSTEXT(STATUS-MESSAGE)
                 CLNTCODEPAGE(CODEPAGE-ASCII)
    END-EXEC.
```

The WEB STARTBROWSE FORMFIELD command

Function

Web services. (TS 2.1 and later) The WEB STARTBROWSE FORMFIELD command starts a browse process for a set of name-value pairs in an HTML form. The HTML form is in the body of the HTTP request being processed by the current task. Once this command is executed, you can use the WEB READNEXT FORMFIELD command to read the first and subsequent name-value pairs in the HTML form.

Syntax

```
EXEC CICS
    WEB STARTBROWSE    FORMFIELD(data-area)
                       NAMELENGTH(data-area)
                  [ CLNTCODEPAGE(name)
                         HOSTCODEPAGE(name) ]
    END-EXEC.
```

Options

FORMFIELD	A data area that specifies the name of the form field where the browse is to start. Subsequent WEB READNEXT FORMFIELD commands will start retrieving name-value pairs from this point in the HTML form. If a name isn't specified, browsing starts at the first name-value pair in the HTML form.
NAMELENGTH	Specifies a binary fullword (PIC S9(8) COMP) or literal value that gives the length of the name in the FORMFIELD option.
CLNTCODEPAGE	Specifies the 40-character name of the code page used when data is converted from the client code page. When you use this option, you must also specify the HOSTCODEPAGE option.
HOSTCODEPAGE	Specifies the 8-character name of the host code page that's used when the form's data is converted from the ASCII code page. When you use this option, you must also specify the CLNTCODEPAGE option.

Exceptional conditions

Note: The default action for these conditions is to terminate the task.

INVREQ	There is already a WEB STARTBROWSE in progress, the client or server code page can't be found, or the program isn't a CICS Web interface application.
LENGERR	The length on NAMELENGTH is less than or equal to zero.
NOTFND	A form field with the specified name can't be found.

Notes and tips

- IBM introduced the WEB commands in CICS TS 1.3 as a way of simplifying the communication between CICS and an external web environment. Prior to TS 1.3, the HTML template manager was required to process HTTP header and HTML form information.

- The WEB STARTBROWSE FORMFIELD command must be issued before you can issue any WEB READNEXT FORMFIELD commands.

- A host code page and a client code page are used to translate data to the format that's used on the server and the client, respectively. In a IBM environment, usually the host uses EBCDIC code while the clients use ASCII.

Coding example

The following example shows how the WEB STARTBROWSE FORMFIELD command can be used to start a browse process on an HTML document.

```
    3000-PROCESS-HTML-FORM.
*
        EXEC CICS
            WEB STARTBROWSE FORMFIELD
        END-EXEC.

        PERFORM 3100-GET-FIELDS
            UNTIL END-OF-FORM.

        EXEC CICS
            WEB ENDBROWSE FORMFIELD
        END-EXEC.
*
    3100-GET-FIELDS.
*
        PERFORM 3200-READNEXT-FORM-FIELD.
    .
    .
    3200-READNEXT-FORM-FIELD.
    .
    .
        EXEC CICS
            WEB READNEXT  FORMFIELD(FORM-FIELD-NAME)
                          NAMELENGTH(FORM-FIELD-NAME-LEN)
                          VALUE(FORM-FIELD-VALUE)
                          VALUELENGTH(FORM-FIELD-VALUE-LEN)
                          RESP(RESPONSE-CODE)
        END-EXEC.
    .
    .
```

The **WEB STARTBROWSE HTTPHEADER** command

Function

Web services. (TS 2.1 and later) The WEB STARTBROWSE HTTPHEADER command starts a browse operation for HTTP headers. Once this command is executed, you can use the WEB READNEXT HTTPHEADER command to read the first and any subsequent HTTP headers from the HTTP request.

Syntax

```
EXEC CICS
    WEB STARTBROWSE HTTPHEADER
END-EXEC.
```

Options

The WEB STARTBROWSE HTTPHEADER command has no options.

Exceptional condition

INVREQ   The program is a non-CICS Web interface application, or the command is being issued for a non-HTTP request. The default action for this condition is to terminate the task.

Notes and tips

- IBM introduced the WEB commands in CICS TS 1.3 as a way of simplifying the communication between CICS and an external web environment. Prior to TS 1.3, the HTML template manager was required to process HTTP header and HTML form information.

- The WEB STARTBROWSE HTTPHEADER command must be issued before you can issue any WEB READNEXT HTTPHEADER commands.

Coding example

The following example shows how the WEB STARTBROWSE HTTPHEADER
command can be used to start a browse process on the HTTP headers.

```
      .
      .
      EXEC CICS
            WEB STARTBROWSE HTTPHEADER
      END-EXEC.

      PERFORM 2100-GET-HEADERS
          UNTIL END-OF-HEADERS.

      EXEC CICS
            WEB ENDBROWSE HTTPHEADER
      END-EXEC.
      .
      .
  2100-GET-HEADERS.
*
          PERFORM 2200-READNEXT-HTTPHEADER.
      .
      .
```

The WEB WRITE HTTPHEADER command

Function

Web services. (TS 1.3 and later) The WEB WRITE HTTPHEADER command lets you add HTTP header information to an HTTP response.

Syntax

```
EXEC CICS
    WEB WRITE    HTTPHEADER(data-area)
               [ NAMELENGTH(data-value) ]
                 VALUE(data-area)
               [ VALUELENGTH(data-value) ]
    END-EXEC.
```

Options

HTTPHEADER	Specifies a data area that contains the name of the HTTP header to be created. The name specified should conform to standard HTTP protocols.
NAMELENGTH	Specifies a binary fullword (PIC S9(8) COMP) or literal value that gives the length of the name in the HTTPHEADER option.
VALUE	Specifies a data area that contains the HTTP header value.
VALUELENGTH	Specifies a binary fullword (PIC S9(8) COMP) or literal value that gives the length of the HTTP header value.

Exceptional condition

INVREQ	The program is a non-CICS Web interface application. The default action for this condition is to terminate the task.

Notes and tips

- IBM introduced the WEB commands in CICS TS 1.3 as a way of simplifying the communication between CICS and an external web environment. Prior to TS 1.3, the HTML template manager was required to process HTTP header and HTML form information.
- The WEB WRITE HTTPHEADER command is seldom used. In most cases, the standard generated header is adequate.

The WRITE command

Function

File control. The WRITE command writes a new record to a file. The file can be a VSAM KSDS, ESDS, RRDS, or path. (CICS also supports BDAM files, but the BDAM options aren't covered in this book.)

Syntax

```
EXEC CICS
    WRITE    FILE(filename)
             FROM(data-area)
             RIDFLD(data-area)
        [ { LENGTH(data-value) }
          { SYSID(systemname) LENGTH(data-value) } ]
        [ KEYLENGTH(data-value) ]
        [ RBA | RRN ]
        [ MASSINSERT ]
        [ NOSUSPEND ]
    END-EXEC.
```

Options

FILE	Specifies the 1- to 8-character name of the data set that will contain the record to be written.
FROM	Specifies the data area that contains the data record to be written.
RIDFLD	Specifies a data area that identifies the record to be written. The content of the RIDFLD field depends on whether RBA or RRN is specified. If neither is specified, the RIDFLD field contains a key for a VSAM KSDS or path.
LENGTH	Specifies a binary halfword (PIC S9(4) COMP) or literal value that indicates the length of the record to be written. Not required if the file has fixed-length records. Required if the SYSID option is specified.
SYSID	Specifies the 1- to 4-character name of a remote system that contains the file.
KEYLENGTH	Specifies a binary halfword (PIC S9(4) COMP) or literal value that indicates the length of the key. Used only when the SYSID option is specified and RBA or RRN is not specified.
RBA	Specifies that the RIDFLD field is a relative byte address (RBA) for a VSAM ESDS. An RBA is a binary fullword (PIC S9(8) COMP). Since ESDS records are always written to the end of the file, the initial value of the RIDFLD field doesn't matter. When control returns, however, the RIDFLD field contains the RBA of the record that was written.
RRN	Specifies that the RIDFLD is a relative record number (RRN) for a VSAM RRDS. An RRN is a binary fullword (PIC S9(8) COMP). The RRN of the first record in an RRDS is 1.

| MASSINSERT | Specifies that the WRITE command is a part of a VSAM mass sequential insertion, which improves performance when many records are to be written to the file from a single task. |
| NOSUSPEND | (RLS only) The WRITE request will not wait if the key for the record is being created, modified, or deleted by another task. |

Exceptional conditions

Note: The default action for these conditions is to terminate the task.

DISABLED	The data set is disabled, probably as a result of the master terminal operator explicitly disabling the file using CEMT SET DISABLE.
DUPREC	A record with the specified key is already in the file. Can also occur if the record contains an alternate key value that already exists, the alternate index does not allow duplicate keys, and the alternate index is a part of the file's upgrade set or access is via the path.
FILENOTFOUND	The data set name specified in the FILE option isn't defined in the File Control Table.
ILLOGIC	A serious VSAM error occurred.
INVREQ	The WRITE request is prohibited by the file's FCT entry. Can also occur if the key value specified in the RIDFLD field doesn't agree with the key value contained within the record to be written, the KEYLENGTH value is incorrect, or a READ, READNEXT, or READPREV command with the UPDATE option has exclusive control of the file.
IOERR	An I/O error occurred.
ISCINVREQ	An undeterminable error occurred on the remote system specified in the SYSID option.
LENGERR	The length specified in the LENGTH option exceeds the maximum record length allowed for the file.
LOADING	(TS 1.1 and later) The WRITE request was made against a data table that is still being loaded into the CICS system.
NOSPACE	There is not enough space allocated to the data set to contain the record.
NOTAUTH	The transaction's PCT entry specified that resource security checking should be done, and the operator is not authorized to access the data set.
NOTOPEN	The file is not open.
SYSIDERR	The system identified by SYSID could not be located or accessed.

Notes and tips

- When you write a record to an ESDS, the record is always added to the end of the file. In that case, the initial value of the RIDFLD is ignored; CICS returns the RBA value of the record that was written in this field.

- If you need to write several records in ascending key sequence, you should use the MASSINSERT option. MASSINSERT changes the technique VSAM uses to split control intervals and can be more efficient when records are written in sequential order. A MASSINSERT operation is not considered complete until you issue an UNLOCK command or a SYNCPOINT command, or you terminate your task. Usually, that's not significant. But if the same program (that is, the same task) reads records from the file after writing records with the MASSINSERT option, it should first issue an UNLOCK command.

- The only exceptional condition you usually need to check for a WRITE command is DUPREC.

Coding example (fixed-length VSAM KSDS records)

This example writes a fixed-length record to a VSAM KSDS. The record is contained in the field named ACCOUNT-RECORD, and AR-ACCOUNT-NUMBER, which is a part of ACCOUNT-RECORD, contains the record's key value. The DUPREC condition is handled in case the record already exists.

```
3100-WRITE-ACCOUNT-RECORD.
*
    EXEC CICS
        WRITE FILE('ACCOUNT')
              FROM(ACCOUNT-RECORD)
              RIDFLD(AR-ACCOUNT-NUMBER)
              RESP(RESPONSE-CODE)
    END-EXEC.

    IF RESPONSE-CODE = DFHRESP(NORMAL)
        MOVE 'N' TO DUPLICATE-RECORD-SW
    ELSE
        IF RESPONSE-CODE = DFHRESP(DUPREC)
            MOVE 'Y' TO DUPLICATE-RECORD-SW
        ELSE
            PERFORM 9999-TERMINATE-PROGRAM
        END-IF
    END-IF.
```

Coding example (variable-length VSAM ESDS records)

This example writes a record to a variable-length VSAM ESDS. The record is contained in ACCOUNT-RECORD, and ACCOUNT-RECORD-LENGTH indicates the record's length (in this case, 250 bytes). After the READ command completes, ACCOUNT-RECORD-RBA will contain the RBA of the record that was written.

```
3100-WRITE-ACCOUNT-RECORD.
*
    MOVE 250 TO ACCOUNT-RECORD-LENGTH.

    EXEC CICS
        WRITE FILE('ACCOUNT')
              FROM(ACCOUNT-RECORD)
              LENGTH(ACCOUNT-RECORD-LENGTH)
              RIDFLD(ACCOUNT-RECORD-RBA)
              RBA
    END-EXEC.
```

The WRITE JOURNALNAME command

Function

Journaling. (TS 1.1 and later) The WRITE JOURNALNAME command writes a record to a journal file.

Syntax

```
EXEC CICS
    WRITE    JOURNALNAME(data-value)
             JTYPEID(data-value)
             FROM(data-area)
        [ FLENGTH(data-value) ]
        [ REQID(data-area) ]
        [ PREFIX(data-value)
            [ PFXLENG(data-value) ] ]
        [ WAIT ]
        [ NOSUSPEND ]
    END-EXEC.
```

Options

JOURNALNAME	Specifies a 1- to 8-character name that identifies the journal where the journal record is to be written. Lowercase letters in the name are not allowed. CICS will search the installed JOURNALMODEL definitions to find a matching journal name. If one isn't found, CICS will attempt to use a default log stream name.
JTYPEID	Specifies a 2-character code that's placed in the journal record to identify the record.
FROM	Specifies the data area that contains the record to be written.
FLENGTH	Specifies a binary fullword (PIC S9(8) COMP) or literal value that indicates the length of the record to be written.
REQID	Specifies a binary fullword (PIC S9(8) COMP) where CICS will place a unique value to identify the journal record. You can use this value later in a WAIT JOURNALNAME command.
PREFIX	Specifies the data area that contains the user prefix that's to be included in the journal record.
PFXLENG	Specifies a binary halfword (PIC S9(4) COMP) or literal value that contains the length of the PREFIX field.
WAIT	Specifies that the journal record is to be written synchronously; that is, control is not returned to your task until the journal record has been successfully written. If WAIT is omitted, the journal record is written asynchronously, so control is returned to your program immediately.
NOSUSPEND	Specifies that if there's not enough room in the journal buffer, control should be returned immediately to the program at the point following the WRITE JOURNALNAME command.

Exceptional conditions

Note: The default action for all of these conditions except NOJBUFSP is to terminate the task. The default action for the NOJBUFSP condition is to suspend the task until buffer space becomes available.

INVREQ   The command isn't valid for processing by CICS.

IOERR   An I/O error occurred.

JIDERR   A log stream does not exist for the specified journal name.

LENGERR   The journal record is larger than the journal buffer.

NOJBUFSP   There isn't enough room in the buffer to hold the journal record. Normally, this causes the task to be suspended until the buffer is written to the file. However, you can override this action by specifying NOSUSPEND on the WRITE JOURNALNUM command.

NOTAUTH   The transaction's PCT entry specified that resource security checking should be done, and the operator is not authorized to access the journal.

NOTOPEN   The journal data set is not open.

Notes and tips

- Journal records have a standardized format that includes several prefix areas. The system header identifies the journal record type, that is, whether it was written automatically by CICS or by a user program. The system prefix contains information about the task that wrote the journal record: its task number, transaction-id, terminal-id, and a time stamp. These prefixes, which are generated automatically by CICS, are followed by an optional user prefix that can contain similar information. Finally, the user prefix is followed by user data.

- Journal records can be written in one of two ways: synchronously or asynchronously. When you write a journal record synchronously, your task waits until the record has been written to disk before continuing. When you write a journal record asynchronously, control returns to your task as soon as the record has been placed in a buffer; the record will be written to disk later (usually within one second). If necessary, you can issue a WAIT JOURNALNAME command to suspend your task until a previously written journal record is actually written to disk. Asynchronous journal output is more efficient and should be used whenever possible.

- NOJBUFSP is one of the few exceptional conditions that does not cause your task to be terminated. Instead, its action depends on whether you handle the condition (using the RESP option or a HANDLE CONDITION command) and whether you specify NOSUSPEND on the WRITE JOURNALNAME command. If you do neither, NOJBUFSP simply causes your task to be suspended until the buffer space becomes available; then, control returns to your program at the first statement following the WRITE JOURNALNAME command. If your program handles the NOJBUFSP condition, the specified error processing is done, but to write the journal record, the program must issue the WRITE JOURNALNAME command again. If you specify NOSUSPEND, control is returned to the statement following the WRITE JOURNALNAME command if the buffer space is unavailable; again, you'll have to issue another WRITE JOURNALNAME command to write the journal record later.

Coding example (synchronous journal output)

This example shows how to delete a data set record after first recording the record in a journal. Synchronous journal output is used, so the data set record isn't deleted until the journal record is written.

```
3100-DELETE-CUSTOMER-RECORD.
*
    EXEC CICS
        WRITE JOURNALNAME('CUSTOMER')
              JTYPEID('CD')
              FROM(CUSTOMER-MASTER-RECORD)
              WAIT
    END-EXEC.
    EXEC CICS
        DELETE FILE('CUSTMAS')
               RIDFLD(CM-CUSTOMER-NUMBER)
    END-EXEC.
```

Coding example (asynchronous journal output)

This example shows how to delete a data set record after first recording the record in a journal. Asynchronous journal output is used, so the program doesn't wait for the journal record to be written before it deletes the data set record. However, a WAIT JOURNALNAME command is issued so that the program will not continue beyond the DELETE command before the journal record is written.

```
3100-DELETE-CUSTOMER-RECORD.
*
    EXEC CICS
        WRITE JOURNALNAME('CUSTOMER')
              JTYPEID('CD')
              FROM(CUSTOMER-MASTER-RECORD)
              FLENGTH(97)
              REQID(WS-REQID)
    END-EXEC.

    EXEC CICS
        DELETE FILE('CUSTMAS')
               RIDFLD(CM-CUSTOMER-NUMBER)
    END-EXEC.

    EXEC CICS
        WAIT JOURNALNAME('CUSTOMER')
             REQID(WS-REQID)
    END-EXEC.
```

The WRITE JOURNALNUM command

Function

Journaling. The WRITE JOURNALNUM command writes a record to a journal file.

Note: The WRITE JOURNALNUM command is supported for compatibility purposes with earlier releases of CICS. It's been replaced by the WRITE JOURNALNAME command.

The WRITE OPERATOR command

Function

Console support. The WRITE OPERATOR command writes a message to one or more system consoles.

Syntax

```
EXEC CICS
    WRITE OPERATOR    TEXT(data-value)
                    [ TEXTLENGTH(data-value) ]
                    [ ROUTECODES(data-value)
                          NUMROUTES(data-value) ]
                    [ { ACTION(data-value) }
                      { EVENTUAL }
                      { IMMEDIATE }
                      { CRITICAL }
                      { REPLY(data-area)
                            MAXLENGTH(data-value)
                        [ REPLYLENGTH(data-area) ]
                        [ TIMEOUT(data-value) ]    } ]
END-EXEC.
```

Options

TEXT	The message to be sent to the operator.
TEXTLENGTH	The length of the TEXT message. Must be 690 or less.
ROUTECODES	A list of 1-byte route codes that indicate which operator consoles the message should be sent to. Each route code is a binary number in the range 1 to 28. The default is a single byte set to 2.
NUMROUTES	A binary fullword (PIC S9(8) COMP) or literal value that indicates the number of route codes specified in the ROUTECODES option. Required if ROUTECODES is specified.
ACTION	A binary fullword (PIC S9(8) COMP) or literal value that indicates that the message requires operator action. Possible values are:
	2 Immediate
	3 Eventual
	11 Critical
EVENTUAL	The message requires eventual action by the operator.
IMMEDIATE	The message requires immediate action by the operator.
CRITICAL	The message requires eventual action by the operator, but will not be scrolled off the screen until deleted.
REPLY	The message requires an operator reply, which will be placed in the data area supplied. The task will be suspended until the reply has been received or the timeout period has elapsed.

MAXLENGTH	A binary fullword (PIC S9(8) COMP) or literal value that specifies the maximum length of the reply. Required if REPLY is coded.
REPLYLENGTH	A binary fullword (PIC S9(8) COMP) where CICS places the length of the operator's reply.
TIMEOUT	A binary fullword (PIC S9(8) COMP) or literal value that specifies how many seconds CICS should wait for a reply. The maximum is 86,400 (24 hours).

Exceptional conditions

Note: The default action for these conditions is to terminate the task.

EXPIRED	The TIMEOUT period has expired without an operator reply.
INVREQ	One of the values specified in the WRITE OPERATOR command is invalid.
LENGERR	The operator's reply is longer than the MAXLENGTH value.

Coding example

The following example writes the message "PR74X1 FINISHED." to the default operator console.

```
    EXEC CICS
        WRITE OPERATOR TEXT('PR74X1 FINISHED.')
                       TEXTLENGTH(16)
                       EVENTUAL
    END-EXEC.
```

The WRITEQ TD command

Function

Transient data. The WRITEQ TD command writes a record to a specified transient data queue.

Syntax

```
EXEC CICS
    WRITEQ TD   QUEUE(name)
                FROM(data-area)
              [ LENGTH(data-value) ]
              [ SYSID(systemname) ]
END-EXEC.
```

Options

QUEUE	Specifies the 1- to 4-character name of the transient data queue where the data is to be written.
FROM	Specifies the data area that contains the record to be written.
LENGTH	Specifies a binary halfword (PIC S9(4) COMP) or literal value that indicates the length of the record to be written.
SYSID	Specifies the 1- to 4-character name of the remote system that contains the destination.

Exceptional conditions

Note: The default action for these conditions is to terminate the task.

DISABLED	The destination is disabled.
INVREQ	The extrapartition destination is open for input.
IOERR	An I/O error occurred.
ISCINVREQ	An undeterminable error occurred on the remote system specified in the SYSID option.
LENGERR	The length specified in the LENGTH option exceeds the maximum record length allowed for the destination.
LOCKED	The use of the queue has been restricted.
NOSPACE	There is not enough space allocated to the destination to contain the record.
NOTAUTH	The transaction's PCT entry specified that resource security checking should be done, and the user is not authorized to access the destination.
NOTOPEN	The destination is not open.
QIDERR	The destination specified in the QUEUE option isn't defined in the Destination Control Table (DCT).
SYSIDERR	The system identified by SYSID could not be located or accessed.

Notes and tips

- There are two types of transient data queues: intrapartition and extrapartition. All intrapartition destinations are stored in a VSAM file called DFHNTRA, and access to them is efficient. Extrapartition destinations, however, are QSAM files managed not by CICS, but by the operating system. Because of the way CICS uses QSAM, extrapartition destinations are relatively inefficient, so use them only when appropriate. (The syntax of the WRITEQ TD command is the same for both types of destinations.)

- An intrapartition destination can be used with automatic transaction initiation (ATI) so that a transaction is started as soon as the number of records in the destination reaches a specified trigger level. Because of this feature, intrapartition destinations are often used for applications where data from one program needs to be gathered temporarily so it can be processed by another program.

- One common use of ATI is for printer applications. An ATI transaction reads records from a destination, formats the data, and sends it to a printer. This technique removes detailed printer considerations from the application program that creates the data to be printed. All that program has to do is issue WRITEQ TD commands to write records to the proper destination.

- The transient data facility provides no mechanism for holding a destination for exclusive use. If you need to write several uninterrupted records to a destination, use the ENQ and DEQ commands.

Coding example

This example shows how to write a record to a destination. The destination's name is stored in a 4-character alphanumeric field named DESTINATION-ID, and the record is in PRINT-AREA.

```
    2220-WRITE-QUEUE-RECORD.
*
        EXEC CICS
            WRITEQ TD QUEUE(DESTINATION-ID)
                      FROM(PRINT-AREA)
        END-EXEC.
```

The WRITEQ TS command

Function

Temporary storage control. The WRITEQ TS command writes a record to a specified temporary storage queue.

Syntax

```
EXEC CICS
    WRITEQ TS { QUEUE(name) | QNAME(name) }
              FROM(data-area)
              [ LENGTH(data-value) ]
              [ { ITEM(data-area)
                    [ REWRITE ] }
                { NUMITEMS(data-area) } ]
              [ SYSID(systemname) ]
              [ MAIN | AUXILIARY ]
              [ NOSUSPEND ]
    END-EXEC.
```

Options

QUEUE	Specifies the 1- to 8-character name of the temporary storage queue where data is to be written.
QNAME	Specifies the 1-to 16-character name of the temporary storage queue that contains the data to be retrieved. QNAME is an alternative to the QUEUE command.
FROM	Specifies the data area that contains the record to be written.
LENGTH	Specifies a binary halfword (PIC S9(4) COMP) or literal value that indicates the length of the record to be written. Required under OS/VS COBOL for queues with variable-length records.
ITEM	Specifies a binary halfword (PIC S9(4) COMP). If you specify RE-WRITE, ITEM specifies the item number of the record you want to rewrite. If you don't specify REWRITE, the initial contents of ITEM are ignored; CICS returns the item number of the record in this field.
REWRITE	Specifies that the record should be rewritten.
NUMITEMS	Specifies a binary halfword (PIC S9(4) COMP) where CICS places a count of the number of items in the queue, including the item just written. Not valid if ITEM is coded.
SYSID	Specifies the 1- to 4-character name of the remote system that contains the destination.
MAIN	Specifies that the record should be held in main storage.
AUXILIARY	Specifies that the record should be written to the temporary storage data set.

NOSUSPEND   Specifies that if there is not enough space for the record, control should be returned immediately to the program at the point following the WRITEQ TS command.

Exceptional conditions

Note: The default action for all of these conditions except NOSPACE is to terminate the task. The default action for the NOSPACE condition is to suspend the task until space becomes available.

INVREQ   The queue name is invalid, or the queue was created for internal use by CICS and therefore can't be written to by a user program.

IOERR   An I/O error occurred.

ISCINVREQ   An undeterminable error occurred on the remote system specified in the SYSID option.

ITEMERR   No record exists for the item number specified.

LENGERR   A length error has occurred.

NOSPACE   There is not enough temporary storage space to contain the record.

NOTAUTH   The transaction's PCT entry specified that resource security checking should be done, and the operator is not authorized to access the queue.

QIDERR   The specified queue does not exist.

SYSIDERR   The system identified by SYSID could not be located or accessed.

Notes and tips

- Temporary storage queues are automatically created when you write a record to a queue that doesn't exist. As a result, no special coding is required to create a queue.

- The MAIN and AUXILIARY options let you specify whether you want the record stored in virtual storage or on disk. If the data is going to exist for more than a few seconds, you should specify AUXILIARY.

- Temporary storage is often used instead of the communication area to save data between executions of a pseudo-conversational program. In general, I recommend you use communication area unless the amount of data you're saving is large; then you're better off using a temporary storage record.

- In many applications that use temporary storage queues, you'll want the queue names to be unique. To ensure that a queue name is unique, use the terminal-id of the terminal that's attached to your task as a part of the name. The terminal-id is always available in the Execute Interface Block field EIBTRMID.

- The QNAME option provides an alternative way of identifying a temporary storage queue by allowing a name of up to 16 bytes. In practice though, the QUEUE option is large enough to store a unique queue name.

- NOSPACE is one of the few exceptional conditions that does not cause your task to be terminated. Instead, its action depends on whether you handle the condition (using the RESP option or a HANDLE CONDITION command) and whether you specify NOSUSPEND on the WRITEQ TS command. If you do neither, NOSPACE simply causes your task to be suspended until the temporary storage space becomes available; then, control returns to your program at the first statement following the WRITEQ TS command. If your program handles the NOSPACE condition, the specified error processing is done, but to write the temporary storage record, the program must issue the WRITEQ TS command again. If you specify NOSUSPEND, control is returned to the statement following the WRITEQ TS command if the temporary storage space is unavailable; again, you'll have to issue another WRITEQ TS command to write the temporary storage record later.

Coding example (write a record)

This example shows how to write a record to a temporary storage queue. The queue's name is stored in an 8-character alphanumeric field named TS-QUEUE-NAME, and the record is in TS-CUSTOMER-RECORD. No exceptional conditions are checked.

```
8100-WRITE-QUEUE-RECORD.
*
    EXEC CICS
        WRITEQ TS QUEUE(TS-QUEUE-NAME)
                  FROM(TS-CUSTOMER-RECORD)
    END-EXEC.
```

Coding example (rewrite a record)

This example shows how to rewrite a record in a queue. Here, TS-ITEM-NUMBER is set to 1 so that the first record in the queue is rewritten.

```
1220-REWRITE-QUEUE-RECORD.
*
    EXEC CICS
        WRITEQ TS QUEUE(TS-QUEUE-NAME)
                  FROM(CUSTOMER-MASTER-RECORD)
                  ITEM(TS-ITEM-NUMBER)
                  REWRITE
    END-EXEC.
```

The XCTL command

Function

Program control. The XCTL command terminates the program that's currently executing and invokes the specified program. Data can be passed to the invoked program. When the invoked program ends, control is not returned to the program that issued the XCTL command.

Syntax

```
EXEC CICS
    XCTL   PROGRAM(name)
         [ COMMAREA(data-area)
             [ LENGTH(data-value) ] ]
         [ INPUTMSG(data-area)
             [ INPUTMSGLEN(data-value) ] ]
    END-EXEC.
```

Options

PROGRAM	Specifies the 1- to 8-character name of the program to be invoked. This name must be defined in the Processing Program Table (PPT).
COMMAREA	Specifies a data area that's passed to the invoked program as a communication area. The invoked program accesses the communication area via its DFHCOMMAREA field, which addresses a separate area of storage where a copy of the specified data area has been placed. (This works differently than it does for a LINK command; see the description of that command for details.)
LENGTH	Specifies a binary halfword (PIC S9(4) COMP) or literal value that indicates the length of the data area specified in the COMMAREA option.
INPUTMSG	Specifies a data area that supplies input data for the first RECEIVE command issued by the invoked program.
INPUTMSGLEN	Specifies a binary halfword (PIC S9(4) COMP) or literal value that specifies the length of the INPUTMSG field.

Exceptional conditions

Note: The default action for these conditions is to terminate the task.

INVREQ	You coded the INPUTMSG option for a task that's not associated with a terminal.
LENGERR	A length error occurred.
NOTAUTH	The transaction's PCT entry specified that resource security checking should be done, and the operator is not authorized to access the program.
PGMIDERR	The program is not defined in the Processing Program Table (PPT).

Notes and tips

- The XCTL command is commonly used to implement menu applications. The menu program itself uses an XCTL command to transfer control to a program selected by the user. And application programs return control to the menu program by issuing an XCTL command.

- If you need to return control to the invoking program, you may want to use LINK instead of XCTL. If you invoke a program with LINK, you can return control to the point following the LINK command by issuing a RETURN command.

- In menu applications, you might want to check for the PGMIDERR condition and simply notify the operator that an application is not available if it occurs. And you might want to check for the NOTAUTH condition and notify the user that he or she isn't authorized to access the application if it occurs.

Coding example

This example shows how the XCTL command might be used in a menu application to transfer control to a program selected by the operator. Since users who are authorized to use the menu may not be authorized to use all of its selections, the NOTAUTH condition is checked. And PGMIDERR is checked to make sure the program is available. In the XCTL command, OPERATOR- SELECTED-PROGRAM is an 8-byte working-storage field that contains the name of the program to be invoked. A communication area is passed to the invoked program.

```
    1000-XFER-TO-APPLICATION.
*
    EXEC CICS
        XCTL PROGRAM(OPERATOR-SELECTED-PROGRAM)
            COMMAREA(COMMUNICATION-AREA)
            RESP(RESPONSE-CODE)
    END-EXEC.

    IF RESPONSE-CODE = DFHRESP(NOTAUTH)
        MOVE 'Y' TO PROGRAM-ERROR-SW
        MOVE 'You are not authorized to run that application.'
            TO MSGO
    ELSE
        IF RESPONSE-CODE = DFHRESP(PGMIDERR)
            MOVE 'Y' TO PROGRAM-ERROR-SW
            MOVE 'That application is not available.'
                TO MSGO
        ELSE
            PERFORM 9999-TERMINATE-PROGRAM
        END-IF
    END-IF.
```

Basic Mapping Support

Unit 9

BMS mapset definition for 3270 displays

If you're developing traditional CICS programs or modular programs in which the presentation logic is implemented in a 3270 display environment, you'll use basic mapping support (BMS) to manage terminal input and output. To use BMS, you have to code assembler language macros to create a *mapset.* The mapset defines the screens used by your program.

After you've coded your mapset, you must assemble it twice: once to create a *physical mapset* and again to create a *symbolic*, or *logical, mapset.* The physical mapset is a load module BMS uses to map data transmitted to and received from the display station. The symbolic mapset is a COBOL copy member that you copy into your program, and it defines the format of the screen data as it's processed by your program. The procedure for assembling BMS mapsets is found in Unit 3.

Most shops use *screen painters,* or *mapset generators,* to simplify BMS mapset creation. Simply put, a screen painter is a program that lets you design the screen layout at your terminal interactively. The screen painter then converts that data into appropriate BMS macro instructions. If you have a screen painter, by all means use it. It can save you a lot of work. On the other hand, you still need to know how to define your own BMS mapsets to use BMS effectively.

Characteristics of 3270 displays

Data displayed by BMS on a 3270 terminal is organized into *fields*. Each field has specific attributes that control its appearance and operation. Field attributes for 3270s can be divided into two classes: *standard attributes*, which are available on all 3270 models, and *extended attributes*, which are available only on more advanced 3270 models. One of the basic functions of a BMS mapset is to specify the attributes of fields.

Today, most 3270 displays are emulated on PCs. In other words, emulation software allows you to access CICS programs on a mainframe server from your PC as though it were a 3270 terminal. In most cases, the emulation program you use will simulate a standard 3270 display capable of displaying base (limited) color and highlighting combinations.

Standard attributes

- Standard 3270 field attributes are specified by a single byte, called an *attribute byte*. An attribute byte occupies the character location on the screen that's immediately before the field it affects, as shown by the shading in figure 9-1.

- On a 3270, fields have no explicit length. The end of one field is indicated by the presence of an attribute byte for the next field. If there's no subsequent attribute byte, the field continues to the end of the screen.

- To keep data entry fields from continuing on too long, it's common to define an attribute byte (a new field) immediately after the last character. Many programmers darken the space that follows each entry field in their screen layouts, to remind themselves to define this attribute byte (see the customer number field below).

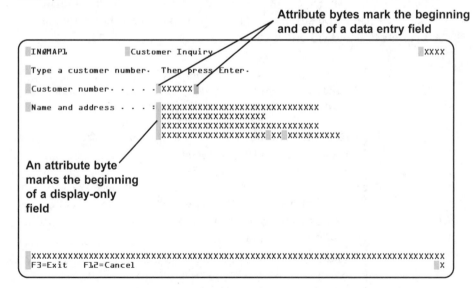

Attribute bytes mark the beginning and end of a data entry field

An attribute byte marks the beginning of a display-only field

Figure 9-1

Standard field attributes

Protection	Shift	Intensity
Unprotected	Alphanumeric	Normal
Protected	Numeric	Bright
Auto-skip		Dark (No-display)

Figure 9-2

- Figure 9-2 lists the three basic field characteristics that are controlled by the standard attribute.

- The *protection attribute* specifies whether or not an operator can enter data into a field. Users can key data into an *unprotected field*, but not into a *protected field*. In contrast, a *skip field*, defined with the auto-skip protection option, is skipped over and causes the cursor to automatically advance to the next unprotected field.

- Generally, protected fields are used for constants (like titles or messages), while unprotected fields are used for data entry. Auto-skip attribute bytes are normally used to mark the end of unprotected data entry fields so that the cursor moves automatically to the next data entry field.

- The *shift attribute* specifies whether the keyboard is in numeric or alphanumeric shift (it has nothing to do with uppercase or lowercase letters).

- When the numeric attribute is specified, the operator can enter numeric data consisting only of numerals, a sign, and a decimal point. This doesn't ensure that the data is entered in a correct numeric format, but it helps.

- The *intensity attribute* specifies the display intensity for the field. Normal and bright intensity are used in some shops to distinguish constants from variable data. Bright intensity is also often used to draw attention to error messages.

- A dark, or no-display, field displays only spaces, no matter what characters the field contains.

The format and contents of an attribute byte

- Figure 9-3 shows the format of a standard 3270 attribute byte, indicating the bit positions that are responsible for each attribute setting. The bit positions within a byte are always numbered from zero.

- The settings in an attribute byte are initially based on the values you code for the field in the BMS mapset. However, you can change these settings from within the COBOL program.

- The last bit in an attribute byte, the *Modified Data Tag* (*MDT*), doesn't control the appearance of the data in the field. Instead, it's used to indicate whether the field should be transmitted to the host system when the operator presses an AID key. If the MDT is on, the field is sent; otherwise, it's not.

- The MDT can be turned on by the application program when it sends data to the terminal. In addition, whenever an operator changes the data in a field, that field's MDT is turned on automatically.

- One other important function of the standard attribute byte is selecting the display color for base color display terminals. A base color terminal can display data in one of four colors (blue, white, green, and red). The color for each field is determined by the combination of the field's protection and intensity attributes.

The bit positions in an attribute byte

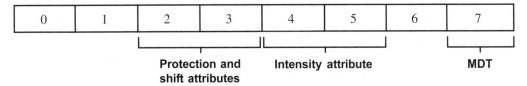

The contents of an attribute byte

Bit positions	Functions	Bit settings
0-1		Depends on the contents of bits 2-7
2-3	Protection and shift	00 = Unprotected alphanumeric 01 = Unprotected numeric 10 = Protected 11 = Protected skip
4-5	Intensity	00 = Normal 01 = Normal 10 = Bright 11 = Dark (No-display)
6		Must be 0
7	MDT	0 = Field has not been modified 1 = Field has been modified

Figure 9-3

Extended attributes

Many terminals allow for *extended attributes* that give more control over the look and operation of a field than the standard attributes, as shown in figure 9-4. Unlike the standard attributes, an extended attribute does *not* take up a position on the screen. If extended attributes are specified but the terminal doesn't support them, they're ignored.

- Many of the *extended color* and *highlighting* options are used in the IBM guidelines for formatting easy-to-use screens (see figure 9-6).

- The *validation* options are not available on a wide variety of terminals, so you may never need them.

- Terminals that support *programmed symbols* can display characters from any of up to six user-defined character sets. This feature is useful for engineering or other graphics applications. The alternate character sets are usually loaded into the terminal before the application program begins. Then, extended attributes are used to specify which character set should be used to display data.

- Terminals that support *field outlining* let you construct boxes around text fields. By setting the outline attribute, you can place a line on any or all sides of a field.

- Terminals that support *SO/SI* let you mix single- and *double-byte character sets* (*DBCS*) in the same field. The SO/SI attribute indicates whether a field can contain DBCS data.

- Terminals that support *background transparency* can display text and graphics at the same time. When the background transparency attribute is on, the graphic image behind a text field is visible.

Type of attribute	Options			
Extended color	Blue	Red	Pink	Green
	Turquoise	Yellow	Neutral (white)	
Extended highlighting	Blinking	Causes the field to flash on the screen.		
	Reverse video	Displays the field in dark characters against a light background—the opposite of the usual display.		
	Underline	Underlines the field.		
Validation	Must enter	The user must enter at least one character of data into the field.		
	Must fill	The user must enter data into each character position of the field.		
	Trigger	The terminal transmits the field's contents as soon as the user moves the cursor out of the field.		
Programmed symbols	Up to 6 alternate user-definable character sets.			
Field outlining	Box	Places a box around the field.		
	Left, Right, Over, Under	Places lines around the field, in any combination.		
SO/SI	Yes or No	Specifies whether the field can contain double-byte characters as well as EBCDIC characters.		
Background transparency	Yes	The background of the field is transparent, so an underlying graphic can show through.		
	No	The background of the field is opaque.		

Figure 9-4

Recommendations for formatting screen displays

- IBM promotes a user interface standard called *CUA*, which stands for *Common User Access*. The goal of CUA is to standardize screen displays so they're easy for users to work with.

- CUA provides three distinct interface models. The *Entry Model* is for non-programmable terminals like the ones most often used for CICS applications. The *Graphical Model* is for programmable workstations such as PCs, and it provides for features like pull-down menus, pop-up dialog boxes, and scroll bars. The *Text Subset of the Graphical Model* provides a standard way of implementing elements of the Graphical Model on non-programmable terminals.

- Figure 9-5 shows typical types of screen fields, and the top part of figure 9-6 summarizes the CUA Entry Model standards for field placement and formatting.

- The CUA standards also encourage the uniform use of function keys throughout an installation, as shown in the bottom part of figure 9-6. Function key assignment is critical to application and screen design, so unless your shop has other standards in place, adhere to the function key guidelines listed whenever possible.

- If your shop has other standards for screen design, be sure to follow them. Your goal is to create interfaces that are consistent with the other applications in your shop so that users can do their work more easily.

Typical fields on a display screen

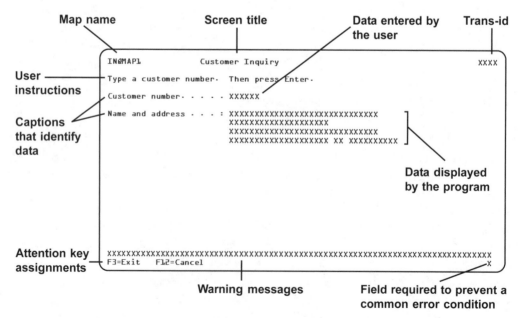

Figure 9-5

CUA guidelines for the color and position of screen fields

Field type	Design
Screen ID (often the trans-id or map name)	Line 1; Blue
Screen titles	Line 1; Green
Instructions and emphasized text	White
Captions (constants) that identify fields	Green; Those that precede display-only fields end with a colon, while those that precede data entry fields end with a period
Variable data that the user enters (data entry fields)	Turquoise; Underline fields so users can see them easily
Variable data displayed by the program that can change as the program executes (display-only fields)	Turquoise
User entry errors	Reverse video
Warning messages	Line 23; Yellow with bright intensity
Attention key assignments	Line 24; Blue

Note: When designing screens for monochrome terminals, substitute the bright intensity attribute for all colors other than blue and green.

CUA guidelines for function key assignments

Key	Assignment
F1	Help: Provide online help for the program
F3	Exit: Exit from the program
F7	Backward: Display the previous screen or record, or scroll up when there's more information than will fit on a screen
F8	Forward: Display the next screen or record, or scroll down when there's more information than will fit on a screen
F12	Cancel: Return to previous screen or exit from the program if it's the first screen
Clear	Clear: Erase any data from the unprotected fields on the screen
F2, F4, F5, F6, F9, F10, F11	Unassigned: Use these keys for program-specific needs

Figure 9-6

How to code a BMS mapset

As you know, a BMS mapset is assembler language code that consists of a number of macro instructions that are expanded by the assembler into a physical mapset and a symbolic mapset. Although you have to follow the assembler's coding rules in your mapset, you don't have to know how to write assembler language programs to develop a mapset. You just have to know how to code two assembler commands (PRINT and END) and three BMS macro instructions (DFHMSD, DFHMDI, and DFHMDF).

The commands and macros in a BMS mapset

Command or macro	Usage
PRINT NOGEN	Coded once at the beginning of the mapset; tells the assembler not to print the statements generated as a result of expanding the BMS macros that follow.
END	Must be the last statement in the input stream; tells the assembler that there are no more source statements.
DFHMSD	Coded once; supplies values that apply to the entire mapset.
DFHMDI	Coded once for each map within the mapset; supplies values that apply to a single map.
DFHMDF	Coded once for each field (or attribute byte) within the map; specifies the position, length, and attributes of a screen field.
DFHMSD TYPE=FINAL	Coded after the last map in the mapset, right before the END command; tells BMS that the mapset is complete.

- If you don't include the PRINT NOGEN command in your mapset, the resulting assembler listing will contain hundreds of lines that aren't important to you. So always start your mapsets with PRINT NOGEN.

- Each mapset should contain one DFHMSD macro instruction. It supplies values that apply to the entire mapset.

- Each map within the mapset begins with a DFHMDI macro instruction. It supplies values that apply to a single map.

- For each field in a map, you code a DFHMDF macro instruction to define the field's attributes. In other words, you code a DFHMDF macro for each attribute byte on the screen. That means you usually code two DFHMDF macros for data entry fields: one for the attribute byte at the beginning of the field, the other for the attribute byte that marks the end of the field (the second attribute byte isn't necessary if the data entry field is followed immediately by the attribute byte for a subsequent field).

- If there's more than one map in the mapset, the next occurrence of a DFHMDI macro marks the end of one map and the beginning of the next. To mark the end of the entire mapset, however, you must code another DFHMSD macro instruction, this time specifying TYPE=FINAL.

- The last line of the mapset is a required assembler command, END.

Assembler language syntax

All BMS macro instructions must follow the assembler's syntax rules. The general syntax for an assembler language statement is as follows:

```
[label]   op-code parameters...
```

- The *label*, when required, begins in column 1 and supplies a symbolic name for the statement. For a BMS macro, the label must begin with a letter and can be up to 7 characters long. An exception is the label for a DFHMDF macro, which can be up to 29 characters long.

- The *op-code* specifies the instruction to be executed and begins in column 10.

- The *parameters* (or *operands*) provide the information the instruction requires to work properly. They're separated from one another by commas with no intervening spaces and can be coded in any order. The first parameter should follow the op-code after one space.

- To specify a parameter's value, use an equals sign. If more than one value is required, separate the values with commas and enclose them in parentheses:

```
COLOR=TURQUOISE
```

```
ATTRB=(NORM,UNPROT)
```

- If a parameter value contains special characters or spaces, enclose it in single quotes. And to include an apostrophe in a value, code two consecutive apostrophes where you want the single apostrophe to appear:

```
INITIAL='CUSTOMER''S NAME'
```

- To make your mapset easier to read, you can code just one parameter per line. Then, to continue the statement on the next line, code a comma after the parameter, place any non-blank character in column 72, and code the next parameter starting in column 16 of the following line (called a *continuation line*).

- You can also use *comment lines* to improve the readability of your mapsets. A comment line is any line with an asterisk in column 1 and a blank in column 72.

- With the exception of comment lines and values in the INITIAL parameter of the DFHMDF macro, you must code assembler statements using uppercase characters.

The DFHMSD macro instruction

Function

The DFHMSD macro instruction has two formats. Format 1 defines a mapset. It supplies the mapset's name and other important information, such as the type of terminal it applies to, the source language it's used with, and whether or not it supports extended attributes. Format 2 marks the end of a mapset. The parameters listed are the ones that you're most likely to use.

Syntax (format 1)

```
name   DFHMSD   TYPE= { &SYSPARM | DSECT | MAP }
                [, LANG= { COBOL | COBOL2 | ASM | PLI | C } ]
                [, MODE= { IN | OUT | INOUT } ]
                [, TERM=terminal-type ]
                [, CTRL=(option,option...) ]
                [, STORAGE=AUTO ]
                [, TIOAPFX= { YES | NO } ]
                [, DSATTS=(type,type...) ]
                [, MAPATTS=(type,type...) ]
                [, EXTATT= { YES | NO | MAPONLY } ]
                [, COLOR= { color | DEFAULT } ]
                [, HILIGHT= { OFF | BLINK | REVERSE | UNDERLINE } ]
                [, VALIDN= { MUSTENTER | MUSTFILL | TRIGGER | USEREXIT } ]
                [, CURSLOC= { YES | NO } ]
                [, OUTLINE= { BOX | ( [,LEFT] [,RIGHT] [,OVER] [,UNDER] ) } ]
                [, SOSI= { YES | NO } ]
                [, TRANSP= {YES | NO } ]
```

Syntax (format 2)

```
DFHMSD TYPE=FINAL
```

Parameters

name	The 1- to 7-character name of the mapset. The mapset name must be unique within a CICS system.
TYPE	For format 1, specifies whether a physical mapset (TYPE=MAP) or a symbolic mapset (TYPE=DSECT), or both (&SYSPARM) will be generated. TYPE=&SYSPARM, which is the usual way to code this parameter, lets you specify this option at execution time via JCL.
	For format 2, TYPE=FINAL indicates the end of the mapset.
LANG	Specifies the source language to be used for the symbolic maps. The default is ASM, so you need to code LANG=COBOL if you're working in COBOL.
MODE	Specifies whether the mapset is used for input, output, or both. There's no performance advantage to specifying just input or output, so you'll usually code MODE=INOUT.

TERM	Specifies the type of terminal that can be used with this mapset. Common values are:

ALL	Any terminal
3270	Same as ALL
3270-1	3270 model-1 terminal (40-column display)
3270-2	3270 model-2 terminal (80-column display)

The IBM manual, *CICS Application Programming Reference*, documents other values you can code for more obscure terminal types. Usually, you'll code TERM=3270-2.

CTRL	Specifies a list of control options in effect for each map in the mapset. Valid options are:

FREEKB	Unlocks the terminal keyboard after each output operation.
FRSET	Turns off the MDT bit in each attribute byte in the terminal's buffer before each output operation. Use this option if you want the terminal to transmit only data that the operator modifies.
ALARM	Sounds the terminal's audible alarm during each output operation.
PRINT	Causes a 3270 printer to print the data in its buffer (after the output operation completes).
length	Specifies how line endings are to be formatted for printed data. L40, L64, and L80 cause a new line to be formatted every 40, 64, or 80 characters, and HONEOM honors the printer's default line length.

STORAGE	If STORAGE=AUTO is coded, the symbolic maps for each map in the mapset occupy separate storage locations. Otherwise, they share the same storage (via a COBOL REDEFINES clause).
TIOAPFX	YES generates a 12-byte FILLER item at the beginning of each symbolic map. It should always be specified for COBOL programs. NO is the default.
DSATTS	Specifies which extended attributes are to be supported in the symbolic maps for this mapset. You can specify any or all of the following:

COLOR	Extended color
HILIGHT	Extended highlighting
OUTLINE	Field outlining
PS	Programmed symbols
SOSI	Two-byte SO/SI characters
TRANSP	Background transparency
VALIDN	Validation

MAPATTS	Specifies which extended attributes are to be supported in the physical maps for this mapset. You can specify any or all of the same types that are valid for the DSATTS parameter. You can specify physical map support for an attribute type that's not specified in the DSATTS parameter, but not the other way around: Any attribute type you specify in the DSATTS parameter should also be specified in the MAPATTS parameter.

EXTATT   Supported for compatibility with releases of CICS before 1.7; for new programs, use DSATTS and MAPATTS instead. Specifies whether or not the maps in the mapset should support extended attributes. If you specify EXTATT=YES, provision is made in both the physical and symbolic maps for attributes for extended color, extended highlighting, programmed symbols, and validation.

COLOR   Specifies a default extended color for the mapset. You may specify DEFAULT for the terminal's default color, or you may specify BLUE, RED, PINK, GREEN, TURQUOISE, YELLOW, or NEUTRAL (white).

HILIGHT   Specifies a default extended highlighting for the mapset. You may specify OFF for no highlighting, or BLINK, REVERSE, or UNDERLINE.

VALIDN   Specifies a default field validation for the mapset. MUSTENTER means the operator must enter some data into each field; MUSTFILL means the operator must completely fill each field; TRIGGER means that fields are transmitted from the terminal one at a time as data is entered into them; and USEREXIT means that fields are processed by the BMS global user exits, XBMIN and XBMOUT.

CURSLOC   Specifies whether or not BMS is to indicate the location of the cursor on an input operation by placing a flag value in the symbolic map following a RECEIVE MAP command. If you code CURSORLOC=YES, the program can test to see if the user placed the cursor in a field by testing that field's flag byte (suffix F) against the BMS constant DFHCURSR.

OUTLINE   Specifies that lines should be included around the fields. If you specify BOX, a box is drawn around the fields. You can also use the LEFT, RIGHT, OVER, and UNDER parameters in any combination to place lines around the fields.

SOSI   If YES is specified, it indicates that the fields may contain a mixture of EBCDIC and DBCS data.

TRANSP   Specifies whether the background of an alphanumeric field is transparent or opaque. YES allows an underlying graphic to be visible behind the characters.

Coding example (no extended attributes)

This example shows the basic parameters you should always code in a DFHMSD macro. You can use this as a model for your own mapsets if you don't need extended highlighting.

```
TTRSET1   DFHMSD TYPE=&SYSPARM,                                 X
                 LANG=COBOL,                                    X
                 MODE=INOUT,                                    X
                 TERM=3270-2,                                   X
                 CTRL=FREEKB,                                   X
                 STORAGE=AUTO,                                  X
                 TIOAPFX=YES
```

Coding example (extended attributes)

This example shows how to provide for extended color and highlighting attributes in both the physical and the symbolic mapsets.

```
TTRSET1   DFHMSD TYPE=&SYSPARM,                                 X
                 LANG=COBOL,                                    X
                 MODE=INOUT,                                    X
                 TERM=3270-2,                                   X
                 CTRL=FREEKB,                                   X
                 STORAGE=AUTO,                                  X
                 TIOAPFX=YES,                                   X
                 DSATTS=(COLOR,HILIGHT),                        X
                 MAPATTS=(COLOR,HILIGHT)
```

The DFHMDI macro instruction

Function

The DFHMDI macro instruction defines a map within a mapset. It supplies the map's name and other important information, such as the map's size and position. In addition, the DFHMDI macro can override defaults specified in a DFHMSD macro. The parameters listed are the ones that you're most likely to use. (By the way, since all the parameters are optional and can be coded in any order, they all start with a comma to show you have to separate parameters with commas. However, you don't code a comma before the first parameter you use.)

Syntax

```
name DFHMDI  [, SIZE=(line,column) ]
             [, LINE= { line-number | NEXT | SAME } ]
             [, COLUMN= { column-number | NEXT | SAME } ]
             [, JUSTIFY=( [ LEFT | RIGHT ][, FIRST | LAST ] ) ]
             [, HEADER=YES ]
             [, TRAILER=YES ]
             [, FIELDS=NO ]
             [, CTRL=(option,option...) ]
             [, TIOAPFX= { YES | NO } ]
             [, DSATTS=(type,type...) ]
             [, MAPATTS=(type,type...) ]
             [, EXTATT= { YES | NO | MAPONLY } ]
             [, COLOR= { color | DEFAULT } ]
             [, HILIGHT= { OFF | BLINK | REVERSE | UNDERLINE } ]
             [, VALIDN= { MUSTENTER | MUSTFILL | TRIGGER | USEREXIT } ]
             [, CURSLOC= { YES | NO } ]
             [, OUTLINE= { BOX | ( [,LEFT] [,RIGHT] [,OVER] [,UNDER] ) } ]
             [, SOSI= { YES | NO } ]
             [, TRANSP= { YES | NO } ]
```

Parameters

name	The 1- to 7-character name of the map. Each map within a mapset must have a unique name.
SIZE	Specifies the size of the map in lines and columns. Common 3270 screen sizes are SIZE=(24,80) and SIZE=(43,80).
LINE	Specifies the starting line number for the map. Usually coded LINE=1. LINE=NEXT tells BMS to place the map on the next available line on the screen. LINE=SAME tells BMS to place the map in the next available position on the same line as the last map sent to the terminal.
COLUMN	Specifies the starting column number for the map. Usually coded COLUMN=1. COLUMN=NEXT tells BMS to place the map in the next available screen column. COLUMN=SAME tells BMS to use the COLUMN parameter from the most recently sent map that specifies the same combination of JUSTIFY options.

JUSTIFY	Specifies how the map should be aligned on the screen. The first set of JUSTIFY options (LEFT and RIGHT) specifies whether the COLUMN parameter refers to columns counted from the left or right edge of the screen. The second set of JUSTIFY options (FIRST and LAST) specifies whether the map should be placed at the top or bottom of the screen, allowing for header or trailer maps.
HEADER	If you code HEADER=YES, the map is treated as a header map. Used in building logical messages.
TRAILER	If you code TRAILER=YES, the map is treated as a trailer map. Used in building logical messages.
FIELDS	If you code FIELDS=NO, it specifies that the map has no fields.
CTRL	Specifies a list of control options in effect for the map. Valid options are:

	FREEKB	Unlocks the terminal keyboard after each output operation.
	FRSET	Turns off the MDT bit in each attribute byte in the terminal's buffer before each output operation. Use FRSET if you want the terminal to transmit only data that the operator modifies.
	ALARM	Sounds the terminal's alarm.
	PRINT	Causes a 3270 printer to start printing.
	length	Specifies how line endings are to be formatted for printed data. L40, L64, and L80 cause a new line to be formatted every 40, 64, or 80 characters, and HONEOM honors the printer's default line length.

TIOAPFX	YES generates a 12-byte FILLER item at the beginning of each symbolic map. It should always be specified for COBOL programs, although it can be specified on the DFHMSD macro instead of here. NO is the default.
DSATTS	Specifies which extended attributes are to be supported in the symbolic map. You can specify any or all of the following:

COLOR	Extended color
HILIGHT	Extended highlighting
OUTLINE	Field outlining
PS	Programmed symbols
SOSI	Two-byte SO/SI characters
TRANSP	Background transparency
VALIDN	Validation

MAPATTS	Specifies which extended attributes are to be supported in the physical map. You can specify any or all of the same types that are valid for the DSATTS parameter. You can specify physical map support for an attribute type that's not specified in the DSATTS parameter, but not the other way around: Any attribute type you specify in the DSATTS parameter should also be specified in the MAPATTS parameter.
EXTATT	Supported for compatibility with releases of CICS before 1.7; for new programs, use DSATTS and MAPATTS instead. Specifies whether or not the map should support extended attributes. If you specify EXTATT=YES, both the physical and symbolic map support attributes for extended color, extended highlighting, programmed symbols, and validation.

COLOR	Specifies a default extended color for the map. You may specify DEFAULT for the terminal's default color, or you may specify BLUE, RED, PINK, GREEN, TURQUOISE, YELLOW, or NEUTRAL (white).
HILIGHT	Specifies a default extended highlighting for the map. You may specify OFF for no highlighting, or BLINK, REVERSE, or UNDERLINE.
VALIDN	Specifies a default field validation for the map. MUSTENTER means the operator must enter some data into each field; MUSTFILL means the operator must completely fill each field; TRIGGER means that fields are transmitted from the terminal one at a time as data is entered into them; and USEREXIT means that fields are processed by the BMS global user exits, XBMIN and XBMOUT.
CURSLOC	Specifies whether or not BMS is to indicate the location of the cursor on an input operation by placing a flag value in the symbolic map following a RECEIVE MAP command. If you code CURSORLOC=YES, the program can test to see if the user placed the cursor in a field by testing that field's flag byte (suffix F) against the BMS constant DFHCURSR.
OUTLINE	Specifies that lines should be included around the fields. If you specify BOX, a box is drawn around the fields. You can also use the LEFT, RIGHT, OVER, and UNDER parameters in any combination to place lines around the fields.
SOSI	If YES is specified, it indicates that the fields may contain a mixture of EBCDIC and DBCS data.
TRANSP	Specifies whether the background of an alphanumeric field is transparent or opaque. YES allows an underlying graphic to be visible behind the characters.

Coding example (no extended attributes or message building)

This example shows you how to define a full-screen (24 by 80) map that doesn't require extended attributes or message building facilities. Just three parameters are specified: SIZE, LINE, and COLUMN.

```
MNTMAP1  DFHMDI SIZE=(24,80),                                    X
                LINE=1,                                          X
                COLUMN=1
```

Coding example (extended attributes)

This example shows how to provide for extended color and highlight attributes in both the physical and symbolic map.

```
MNTMAP1  DFHMDI SIZE(24,80),                                     X
                LINE=1,                                          X
                COLUMN=1,                                        X
                DSATTS=(COLOR,HILIGHT),                          X
                MAPATTS=(COLOR,HILIGHT)
```

Coding example (message building)

This example shows three DFHMDI macros for a message building application. When BMS message building is used (and it's not a common application), the purpose is usually to produce reports that are displayed or printed on 3270 devices. As a result, messages typically include header and trailer information before and after the body of the report. So in this example, the first DFHMDI macro is for a header map, the second is for a one-line detail map, and the third is for a trailer map. The header map is positioned at the top of the screen; the detail map is positioned in the first column of the next available line; and the trailer map is positioned at the bottom of the screen.

```
LSTMAP1  DFHMDI SIZE=(5,80),                                     X
                JUSTIFY=FIRST,                                   X
                HEADER=YES
         .
         .
LSTMAP2  DFHMDI SIZE=(1,80),                                     X
                LINE=NEXT,                                       X
                COLUMN=1
         .
         .
LSTMAP3  DFHMDI SIZE=(2,80),                                     X
                JUSTIFY=LAST,                                    X
                TRAILER=YES
```

The DFHMDF macro instruction

Function

The DFHMDF macro instruction defines a map field by specifying its position, length, and attributes. Actually, DFHMDF defines an attribute byte. To define a protected field, you code one DFHMDF macro, since a protected field can continue all the way to the next field without its contents being affected. But to define an unprotected field that's not followed immediately by another field, you code two DFHMDF macros: one to mark the beginning of the field and the other to mark the end. The parameters listed are the ones that you're most likely to use.

Syntax

```
name   DFHMDF POS= { (line,column) | number }
              [, LENGTH=field-length ]
              [, ATTRB=( [, { NORM | BRT | DRK } ]
                         [, { ASKIP | PROT | UNPROT [, NUM ] } ]
                         [, IC ] [, FSET ] [, DET ] ) ]
              [, { INITIAL='literal' | XINIT=hex-value | GINIT=dcbs-value } ]
              [, OCCURS=number ]
              [, GRPNAME=group-name ]
              [, PICIN='picture-string' ]
              [, PICOUT='picture-string' ]
              [, COLOR= { color | DEFAULT } ]
              [, HILIGHT= { OFF | BLINK | REVERSE | UNDERLINE } ]
              [, VALIDN= { MUSTENTER | MUSTFILL | TRIGGER | USEREXIT } ]
              [, OUTLINE= { BOX | ( [,LEFT] [,RIGHT] [,OVER] [,UNDER] ) } ]
              [, SOSI= { YES | NO } ]
              [, TRANSP= {YES | NO } ]
```

Parameters

name	The 1- to 29-character name for the field. If omitted, the field is not included in the symbolic map.
POS	Specifies the line and column position of the field's attribute byte. If *number* is used, it specifies the displacement of the field's attribute byte (relative to zero) from the beginning of the map.
LENGTH	Specifies the length of the field, or group of fields, not including the attribute byte. This length is used in the symbolic map, but doesn't imply any specific field length on the display. So the attributes specified for a particular field continue until the attribute byte for the next field is encountered.

ATTRB
Specifies one or more attribute byte settings for the field. If omitted, the default is NORM,ASKIP. If any options are specified, the default becomes NORM,UNPROT.

NORM	The field is displayed with regular intensity.
BRT	The field is displayed with high intensity.
DRK	The field is not displayed on the screen.
ASKIP	The field is protected, and the cursor will automatically skip over it.
PROT	The field is protected, so data may not be keyed into it.
UNPROT	The field is unprotected, so data may be keyed into it.
NUM	The field is numeric and is right-justified and zero-filled. If omitted, the field is assumed to be alphanumeric and is left-justified and space-filled.
IC	Specifies that the cursor should be located at the start of the data field.
FSET	Specifies that the MDT bit in the attribute byte should be turned on before the map is sent to the terminal.
DET	Specifies that the field is detectable. The first character of a 3270 detectable field must be a question mark (?), greater-than sign (>), ampersand (&), blank, or null. This option is used with two hardware features, the cursor select key and the light pen. It cannot be specified if DRK is specified.

INITIAL
Specifies the starting value of the field.

XINIT
Specifies a hexadecimal initial value for the field. The hex value can be one or more two-character hex numbers, like XINIT=7EC1.

GINIT
Specifies a DBCS character string as the initial value for the field.

OCCURS
Specifies that the indicated number of entries for this field should be generated in the symbolic map as an array. That way, the field occurrences can then be subscripted in the program and the need for a unique name for each field is bypassed. The OCCURS and GRPNAME parameters are mutually exclusive.

GRPNAME
Specifies that the field should be grouped in the symbolic map with other fields with the same GRPNAME. All fields within a group must be coded in sequence in the mapset and must have labels. The ATTRB parameter specified in the first field of the group will apply to all of the fields within the group.

PICIN
Specifies a COBOL PICTURE string that defines the format of the data on input. Example: PICIN='999V99'. The length defined by PICIN must agree with the LENGTH parameter. If omitted, PICIN='X(n)' will be assumed, where *n* is the value specified for the LENGTH parameter.

PICOUT
Specifies a COBOL PICTURE string defining the format of the data on output. Example: PICOUT='Z9.99'. The length defined by PICOUT must agree with the LENGTH parameter.

COLOR
Specifies an extended color for the field. You may specify DEFAULT for the terminal's default color, or you may specify BLUE, RED, PINK, GREEN, TURQUOISE, YELLOW, or NEUTRAL (white).

HILIGHT   Specifies extended highlighting for the field. You may specify OFF for no highlighting, or BLINK, REVERSE, or UNDERLINE.

VALIDN   Specifies field validation for the field. MUSTENTER means the operator must enter some data into the field; MUSTFILL means the operator must completely fill the field; TRIGGER means that the field is transmitted from the terminal as soon as data is entered into it; and USEREXIT means that the field is processed by the BMS global user exits, XBMIN and XBMOUT.

OUTLINE   Specifies that lines should be included around the field. If you specify BOX, a box is drawn around the field. You can also use the LEFT, RIGHT, OVER, and UNDER parameters in any combination to place lines around the field.

SOSI   If YES is specified, it indicates that the field may contain a mixture of EBCDIC and DBCS data.

TRANSP   Specifies whether the background of an alphanumeric field is transparent or opaque. YES allows an underlying graphic to be visible behind the characters.

Coding example (constant field)

In this example, two DFHMDF macros define a heading in line 1 of the screen that contains the word "INQMAP1" in columns 2 through 8 and the words "Customer Inquiry" in columns 21 through 36.

```
DFHMDF POS=(1,1),                                               X
       LENGTH=7,                                                X
       ATTRB=(NORM,PROT),                                       X
       COLOR=BLUE,                                              X
       INITIAL='INQMAP1'
DFHMDF POS=(1,20),                                              X
       LENGTH=16,                                               X
       ATTRB=(NORM,PROT),                                       X
       COLOR=GREEN,                                             X
       INITIAL='Customer Inquiry'
```

Coding example (alphanumeric data entry field)

This example shows how to code three DFHMDF macros for an alphanumeric data entry field: one for the field's caption (a constant field), one to mark the start of the field, and one to mark the end of the field. The last DFHMDF macro specifies ATTRB=ASKIP, so the cursor will advance to the next unprotected screen field when it reaches the end of this field. Only the data field will be manipulated in the CICS program, so it's the only field that's given a name.

```
          DFHMDF POS=(2,1),                             X
                 LENGTH=26,                              X
                 ATTRB=(NORM,PROT),                      X
                 COLOR=GREEN,                            X
                 INITIAL='Customer number. . . . . .'
CUSTNO    DFHMDF POS=(2,28),                             X
                 LENGTH=6,                               X
                 ATTRB=(NORM,UNPROT),                    X
                 COLOR=TURQUOISE,                        X
                 INITIAL='_____'
          DFHMDF POS=(2,35),                             X
                 LENGTH=1,                               X
                 ATTRB=ASKIP
```

Coding example (numeric data entry field)

This example shows how to code a numeric data entry field. Like the non-numeric data entry field, three DFHMDF macros are required: one to define the caption, one to define the start of the field, and one to define the end of the field. The ATTRB parameter of the second DFHMDF macro specifies the NUM option to enable numeric data entry.

```
          DFHMDF POS=(2,1),                             X
                 LENGTH=24,                              X
                 ATTRB=(NORM,PROT),                      X
                 COLOR=GREEN,                            X
                 INITIAL='Quantity . . . . . . . .'
QTY       DFHMDF POS=(2,26),                             X
                 LENGTH=5,                               X
                 ATTRB=(NORM,NUM,UNPROT),                X
                 COLOR=TURQUOISE,                        X
                 INITIAL='_____'
          DFHMDF POS=(2,32),                             X
                 LENGTH=1,                               X
                 ATTRB=ASKIP
```

Coding example (alphanumeric display-only data field)

This example shows how to define a field for alphanumeric output data that changes during the course of the program. Two DFHMDF macros are coded: one to define the field's caption, the other to define the field itself. The data to be displayed in this field will be supplied by the COBOL program via the symbolic map.

```
          DFHMDF POS=(2,1),                              X
                 LENGTH=24,                              X
                 ATTRB=(NORM,PROT),                      X
                 COLOR=GREEN,                            X
                 INITIAL='Name and address . . . . :'
LNAME     DFHMDF POS=(2,26),                             X
                 LENGTH=30,                              X
                 ATTRB=(NORM,PROT),                      X
                 COLOR=TURQUOISE
```

Coding example (numeric display-only data field)

This example shows how to define a field for numeric output data. The only real difference between this definition and the one for the alphanumeric field above is the addition of the PICOUT parameter. It formats the numeric display.

```
          DFHMDF POS=(2,1),                              X
                 LENGTH=24,                              X
                 ATTRB=(NORM,PROT),                      X
                 COLOR=GREEN,                            X
                 INITIAL='Balance due. . . . . . :'
BALDUE    DFHMDF POS=(2,26),                             X
                 LENGTH=13,                              X
                 ATTRB=(NORM,PROT),                      X
                 COLOR=TURQUOISE,                        X
                 PICOUT='ZZ,ZZZ,ZZ9.99'
```

Coding example (message area)

This example shows how to code the DFHMDF macro instructions to define a two-line message area: line 23 is used for warning messages, and line 24 is used to display attention key assignments. The third DFHMDF statement, labeled DUMMY, defines a one-byte field whose attributes are set to dark, protected, and FSET. This field serves one purpose: It prevents the MAPFAIL condition from being raised unless the user presses the Clear key or a PA key. I suggest you include a field like this in all your maps.

```
MESSAGE    DFHMDF POS=(23,1),                                    X
                  LENGTH=79,                                     X
                  ATTRB=(BRT,PROT),                              X
                  COLOR=YELLOW
           DFHMDF POS=(24,1),                                    X
                  LENGTH=19,                                     X
                  ATTRB=(NORM,PROT),                             X
                  COLOR=BLUE,                                    X
                  INITIAL='F3=Exit   F12=Cancel'
DUMMY      DFHMDF POS=(24,79),                                   X
                  LENGTH=1,                                      X
                  ATTRB=(DRK,PROT,FSET),                         X
                  INITIAL=' '
```

The symbolic map

You use a symbolic map in a COBOL program to access data sent to and received from a terminal screen. When you assemble a mapset, a symbolic map is created for each map in the mapset and placed in a copy library. Then, you use the Copy statement to include the symbolic maps in the Working-Storage Section of your COBOL program.

BMS-generated symbolic maps

When BMS generates a symbolic map, it uses the 7-character names you supply in the mapset to form 8-character data names. In other words, a one-character suffix is added to the end of each name to identify the data name's function. In the symbolic map, the 8-character data names are coded in a specific order to match the data structure BMS requires. To use a BMS-generated symbolic map, however, you don't have to know the details of that structure. You just have to know what the generated data names mean.

- For each named DFHMDF macro in a map, BMS generates several data names. Figure 9-7 gives the suffix associated with each data name, a brief description of the field, and an example of the complete data name for two map fields named CUSTNO and LNAME.

- You can use the data names in the symbolic map in your COBOL program as needed. For example, to format the last-name output field with data from a customer master record so it can be displayed on the screen, you could code a statement like this:

    ```
    MOVE CM-LAST-NAME TO LNAMEO
    ```

- The A and F (for *flag byte*) fields define the same byte of the symbolic map data area. As a result, you can use these data names interchangeably.

- For each DFHMDI macro in a mapset, BMS adds I and O to the end of the map name to form group names that are used to define the entire symbolic map for input (I) and output (O). This is shown in the symbolic map in figure 9-8. Here, INQMAP1 was the map name coded on the DFHMDI macro, so BMS generated the group names INQMAP1I and INQMAP1O.

- A Redefines clause is used so that both the 01-level names for a map refer to the same storage. That means that the 03-level I and O fields—like LNAMEI and LNAMEO—occupy the same storage location. This allows the Picture clauses to differ according to the PICIN and PICOUT parameters on the DFHMDF macro.

The data name suffixes used for DFHMDF fields in a symbolic map

Suffix	Example	Usage
L	CUSTNOL LNAMEL	A binary halfword (PIC S9(4) COMP) that contains the length of the data sent from the screen field to the program. This may be different from the length of the field specified in the DFHMDF LENGTH parameter, depending on how many characters the user actually entered into the field. If the user doesn't enter any data, the length field is set to zero.
F	CUSTNOF LNAMEF	A single-character field (PIC X) that contains hexadecimal 80 if the user made a change to the field, but no data was transmitted (for example, the user used the Delete key to clear the field). Otherwise, it contains LOW-VALUE.
A	CUSTNOA LNAMEA	A single-character field that contains the attribute byte for output operations. Occupies the same storage location as the F field.
C	CUSTNOC LNAMEC	A single-character field that contains the attribute for extended color. Generated only if DSATTS=COLOR is specified.
P	CUSTNOP LNAMEP	A single-character field that contains the attribute for programmed symbols. Generated only if DSATTS=PS is specified.
H	CUSTNOH LNAMEH	A single-character field that contains the attribute for extended highlighting. Generated only if DSATTS=HILIGHT is specified.
V	CUSTNOV LNAMEV	A single-character field that contains the attribute for validation. Generated only if DSATTS=VALIDN is specified.
M	CUSTNOM LNAMEM	A single-character field that contains the attribute for SO/SI characters. Generated only is DSATTS=SOSI is specified.
T	CUSTNOT LNAMET	A single-character field that contains the attribute for background transparency. Generated only if DSATTS=TRANSP is specified.
U	CUSTNOU LNAMEU	A single-character field that contains the attribute for field outlining. Generated only if DSATTS=OUTLINE is specified.
I	CUSTNOI LNAMEI	The input data field.
O	CUSTNOO LNAMEO	The output data field. Occupies the same storage location as the input field.

Figure 9-7

A BMS-generated symbolic map

```
01  INQMAP1I.
    03  FILLER                          PIC X(12).
    03  TRANIDL                         PIC S9(4) COMP.
    03  TRANIDF                         PIC X.
    03  FILLER REDEFINES TRANIDF.
        05  TRANIDA                     PIC X.
    03  TRANIDI                         PIC X(4).
    03  CUSTNOL                         PIC S9(4) COMP.
    03  CUSTNOF                         PIC X.
    03  FILLER REDEFINES CUSTNOF.
        05  CUSTNOA                     PIC X.
    03  CUSTNOI                         PIC X(6).
    03  LNAMEL                          PIC S9(4) COMP.
    03  LNAMEF                          PIC X.
    03  FILLER REDEFINES LNAMEF.
        05  LNAMEA                      PIC X.
    03  LNAMEI                          PIC X(30).
    03  FNAMEL                          PIC S9(4) COMP.
    03  FNAMEF                          PIC X.
    03  FILLER REDEFINES FNAMEF.
        05  FNAMEA                      PIC X.
    03  FNAMEI                          PIC X(20).
    03  ADDRL                           PIC S9(4) COMP.
    03  ADDRF                           PIC X.
    03  FILLER REDEFINES ADDRF.
        05  ADDRA                       PIC X.
    03  ADDRI                           PIC X(30).
    03  CITYL                           PIC S9(4) COMP.
    03  CITYF                           PIC X.
    03  FILLER REDEFINES CITYF.
        05  CITYA                       PIC X.
    03  CITYI                           PIC X(20).
    03  STATEL                          PIC S9(4) COMP.
    03  STATEF                          PIC X.
    03  FILLER REDEFINES STATEF.
        05  STATEA                      PIC X.
    03  STATEI                          PIC X(2).
    03  ZIPCODEL                        PIC S9(4) COMP.
    03  ZIPCODEF                        PIC X.
    03  FILLER REDEFINES ZIPCODEF.
        05  ZIPCODEA                    PIC X.
    03  ZIPCODEI                        PIC X(10).
    03  MESSAGEL                        PIC S9(4) COMP.
    03  MESSAGEF                        PIC X.
    03  FILLER REDEFINES MESSAGEF.
        05  MESSAGEA                    PIC X.
    03  MESSAGEI                        PIC X(79).
    03  DUMMYL                          PIC S9(4) COMP.
    03  DUMMYF                          PIC X.
    03  FILLER REDEFINES DUMMYF.
        05  DUMMYA                      PIC X.
    03  DUMMYI                          PIC X(1).
```

Figure 9-8 (part 1 of 2)

A BMS-generated symbolic map   **Page 2**

```
01  INQMAP1O REDEFINES INQMAP1I.
    03  FILLER                        PIC X(12).
    03  FILLER                        PIC X(3).
    03  TRANIDO                       PIC X(4).
    03  FILLER                        PIC X(3).
    03  CUSTNOO                       PIC X(6).
    03  FILLER                        PIC X(3).
    03  LNAMEO                        PIC X(30).
    03  FILLER                        PIC X(3).
    03  FNAMEO                        PIC X(20).
    03  FILLER                        PIC X(3).
    03  ADDRO                         PIC X(30).
    03  FILLER                        PIC X(3).
    03  CITYO                         PIC X(20).
    03  FILLER                        PIC X(3).
    03  STATEO                        PIC X(2).
    03  FILLER                        PIC X(3).
    03  ZIPCODEO                      PIC X(10).
    03  FILLER                        PIC X(3).
    03  MESSAGEO                      PIC X(79).
    03  FILLER                        PIC X(3).
    03  DUMMYO                        PIC X(1).
```

Figure 9-8 (part 2 of 2)

How to create your own symbolic map

In some cases, you'll need to discard the symbolic map generated by BMS and code your own (this is illustrated by the order entry program in Unit 6). Figure 9-9 shows a symbolic map that replaces the one shown in figure 9-8. Here are some simple rules to follow when you create a symbolic map:

1. Code only one 01-level item, rather than separate 01-level items that redefine one another for input and output purposes.

2. Code a 12-byte FILLER item at the beginning of each map.

3. For each labeled map field, code a group of 05-level items, following these rules to create the data names:

   a. Start each name with a 2- or 3-character prefix that relates the data name to the 01-level item.

   b. Include one character to identify the field's function: L for the length field, A for the attribute field, and D for the data field.

   c. If you need different pictures for input and output, create a fourth data name that redefines the data field. Then, identify the input and output data fields with the characters I and O.

   d. If you use extended attributes, you'll have to code additional attribute fields. If you use the DSATTS parameter, add attribute byte fields for the attributes specified on the parameter between the basic attribute field and the data field. Use the characters C and H to identify extended color and extended highlighting attributes. If it's an older mapset that specifies EXTATT=YES, add four attribute byte fields. Use the characters C, P, H, and V, in that order, to identify extended color, highlighting, programmed symbols, and validation attributes.

4. Separate each set of data names with a blank comment line.

5. Align the elements of the symbolic map so it's easy to read.

A programmer-generated symbolic map

```
 01  INQMAP1.
*
     05  FILLER              PIC X(12).
*
     05  INQ-L-TRANID1       PIC S9(4) COMP.
     05  INQ-A-TRANID1       PIC X.
     05  INQ-D-TRANID1       PIC X(4).
*
     05  INQ-L-CUSTNO        PIC S9(4) COMP.
     05  INQ-A-CUSTNO        PIC X.
     05  INQ-D-CUSTNO        PIC X(6).
*
     05  INQ-L-LNAME         PIC S9(4) COMP.
     05  INQ-A-LNAME         PIC X.
     05  INQ-D-LNAME         PIC X(30).
*
     05  INQ-L-FNAME         PIC S9(4) COMP.
     05  INQ-A-FNAME         PIC X.
     05  INQ-D-FNAME         PIC X(20).
*
     05  INQ-L-ADDR          PIC S9(4) COMP.
     05  INQ-A-ADDR          PIC X.
     05  INQ-D-ADDR          PIC X(30).
*
     05  INQ-L-CITY          PIC S9(4) COMP.
     05  INQ-A-CITY          PIC X.
     05  INQ-D-CITY          PIC X(20).
*
     05  INQ-L-STATE         PIC S9(4) COMP.
     05  INQ-A-STATE         PIC X.
     05  INQ-D-STATE         PIC X(2).
*
     05  INQ-L-ZIPCODE       PIC S9(4) COMP.
     05  INQ-A-ZIPCODE       PIC X.
     05  INQ-D-ZIPCODE       PIC X(10).
*
     05  INQ-L-MESSAGE       PIC S9(4) COMP.
     05  INQ-A-MESSAGE       PIC X.
     05  INQ-D-MESSAGE       PIC X(79).
*
     05  INQ-L-DUMMY         PIC S9(4) COMP.
     05  INQ-A-DUMMY         PIC X.
     05  INQ-D-DUMMY         PIC X.
```

Note: When you create your own symbolic map, it's up to you to make sure that any changes to the mapset are reflected in your symbolic map. This can be a problem as an application is maintained over time. So check whether your installation allows you to create your own symbolic maps before you get started.

Figure 9-9

A complete BMS mapset

Figure 9-10 is the BMS mapset for the Customer Inquiry screen shown in figure 9-5 that resulted in the symbolic map shown in figure 9-8. This mapset includes only one map. But Unit 5 gives you an example of a mapset that has two maps, so you can see how multiple maps affect the code. Unit 6 gives you three additional mapsets to use as models in your own work. And Unit 10 shows you two macros you can add to your mapsets when you use them to create HTML documents instead of 3270 displays.

The BMS mapset for a 3270 display   Page 1

```
PRINT NOGEN
INQSET1   DFHMSD TYPE=&SYSPARM,                                          X
                 LANG=COBOL,                                            X
                 MODE=INOUT,                                            X
                 TERM=3270-2,                                           X
                 CTRL=FREEKB,                                           X
                 STORAGE=AUTO,                                          X
                 TIOAPFX=YES
************************************************************************
INQMAP1   DFHMDI SIZE=(24,80),                                          X
                 LINE=1,                                                X
                 COLUMN=1
************************************************************************
          DFHMDF POS=(1,1),                                             X
                 LENGTH=7,                                              X
                 ATTRB=(NORM,PROT),                                     X
                 COLOR=BLUE,                                            X
                 INITIAL='INQMAP1'
          DFHMDF POS=(1,20),                                            X
                 LENGTH=16,                                             X
                 ATTRB=(NORM,PROT),                                     X
                 COLOR=GREEN,                                           X
                 INITIAL='Customer Inquiry'
TRANID    DFHMDF POS=(1,76),                                            X
                 LENGTH=4,                                              X
                 ATTRB=(NORM,PROT),                                     X
                 COLOR=BLUE,                                            X
                 INITIAL='XXXX'
************************************************************************
          DFHMDF POS=(3,1),                                             X
                 LENGTH=42,                                             X
                 ATTRB=(NORM,PROT),                                     X
                 COLOR=NEUTRAL,                                         X
                 INITIAL='Type a customer number.  Then press Enter.'
          DFHMDF POS=(5,1),                                             X
                 LENGTH=24,                                             X
                 ATTRB=(NORM,PROT),                                     X
                 COLOR=GREEN,                                           X
                 INITIAL='Customer number. . . . .'
```

Figure 9-10 (part 1 of 2)

The BMS mapset for a 3270 display   Page 2

```
CUSTNO     DFHMDF POS=(5,26),                                         X
                  LENGTH=6,                                           X
                  ATTRB=(NORM,UNPROT,IC),                             X
                  COLOR=TURQUOISE,                                    X
                  INITIAL='_____'
           DFHMDF POS=(5,33),                                         X
                  LENGTH=1,                                           X
                  ATTRB=ASKIP
*******************************************************************
           DFHMDF POS=(7,1),                                          X
                  LENGTH=24,                                          X
                  ATTRB=(NORM,PROT),                                  X
                  COLOR=GREEN,                                        X
                  INITIAL='Name and address . . . :'
LNAME      DFHMDF POS=(7,26),                                         X
                  LENGTH=30,                                          X
                  ATTRB=(NORM,PROT),                                  X
                  COLOR=TURQUOISE
FNAME      DFHMDF POS=(8,26),                                         X
                  LENGTH=20,                                          X
                  ATTRB=(NORM,PROT),                                  X
                  COLOR=TURQUOISE
ADDR       DFHMDF POS=(9,26),                                         X
                  LENGTH=30,                                          X
                  ATTRB=(NORM,PROT),                                  X
                  COLOR=TURQUOISE
CITY       DFHMDF POS=(10,26),                                        X
                  LENGTH=20,                                          X
                  ATTRB=(NORM,PROT),                                  X
                  COLOR=TURQUOISE
STATE      DFHMDF POS=(10,47),                                        X
                  LENGTH=2,                                           X
                  ATTRB=(NORM,PROT),                                  X
                  COLOR=TURQUOISE
ZIPCODE    DFHMDF POS=(10,50),                                        X
                  LENGTH=10,                                          X
                  ATTRB=(NORM,PROT),                                  X
                  COLOR=TURQUOISE
*******************************************************************
MESSAGE    DFHMDF POS=(23,1),                                         X
                  LENGTH=79,                                          X
                  ATTRB=(BRT,PROT),                                   X
                  COLOR=YELLOW
           DFHMDF POS=(24,1),                                         X
                  LENGTH=20,                                          X
                  ATTRB=(NORM,PROT),                                  X
                  COLOR=BLUE,                                         X
                  INITIAL='F3=Exit    F12=Cancel'
DUMMY      DFHMDF POS=(24,79),                                        X
                  LENGTH=1,                                           X
                  ATTRB=(DRK,PROT,FSET),                              X
                  INITIAL=' '
*******************************************************************
           DFHMSD TYPE=FINAL
           END
```

Figure 9-10 (part 2 of 2)

Unit 10

Creating HTML documents from BMS mapsets

With IBM's 3270 Bridge facility, all you have to do to web-enable your CICS applications is convert your BMS mapsets to *HTML templates* that format HTML pages instead of 3270 displays. Then, all of the CICS application code stays the same, but the screen display is suitable for a web browser. Although there are other ways to web-enable CICS applications that provide more flexibility, this approach is the easiest. So this unit shows you how to create HTML templates from BMS source code, and how to enhance the HTML output in some basic ways.

How to prepare an HTML template

Beginning with CICS TS 1.3, IBM added a JCL cataloged procedure named DFHMAPT that allows you to generate an HTML template from BMS macro source code. You use this procedure instead of DFHMAPS to assemble your mapset, as shown in figure 10-1. Figure 10-2 shows you how to invoke the procedure, and figure 10-3 shows you the procedure itself (the beginning of the new assembly step is shaded).

The conversion process

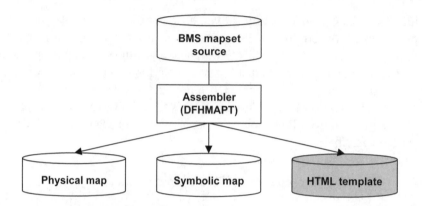

- If your BMS mapset specifies TYPE=&SYSPARM in the DFHMSD macro, the DFHMAPT procedure will produce an HTML template as well as the physical and symbolic map. Otherwise, you need to code TYPE=TEMPLATE to produce the HTML template.

Figure 10-1

JCL that invokes the DFHMAPT procedure

```
//MM01HTML JOB 36512,'R.MENENDEZ',NOTIFY=MM01
//JOBPROC  JCLLIB ORDER=CICSTS13.CICS.SDFHPROC
//MAPASM   EXEC DFHMAPT,
//              MAPLIB='MM01.CICS.LOADLIB',    TARGET LOADLIB FOR MAP
//              DSCTLIB='MM01.CICS.COPYLIB',   TARGET COPYLIB FOR DSECT
//              TEMPLIB='MM01.CICS.TEMPLIB',   TARGET FOR TEMPLATE
//              MAPNAME=INQSET1                MAPSET NAME
//COPY.SYSUT1 DD DSN=MM01.CICS.SOURCE(INQSET1),DISP=SHR    MAPSET SOURCE
/*
```

- Most of the JCL is the same as for invoking DFHMAPS. But besides specifying DFHMAPT in the EXEC statement, you may need to add a TEMPLIB parameter to identify the library that will contain the HTML template. You may also want to include a JCLLIB statement to specify the library where DFHMAPT is stored. And if your mapset includes a macro for customizing the HTML output, you may need to add a PARM parameter for the ASMTEMPL step (you'll see how to do this later in this unit).

Figure 10-2

The DFHMAPT procedure

```
//DFHMAPT PROC INDEX='CICSTS13.CICS',  FOR SDFHMAC
//              MAPLIB='CICSTS13.CICS.SDFHLOAD',  TARGET FOR MAP
//              DSCTLIB='CICSTS13.CICS.SDFHMAC',  TARGET FOR DSECT
//              TEMPLIB='CICSTS13.CICS.SDFHHTML', TARGET FOR TEMPLATES
//              MAPNAME=,                    NAME OF MAPSET - REQUIRED
//              A=,                          A=A FOR ALIGNED MAP
//              RMODE=24,                    24/ANY
//              ASMBLR=ASMA90,               ASSEMBLER PROGRAM NAME
//              REG=2048K,                   REGION FOR ASSEMBLY
//              OUTC=A,                      PRINT SYSOUT CLASS
//              WORK=SYSDA                   WORK FILE UNIT
//COPY      EXEC PGM=IEBGENER
//SYSPRINT DD SYSOUT=&OUTC
//SYSUT2    DD DSN=&&TEMPM,UNIT=&WORK,DISP=(,PASS),
//              DCB=(RECFM=FB,LRECL=80,BLKSIZE=400),
//              SPACE=(400,(50,50))
//SYSIN     DD DUMMY
//* SYSUT1 DD * NEEDED FOR THE MAP SOURCE
//ASMMAP    EXEC PGM=&ASMBLR,REGION=&REG,
//   PARM='SYSPARM(&A.MAP),DECK,NOOBJECT'
//SYSPRINT DD SYSOUT=&OUTC
//SYSLIB    DD DSN=&INDEX..SDFHMAC,DISP=SHR
//          DD DSN=SYS1.MACLIB,DISP=SHR
//SYSUT1    DD UNIT=&WORK,SPACE=(CYL,(5,5))
//SYSUT2    DD UNIT=&WORK,SPACE=(CYL,(5,5))
//SYSUT3    DD UNIT=&WORK,SPACE=(CYL,(5,5))
//SYSPUNCH DD DSN=&&MAP,DISP=(,PASS),UNIT=&WORK,
//              DCB=(RECFM=FB,LRECL=80,BLKSIZE=400),
//              SPACE=(400,(50,50))
//SYSIN     DD DSN=&&TEMPM,DISP=(OLD,PASS)
//LINKMAP   EXEC PGM=IEWL,PARM='LIST,LET,XREF,RMODE(&RMODE)'
//SYSPRINT DD SYSOUT=&OUTC
//SYSLMOD   DD DSN=&MAPLIB(&MAPNAME),DISP=SHR
//SYSUT1    DD UNIT=&WORK,SPACE=(1024,(20,20))
//SYSLIN    DD DSN=&&MAP,DISP=(OLD,DELETE)
//ASMDSECT EXEC PGM=&ASMBLR,REGION=&REG,
//   PARM='SYSPARM(&A.DSECT),DECK,NOOBJECT'
//SYSPRINT DD SYSOUT=&OUTC
//SYSLIB    DD DSN=&INDEX..SDFHMAC,DISP=SHR
//          DD DSN=SYS1.MACLIB,DISP=SHR
//SYSUT1    DD UNIT=&WORK,SPACE=(CYL,(5,5))
//SYSUT2    DD UNIT=&WORK,SPACE=(CYL,(5,5))
//SYSUT3    DD UNIT=&WORK,SPACE=(CYL,(5,5))
//SYSPUNCH DD DSN=&DSCTLIB(&MAPNAME),DISP=OLD
//SYSIN     DD DSN=&&TEMPM,DISP=(OLD,PASS)
//ASMTEMPL EXEC PGM=&ASMBLR,REGION=&REG,
//   PARM='SYSPARM(TEMPLATE),DECK,NOOBJECT'
//SYSPRINT DD SYSOUT=&OUTC
//SYSLIB    DD DSN=&INDEX..SDFHMAC,DISP=SHR
//          DD DSN=SYS1.MACLIB,DISP=SHR
//SYSUT1    DD UNIT=&WORK,SPACE=(CYL,(5,5))
//SYSUT2    DD UNIT=&WORK,SPACE=(CYL,(5,5))
//SYSUT3    DD UNIT=&WORK,SPACE=(CYL,(5,5))
//SYSPUNCH DD UNIT=&WORK,SPACE=(CYL,(5,5)),DISP=(,PASS)
//SYSIN     DD DSN=&&TEMPM,DISP=(OLD,DELETE)
//UPDTEMPL EXEC PGM=IEBUPDTE,REGION=&REG,PARM=NEW
//SYSPRINT DD SYSOUT=&OUTC
//SYSIN     DD DSN=*.ASMTEMPL.SYSPUNCH,DISP=(OLD,DELETE)
//SYSUT2    DD DSN=&TEMPLIB,DISP=SHR
```

Figure 10-3

Generated HTML output

Although generating an HTML template from a BMS mapset requires no additional BMS coding, chances are, you won't be happy with the result. That's because DFHMAPT simply translates the BMS macro code "as is," resulting in a basic screen that is not too appealing. Fortunately, IBM provides additional BMS macros that you can use to enhance the appearance of the HTML page.

Standard output

Figure 10-4 shows an example of the HTML template that's generated when you run DFHMAPT without adding any code to the BMS mapset. The HTML template contains all of the fields from the BMS mapset and functions in a manner similar to its 3270-display counterpart. In general, a standard generation will produce the following:

- Labels and fields from the map.

- Buttons for the Enter and Clear keys, PA1, PA2, and PA3 keys, function keys PF1 to PF24, and the Reset key.

- Additional hidden variables used to manage the HTML page.

- A JavaScript function called dfhsetcursor that sets the cursor position to the field whose name is the value in the DFH_CURSOR hidden variable.

Generated HTML output without any customization

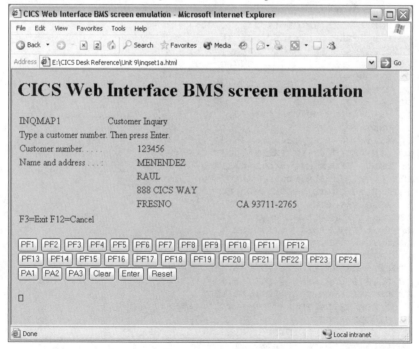

Figure 10-4

Customized output

Figure 10-5 shows the HTML template from figure 10-4 with some customization. There are two additional macro commands you can add to your BMS source code to customize an HTML template. If all you want to do is add text to the HTML template that will not be seen on the 3270 display, you simply code a DFHWBOUT macro at the place in the mapset where you want the text to appear.

However, if you want to add options that affect the look and feel of the HTML display, you use the DFHMDX macro. And to do that, you have to write your own macro definition, as summarized in the next topic. Among other things, the parameters of the DFHMDX macro allow you to:

- Modify the BMS colors for the text.
- Change the background color or specify a special background.
- Provide an HTML title for the HTML page.
- Suppress the generation of buttons for attention keys the program doesn't use.
- Change the appearance of the button keys, including the text associated with them.
- Include a masthead graphic for the HTML page.

Generated HTML output customized with the DFHMDX macro

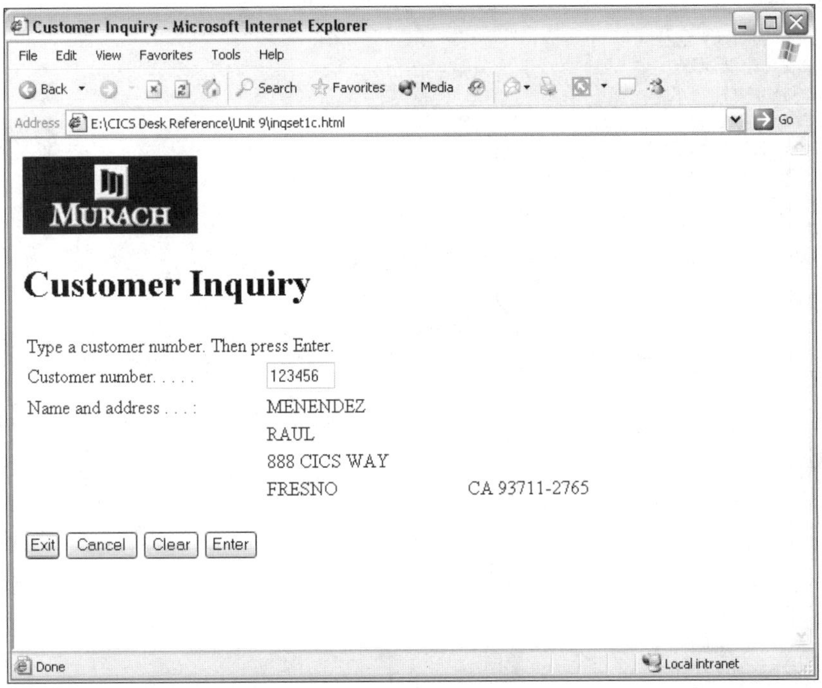

Note: You can customize the HTML template manually by editing the HTML code, but be careful! The order in which the fields appear on the HTML page must be kept. Otherwise, the 3270 Bridge facility won't be able to process the page.

Figure 10-5

How to create a customizing macro definition with DFHMDX

To customize an HTML template using the DFHMDX macro, you have to supply a complete macro definition that is invoked by the CICS-supplied assembler macros for BMS mapsets. This customizing macro definition must contain the following elements:

1. A MACRO statement to begin the definition.

2. The name of the macro. CICS assumes a default name of DFHMSX, so if you use a different name, you need to include a PARM parameter for the template assembly step in the JCL that invokes the DFHMAPT procedure, like this:

   `PARM.ASMTEMPL='SYSPARM(TEMPLATE,macro-name),DECK,NOOBJECT'`

3. Any number of DFHMDX macros.

4. A MEND statement to end the definition.

Figure 10-6 shows the customizing macro definition for the HTML page in figure 10-5. Like standard BMS macro definitions, a continuation character must be placed in column 72 to continue a macro on more than one line.

The definition of a customizing macro named DFHMSX

```
MACRO
DFHMSX
DFHMDX MAPSET=*,                                                       X
       MAP=INQMAP1,                                                    X
       ENTER='Enter',                                                  X
       RESET=NO,                                                       X
       CLEAR='Clear',                                                  X
       PF3='Exit',PF12='Cancel',                                       X
       TITLE='Customer Inquiry',                                       X
       BGCOLOR=WHITE,                                                  X
       SUPPRESS=((1,*),(24,*)),                                        X
       MASTHEAD=www.murach.com/images/murachlogo.gif
MEND
```

Figure 10-6

The DFHMDX macro

Function

The DFHMDX macro lets you customize the HTML template generated from the BMS macro code. With the exception of the MAPSET and MAP parameters, all of the parameters are optional.

Syntax

```
DFHMDX  MAPSET= { name | * }
        ,MAP= { name | * }
     [, MODULE=name ]
     [, DOCTYPE=doctype ]
     [, TITLE='title-text' ]
     [, MASTHEAD= { url | url,'alternate-text' } ]
     [, BACKGROUND=url ]
     [, BGCOLOR=color ]
     [, TEXT=color ]
     [, LINK=color ]
     [, VLINK=color ]
     [, ALINK=color ]
     [, bmscolor=color ]
     [, key=button ]
     [, RESET= { YES | NO | 'text' } ]
     [, SUPPRESS= ( (line,column...)[,...] [,HEAD] [,FOOT] ) ]
     [, ONLOAD='text' ]
     [, ONUNLOAD='text' ]
     [, PROPFONT= { NO | YES } ]
     [, CODEPAGE(data-value) ]
```

Parameters

MAPSET	Specifies the name of the mapset that contains the map the other parameters refer to. If you specify MAPSET=*, any parameters used become the default for subsequent mapsets within the same source file unless another DFHMDX macro is encountered.
MAP	Specifies the name of the map that the other parameters refer to. If you specify MAP=*, any parameters used become the default for subsequent maps within the same mapset unless another DFHMDX macro is encountered.
MODULE	Specifies the name of the link-edited load module.
DOCTYPE	Specifies the DTD (Document Type Definition) public identifier part of the <!doctype> tag that will appear in the HTML page.
TITLE	Specifies the value of the HTML title used in the first <h1> tag of the HTML page.
MASTHEAD	Specifies the URL location of a masthead graphic that's inserted into the HTML page before the first <h1> tag. If you specify a value for *alternate-text*, that text is inserted instead if the graphic can't be found.

BACKGROUND	Specifies the URL location of a graphic file that's used as a background for the HTML page.
BGCOLOR	Specifies the color of the HTML page background.
TEXT	Specifies the color for normal text.
LINK	Specifies the color for unvisited hypertext links on the HTML page.
VLINK	Specifies the color for visited hypertext links on the HTML page.
ALINK	Specifies the color for activated hypertext links on the HTML page.
bmscolor	Specifies a substitute color that replaces the bmscolor on the BMS map. For example:
	BLUE=green
	Valid bmscolors are BLUE, GREEN, NEUTRAL, PINK, RED, TURQUOISE, and YELLOW.
key	Specifies the text or image that's assigned to the simulated button for the corresponding 3270 attention key. For example:
	PF1='HELP'
	Valid key names are PF1-PF24, PA1-PA3, CLEAR, ENTER, and PEN.
RESET	Specifying YES allows the HTML reset function to be supported, so a Reset button is placed on the HTML page. You can also specify your own text to replace the default legend for the button.
SUPPRESS	Allows you to suppress map fields that you don't want to appear on the HTML page. The basic *line,column* format is the same as that for the POS option on the DFHMDF macro. You can specify an entire line by coding an * for the column value. You can also code multiple *line,column* pairs by enclosing each pair in parentheses, and separating them with commas. The HEAD and FOOT keywords let you suppress the heading and footer information for the HTML page.
ONLOAD	Specifies the JavaScript text that replaces the standard onLoad exception handler for the HTML page.
ONUNLOAD	Specifies the JavaScript text that's used as the onUnload exception handler for the HTML page.
PROPFONT	Specifying YES causes the text to be displayed in a proportional font where consecutive spaces are reduced to just a single space.
CODEPAGE	Specifies the IBM code page number specified in either the HOSTCODEPAGE option of a CICS DOCUMENT command or the SRVERCP option of the DFHCNV macro selected by the analyzer program.

Coding example (a single DFHMDX macro)

In this example, lines 1 and 24 of the maps within the INQSET2 mapset will not be displayed on the HTML page. Typically, you'll do this to remove any text that may be specific to the 3270 display.

```
DFHMDX MAPSET=INQSET2,MAP=*,SUPPRESS=((1,*),(24,*))
```

Coding example (multiple DFHMDX macros)

This example shows how two DFHMDX macros are applied to a map named INQMAP2. The first invocation of DFHMDX sets the default values that will be applied to all of the maps in this and subsequent mapsets. In this case, the PF3 button on all subsequent maps will display "Exit" and a Reset button won't be included in any of the maps. The second invocation of DFXMDX applies only to INQMAP2. It assigns name values to additional attention keys found only on that map, assigns an H1 title and a masthead company logo to be displayed at the top of the HTML page, and sets the page background color to neutral (white).

```
DFHMDX MAPSET=*,                                          X
       MAP=*,                                             X
       PF3='Exit',                                        X
       RESET=NO
DFHMDX MAPSET=*,                                          X
       MAP=INQMAP2,                                       X
       ENTER='Enter',                                     X
       PF5='First',PF6='Last',                            X
       PF7='Prev',PF8='Next',                             X
       PF12='Cancel',                                     X
       TITLE='Customer Inquiry',                          X
       MASTHEAD=www.murach.com/images/murachlogo.gif,     X
       BGCOLOR=NEUTRAL
```

The DFHWBOUT macro

Function

The DFHWBOUT macro lets you add text to an HTML page that does not appear on a 3270 display. If the macro is used before the first occurrence of a DFHMDF macro in a map, the text is placed in the <head> section of the HTML page. Otherwise, the text is placed in the body of the HTML page immediately following any text generated by a preceding DFHMDF macro.

Syntax

```
DFHWBOUT 'text'
        [, SOSI= { YES | NO } ]
```

Parameters

text	The text that's inserted into the HTML page.
SOSI	Specify YES if the text contains DBCS characters.

Coding example

In this example, a text message is inserted after a constant field. As you can see, this is a message that's appropriate for an HTML display, but not for a 3270 display.

```
DFHMDF POS=(1,20),                              X
       LENGTH=16,                               X
       ATTRB=(NORM,PROT),                       X
       COLOR=BLUE,                              X
       INITIAL='Customer Inquiry'
DFHWBOUT 'Do not use the browser Back button'
```

CICS program development aids

Unit 11

AMS commands to define and manipulate VSAM files

As an applications programmer, you often need to use *Access Method Services* (*AMS* or *IDCAMS*) to define and work with VSAM files. That's why this unit summarizes 9 of the AMS commands. Before that, though, this unit summarizes the coding rules for AMS commands and shows you how to use JCL to invoke AMS. If you have any trouble understanding the JCL or the AMS commands, please refer to *Murach's OS/390 and z/OS JCL* for an in-depth tutorial presentation.

How to code AMS commands

AMS commands have relatively complicated formatting requirements. To begin with, you can code AMS commands anywhere in columns 2 through 72. It's easy to code your commands in column 1, so be sure to avoid that common mistake.

Each AMS command follows this general format:

```
verb    parameters ...
```

Verb is the name of a command (like DEFINE CLUSTER or LISTCAT) and the *parameters* supply additional information that tells AMS what you want it to do.

Parameters, continuation lines, and abbreviations

- Most AMS commands require more than one parameter, and many of them require more parameters than you can code on a single line. To continue an AMS command from one line to the next, end the current line with one or more spaces followed by a hyphen, then continue coding on the next line. The hyphen can be in any position, but it must be the last character in the line or AMS will reject your command.

- There's no limit to the number of continuation lines you can use for a command. So I recommend that you code only one parameter on each line. That makes your AMS code much easier to read and modify.

- Most AMS parameters have one or more abbreviated forms. For example, you can abbreviate RECORDS as REC, and CONTROLINTERVALSIZE as CISZ or CNVSZ. Most of the abbreviations are more trouble to remember than they're worth. So I only use abbreviations for long parameters like CONTROLINTERVALSIZE or ALTERNATEINDEX.

Parameter values and subparameter lists

- Most parameters require values in parentheses, such as RECORDS(500).

- If a parameter requires more than one value, you code a subparameter list, separating the values with a space or comma, as in KEYS(5 0).

- Some parameters allow multiple sets of subparameter lists. For example, this KEYRANGES parameter consists of two subparameter lists, each containing two values:

```
KEYRANGES((0001 4000) (4001 7000))
```

Parameter groups and parentheses

Often, entire groups of parameters must be grouped together by parentheses, as shown in this command:

```
DEFINE CLUSTER ( NAME(AR.TRANS)         -
                 INDEXED                -
                 RECORDSIZE(150 200)    -
                 KEYS(12 0) )           -
          DATA  ( NAME(AR.TRANS.DATA)   -
                 VOLUMES(261 262)       -
                 CYLINDERS(50 50) )     -
         INDEX  ( NAME(AR.TRANS.INDEX)  -
                 VOLUMES(271) )
```

Here, the first four parameters—NAME, INDEXED, RECORDSIZE, and KEYS— are grouped together within parentheses, as required by the DEFINE CLUSTER command. This group is followed by two other groups, labeled DATA and INDEX. Notice that two parameters—NAME and VOLUMES—are coded more than once. AMS interprets the meaning of each depending on the group where the parameter is coded.

Comments

- To code a comment in an AMS command, start it with /* and end it with */, like this:

  ```
  /* THIS IS A COMMENT */
  ```

- Comments can be coded on separate lines or to the right of a command line. When they are coded on the right, the hyphen for a continuation comes after the comment.

How to invoke AMS using JCL

The program name for Access Method Services is IDCAMS. So to invoke AMS, you code an EXEC statement specifying IDCAMS in the PGM parameter. Then, you provide two DD statements: SYSPRINT and SYSIN. SYSPRINT directs AMS printed output, and SYSIN identifies the file that contains the AMS commands. Usually, you'll code the commands in the job stream as instream data, and you'll specify the SYSPRINT DD statement as a SYSOUT data set.

The DD statement for VSAM files

- If one of the AMS commands in your job requires that a VSAM data set be processed, you may have to provide a DD statement for that data set too.

- On the DD statement, you need to specify just two parameters: DSNAME to identify the file's name and DISP=SHR to specify that the file can be shared. The first qualifier of the data set name identifies the catalog that owns the file, as in this example:

```
//CUSTMAST   DD   DSNAME=MMA2.CUSTMAST,DISP=SHR
```

- If the data set that's being processed is identified by the AMS command, you don't need to code a DD statement for it. This is often what happens.

Coding example

The following example shows how to invoke AMS using OS/390 or z/OS JCL.

```
//LISTCAT    JOB   (job accounting information)
//           EXEC  PGM=IDCAMS
//SYSPRINT   DD    SYSOUT=A
//SYSIN      DD    *
  LISTCAT  ENTRIES(AR.OPEN.ITEMS)    -
         VOLUME
/*
//
```

The DEFINE CLUSTER command

Function

The DEFINE CLUSTER command defines a VSAM data set, specifying the file's name, organization, space requirements, and other characteristics.

Syntax

```
DEFINE CLUSTER (    NAME(entry-name)
                 [ OWNER(owner-id) ]
                 [ FOR(days) | TO(date) ]
                 [ INDEXED | NONINDEXED | NUMBERED ]
                 [ RECORDSIZE(avg max) ]
                 [ KEYS(length offset) ]
                 [ SPANNED | NONSPANNED ]
                 [ CISZ(size) ]
                 [ FREESPACE(ci ca) ]
                 [ VOLUMES(vol-ser...) ]
                 [ FILE(ddname) ]

                 [ { CYLINDERS(primary [secondary]) }
                   { KILOBYTES(primary [secondary]) }
                   { MEGABYTES(primary [secondary]) }
                   { TRACKS(primary [secondary])    }
                   { RECORDS(primary [secondary])   } ]

                 [ REUSE | NOREUSE ]
                 [ SHAREOPTIONS(a b) ]
                 [ IMBED | NOIMBED ]         )
                 [ STORAGECLASS(storage-class) ]
                 [ DATACLASS(data-class) ]
                 [ MANAGEMENTCLASS(management-class) ] )
        [ DATA    ( [ NAME(entry-name) ]
                    [ VOLUMES(vol-ser...) ]
                    [ FILE(ddname) ]
                    [ CISZ(size) ]

                    [ { CYLINDERS(primary [secondary]) }
                      { KILOBYTES(primary [secondary]) }
                      { MEGABYTES(primary [secondary]) }
                      { TRACKS(primary [secondary])    }
                      { RECORDS(primary [secondary])   } ] ) ]
        [ INDEX   ( [ NAME(entry-name) ]
                    [ VOLUMES(vol-ser...) ]

                    [ { CYLINDERS(primary [secondary]) }
                      { KILOBYTES(primary [secondary]) }
                      { MEGABYTES(primary [secondary]) }
                      { TRACKS(primary [secondary])    }
                      { RECORDS(primary [secondary])   } ] ) ]
        [ CATALOG(name) ]
```

Parameters

NAME	Specifies the name of the cluster or component.
OWNER	Specifies a 1- to 8-character owner-id. This is for documentation only. If you omit it when you issue a DEFINE CLUSTER command from a TSO terminal, VSAM uses your TSO user-id as the owner-id.
FOR	TO	Specifies a retention period (in the format *dddd*) or an expiration date (in the format *yyyyddd*).
INDEXED	Specifies that a KSDS is being defined.
NONINDEXED	Specifies that an ESDS is being defined.
NUMBERED	Specifies that an RRDS is being defined.
RECORDSIZE	Specifies the average and maximum record size. If omitted, VSAM sets defaults of 4089 for both average and maximum if the records aren't SPANNED; it sets defaults of 4086 and 32600 if the records are SPANNED.
KEYS	Specifies the length and offset of the primary key for a KSDS. The default length is 64 bytes with an offset of 0.
SPANNED NONSPANNED	Specifies whether records can cross control interval boundaries. If the record size is larger than one control interval, you need to code SPANNED.
CISZ	Specifies the size of the control intervals. For most data sets, you can set this at 4096 unless the records are larger than that. For larger records, you can set this at the next multiple of 2K (2048), like 6144 or 8192. If omitted, VSAM sets this size.
FREESPACE	Specifies the percentage of free space to reserve for the control intervals (*ci*) and control areas (*ca*) of the data component. If file additions are likely, you should code this parameter because the default is no free space. The free space that you specify is part of the space allocated to the data component.
VOLUMES	Specifies one or more volumes that will contain the cluster or component. It is required at one of the levels, and it's normally coded at the cluster level of a KSDS so the index and data components are on the same volume. Otherwise, you can code this parameter at both the data and index levels.
FILE	Specifies a ddname that identifies a DD statement that allocates the volume or volumes when the job is run. This is required only for removable DASD volumes.
unit (primary [secondary])	*Primary* specifies the amount of space to allocate initially, expressed in terms of the *unit* (cylinders, kilobytes, megabytes, tracks, or records). *Secondary* specifies the secondary space allocation. If you specify this allocation in cylinders, the control areas will be one cylinder each.

REUSE | NOREUSE	Specifies whether a data set is reusable.
SHAREOPTIONS	Specifies the level of file sharing permitted as summarized below. The default level is 1 3.
IMBED NOIMBED	(KSDS only) Specifies whether sequence set records should be imbedded in the data component. Because this tends to improve performance, IMBED is usually coded.
STORAGECLASS	Specifies the storage class for SMS-managed data sets only.
DATACLASS	Specifies the data class for any data set as long as SMS is installed and active.
MANAGEMENTCLASS	Specifies the management class for SMS-managed data sets only.
CATALOG	Specifies the name of the catalog that will own the cluster. If omitted, the operating system uses its standard search sequence to identify the catalog.

Share options

Cross-region share options (a)

1   The file can be processed simultaneously by multiple jobs as long as all jobs open the file for input only. If a job opens the file for output, no other job can open the file.

2   The file can be processed simultaneously by multiple jobs as long as only one job opens the file for output; all other jobs must open the file for input only.

3   Any number of jobs can process the file simultaneously for input or output, but VSAM does nothing to insure the integrity of the file.

4   Any number of jobs can process the file simultaneously for input or output, but VSAM imposes these restrictions:

  • direct retrieval always reads data from disk even if the desired index or data records are already in a VSAM buffer;

  • data may not be added to the end of the file

  • a control area split is not allowed.

Cross-system share options (b)

3   Any number of jobs on any system can process the file simultaneously for input or output, but VSAM does nothing to insure the integrity of the file.

4   Any number of jobs on any system can process the file simultaneously for input or output, but VSAM imposes the same restrictions as for cross-region share option 4.

Coding example (KSDS)

This example shows how to define a key-sequenced data set named
MMA2.CUSTOMER.MASTER.

```
DEFINE CLUSTER ( NAME(MMA2.CUSTOMER.MASTER)              -
                 INDEXED                                 -
                 RECORDSIZE(200 200)                     -
                 KEYS(6 0)                               -
                 VOLUMES(MPS800)                         -
                 FOR(30)                                 -
                 SHAREOPTIONS(2 3)                       -
                 IMBED )                                 -
       DATA    ( NAME(MMA2.CUSTOMER.MASTER.DATA)         -
                 CYLINDERS(6 0)                          -
                 CISZ(4096) )                            -
       INDEX   ( NAME(MMA2.CUSTOMER.MASTER.INDEX) )
```

Coding example (ESDS)

This example shows how to define an entry-sequenced data set named
MMA2.AR.TRAN.

```
DEFINE CLUSTER ( NAME(MMA2.AR.TRAN)                      -
                 NONINDEXED                              -
                 RECORDSIZE(190 280)                     -
                 VOLUMES(MPS800)                         -
                 FOR(90) )                               -
       DATA    ( NAME(MMA2.AR.TRAN.DATA)                 -
                 CYLINDERS(10 1) )
```

Coding example (RRDS)

This example shows how to define a relative record data set named
MMA2.GL.ACCOUNT.MASTER.

```
DEFINE CLUSTER ( NAME(MMA2.GL.ACCOUNT.MASTER             -
                 NUMBERED                                -
                 RECORDSIZE(502 502)                     -
                 VOLUMES(MPS800)                         -
                 FOR(365)                                -
                 SHAREOPTIONS(1 3) )                     -
       DATA    ( NAME(MMA2.GL.ACCOUNT.MASTER.DATA)       -
                 CYLINDERS(10 1) )
```

The DEFINE ALTERNATEINDEX command

Function

The DEFINE ALTERNATEINDEX command defines an alternate index. The alternate index is related to a base cluster via the RELATE option. However, to process the base cluster via the alternate index, you must create a path using the DEFINE PATH command. Although you can spell it out if you wish, the keyword ALTERNATEINDEX is almost always abbreviated AIX.

Syntax

```
DEFINE AIX      (    NAME(entry-name)
                     RELATE(cluster-name)
                [ OWNER(owner-id) ]
                [ FOR(days) | TO(date) ]
                [ KEYS(length offset) ]
                [ UNIQUEKEY | NONUNIQUEKEY ]
                [ UPGRADE | NOUPGRADE ]
                [ VOLUMES(vol-ser...) ]
                [ FILE(ddname) ]

                [ { CYLINDERS(primary [secondary]) }
                  { KILOBYTES(primary [secondary]) }
                  { MEGABYTES(primary [secondary]) }
                  { TRACKS(primary [secondary])    }
                  { RECORDS(primary [secondary])   } ]

                [ REUSE | NOREUSE ]
                [ SHAREOPTIONS(a b) ]
                [ MODEL(entry-name [cat-name]) ] )

        [ DATA   ( [ NAME(entry-name) ]
                   [ VOLUMES(vol-ser...) ]

                   [ { CYLINDERS(primary [secondary]) }
                     { KILOBYTES(primary [secondary]) }
                     { MEGABYTES(primary [secondary]) }
                     { TRACKS(primary [secondary])    }
                     { RECORDS(primary [secondary])   } ] ) ]

        [ INDEX  ( [ NAME(entry-name) ]
                   [ VOLUMES(vol-ser...) ]

                   [ { CYLINDERS(primary [secondary]) }
                     { KILOBYTES(primary [secondary]) }
                     { MEGABYTES(primary [secondary]) }
                     { TRACKS(primary [secondary])    }
                     { RECORDS(primary [secondary])   } ] ) ]

        [ CATALOG(name) ]
```

Parameters

NAME	Specifies the name of the alternate index or component.
RELATE	Specifies the name of the base cluster to which this alternate index is related.
OWNER	Specifies a 1- to 8-character owner-id for the alternate index.
FOR | TO	Specifies a retention period (in the format *dddd*) or an expiration date (in the format *yyyyddd*) for the alternate index.
KEYS	Specifies the length and offset of the alternate key for a KSDS. An offset of 0 specifies the first position in the key.
UNIQUEKEY	Specifies that duplicate key values aren't allowed.
NONUNIQUEKEY	Specifies that duplicate key values are allowed.
UPGRADE NOUPGRADE	Specifies whether the alternate index is a part of the base cluster's upgrade set. UPGRADE is the default.
VOLUMES	Specifies one or more volumes that will contain the alternate index or component.
FILE	Specifies a ddname that identifies a DD statement that allocates the volume or volumes when the job is run. This is required only for removable DASD volumes.
unit (primary [secondary])	*Primary* specifies the amount of space to allocate initially, expressed in terms of the *unit* (cylinders, kilobytes, megabytes, tracks, or records). *Secondary* specifies the secondary space allocation.
REUSE | NOREUSE	Specifies whether a data set is reusable.
SHAREOPTIONS	Specifies how the alternate index may be shared among regions (a) and among systems (b). See the description of the SHAREOPTIONS values under the DEFINE CLUSTER command for details. Abbreviation: SHR.
MODEL	Specifies the name of an existing alternate index to use as a model.
CATALOG	Specifies the name of the catalog that will own the alternate index. If omitted, the operating system uses its standard search sequence to identify the catalog.

Coding example

This example shows how to define an alternate index named
MMA2.EMPMAST.SSN.AIX for a base cluster named MMA2.EMPMAST. The
alternate key values are employee social security numbers, so the alternate key is 9
bytes long, and it starts in the 13th byte (offset 12) of each record. Duplicates are
not allowed (UNIQUEKEY), and the alternate index is not a part of the base
cluster's upgrade set (NOUPGRADE).

```
DEFINE AIX    ( NAME(MMA2.EMPMAST.SSN.AIX)              -
                RELATE(MMA2.EMPMAST)                    -
                FOR(365)                                -
                KEYS(9 12)                              -
                UNIQUEKEY                               -
                NOUPGRADE                               -
                VOLUMES(MPS800) )                       -
       DATA   ( NAME(MMA2.EMPMAST.SSN.AIX.DATA)         -
                CYLINDERS(1 1) )                        -
       INDEX  ( NAME(MMA2.EMPMAST.SSN.AIX.INDEX) )
```

The DEFINE PATH command

Function

The DEFINE PATH command defines the processing link between an alternate index and its base cluster.

Syntax

```
DEFINE PATH (   NAME(entry-name)
                PATHENTRY(aix-name)
            [ UPDATE | NOUPDATE ]
            [ FOR(days) | TO(date) ]
            [ MODEL(entry-name [cat-name]) ]
            [ RECATALOG | NORECATALOG ] )
      [ CATALOG(name) ]
```

Parameters

NAME	Specifies the name of the path.
PATHENTRY	Specifies the name of the alternate index to which this path is related.
UPDATE NOUPDATE	Specifies whether or not the upgrade set should be updated when this path is processed.
FOR | TO	Specifies a retention period (in the format *dddd*) or an expiration date (in the format *yyyyddd*).
MODEL	Specifies the name of an existing path to use as a model.
RECATALOG	Specifies that a path entry is to be recataloged. The NAME and PATHENTRY parameters must be specified as they were when the path was originally defined.
NORECATALOG	Specifies that a new path entry should be created in a catalog.
CATALOG	Specifies the name of the catalog that contains the alternate index. Required only if the correct catalog can't be found using the standard search sequence.

Coding example

This example shows how to define a path that links an alternate index named MMA2.EMPMAST.SSN.AIX to its base cluster.

```
DEFINE PATH ( NAME(MMA2.EMPMAST.SSN.PATH)      -
              PATHENTRY(MMA2.EMPMAST.SSN.AIX)  -
              UPDATE )
```

The BLDINDEX command

Function

The BLDINDEX command creates the key entries necessary to access a base cluster via a path. You use it initially to load key entries into an alternate index. And you use it periodically to rebuild alternate indexes so they can be processed efficiently.

Syntax

```
BLDINDEX { INDATASET(cluster-name) }
         { INFILE(ddname)          }
         { OUTDATASET(aix-or-path-name) }
         { OUTFILE(ddname)          }
         [ EXTERNALSORT | INTERNALSORT ]
         [ WORKFILES(ddname ddname) ]
         [ CATALOG(name) ]
```

Parameters

INDATASET	Specifies the name of the base cluster.
INFILE	Specifies the name of a DD statement that identifies the base cluster.
OUTDATASET	Specifies the name of the alternate index.
OUTFILE	Specifies the name of a DD statement that identifies the alternate index.
INTERNALSORT	Specifies that the index records should be sorted in virtual storage. This is the default. Then, if VSAM can't find enough virtual storage for an internal sort, it automatically does an external sort.
EXTERNALSORT	Specifies that the index records should be sorted by an external sort program that uses disk work files. It's faster, though, to use the internal sort.
WORKFILES	Supplies the ddnames for the work files that are used by an external sort. If omitted, OS/390 or z/OS uses IDCUT1 and IDCUT2 as the ddnames for these files, and you must provide DD statements for them.
CATALOG	Specifies the name of the catalog that will own the sort work files. If omitted, the standard search sequence is used.

Coding example

This example shows how to build the alternate index that was defined in the coding
example for the DEFINE ALTERNATEINDEX command.

```
//          EXEC PGM=IDCAMS
//SYSPRINT DD   SYSOUT=A
//IDCUT1    DD   UNIT=SYSDA,VOL=SER=MPS800,DISP=SHR
//IDCUT2    DD   UNIT=SYSDA,VOL=SER=MPS800,DISP=SHR
//SYSIN    DD   *
 BLDINDEX INDATASET(MMA2.EMPMAST)              -
          OUTDATASET(MMA2.EMPMAST.SSN.AIX)    -
          CATALOG(MMA2)
/*
```

The LISTCAT command

Function

The LISTCAT command lists information about data sets and other VSAM objects that are defined in VSAM catalogs.

Syntax

```
LISTCAT  [ CATALOG(name) ]
         [ {ENTRIES(entry-name...)}
           {LEVEL(level)} ]
         [ entry-type... ]
         [ NAME | HISTORY | VOLUME | ALLOCATION | ALL ]
```

Parameters

CATALOG	Specifies the name of the catalog from which entries are to be listed. If omitted, the standard search sequence is used.
ENTRIES	Specifies the names of the entries you want to list. You can specify a generic entry name by replacing one or more of the file name levels with an asterisk.
LEVEL	Specifies one or more levels of qualification. Any data sets whose names match those levels are listed.
entry-type	Specifies the type of entries you want listed (you can code more than one type):
	ALIAS
	ALTERNATEINDEX or AIX
	CLUSTER
	DATA
	GENERATIONDATAGROUP or GDG
	INDEX
	NONVSAM
	PAGESPACE
	PATH
	USERCATALOG
NAME	Specifies that only the names and types of the specified entries be listed. This is the default.
HISTORY	Specifies that the NAME information plus the history information (such as creation and expiration dates) be listed.
VOLUME	Specifies that the HISTORY information plus the volume locations of the specified entries be listed.
ALLOCATION	Specifies that the VOLUME information plus detailed extent information be listed.
ALL	Specifies that all catalog information be listed.

Coding examples

The following example shows how to list the names of all data sets that begin with MMA2.

```
LISTCAT LEVEL(MMA2) -
        NAME
```

The following example shows how to list the volume information for the cluster, data, and index components of a data set named MM01.CUSTOMER.MASTER.

```
LISTCAT ENTRIES (MM01.CUSTOMER.MASTER) -
        VOLUME
```

The following example shows how to list the allocation information for all data sets in the catalog named MM01 whose names begin with the qualifier MM01 and end with the qualifier MASTER.

```
LISTCAT CATALOG(MM01)            -
        ENTRIES(MM01.*.MASTER) -
        ALLOCATION
```

The following example shows how to list the history information for all data and index components in the catalog named PRDTST1.

```
LISTCAT CATALOG(PRDTST1) -
        DATA            -
        INDEX           -
        HISTORY
```

The ALTER command

Function

The ALTER command lets you change a VSAM file's name, volume allocation, and other characteristics assigned to the file when you defined it.

Syntax

```
ALTER    entry-name
     [ CATALOG(name) ]
     [ NEWNAME(entry-name) ]
     [ ADDVOLUMES(vol-ser...) ]
     [ REMOVEVOLUMES(vol-ser...) ]
```

Parameters

Note: Although they aren't included in the syntax above, you can also specify many of the DEFINE CLUSTER options, like FREESPACE or SHAREOPTIONS. However, there are restrictions to the use of some of these, so be sure to consult your systems programmer or the appropriate AMS reference manual before using them.

entry-name	Specifies the name of the object whose catalog entry is to be altered.
CATALOG	Identifies the catalog that contains the object to be altered. Required only if the catalog can't be located by the standard search sequence.
NEWNAME	Specifies a new entry name for the entry.
ADDVOLUMES	Adds the specified volumes to the list of volumes where space may be allocated to the data component. Can't be used with a cluster.
REMOVEVOLUMES	Removes the specified volumes from the list of volumes where space may be allocated to the data component. Ignored if space has already been allocated on the specified volumes. Can't be used with a cluster.

Coding examples

The following example changes the name of the data set from MM01.CUSTOMER.MASTER to MM01.CUSTMAST.

```
ALTER MM01.CUSTOMER.MASTER    -
      NEWNAME(MM01.CUSTMAST)
```

The following example adds two volumes to the allocation for a data set. In this case, you need to specify the data component as the entry to be altered, not the cluster.

```
ALTER MM01.CUSTOMER.MASTER.DATA    -
      ADDVOLUMES (VOL291 VOL292)
```

The DELETE command

Function

The DELETE command deletes a VSAM file or other object.

Syntax

```
DELETE    (entry-name...)
          [ CATALOG(name)   ]
          [ entry-type... ]
          [ PURGE | NOPURGE ]
          [ ERASE | NOERASE ]
```

Parameters

entry-name	Specifies the name of the entry or entries to be deleted. If you specify more than one entry name, you must enclose the list in parentheses.
CATALOG	Specifies the name of the catalog that owns the entries to be deleted. Required only if the correct catalog can't be found using the standard search sequence.
entry-type	Specifies that only entries of the listed types should be deleted. The valid entry types are the same as for the LISTCAT command.
PURGE NOPURGE	PURGE means that an object should be deleted even if its retention period has not expired. NOPURGE means to delete entries only if their expiration dates have passed (the default).
ERASE NOERASE	ERASE means that the data component of a cluster or alternate index should be erased (overwritten with binary zeros). NOERASE means that the data component should not be erased (the default).

Coding example

This example shows two DELETE commands. The first one deletes three entries, regardless of their expiration dates. The second deletes all alternate indexes whose names follow the form MMA2.CUSTMAST.*.AIX.

```
DELETE (MMA2.CUSTOMER.MASTER           -
        MMA2.CUSTMAST.DISTRICT.AIX     -
        MMA2.CUSTMAST.DISTRICT.PATH)   -
        PURGE
DELETE MMA2.CUSTMAST.*.AIX             -
       ALTERNATEINDEX
```

The PRINT command

Function

The PRINT command prints all, or a specified portion, of a VSAM file in character, hex, or dump format.

Syntax

```
PRINT { INDATASET(entry-name) }
      { INFILE(ddname)         }
      [ CHARACTER | HEX | DUMP ]
      [ OUTFILE(ddname) ]
      [ { SKIP(count)          }
        { FROMKEY(key)         }
        { FROMNUMBER(number)   }
        { FROMADDRESS(address) } ]
      [ { COUNT(count)         }
        { TOKEY(key)           }
        { TONUMBER(number)     }
        { TOADDRESS(address)   } ]
```

Parameters

INDATASET	Specifies the name of the data set to be printed.
INFILE	Specifies the name of a DD statement that identifies the data set to be printed.
CHARACTER	Specifies that the data should be printed in character format.
HEX	Specifies that the data should be printed in hexadecimal format.
DUMP	Specifies that the data should be printed in both character and hex format.
OUTFILE	Specifies an output file other than the default SYSPRINT.
SKIP	Specifies the number of records to be skipped before the records are printed.
FROM...	Specifies the key (KSDS), relative record number (RRDS), or relative-byte address (ESDS) of the first record to be printed.
COUNT	Specifies the number of records to be printed.
TO...	Specifies the key (KSDS), relative record number (RRDS), or relative byte address (ESDS) of the last record to be printed.

Coding examples

This example shows how to print the contents of a VSAM file in character format.

```
PRINT INDATASET(MMA2.CUSTOMER.MASTER)    -
      CHARACTER
```

This example shows how to print records 29, 30, and 31 in dump format.

```
PRINT INDATASET(MMA2.CUSTOMER.MASTER)    -
      SKIP(28)                           -
      COUNT(3)
```

This example shows how to print the records from key 1000 to key 1200 in hex format.

```
PRINT INDATASET(TEST.CUSTOMER.MASTER)    -
      HEX                                -
      FROMKEY(1000)                      -
      TOKEY(1200)
```

The REPRO command

Function

The REPRO command copies the contents of a data set into another data set. Usually, you use it to copy one VSAM file to another or to copy a non-VSAM file to a VSAM file. If the output file is a VSAM file, it must first be defined with a DEFINE CLUSTER command. If the output file is empty, the records are simply copied in from the input file. If the output file contains records, the records from the input file are merged with the output file records depending on the data set's organization.

Syntax

```
REPRO { INDATASET(entry-name)  }
      { INFILE(ddname)         }
      { OUTDATASET(entry-name) }
      { OUTFILE(ddname)        }
      [ { SKIP(count)          }
        { FROMKEY(key)         }
        { FROMNUMBER(number)   }
        { FROMADDRESS(address) } ]
      [ { COUNT(count)         }
        { TOKEY(key)           }
        { TONUMBER(number)     }
        { TOADDRESS(address)   } ]
      [ REUSE | NOREUSE ]
      [ REPLACE | NOREPLACE ]
```

Parameters

INDATASET	Specifies the name of the data set to be copied.
INFILE	Specifies the name of a DD statement that identifies the data set to be copied.
OUTDATASET	Specifies the name of the output data set.
OUTFILE	Specifies the name of a DD statement that identifies the output data set.
SKIP	Specifies the number of records to be skipped before copying begins.
FROM...	Specifies the key (KSDS), relative record number (RRDS), or relative byte address (ESDS) of the first record to be copied.
COUNT	Specifies the number of records to be copied.
TO...	Specifies the key (KSDS), relative record number (RRDS), or relative byte address (ESDS) of the last record to be copied.

REUSE NOREUSE	Specifies whether or not a reusable output file should be reset. If REUSE is specified, the input records overwrite the existing records in the output file. If NOREUSE is specified, the input records are merged with the existing records in the output file.
REPLACE NOREPLACE	Specifies whether or not duplicate records should be replaced. If NOREPLACE is specified, the duplicate records in the output data set are retained and the duplicate input records are discarded.

Coding example

This example shows how to copy the first 1000 records in a data set named MMA2.CUSTOMER.MASTER to MMA2.CUSTOMER.MASTER.TEST. Note that MMA2.CUSTOMER.MASTER.TEST must first be defined with a DEFINE CLUSTER command.

```
REPRO  INDATASET(MMA2.CUSTOMER.MASTER)          -
       OUTDATASET(MMA2.CUSTOMER.MASTER.TEST)  -
       COUNT(1000)
```

Unit 12

CICS resource definition

For a CICS application to operate, CICS must know about the transactions, programs, maps, files, and other resources required for the application. Systems programmers will typically define most of these resources for you. However, you may occasionally have to define your own resources in order to test your application properly. There are two ways to do this: using an online facility called *Resource Definition Online*, or *RDO*, or using a batch facility called *DFHCSDUP*. This unit shows you how to use the RDO facility to define maps, programs, transactions, and files.

Resource Definition Online (RDO) basics

The RDO facility allows you to define CICS resources to the *CICS system definition file* (*CSD file*) for a specific CICS region. You'll typically use this facility in a test region to define the resources for new CICS applications you write.

RDO transactions

RDO offers three transactions you can use to define resources in a CICS region, each with a different level of functionality. In fact, as you can see in the table below, the CEDB and CEDC transactions are subsets of the CEDA transaction. In the examples that follow, I'll use the CEDA transaction because it allows the most flexibility.

RDO transaction	Description
CEDA	All RDO commands. These commands allow you to perform three basic functions: display data from the CSD; change data in the CSD; and install changed resource definitions so they become effective.
CEDB	All RDO commands except INSTALL. This means you can display or change CSD definitions, but you can't install them.
CEDC	DISPLAY, EXPAND, and VIEW commands only. This means you can display resource definitions, but you can't change or install them.

How to enter CEDA commands

- You can start a CEDA session just by keying in the trans-id CEDA and then pressing Enter. The initial panel that's displayed lists the commands you can use, as shown in figure 12-1.

- You can also start a CEDA session from a blank screen by entering CEDA followed by a CEDA command, as shown in figure 12-2.

- Once you've started CEDA, you can enter commands in the command line (at the top of the display) or you can overtype data directly on the data display.

- If you don't enter complete information for a CEDA command, CEDA responds by displaying a panel that allows you to enter the additional information needed to complete the operation.

The initial CEDA panel that's displayed when you enter CEDA and press the Enter key

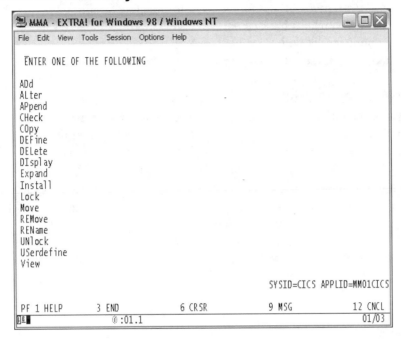

Figure 12-1

A DEFINE command entered at a blank screen that will start CEDA and display the program definition panel

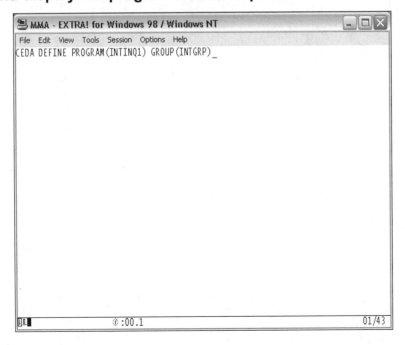

Figure 12-2

The CEDA DEFINE command

- To define maps, programs, transactions, and files to a CICS region, you use the CEDA DEFINE command. For example, to define a program named INTINQ1, you enter a command like this:

```
DEFINE PROGRAM(INTINQ1) GROUP(INTGRP)
```

- Every resource you define must belong to a group, as specified in the GROUP option of the DEFINE command. For example, in the DEFINE command shown above, the INTINQ1 program is assigned to the group named INTGRP. CICS can then use this group name to collect related resources on the CSD file. If the group name you specify doesn't exist, it's automatically created.

- The resource definition screen that's displayed in response to a DEFINE command lists a number of options and their defaults. The options vary depending on what resource is being defined, as you'll see in the examples in this unit. In general, the defaults will be adequate for testing purposes. What's more, your installation standards may limit which options you can change, so be sure to follow those guidelines.

How to define mapsets

To define new mapsets in a CICS region, you use the CEDA DEFINE command with the MAPSET option, as shown in figure 12-3. The values you can code for each option are listed to the right of the option. Although you'll use the default values for most options, it's a good idea to enter a description of the resource for documentation purposes.

The command to define a mapset entry in a CICS region

```
DEFINE MAPSET(INTSET1) GROUP(INTGRP)
```

The mapset definition screen that's displayed in response

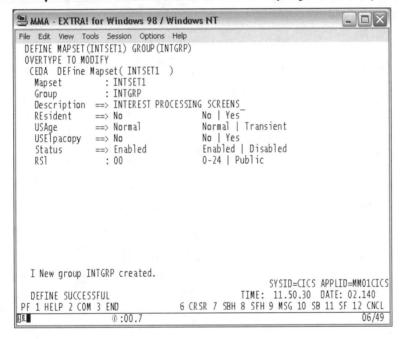

```
MMA - EXTRA! for Windows 98 / Windows NT

File  Edit  View  Tools  Session  Options  Help
 DEFINE MAPSET(INTSET1) GROUP(INTGRP)
 OVERTYPE TO MODIFY
  CEDA  DEFine Mapset( INTSET1  )
   Mapset      : INTSET1
   Group       : INTGRP
   Description  ==> INTEREST PROCESSING SCREENS_
   REsident    ==> No            No | Yes
   USAge       ==> Normal        Normal | Transient
   USElpacopy  ==> No            No | Yes
   Status      ==> Enabled       Enabled | Disabled
   RSl         : 00              0-24 | Public




   I New group INTGRP created.
                                       SYSID=CICS  APPLID=MM01CICS
   DEFINE SUCCESSFUL                   TIME:  11.50.30  DATE: 02.140
 PF 1 HELP 2 COM 3 END       6 CRSR 7 SBH 8 SFH 9 MSG 10 SB 11 SF 12 CNCL
                    :00.7                                  06/49
```

Figure 12-3

How to define programs

Defining a program is similar to defining a mapset, as shown in figure 12-4. Just be sure that COBOL is specified in the Language option before you press Enter to accept the definition.

The command to define a program entry in a CICS region

```
DEFINE PROGRAM(INTINQ1) GROUP(INTGRP)
```

The program definition screen that's displayed in response

```
MMA - EXTRA! for Windows 98 / Windows NT                    _ □ ✕
File  Edit  View  Tools  Session  Options  Help
 DEFINE PROGRAM(INTINQ1) GROUP(INTGRP)
 OVERTYPE TO MODIFY
  CEDA  DEFine PROGram( INTINQ1  )
   PROGram        : INTINQ1
   Group          : INTGRP
   DEscription  ==> INTEREST PROCESSING INQUIRY
   Language     ==> COBOL_           CObol | Assembler | Le370 | C | Pli
                                     | Rpg
   RELoad       ==> No               No | Yes
   RESident     ==> No               No | Yes
   USAge        ==> Normal           Normal | Transient
   USElpacopy   ==> No               No | Yes
   Status       ==> Enabled          Enabled | Disabled
   RSl          : 00                 0-24 | Public
   Cedf         ==> Yes              Yes | No
   DAtalocation ==> Below            Below | Any
   EXECKey      ==> User             User | Cics
  REMOTE ATTRIBUTES
   REMOTESystem ==>
 + REMOTEName   ==>

                                    SYSID=CICS APPLID=MM01CICS
  DEFINE SUCCESSFUL                 TIME: 11.57.58 DATE: 02.140
 PF 1 HELP 2 COM 3 END      6 CRSR 7 SBH 8 SFH 9 MSG 10 SB 11 SF 12 CNCL
 █▌█                @:00.7                                    07/27
```

Figure 12-4

How to define transactions

Defining transactions in a CICS region is similar to defining programs and mapsets, as shown in figure 12-5. The main difference is that you must supply the name of the program that is to execute when a user types in the transaction-id.

The command to define a transaction in a CICS region

```
DEFINE TRANSACTION(INT1) GROUP(INTGRP)
```

The transaction identifier definition screen that's displayed in response

```
MMA - EXTRA! for Windows 98 / Windows NT                    [_][□][X]
File  Edit  View  Tools  Session  Options  Help

 OVERTYPE TO MODIFY
  CEDA  DEFine  TRANSaction( INT1 )
   TRANSaction    : INT1
   Group          : INTGRP
   DEscription  ==> INTEREST PROCESSING INQUIRY TRAN-ID
   PROGram      ==> INTINQ1
   TWasize      ==> 00000          0-32767
   PROFile      ==> DFHCICST
   PArtitionset ==>
   STAtus       ==> Enabled        Enabled | Disabled
   PRIMedsize     : 00000          0-65520
   TASKDATALoc  ==> Below          Below | Any
   TASKDATAKey  ==> User           User | Cics
   STOrageclear ==> No             No | Yes
   RUnaway      ==> System         System | 0-2700000
   SHutdown     ==> Disabled       Disabled | Enabled
   ISolate      ==> Yes            Yes | No
  REMOTE ATTRIBUTES
 + DYnamic      ==> No       _     No | Yes

                                       SYSID=CICS APPLID=MM01CICS
  DEFINE SUCCESSFUL                    TIME: 12.08.24  DATE: 02.140
 PF 1 HELP 2 COM 3 END       6 CRSR 7 SBH 8 SFH 9 MSG 10 SB 11 SF 12 CNCL
 ▉▊▋               ☺ :00.5                               19/34
```

Figure 12-5

How to define files

To define a file to a CICS region, you must provide more information than you do for mapsets, programs, or transactions, as shown in figure 12-6.

- You supply the name of the VSAM file in the DSName option.

- You specify what type of permissions this CICS region will have for the VSAM file in the Operations options. The default is read-only, but you can also authorize add, browse, delete, and update operations by typing YES in the fields provided.

- If the file contains fixed-length records, you can change the RecordFormat option from V to F.

- To scroll down the screen, you use the PF8 key.

The command to define a file entry in a CICS region

```
DEFINE FILE(INTMST) GROUP(INTGRP)
```

The file definition screen that's displayed in response

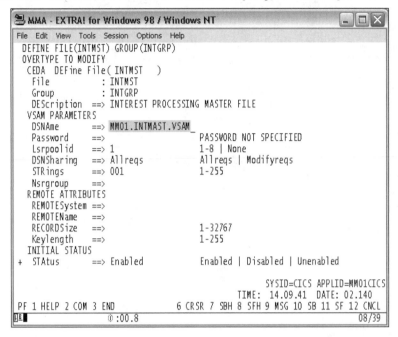

Setting VSAM file permissions

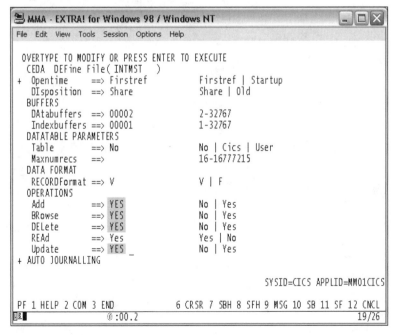

Figure 12-6

Unit 13

CICS service transactions

To use CICS effectively for program development, you need to know how to use the various *service transactions* that are supplied with CICS. This unit provides reference information for service transactions designed for CICS terminal operators. These transactions let you perform master terminal operations (CEMT and CEOT), browse temporary storage (CEBR), route messages (CMSG), and retrieve message pages (CSPG). Other important CICS service transactions covered in this book can be found in Unit 4 (CESN, CESF, CECI, and CEDF) and Unit 12 (CEDA, CEDB, and CEDC).

The Master Terminal Transaction (CEMT)

CEMT lets you display and change the status of resources, including programs, transactions, data sets, queues, and terminals. You'll use CEMT in a CICS test environment often to refresh a copy of a program, allocate and deallocate a file, or just inquire on the status of a given resource. In addition, you use CEMT to shut down a CICS system.

Operation

- To invoke CEMT, you enter the trans-id CEMT with or without a command. Once you've started CEMT, you can enter commands in the command line (at the top of the display) or you can overtype data directly on the data display.

- If you don't enter complete information for a CEMT command, CEMT prompts you for the additional information, showing all of the valid choices.

- You can abbreviate any CEMT command option with as few characters as are required to make the abbreviation unique within the context. For the keyword PERFORM, for example, you can enter P, PE, PER, PERF, and so on. However, if another keyword *at the same level* begins with the letter P, you would have to use at least two letters in the abbreviation.

- The three basic CEMT commands you're likely to use are INQUIRE (usually abbreviated INQ), SET, and PERFORM.

INQUIRE command syntax

```
CEMT INQUIRE FILE [(name)]
             PROGRAM [(name)]
             QUEUE [(name)]
             TASK [(number)]
             TERMINAL [(term-id)]
             TRANSACTION [(trans-id)]
```

Commonly used SET command syntax

```
CEMT SET    FILE(name)
            { ENABLED | DISABLED }
            { OPEN | CLOSED }

CEMT SET    PROGRAM(name)
            { ENABLED | DISABLED }
            [ NEWCOPY ]
            [ DPLSUBSET ]

CEMT SET    QUEUE(name)
            { ENABLED | DISABLED }
            { OPEN | CLOSED }
            [ TRIGGER(number) ]

CEMT SET    TASK(number)
            { PURGE | FORCEPURGE }

CEMT SET    TERMINAL(term-id)
            { INSERVICE | OUTSERVICE }
            { PURGE | FORCEPURGE }
            { PAGEABLE | AUTOPAGEABLE }
            { ATI | NOATI }

CEMT SET    TRANSACTION(trans-id)
            { ENABLED | DISABLED }
```

PERFORM SHUTDOWN command syntax

```
CEMT PERFORM SHUTDOWN [ IMMEDIATE ]
```

Options

Note: You can use the asterisk wildcard (*) in specifying the names or ids of any of the resources. Then, CEMT will let you display or change the status of any resource that matches the specified pattern.

FILE	Retrieves or sets data set information. If you omit the file name, CEMT displays a list of all data sets.
PROGRAM	Retrieves or sets program information. If you omit the program name, CEMT displays a list of all programs.
QUEUE	Retrieves or sets transient data information. If you omit the destination name, CEMT displays a list of all transient data queues.
TASK	Retrieves or sets task information. If you omit the task identifier, CEMT displays a list of all active tasks.
TERMINAL	Retrieves or sets terminal information. If you omit the terminal-id, CEMT displays a list of all terminals.
TRANSACTION	Retrieves or sets transaction information. If you omit the trans-id, CEMT displays a list of all transactions.

ENABLED DISABLED	Changes the status of the resource to ENABLED or DISABLED. Disabling a resource is often a good way to get out of a processing loop. For example, if your terminal is tied up by a pseudo-conversational transaction that keeps restarting itself, simply disable the transaction from another terminal.
OPEN CLOSED	Changes the status of a data set or queue to OPEN or CLOSED. A data set must be closed before you can update it outside of the CICS environment.
NEWCOPY	Establishes a new copy of a program or mapset. You should issue CEMT SET PROGRAM(name) NEWCOPY each time you recompile or reassemble a program or mapset.
DPLSUBSET	Specifies that a program run in a local CICS region is restricted to the Distributed Link Program API subset. In this mode, a program isn't allowed to issue any CICS commands that access a terminal, which is useful for testing business logic programs.
TRIGGER	Changes the trigger level for an ATI task associated with a transient data queue.
INSERVICE OUTSERVICE	Specifies whether or not the terminal is available for use.
PURGE FORCEPURGE	Cancels a running task: For SET TASK, cancels the task indicated by the task identifier; for SET TERMINAL, cancels the task associated with the terminal. PURGE cancels the task only if CICS can ensure system and data integrity; FORCEPURGE cancels a task without regard to integrity. Always try PURGE first.
PAGEABLE AUTOPAGEABLE	Specifies how a terminal handles multiple page messages. If PAGEABLE is specified, the operator must retrieve message pages with the CSPG transaction; if AUTOPAGEABLE is specified, message pages are delivered one after another. PAGEABLE is usually specified for display devices, and AUTOPAGEABLE is usually specified for printer devices.
ATI NOATI	ATI means that the terminal can be used for transactions that are invoked via Automatic Transaction Initiation (ATI) facilities or for Intersystem Communication (ISC) transactions. NOATI means that the terminal can not be used for those transactions.
SHUTDOWN	Terminates the CICS system.
IMMEDIATE	Specifies that CICS should be terminated immediately, even if there are tasks still running. If you omit IMMEDIATE, CICS waits until any active tasks are completed.

The terminal status transaction (CEOT)

CEOT is designed to let terminal users who aren't authorized to use CEMT inquire into and change the status of a terminal. Using CEOT, you can display the status of any terminal, but you can change the status only of your own.

Operation

- If you enter the CEOT trans-id without any options, CEOT displays the current status of your terminal and prompts you for more information.

Syntax

```
CEOT [ PAGEABLE | AUTOPAGEABLE ]
     [ ATI | NOATI ]
     [ TTI | NOTTI ]
```

Options

PAGEABLE AUTOPAGEABLE	If you specify PAGEABLE, pages of a multiple-page message are displayed only when you request them using the CSPG transaction. If you specify AUTOPAGEABLE, pages are automatically sent to the terminal. AUTOPAGEABLE should never be used with a display device.
ATI NOATI	If you specify ATI, the terminal can be used for transactions that are invoked via Automatic Transaction Initiation (ATI) facilities or for Intersystem Communication (ISC) transactions. NOATI means that the terminal can not be used for those transactions.
TTI NOTTI	If you specify TTI, transactions can be initiated from the terminal. In other words, CICS accepts and processes input from the terminal. NOTTI means that the terminal is output only; no input data is accepted from it.

The temporary storage browse transaction (CEBR)

CEBR lets you browse the contents of a specified temporary storage queue, which you may need to do if you're testing a program that uses temporary storage. In addition, CEBR lets you delete the temporary storage queue. And it lets you write the contents of the temporary storage queue to a transient data queue or read the contents of a transient data queue into the temporary storage queue.

Operation

- If you enter the CEBR trans-id without a queue name, CEBR uses a default queue name that consists of the letters CEBR followed by your terminal's term-id. So if you're using terminal L1T4, the default queue name is CEBRL1T4.

- CEBR's data display shows each record in the queue and lets you use PF keys to scroll forward or backward through it (the meaning of each PF key is displayed at the bottom of the screen). At the top of the screen is a command line where you can enter any of the commands listed below.

Syntax

```
CEBR [ queue-name ]
```

CEBR commands

QUEUE queue-name	Changes the display to the temporary storage queue you specify. You can specify a name that's up to 16 characters long.
TERMINAL xxxx	Changes the last 4 characters of the queue's name to the characters you specify.
PURGE	Deletes the queue.
TOP	Scrolls to the first record in the queue.
BOTTOM	Scrolls to the last record in the queue.
FIND /string/	Searches for the string enclosed within the delimiters. You can use any character for the delimiter as long as that character isn't in the search string. If the search string doesn't contain spaces, you can omit the second delimiter character.
LINE nnnn	Scrolls to the specified line.
COLUMN nnnn	Scrolls to the specified column.
GET xxxx	Reads the specified transient data queue into the current temporary storage queue. Remember that when you do this, the records in the destination are effectively deleted.
PUT xxxx	Writes the contents of the current temporary storage queue to the specified transient data queue.
SYSID xxxx	Changes the name of the remote system or storage pool where the queue can be found.

The message switching transaction (CMSG)

The CMSG transaction lets you send a message to other CICS users. You can specify that the message is to be sent to a specific terminal or operator or to all operators of a particular class. And you can specify that the message should be delivered immediately or in the future.

Operation

- CMSG is somewhat interactive, in that if you don't enter all the required options, you'll be prompted to enter more data. But it doesn't use a full-screen, fill-in-the-blanks approach like CEMT or CECI (CECI is covered in Unit 4).

Syntax

```
CMSG [ MSG= ]'message'
     [, ROUTE=route-list ]
     [, OPCLASS=operator-class-number ]
     [, TIME=time ]
     [, DATE=date ]
     [, FULLDATE ]
     [, ID=(message-title) ]
     [, HEADING={ YES | NO } ]
     [, SEND | CANCEL ]
```

Options

MSG
Specifies the message text, which must be enclosed in quotation marks. The word MSG= is optional. To include a quotation mark in the message, code two quotation marks in a row. If you omit the closing quotation mark, CMSG asks you to continue the message.

ROUTE
Specifies the terminals and/or operators that are to be sent the message. The ROUTE parameter has a complicated format, but it's usually coded in one of these simple forms:

ROUTE=ALL   Send the message to all terminals.

ROUTE=(term-id [,term-id...])
Send the message to the specified terminals.

ROUTE=(/operator [,/operator...])
Send the message to the specified operators. Note that each operator-id must be preceded by a slash.

ROUTE=(.term-list [,.term-list...])
Send the message to all terminals in the specified terminal lists. Note that each term-list identifier must be preceded by a period. Terminal lists are defined in a system table called the Terminal List Table (TLT) and are used to group related terminals.

OPCLASS	Specifies one or more operator classes. The message will be delivered only to operators of the specified class. The operator class numbers can be from 1 to 24.
TIME	Specifies when the message should be delivered. You can specify a time of day as *hhmm*, or you can specify a relative time as *+hhmm*, *+mm*, or *+m*.
DATE	Specifies the date when the message should be delivered. You can specify the date in the form *yy.ddd*, *mm/dd*, *mm/dd/yy*, or *+d*.
FULLDATE	Specifies a date, with a four-digit year, when the message should be delivered. You can specify the FULLDATE in the form *yyyy.ddd*, *mm/dd*, *mm/dd/yyyy*, or *+d*.
ID	Specifies a title of up to 62 characters (enclosed in parentheses). This title is associated with the message and is displayed when the terminal operator requests a list of pending messages.
HEADING	HEADING=YES adds a heading to the message. The heading includes the current time and date and the terminal-id of the terminal where the message originated.
SEND CANCEL	SEND tells CICS to send the message; CANCEL tells CICS to cancel the message request. If you don't code SEND or CANCEL, CMSG prompts you to enter additional parameters.

Abbreviations

You can abbreviate all CMSG parameters except CANCEL to a single letter, as follows:

D	DATE
F	FULLDATE
H	HEADING
I	ID
M	MSG
O	OPCLASS
R	ROUTE
S	SEND
T	TIME

Coding examples

Example 1

This example sends a message to terminal L401. The message is delivered immediately.

```
CMSG 'THE BMS MAPSET ASSEMBLY IS COMPLETED',R=L401
```

Example 2

This example sends a message to all terminal users. The message is delivered at 5:30 pm (1730).

```
CMSG 'CICS WILL BE SHUT DOWN IN 30 MINUTES',R=ALL,T=1730
```

Example 3

This example sends a message to all terminals specified in the terminal list table entry named ADMIN1A. Because the message is long, two terminal interactions are used. After the operator enters the first line, CMSG responds with

```
CONTINUE INPUT
```

Then, the operator enters the second line. Notice that the closing apostrophe is omitted on the first line so that the message can be continued on the second line.

```
CMSG 'DON''T FORGET—TODAY IS THE LAST DAY TO SUBMIT VOUCHERS
CMSG '  PLEASE HAVE YOUR SUBMISSIONS IN BY NOON',R=(.ADMIN1A)
```

The page retrieval transaction (CSPG)

CICS page retrieval functions let a terminal operator manage the display of multi-page messages by entering page retrieval commands. Although you don't normally invoke page retrieval functions using a trans-id like you invoke other service transactions, the page retrieval functions are implemented as a single transaction named CSPG. CICS itself interprets page retrieval commands the operator enters and invokes the CSPG transaction when necessary.

Operation

- A facility called *Single Keystroke Retrieval*, or *SKR*, lets an installation specify PF key assignments for certain page retrieval commands. For example, your shop might specify that PF1 retrieves the next page in sequence, while PF3 ends the page retrieval session. Since those PF key assignments are installation dependent, you'll have to find out how your shop uses them.

- There are two basic page retrieval commands you're likely to use: Getpage to retrieve pages and Msgterm to end the session. Both commands can be associated with a prefix determined by the installation. Usually, the prefix for the Getpage command is P/ and the prefix for the Msgterm command is T/. If your shop uses a different prefix, use it wherever you see P/ or T/ in the following commands.

The Getpage command

P/n	Retrieve page *n*.
P/+n	Retrieve the page that's *n* pages past the current page.
P/-n	Retrieve the page that's *n* pages before the current page.
P/L	Retrieve the last page.
P/N	Retrieve the next page.
P/P	Retrieve the previous page.
P/C	Redisplay the current page.
P/x, message-id	Retrieve a page from the specified message; *x* can be any of the above options (n, +n, -n, L, N, P, or C), and message-id is the message identifier for the message you want to display. You can determine the message identifier of an undelivered message by issuing the P/Q command.
P/Q	Display a list of pending messages for this terminal.

The Msgterm command

T/A	Terminate the page retrieval session and purge any messages destined for or currently being displayed at that terminal.
T/B	Terminate the page retrieval session and purge the message being displayed.

Unit 14

Reference tables

In this unit, you'll find several reference tables that will help you out from time to time. The hex and EBCDIC tables are generic to any IBM mainframe application, of course, while the last three tables provide information that's specific to CICS.

Hex/binary equivalents

Hex digit	Bit pattern	Hex digit	Bit pattern
0	0000	8	1000
1	0001	9	1001
2	0010	A	1010
3	0011	B	1011
4	0100	C	1100
5	0101	D	1101
6	0110	E	1110
7	0111	F	1111

EBCDIC code table

Dec	Hex	EBCDIC		Dec	Hex	EBCDIC
0	00	NUL		41	29	SFE
1	01	SOH		42	2A	SM/SW
2	02	STX		43	2B	CSP
3	03	ETX		44	2C	MFA
4	04	SEL		45	2D	ENQ
5	05	HT		46	2E	ACK
6	06	RNL		47	2F	BEL
7	07	DEL		48	30	
8	08	GE		49	31	
9	09	SPS		50	32	SYN
10	0A	RPT		51	33	IR
11	0B	VT		52	34	PP
12	0C	FF		53	35	TRN
13	0D	CR		54	36	NBS
14	0E	SO		55	37	EOT
15	0F	SI		56	38	SBS
16	10	DLE		57	39	IT
17	11	DC1		58	3A	RFF
18	12	DC2		59	3B	CU3
19	13	DC3		60	3C	DC4
20	14	RES/ENP		61	3D	NAK
21	15	NL		62	3E	
22	16	BS		63	3F	SUB
23	17	POC		64	40	space
24	18	CAN		65	41	RSP
25	19	EM		66	42	
26	1A	UBS		67	43	
27	1B	CU1		68	44	
28	1C	IFS		69	45	
29	1D	IGS		70	46	
30	1E	IRS		71	47	
31	1F	ITB/IUS		72	48	
32	20	DS		73	49	
33	21	SOS		74	4A	¢
34	22	FS		75	4B	.
35	23	WUS		76	4C	<
36	24	BYP/INP		77	4D	(
37	25	LF		78	4E	+
38	26	ETB		79	4F		
39	27	ESC		80	50	&
40	28	SA		81	51	

Dec	Hex	EBCDIC		Dec	Hex	EBCDIC
82	52			127	7F	"
83	53			128	80	
84	54			129	81	a
85	55			130	82	b
86	56			131	83	c
87	57			132	84	d
88	58			133	85	e
89	59			134	86	f
90	5A	!		135	87	g
91	5B	$		136	88	h
92	5C	*		137	89	i
93	5D	)		138	8A	
94	5E	;		139	8B	
95	5F			140	8C	
96	60	-		141	8D	
97	61	/		142	8E	
98	62			143	8F	
99	63			144	90	
100	64			145	91	j
101	65			146	92	k
102	66			147	93	l
103	67			148	94	m
104	68			149	95	n
105	69			150	96	o
106	6A	|		151	97	p
107	6B	,		152	98	q
108	6C	%		153	99	r
109	6D	_		154	9A	
110	6E	>		155	9B	
111	6F	?		156	9C	
112	70			157	9D	
113	71			158	9E	
114	72			159	9F	
115	73			160	A0	
116	74			161	A1	~
117	75			162	A2	s
118	76			163	A3	t
119	77			164	A4	u
120	78			165	A5	v
121	79	`		166	A6	w
122	7A	:		167	A7	x
123	7B	#		168	A8	y
124	7C	@		169	A9	z
125	7D	`		170	AA	
126	7E	=		171	AB	

Dec	Hex	EBCDIC	Dec	Hex	EBCDIC
172	AC		214	D6	O
173	AD		215	D7	P
174	AE		216	D8	Q
175	AF		217	D9	R
176	B0		218	DA	
177	B1		219	DB	
178	B2		220	DC	
179	B3		221	DD	
180	B4		222	DE	
181	B5		223	DF	
182	B6		224	E0	\
183	B7		225	E1	NSP
184	B8		226	E2	S
185	B9		227	E3	T
186	BA		228	E4	U
187	BB		229	E5	V
188	BC		230	E6	W
189	BD		231	E7	X
190	BE		232	E8	Y
191	BF		233	E9	Z
192	C0	{	234	EA	
193	C1	A	235	EB	
194	C2	B	236	EC	
195	C3	C	237	ED	
196	C4	D	238	EE	
197	C5	E	239	EF	
198	C6	F	240	F0	0
199	C7	G	241	F1	1
200	C8	H	242	F2	2
201	C9	I	243	F3	3
202	CA	SHY	244	F4	4
203	CB		245	F5	5
204	CC		246	F6	6
205	CD		247	F7	7
206	CE		248	F8	8
207	CF		249	F9	9
208	D0	}	250	FA	
209	D1	J	251	FB	
210	D2	K	252	FC	
211	D3	L	253	FD	
212	D4	M	254	FE	
213	D5	N	255	FF	EO

Attribute bytes

Protection	Shift	Intensity	MDT	Hex	Character
Unprot				40	SPACE
Unprot			On	C1	A
Unprot		Bright		C8	H
Unprot		Bright	On	C9	I
Unprot		Dark		4C	<
Unprot		Dark	On	4D	(
Unprot	Num			50	&
Unprot	Num		On	D1	J
Unprot	Num	Bright		D8	Q
Unprot	Num	Bright	On	D9	R
Unprot	Num	Dark		5C	*
Unprot	Num	Dark	On	5D	)
Prot				60	-
Prot			On	61	/
Prot		Bright		E8	Y
Prot		Bright	On	E9	Z
Prot		Dark		6C	%
Prot		Dark	On	6D	_
Prot	Skip			F0	0
Prot	Skip		On	F1	1
Prot	Skip	Bright		F8	8
Prot	Skip	Bright	On	F9	9
Prot	Skip	Dark		7C	@
Prot	Skip	Dark	On	7D	QUOTE

Execute Interface Block fields

Field name	COBOL PIC	Description
EIBAID	X(1)	Most recent AID character
EIBATT	X(1)	RU attach header flag
EIBCALEN	S9(4) COMP	Length of DFHCOMMAREA
EIBCOMPL	X(1)	RECEIVE command completion flag
EIBCONF	X(1)	APPC confirmation flag
EIBCPOSN	S9(4) COMP	Most recent cursor address, given as displacement value
EIBDATE	S9(7) COMP-3	Task start date in the format 0CYYDDD (day in year, where *C* identifies the century with 0 for the 1900s, 1 for the 2000s)
EIBDS	X(8)	Most recent data set name
EIBEOC	X(1)	RU end-of-chain flag
EIBERR	X(1)	APPC error flag
EIBERRCD	X(4)	APPC error code (when EIBERR is set)
EIBFMH	X(1)	FMH flag
EIBFN	X(2)	Most recent CICS command code
EIBFREE	X(1)	Free facility flag
EIBNODAT	X(1)	APPC no data flag
EIBRCODE	X(6)	CICS response code
EIBRECV	X(1)	RECEIVE command more-data flag
EIBREQID	X(8)	Interval control request-id
EIBRESP	S9(8) COMP	Exceptional condition code
EIBRESP2	S9(8) COMP	Exceptional condition extended code
EIBRLDBK	X(1)	Rollback flag
EIBRSRCE	X(8)	Last resource used (map name for a SEND MAP or RECEIVE MAP command, program name for a LINK or XCTL command, file name for a file control command, etc.)
EIBSIG	X(1)	SIGNAL flag
EIBSYNC	X(1)	Syncpoint flag
EIBSYNRB	X(1)	Syncpoint rollback flag
EIBTASKN	S9(7) COMP-3	Task number
EIBTIME	S9(7) COMP-3	Task starting time in the format 0HHMMSS (hours, minutes, seconds; assumes a 24-hour clock)
EIBTRMID	X(4)	Terminal-id
EIBTRNID	X(4)	Transaction-id

DFHAID field names for EIBAID values

Field name	Refers to use of
DFHENTER	ENTER key
DFHCLEAR	CLEAR key
DFHPA1-DFHPA3	PA1-PA3 keys
DFHPF1-DFHPF24	PF1-PF24 keys
DFHOPID	OPERID or MSR
DFHMSRE	Extended (standard) MSR
DFHTRIG	Trigger field
DFHPEN	SELECTOR PEN or CURSOR SELECT key
DFHCLRP	CLEAR PARTITION key
DFHSTRF	Structured field pseudo-AID

Index

E

O

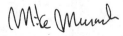